Sports Personal Injury: Law & Practice

By

Tim Kevan, B.A. (Hons)
Dominic Adamson, B.A. (Hons)
Stephen Cottrell, B.A. (Hons)

Barristers, 1 Temple Gardens

Published in 2002 by
Sweet & Maxwell Limited of
100 Avenue Road, Swiss Cottage, London NW3 3PF
(*http://www.sweetandmaxwell.co.uk*)

Printed and bound in Great Britain by
MPG Books Ltd, Bodmin, Cornwall

No natural forests were destroyed to make this product;
only farmed timber was used and replanted

ISBN 0421 778 407

A catalogue record for this book
is available from the British Library

To our parents

Foreword

I am delighted to have the opportunity to introduce this textbook on sports injury law by among others, my friend Tim Kevan.

Sport and the law have had a somewhat rocky relationship in the past with many saying that it should have no part to play over and above the decision of the referee. Experience has proved this not to be the case and it is now clear that the law is an essential backdrop to all sports and ensures not only fair play but more importantly, safety.

I have seen this first hand through my experiences in boxing. The decision by the Court of Appeal in finding the British Boxing Board of Control liable for failing to provide sufficient medical resources to Michael Watson was a watershed in the history of sports safety. Not only did this provide Michael with a legal remedy, it also resulted in closer scrutiny of the safety procedures at fights.

However, the decision also highlighted the need for compulsory insurance in order that that remedy can have a practical effect. Ironically, it is other sports which cause the vast majority of injuries and therefore this need for insurance is essential for all sporting events and at all levels.

It is with this in mind that I recommend this book not only to those who practise the art of law but also to laymen such as myself. It is a guide both for those clubs and organisers who have a potential liability and also for those who injure themselves in the sporting context.

BARRY McGUIGAN
Former featherweight boxing world champion
Founder and President of the British Boxers' Association
May 2002

Preface

"City till I die, City till I die, I know I am, I'm sure I am, I'm City till I die."
Song of the long-suffering Manchester City faithful.

Originally, this book came from a chance conversation between myself and Carl Waring of Waring and Co. Solicitors in which we agreed that whilst we had both failed to achieve our ambition of scoring a hat trick for Manchester City in a Wembley FA Cup Final victory over United, we could at least try and represent City off the field. Whilst that has not yet happened (still open to offers), it did lead Carl and I into expanding our practice into sports injury law.

It soon became apparent that very little had been written on the subject and following an article I wrote for the *Journal of Personal Injury Law*, Sweet and Maxwell approached me with the idea of expanding the topics covered into a book. From there I brought Dominic Adamson and Stephen Cottrell of 1 Temple Gardens onto the team along with Carl Waring, the latter providing valuable research and practical advice.

It is believed that this is the first book exclusively devoted to the personal injury aspects of sports law. It is aimed primarily at personal injury practitioners ranging from unqualified claims assessors, to solicitors and their employees and barristers. However, it is also intended to assist those involved in the organisation of sport ranging from professional and amateur clubs, to schools, local authorities and other organisers of sporting activities. No doubt, though, given the topical nature of the subject-matter, it will also appeal to many others who have an interest in sport and particularly those who participate in sport.

It is intended that this will be the first of several editions which will keep up-to-date with on-going developments. As to the timing, I take it as a good sign that this book goes to publication at the time that Manchester City enter the Premier League as First Division Champions.

It should be noted that the examples which have been provided are entirely fictional. Further, they are intended to highlight the issue raised rather than to answer a particular problem.

We have referred to various sources throughout this book. In addition, for more general reference, we would refer the reader to the following books which we have found useful: *Sports Law and Litigation* by Craig Moore (2nd ed., CLT Professional Publishing, 2000); *Sports Law*, by Gardiner *et al.*, (1st ed., Cavendish Publishing Ltd, 1998); (2nd ed., 2000); *Sport and the Law* by Edward Grayson (3rd ed., Butterworths, 2000); *Sports Law* by

Beloff, Kerr and Demetriou (1st ed., Hart Publishing, 1999); *Law and the Business of Sport* by David Griffith-Jones and Adrian Barr-Smith (Butterworths, 1997); *Clerk & Lindsell on Torts* (18th ed., Sweet and Maxwell, 2000); *Charlesworth and Percy on Negligence* by R.A. Percy and C.T. Walton (10th ed., Sweet and Maxwell, 1997) and *Bingham's Negligence Cases* by His Honour David Maddison J., His Honour Christopher Tetlow J. and Graham N. Wood (4th ed., Sweet and Maxwell, 1996).

The law is stated as it is understood by the authors as at April 30, 2002. Any errors are the authors' own for which we apologise and would hope to correct by the second edition. The purpose of this book is to highlight the various areas of law potentially associated with sports injuries. It is not intended to be a substitute for legal advice and readers researching a particular problem should not rely upon its contents in isolation but should instead refer to textbooks on the particular aspect of the problem and to legally qualified professionals. All brand and product names used in this book are recognised as trademarks, or registered trademarks, of their respective companies.

I should like to thank the following people who have helped in the production of this work: Carl Waring of Waring and Co. Solicitors who has been involved with the project from the beginning and has provided practical advice as well as invaluable help on all aspects from research to proofreading; Nick Collins at Ford and Warren Solicitors; Alex Padfield at Hextalls Solicitors; Jayne Andrews and Karen Green at McGoldricks Solicitors; Perrin Gibbons, a Barrister at 9 Gough Square; and Sweet and Maxwell for giving us the opportunity to publish.

TIM KEVAN
1 Temple Gardens
Temple
London EC4Y 9BB
April 30, 2002

Contents

Part I: General

Part II: Sporting Liabilities

Part III: Criminal and Other Disciplinary Jurisdictions

Part IV: Practice and Procedure

Part V: Conclusion

Table of Cases

Table of Cases

Table of Statutes

Table of Statutory Instruments

Table of European Legislation

Table of Civil Procedure Rules

Table of International Conventions

Part I

General

Chapter 1

Introduction

"Games might be and [are] the serious business of life to many people. It would be extraordinary to say that people could not recover from injuries sustained in the business of life, whether that was football, or motor racing, or any other of those pursuits which were instinctively classed as games but which everyone knew quite well to be serious business transactions for the persons engaged therein."

Swift J., *Cleghorn v. Oldham.*[1]

Some would say that sport is a reflection of life itself. For some it is a way **1.01** of life, for others a means of earning a living. For others it is a way of keeping fit, making friends, competing. Then there are the arm-chair sportsmen who enjoy nothing better than kicking back on a summer's day and watching the Aussies get thrashed at cricket (well, we can dream) or getting down the pub and singing for England during the World Cup. For others it may be cheering on Ellen McArthur as she arrives back from another round the world yacht race or Sally Gunnell down the home straight of an Olympic final. Whatever the motivation, it is clear that sport permeates all aspects of peoples' lives.

Sport, in itself, is enormously difficult if not impossible to define. The **1.02** European Sports Charter[2] defines sport as:

"all forms of physical activity which, through casual or organised participation, aim at expressing or improving physical fitness and mental well-being, forming social relationships or obtaining results in competition at all levels."

Such a sterile definition is almost to miss the point of sport for many people as one of the many outlets for their passions. Perhaps, it is better to look at its origins instead. The word itself derives from the French determined Middle English verb *sporten*, to divert[3] and also the Latin term *desporto*, literally "to carry away". The emphasis is therefore on its being a distraction, something that gives pleasure.[4] The nature of sport has changed down the ages deriving no doubt originally from the hunting of wild

---

[1] [1927] 43 T.L.R. 465 at 466.
[2] European Sports Charter, Council of Europe.
[3] *Webster's New Collegiate Dictionary* (Websters Publishing, New York, 1995).
[4] Gardiner *et al.*, *Sports Law*, (1st ed., Cavendish Publishing Ltd, 1998), p. 15.

animals and moving on to a facet of training for war as seen in the spirit of the original Greek Olympics held in 686BC. Going even further back in time, the earliest evidence of the existence of boxing is recorded in Egyptian hieroglyphics around 4000BC.[5]

1.03   From these ancient beginnings sport has diversified like any self-respecting product to suit the demands of almost all those undertaking any form of physical activity from kicking a piece of leather around a grass field to riding the ocean waves. Of course, this has also led to the invention of what might be thought of as the more unusual sports such as bog-snorkling whose world championship is held at Llanwrtyd Wells in Wales each year or snail racing whose world record is held by "Archie" who completed the requisite 13-inch course in two minutes and 20 seconds.[6]

1.04   Thankfully, for the purposes of this book it is not necessary to enter the controversial debate as to what exactly is or is not a sport. Suffice it to say that the authors have chosen what they consider to be either mainstream sports or sports where there is a risk of injury or occasionally sports which merely reflect their own passions. If there are any tiddly-winks players out there having suffered personal injuries from the pursuit and who think that it should have been included we should be happy to consider what they have to say for the second edition of this work.

1.05   Perhaps one of the main attractions of sport is that it reflects the freedom of the human spirit. Free from work and everyday worries. Free from politics, free from government. No wonder people always turn to the back page of a newspaper first when the front page is full of bad news.

1.06   However, there are other perspectives on sport which suggest that it is devisive, reinforcing the principle of winner takes all. Others suggest that sport in some way perpetuates a patriarchal society. From this perspective, it is argued that sports are "gendered" activities. As Coakley, J. states in *Sport in Society: Issues and Controversies*[7]:

> "Feminists describe sports as 'gendered' activities. The fact that organised sports were developed to emphasise competition, efficiency and performance ranking systems and to devalue supportiveness and caring contributions to the 'gendered' character. To say that sports are 'gendered' activities and to say that sports organisations are 'gendered' structures means that they have been socially constructed out of the values and experiences of men."

1.07   Whatever perspective one takes, the question arises as to what has the law, and more importantly those damn lawyers, got to do with sport? As with all aspects of human life, not even sport can exist in a legal vacuum and in the last few years the importance of the law in sport has become increasingly apparent. This may in part be due to the efforts of a few

---

[5] Gardiner *et al.*, above, p. 15.
[6] Sports Law Bulletin, September/October 2001, p. 20.
[7] 1994, at p. 38.

frustrated lawyers who failed to achieve their dreams of becoming one of the world's best footballers and want at least to be involved on the touchline (the authors of this book, for example). Perhaps most importantly, it is due to the increasing commercialisation of professional sport.

However, the regulation of sport is nothing new. The most immediate **1.08** form of regulation can be found in the rules usually found associated with each sport. Generally, these are for either regulating the dynamics of play or for ensuring safety. The latter was clearly the aim in the first rules set down to govern boxing in 1743 (pre-dating those codified under the auspices of the Marquis of Queenbury in 1867) and written by Jack Broughton who two years earlier had killed George Stevenson in a prize-ring in Tottenham Court Road, his patron the Duke of Cumberland a horrified spectator.[8] They provided:

> "That a square of a Yard be chalked in the middle of the Stage; and on every fresh set-to after a fall or being parted from the rails, each Second is to bring his man to the side of the square and place him opposite to the other and till they are fairly set-to at the Lines, it shall not be lawful for one to strike at the other."[9]

The late nineteenth century saw the formal codification of many sports.[10] As **1.09** time has gone on these rules have become ever more sophisticated, no doubt in order to try and close loop-holes which players down the ages have tried to exploit or sometimes to increase the safety of the particular sport.

In conjunction with these developments, sports have always had to work **1.10** within the law of the land and often came to be specifically regulated by the state. Sometimes this has been to regulate safety and sometimes to preserve public order since games could often get out of hand. R. Brasch provides the following example of thirteenth and fourteenth century problems in *How Did Sports Begin?*[11]:

> "In a ball game, probably football, at Ukham Northumberland on Trinity Sunday 1280, Henry de Ellington was accidentally killed when, jostling for the ball, he impaled himself on another player's knife. But ball games could be dangerous even without knives. Three years earlier a 10 year old boy killed a 12 year old companion by hitting him on the ear after a clash of sticks in a hockey game . . . In 1303 an Oxford student from Salisbury was killed—allegedly by Irish fellow students—whilst playing football in the High."

Eventually, in 1314 the Lord Mayor of London issued a proclamation on the King's behalf forbidding rumpuses with large footballs in the public fields. So, too, in answer to political concerns, in 1285, a statute of Edward I referred to "fools who delight in their folly" and banned tournaments and

---

[8] Gardiner *et al.*, above, p. 50.
[9] "Sportsview: Why they can't close school of hard knocks", *The Observer*, October 29, 1995, p. 10.
[10] Gardiner *et al.*, above, p. 51.
[11] Angus and Robinson (Sydney, 1986) p. 32.

swordplay in London as well as prohibiting the teaching of swordsmanship in the city on pain of 40 days' imprisonment.[12]

1.11 State intervention has not only been directed at the players in this regard. A recent example of this followed the Hillsborough disaster and the Taylor report which examined it. A number of specific statutes have been passed since then dealing ever more stringently with football hooliganism.

1.12 On occasions, sport has played host, perhaps unwittingly, to acts which have changed the course of history in some way. Perhaps the greatest example of this was the action of Emily Wilding Davidson on June 8, 1913 when she brought down the horse owned by King George V in the Epsom Derby, Amner, seriously injury its jockey Herbet Jones and ultimately losing her own life in the process. As Dame Christabelle Pankhurst recorded[13]:

> "Emily Davidson paid with her life by making the whole world understand that women were in earnest for the vote. Probably in no other way and no other time could she so effectively have brought the attention of millions to bear upon the cause."

Alongside the direct intervention through statute there has been increasing recourse to the courts in recent years in the sporting arena. In the criminal arena, participants have been made aware that they may end up facing a jail sentence if they go too far during the game. This is illustrated by the three month prison sentence which Duncan Ferguson, a Scottish international footballer, received for head butting during a game in 1994. Challenges have also been made in the courts to the decisions of sports' governing bodies themselves and these are set out in Chapters 22 and 23.

1.13 Perhaps the major development in this area has been the development of the law of negligence into what had previously been unchartered waters. This has come with the increasing commercialisation of professional sport coupled with the rise in personal injury litigation and has led to numerous sports injury cases in the last few years.

Successful claims have now been made by both participants and spectators for injuries suffered during a game. However, it is not the identity of the claimants which has caused any surprise but that of the defendants in many of the recent high profile actions. For example, in *Smoldon v. Whitworth and Nolan*[14] a referee was held liable for injuries sustained as a result of his negligence. In *Watson v. British Boxing Board of Control*,[15] Michael Watson succeeded in his claim that the British Board of Boxing ("BBBC") had been negligent in failing to provide adequate emergency medical facilities at the world middleweight title fight with Chris Eubank.

---

[12] R. Brasch, *How Did Sports Begin?*, Angus and Robinson (Sydney, 1986) p. 32.
[13] In *Unshackled: The Story of How We Won the Vote*, edited by Rt Hon Lord Pethick-Lawrence, 1959.
[14] [1997] P.I.Q.R. 133.
[15] *The Times*, October 12, 1999.

In addition to these developments, the rise in litigation against schools and local authorities has had a direct impact on their potential liabilities in the sporting context. So, too, with the increasing popularity of extreme sports such as surfing, snowboarding and kite-boarding the potential liabilities of the organisers has increased.

Related to this has been an increase in awareness of the need for insurance. For example, in July 2000, the Sports Minister Kate Hoey signalled her support for the introduction of a compulsory insurance scheme to benefit more than 500,000 amateur footballers. Further, the Football Association announced that it was considering funding a scheme to provide both personal injury and public liability cover for all its 43,000 clubs. **1.14**

As to the numbers of sporting injuries, the figures speak for themselves. As noted above, a British Sports Council Survey in 1991, *Epidemiology of Exercise*, into sports related illness concluded that six million new sports injuries required treatment each year. In *Sports Law and Litigation*, Craig Moore states[16] that it has been estimated that 19 million sports injuries occur in England and Wales each year, costing some £500 million in treatment and absence from work.

In 1997, Dr Robin Knill-Jones recorded in the *British Journal of Sports Medicine*[17]:

"Sports related injuries form a significant part of the workload of the National Health Service. Patients with acute injuries account for between 3.9 per cent and 7.1 per cent of total attendance at casualty departments, and a higher proportion of attendance—28 per cent by children."

As Jayne Andrews of McGoldricks Solicitors[18] says:

"With number of injuries along with the legal developments and the rise of no win no fee agreements, litigation over sports injuries is only likely to increase in the future."

---

[16] 2nd ed., CLT Professional Publishing, 2000, p. 145.
[17] June 1997, pp. 95–96.
[18] Contact: sfjc@ukgateway.net.

Chapter 2

General principles

"Serious sport has nothing to do with fair play. It is bound up with hatred, jealousy, boastfulness, disregard of all rules and sadistic pleasure in witnessing violence. In other words, it is war minus the shooting."

George Orwell.

This Chapter provides a brief guide to some of the general principles which **2.01** arise throughout the rest of the book and which are applicable both to personal injury cases in general and sporting personal injury cases in particular. It merely provides a very brief introduction to these principles. Some are covered in more detail in the context of specific situations. Others may be followed up through the standard texts in the area such as *Clerk & Lindsell on Torts* (18th ed., Sweet and Maxwell, 2000); *Charlesworth and Percy on Negligence* by R.A. Percy and C.T. Walton (10th ed., Sweet and Maxwell, 1997) to which the reader is referred.

Negligence

There are four requirements of the tort of negligence, namely[1]:

1. the existence in law of a duty of care situation, *i.e.* one in which the law attaches liability to carelessness. There has to be a recognition by law that the careless infliction of the kind of damage in suit on the class of person to which the claimant belongs by the class of person to which the defendant belongs is actionable;

2. breach of the duty of care by the defendant, *i.e.* that it failed to measure up to the standard set by law;

3. a causal connection between the defendant's careless conduct and the damage;

4. that the particular kind of damage to the particular claimant is not so unforeseeable as to be too remote.

---

[1] *Clerk & Lindsell on Torts* (18th ed., Sweet and Maxwell, 2000), para. 7–04.

The starting point for an analysis as to when a duty of care arises remains the famous dictum of Lord Atkin in *Donoghue v. Stevenson*[2]:

> "You must take reasonable care to avoid acts or omissions which you can reasonably foresee would be likely to injure your neighbour. Who then is my neighbour? The answer seems to be—persons who are so closely and directly affected by my act that I ought reasonably to have them in contemplation as being so affected when I am directing my mind to the acts or omissions which are called into question."

2.02   The test perhaps most quoted by the courts in recent times is the three-stage test set out in *Caparo Industries plc v. Dickman*[3] by Lord Bridge when he said:

> "What emerges is that, in addition to the foreseeability of damage, necessary ingredients in any situation giving rise to a duty of care are that there should exist between the party owing the duty and the party to whom it is owed a relationship characterised by the law as one of "proximity" or 'neighbourhood' and that the situation should be one in which the court considers it fair, just and reasonable that the law should impose a duty of a given scope upon the one party for the benefit of the other."

Commenting on the role of the three criteria in *Caparo*, Lord Oliver said:

> " . . . it is difficult to resist a conclusion that what have been treated as three separate requirements are, at least in most cases, in fact merely facets of the same thing, for in some cases the degree of foreseeability is such that it is from that alone that the requisite proximity can be deduced, whilst in others the absence of that essential relationship can most rationally be attributed simply to the court's view that it would not be fair and reasonable to hold the defendant responsible."[4]

Beyond this, the other requirements of the tort of negligence will be covered as and when they arise in their specific contexts throughout this text.

Volenti non fit injuria

2.03   A principle which is very important to the law of negligence in the sporting context is that described by the maxim *volenti non fit injuria* which describes a defence to a claim in circumstances where it is shown that the claimant had consented to the breach of the duty of care which is alleged

---

[2] [1932] A.C. 562 at 580.
[3] [1990] 2 A.C. 605 at 617–618.
[4] [1990] 2 A.C. 605 at 633.

and had agreed to wave his right of action in respect thereof. Thus, it is often argued that those involved in a game are usually taken to have consented to the everyday rough and tumble which may reasonably be expected.

When the defence of *volenti* applies it is a complete defence; the claimant recovers nothing. There are at least three requirements for it to apply[5]:

1. agreement by the claimant to waive a claim against the defendant;

2. this agreement must be voluntary, not due to compulsion by the defendant or external circumstances; and

3. the claimant should therefore have full knowledge of the nature and extent of the risk.

However, with regard to the law of negligence, the defence is difficult to prove on the law as it currently stands. It was specifically examined in the case of *Smoldon v. Whitworth and Nolan*[6] in the context of an accusation of negligence against a rugby referee for an injury caused by the collapse of a scrum. The Court of Appeal gave short shrift to the argument that the claimant had consented to the risk of injury of the type sustained by him by voluntarily playing in the front row of the scrum and thereby participating in the collapse: **2.04**

" . . . this argument is unsustainable. The plaintiff had of course consented to the ordinary incidents of a game of rugby football of the kind in which he was taking part. Given, however, that the rules were framed for the protection of him and other players in the same position, he cannot possibly be said to have consented to a breach of duty on the part of the official whose duty it was to apply the rules and ensure so far as possible that they were observed."

However, the Court of Appeal did go on to give an indication of a particular set of circumstances in which a *volenti* defence might arise. If the claimant had been identified as a prime culprit in causing the scrum to collapse, then it might have required some consideration as to whether or not, by his actions, he should have consented to the risk of injury and to have waived his right of action against the referee for breach of his duty of care. This case is examined in more detail in Chapter 12.

The demise of the importance of the defence of *volenti* is perhaps partly due to the fact that contributory negligence no longer acts as a complete defence. It is therefore possible that rather than finding the defence of *volenti* which would completely defeat a claim, it may instead turn to the **2.05**

---

[5] *Clerk & Lindsell on Torts* (18th ed., Sweet and Maxwell, 2000), para. 3–72.
[6] [1997] P.I.Q.R. 133.

defence of contributory negligence. As Lord Denning stated in *Nettleship v. Weston*[7]:

> "Now that contributory negligence is not a complete defence, but only a ground for reducing the damages, the defence of *volenti non fit injuria* has been closely considered, and, in consequence, it has been severely limited. Knowledge of the risk of injury is not enough. Nor is a willingness to take the risk of injury. Nothing will suffice short of an agreement to waive any claim for negligence. The plaintiff must agree, expressly or impliedly, to waive any claim for any injury that may befall him due to the lack of reasonable care by the defendant: or, more accurately, due to the failure of the defendant to measure up to the standard of care that the law requires of him."

2.06 Alternatively, the courts appear to have taken the issue of consent into account when initially analysing the duty of care and before even arriving at a consideration of the defences. In *Condon v. Basi*,[8] Lord Donaldson cited with approval the statements made by the High Court of Australia in the case of *Rootes v. Skelton*[9]:

> "By engaging in a sport . . . the participants may be held to have accepted risks which are inherent in that sport . . . : but this does not eliminate all duty of care of the one participant to the other."

In general, therefore, subject perhaps to very specific exceptions, there is limited basis for saying that a participant or spectator must be taken to have accepted the risk of injury caused by negligence. This was effectively put by Lord Denning M.R. in *White v. Blackmore*[10] in the context of a claim by dependents of a spectator killed whilst watching a jalopy race when he stated:

> "No doubt the visitor takes on himself the risks inherent in motor-racing, but he does not take on himself the risk of injury due to the defaults of the organisers."

Example

Champion mountain-biker Lucy Sullivan is taking part in the World Mountain Bike Championships on Exmoor organised by Toby Backhouse. As she enters the final section of the race she is leading from her close rival Kathryn Baker by a wheel. However, as they go into the final sprint Kathryn Baker nudges Lucy Sullivan off her bike and into the mud going on to win the race herself.

Can it be said that Lucy Sullivan consented to the possibility of being pushed off her bike by Kathryn Baker merely by having entered the race?

---

[7] [1971] 2 Q.B. 691 at 701.
[8] [1985] 1 W.L.R. 866.
[9] [1968] A.L.R. 33.
[10] [1972] 2 Q.B. 651 at 663.

Contributory negligence

As mentioned above, contributory negligence no longer acts as a complete   **2.07**
defence to a claim. Instead, section 1(1) of the Law Reform (Contributory
Negligence) Act 1945 provides:

> "Where any person suffers damage as the result partly of his own fault and partly
> of the fault of any other person or persons, a claim in respect of that damage shall
> not be defeated by reason of the fault of the person suffering the damage, but the
> damages recoverable in respect thereof shall be reduced to such extent as the court
> thinks just and equitable having regard to the claimant's share in the responsibility
> for the damage . . . "

Vicarious liability/agency

One of the greatest risks for employers is their potential liability for the   **2.08**
actions of their employees. This is particularly important with respect to
professional sports clubs such as football and rugby clubs. This section sets
out an introduction to the law in this area.

Criminal law

With regard to the criminal law, it is mainly aimed at the perpetrators of
offences, *i.e.* the person who directly carries out the offence. This is not as
relevant in the present context as that of civil liability.

Tort

General
In tort the position is very different. The classic statement of vicarious
liability in this area was made, and has been constantly approved, in *Salmon
on Tort*. This is recorded in the 18th edition as follows:

> "It is clear that the master is responsible for acts actually authorised by him: for
> liability would exist in this case, even if the relation between the parties was
> merely one of agency, and not one of service at all. But a master, as opposed to the
> employer of an independent contract, is liable even for acts which he has author-
> ised that nay rightly be regarded as modes—although improper modes—of doing
> them. In other words, a master is responsible not merely for what he authorises his
> servant to do, but also for the way in which he does it. If a servant does negligently
> that which he was authorised to do carefully, or if he does fraudulently that which
> he was authorised to do honestly, or if he does mistakenly that which he was
> authorised to do correctly, his master will answer for that negligence, fraud or
> mistake. On the other hand, if the unauthorised and wrongful act of the servant
> is not so connected with the authorised act as to be a mode of doing it, but is an

independent act, the master is not responsible: for in such a case the servant is not acting in the course of his employment, but has gone outside of it."

This has, for most part, been applied in all situations whereby course of employment/master—servant is in issue. There must usually be some element of control in some form or fashion. In determining the status of an employee, the Courts will look at all the relevant factors concerned and will not be swayed materially by what the parties have intended or labelled their relationship as.[11]

There are various tests for establishing employment, but in essence all factors need to be appraised and the Court need to make a qualitative assessment of the true nature of the position.

2.09   Whether something is or is not in the course of employment may well hinge upon whether there has been any prohibition upon the activity in question. For instance in *C.P.R. v. Lockhart*[12] an employee was authorised to use his own car in the course of his employment provided that it was insured. The employee had an accident and his car was uninsured. It was held that the company was vicariously liable as the mode of employment was permitted, it was only the way in which he carried out that mode of employment which caused the problem. Contrast this with where the class of acts concerned are prohibited. For instance in *Iqbal v. London Transport Executive*[13] a bus conductor was expressly forbidden to drive buses. When told to get an engineer to move a bus, and instead he did it himself resulting in a tort, the bus company were not held vicariously liable—driving buses was not in the course of his employment.

Beloff, Kerr and Demetriou in *Sports Law*[14] suggest that the deliberate infliction of an injury would result in a player being guilty of assault and that in those circumstances it would be most unlikely for his club to be held to be vicariously liable.[15] However, on the other hand they suggest that if the injury was inflicted negligently or recklessly—"in the sense that the player showed reckless disregard for the safety of the victim, but without intent to injure him"—the club will be vicariously liable on ordinary principles as the employer of the guilty party.[16]

2.10   It should be noted that in the Australian case of *Rogers v. Bugden and Canterbury Bankston Club*,[17] the judgment of the New South Wales Supreme Court Common Law Division after an award of A\$68,154.60 with costs against not only an offending player who broke an opponent's jaw in

---

[11] *Ferguson v. Dawson Partners (Contractors) Ltd* [1976] 1 W.L.R. 1213.
[12] [1942] A.C. 591.
[13] (1973) 16 K.I.R. 39.
[14] 1st ed., Hart Publishing, 1999, para. 5.72.
[15] See, *e.g. Racz v. Home Office* [1994] 2 A.C. 45; *Makanjuola v. Commissioner of Police for the Metropolis* [1989] 2 Admin. L.R. 214.
[16] They refer to *Clerk & Lindsell on Torts* (18th ed., Sweet and Maxwell, 1995), para. 5–20ff.
[17] [1993] Australian Torts Rep 181–248, CA (NSW).

a professional rugby league match, but also the employer club,[18] was subsequently affirmed on appeal with an increase for aggravated damages.

In the light of the case law in this area, clubs employing professional sportsmen are likely to find themselves being vicariously liable for negligent play on the field even though this has not been so authorised.

In order to counter this in the future, as well as clubs taking out insurance to cover such risks they may also add disclaimers into the small print of the employment contracts and therefore sportsmen must be careful to read the small print before signing up.[19] **2.11**

Independent contractors

A different position may arise where a player is merely on loan from another club or has been employed merely to play one game. In those circumstances it may be argued that the player was in effect an independent contractor for which different considerations apply. Generally where an employer has employed an independent contractor of sufficient prima facie competence, then he will not be held responsible for their torts:

> "Unquestionably, no one can be made liable for an act or breach of duty, unless it be traceable to himself or his servant or servants in the course of his or their employment. Consequently, if an independent contractor is employed to do a lawful act, and in the course of the work he or his servants commit some casual act of wrong or negligence, the employer is not answerable".[20]

There are certain exceptions to this in relation to certain non-delegable duties. In some ways they are practical exceptions only rather than technical exceptions as in reality the employer is more in breach of his own duty rather than accepting responsibility for the breach of another's duty. **2.12**

Amateur players

A question which may become increasingly important in the future is whether clubs should be held to be vicariously liable for the actions of their players even if those players are not being paid.

In this regard, *Clerk & Lindsell on Torts* states[21]:

> "For vicarious liability to arise at all, save in exceptional circumstances, save in exceptional circumstances discussed later, the alleged employee or independent contractor must have been employed to work for the employer rather than simply asked, or even ordered, to a perform a gratuity in a context quite different from

---

[18] Unreported, December 14, 1990 and see [1991] All E.R. 246.
[19] See also Gardiner *et al.*, *Sports Law* (2nd ed., Cavendish Publishing Ltd, 2001), Chap. 16 and the American case of *Tomjanovich v. California Sports Inc* [No. H–78–243 (SD Tx 1979)] referred to therein.
[20] *Pickard v. Smith* (1861) 10 C.B. (N.S.) 470, *per* Williams J.
[21] 18th ed., Sweet and Maxwell, 2000, para. 5–02.

that usually understood by the term employment. The schoolboy distributing the mid-morning milk to fellow pupils does so as a pupil obeying his teacher and not as a servant of the school. The school is not vicariously liable for his negligence, but only liable if they are in breach of their duty to make reasonably safe arrangements for the performance of that task and supervise the boy with care.[22] Similarly, the Court of Appeal has accepted that a local authority is not vicariously liable for foster parents' negligence, which caused injury to a child boarded out with them."[23]

2.13   The exceptions to this general statement are set out at paragraphs 5–48 to 5–66 and 5–67 to 5–70 of the same publication. Briefly they include situations where an entity has non-delegable duties either at common law or by statute or where land is involved, for example the withdrawal of support from neighbouring land, the undertaking of operations on a highway, *Rylands v. Fletcher*[24] liability, nuisance and occupier's liability. There are also potential exceptions involving the employer's common law duty to his employee, bailment and the loan of a chattel. However, the exceptions do not involve situations which would commonly involve the actions of sportsmen and they will not therefore be analysed in this chapter.

It may be that on the particular facts of a case a claimant may be able to argue that a club is liable for the acts of an amateur player by virtue of the fact that it comes within one of the exceptions to the general rule.

2.14   An alternative approach is to argue that amateur sportsmen do in fact come within the definition of employment and that there is no actual requirement for payment if the other distinguishing features of an employment relationship, such as control over the player, exist.

This approach was successful in the Australian case of *Kennedy v. Pender & Narooma Rugby League Football Club*[25] in which Mr Justice Blanch ruled that the on-field conduct of a rugby league player not receiving match fees remained the club's responsibility, including injuries caused by foul play.

The case involved Darren Kennedy, a centre for Bega Roosters rugby league club, who had his jaw broken in a tackle by Narooma Red Devils' centre Gary Pender. Mr Pender's elbow met Mr Kennedy's jaw after Mr Kennedy had passed the ball. At the time of the incident, the Roosters received a penalty but Mr Kennedy was unable to continue and X-rays later revealed that he had sustained a serious fracture which ultimately required two operations.

2.15   A claim was filed in the Bega District Court against Gary Pender and the Narooma Rugby League Football Club. Mr Pender was never found and did

---

[22] *Watkins v. Birmingham City Council, The Times*, August 1, 1975; (1976) 126 New L.J. 442, CA.

[23] *S. v. Walsall M.B.C.* [1985] 3 All E.R. 294.

[24] (1866) L.R. 1 EX 265; affirmed (1868) L.R. 3 HL.

[25] New South Wales District Court, Chief Judge Mr Justice Blanch, February 1, 2001. This is referred to at: www.borderattorneys.com.

not appear to defend the claim. Mr Justice Blanch heard evidence that the Narooma Red Devils were not paid match fees during 1997. The club's lawyers argued that the club could not be liable for the actions of volunteer players since they were not strictly employees. But Mr Justice Blanch ruled that when Mr Pender tackled Darren he was doing what the club expected him to do although he was doing so illegally. He therefore ordered Narooma to pay more than A$40,000 in damages plus costs.

Terry O'Riain, the solicitor who acted for Mr Kennedy, stated in a radio interview[26] that:

> "our argument was based simply on the master/servant relationship: are they involved in an organisation and are they doing work to promote the aims of the organisation, or the master if you like; are they working under the direction of the master, or the club, or the organisation, and is it done for the benefit of the club or the organisation or the master. And His Honour had no trouble finding that all of those things were the case."

In the interview, Mr O'Riain also stated that he believed that this was the first time that this sort of decision in the courts had been taken against a sporting club in Australia that did not pay its players.

If such a decision were to be reached in this country the implications for **2.16** amateur sporting organisations in any sport would be substantial. As with many of the areas covered in this book, only time will tell how the law will develop in this area.

Example

Ex-England captain Clive Bryan is now the manager of the amateur Minehead Barbarians Rugby team. Before the start of their game against Toowoomba XV he gives a team talk in which he says that the game is likely to be a physical one and he expects each player to go in hard and make sure that they put Toowoomba in no doubt as to who is in charge. In traditional style he also pours them each a pint of scrumpy cider in the dressing room and gets each player to empty their glass before going on the field. Spurred by the encouragement of Clive Bryan, Minehead's star player "Scrumpy King" Bruce Baker makes a number of heavy tackles which eventually result in him being sent off for 10 minutes. Whilst he is off the field, he and Clive Bryan manage to finish off two more pints of cider each. On returning to the field, Bruce Baker eventually makes a bad tackle which results in one of the Toowoomba players, Peter Kellett, sustaining an injury.

Can it be said that Clive Bryan and the Minehead Barbarians are vicariously liable for the injuries sustained by Peter Kellett?

Agency

In addition to the above, the principles of agency potentially open up the fields of liability even further and also need to be borne in mind. However, it would not appropriate to set these out in this particular text.

---

[26] See www.abc.net.au/rn/talks/8.30/sportsf/stories/s250575.htm for a transcript.

Further cases

The following cases provide some further useful examples in this area[27]:

Brown v. Lewis[28]

Blackburn Rovers Football Club committee were held liable for their own personal negligence in having employed an incompetent person to repair a stand: and a year later in 1897 the club converted its legal status into that of a limited liability company.

Williams v. Curzon Syndicate Ltd[29]

Defendant proprietors of a residential club employed an old and dangerous criminal as a night porter, one Lister, who stole the claimant's jewellery from a safe in the club manager's office. The claimant alleged that the defendants were negligent in employing such a man without taking proper care to ascertain his record. Because they were found not to have used due care in engaging an old lag, they were liable to make good the claimant's loss.

Bradley Egg Farm v. Clifford[30]

The Executive Council of an unincorporated poultry society were held to be personally liable for the damage caused by a servant of the society who performed a contract negligently. Because the society were unincorporated and there was no legal or factual principal on whose behalf the council members could act only those council members (as in the case of the Blackburn Rovers Committee members) would be liable. Other members of the society were not liable.

Thelma (Owners) v. University College School[31]

A pupil acting as a cox for a school eight was held to be the school's agent and the governors were liable for his negligence through defective steering on the River Thames.

Tomjanovich v. California Sports Inc[32]

The injured player, Tomjanovich, did not sue the other player, Kermit Washington. However, a lawsuit was brought against Washington's employer for injuries received when Washington punched Tomjanovich in

---

[27] See E. Grayson, *Sport and the Law* (3rd ed., Butterworths, 2000), pp. 284–286.
[28] (1896) 12 T.L.R. 455.
[29] (1919) 35 T.L.R. 475.
[30] [1943] 2 All E.R. 378 at 386.
[31] [1953] 2 Lloyd's Rep. 613.
[32] No. H–78–243 (SD Text 1979).

the face during the professional basketball game. Substantial damages were awarded by a jury, and settled on appeal: but liability was proved on the principle of the employer's failing to curb the offender's "dangerous tendencies" of what is known as "enforcer" in the National Basketball Association.

Robitaille v. Vancouver Hockey Club Ltd[33]

The British Columbia Court of Appeal upheld the Judge's damages award because of medical neglect of medical staff within control of the club citing *Monen v. Swinton and Pendlebury Borough Council.*[34]

Rogers v. Bugden and Canterbury Bankstown Club[35]

In Australia, the judgment of the New South Wales Supreme Court Common Law Division was reported by Grayson[36] to be en route to appeal after an award of A\$68,154.60 with costs against not only an offending player who broke an opponent's jaw in a professional rugby league game, but also the employer's club.[37]

Related areas

This book deals only with the personal injury aspects of sports law. However, in some actions there will be related causes of action which are pleaded. The reader is referred to the standard textbooks in the particular areas in this regard.   **2.17**

A good example of how wide potential actions can go may be found in the case of *Watson v. Bradford City AFC v. Gray and Huddersfield Town FC*[38] in which the Bradford City player, Gordon Watson, succeeded in his negligence action against Kevin Gray and his club, Huddersfield Town, following an incident in a Nationwide League first division match in February 1997 in which Watson sustained a double fracture of his right leg. This is dealt with in more detail in Chapter 3 below. However, the action also involved a claim by Watson's club for the loss of his services and other associated losses. They argued that Gray had unlawfully interfered with Watson's contract of employment. To that end, it was accepted on behalf of Bradford that it needed to establish recklessness for the purposes of the tort of unlawful interference with contract (a so-called "intentional" tort). In the

---

[33] [1981] D.L.R. (3rd) 288.
[34] [1965] 2 All E.R. 349 at 351.
[35] (Unreported) December 14, 1990 and see (1991) All E.R. Review 246 and E. Grayson, *Sport and the Law* (3rd ed., Butterworths, 2000) at 286.
[36] *Sport and the Law* (3rd ed., Butterworths, 2000), p. 279.
[37] See also, Chap. 27, below.
[38] *The Times*, November 26, 1998.

event, the court found that the tackle was negligent but not reckless, and Bradford's claim therefore failed at the first hurdle. As Craig Moore states in *Sports Law and Litigation*,[39] "It remains to be seen whether a club can recover for losses that it incurs as a result of the loss of one of its players due to the negligent infliction of injury caused by another player".

---

[39] 2nd ed., CLT Professional Publishing, 2000.

Part II

Sporting Liabilities

Chapter 3

Liability of participants to other participants

"Football isn't a contact sport, it's a collision sport. Dancing is a contact sport."

Duffy Daugherty.

This Chapter covers the potential liabilities which may arise between participants in sports events. It briefly touches on assault and battery and then analyses the increasing body of case law concerning negligence in this area.

Assault and battery

Potentially, injury inflicted by one competitor on another may give rise to a   **3.01**
cause of action in assault and battery, in other words, trespass to the person.

An assault is an overt act indicating an immediate intention to commit a battery, coupled with the capacity of carrying that intention into effect.[1] As for battery, Holt C.J. in *Cole v. Turner*[2] stated that it is "The least touching of another in anger".

However, such cases are likely to be rare since in order to establish such an action, a claimant would have to show that the defendant intentionally inflicted the injury. An obvious example would be the stabbing of Monica Seles by a Steffi Graf fan.

As Lord Denning made clear in *Letang v. Cooper*[3]:

"When injury is not inflicted intentionally, but negligently, I would say that the only cause of action is negligence and not trespass."

Craig Moore in *Sports Law and Litigation*[4] refers to *May v. Strong*[5]   **3.02**
where an award of £6,000 was made to a semi-professional footballer who

---

[1] *Stephens v. Myers* (1830) 4 C. & P. 349; *Read v. Coker* (1853) 13 C.B. 850.
[2] (1704) 6 Mod. 149.
[3] [1967] 1 Lloyd's Rep. 488.
[4] 2nd ed., CLT Professional Publishing Ltd, 2000.
[5] [1991] BPILS [2274].

suffered a compound fracture of his fibula and tibia as a result of a very late tackle from behind. He states that it is interesting to note that the trial judge found that the recklessness of the defendant was so great that the tackle amounted to an assault.

Edward Grayson in *Sport and the Law*[6] provides three examples of civil assault cases:

Hamish v. Smailes[7]

Involved a head butt causing a broken nose and black eyes to a 38-year-old local player in a local league match. The defendant was held liabile for civil assault (trespass to the person).

Vermont v. Green[8]

Kick during course of play to opponent causing two nights in hospital adjudicated to have been deliberate on the spur of the moment. Defendant held liable for civil assault (trespass to the person).

May v. Strong[8a]

Serious foul play and violent conduct to a 19-year-old semi-professional footballer. Defendant sent off by referee and recklessness held by the judge to amount to an assault.

Negligence

General

3.03 The question of the potential liability in negligence between participants goes to the very heart of the debate as to how far the law should intrude into the sporting arena. The previous Chapter has already set out some of the general principles with regard to negligence and also with regard to the issue of consent and specifically the defence of *volenti non fit injuria*.

The principles in this Chapter are not limited to sports such as football and rugby but may extend to all sports in which there is the possibility of injury. For example, it may be asked whether Mary Decker would today have a cause of action against Zola Budd for causing her to fall in the 1,500m semi-final at the Los Angeles Olympics.

---

[6] 3rd ed., Butterworths, 2000, p. 279.
[7] (Unreported, Epsom County Court, 1983) Provided to Edward Grayson by H.H.J. John A. Baker DL from Court archives.
[8] (Unreported, Basingstoke, 1989) E. Grayson, *Sport and the Law* (3rd ed., Butterworths, 2000); p. 279; provided to Edward Grayson by Oliver Sie, Barrister.
[8a] Teeside county court, 1990; Halsbury's Laws MRE 92/62 (1991) All E.R. 313; [1991] BPILS 2274.

As mentioned above, there are four requirements of the tort of negligence, namely[9]:

1. the existence in law of a duty of care situation, *i.e.* one in which the law attaches liability to carelessness. There has to be a recognition by the law that the careless infliction of the kind of damage in suit on the class of person to which the claimant belongs by the class of person to which the defendant belongs is actionable;

2. breach of the duty of care by the defendant, *i.e.* that it failed to measure up to the standard set by law;

3. a causal connection between the defendant's careless conduct and the damage;

4. that the particular kind of damage to the particular claimant is not so unforeseeable as to be too remote.

The existence of a duty of care between sports competitors is now well-established[10] and follows from the neighbour principle first articulated by Lord Atkin in *Donoghue v. Stevenson*.[11] As for causation and remoteness of damage this will depend upon the facts of each particular case. To some extent this is dealt with in Chapter 26 of this book. **3.04**

The key question therefore remains as to the standard of care expected of participants to their fellow participants.

Standard of care

Ordinary negligence or reckless disregard

The difficulty here is the fact that it may be said that the players have necessarily consented to the everyday rough and tumble associated with a particular sport. Indeed, having entered the field of play it might be reasonable to expect them to make every effort to win within the rules of the game. This problem is encapsulated in two dicta from Commonwealth courts. In the Australian case of *Rootes v. Skelton*,[12] it was said that: **3.05**

> "By engaging in a sport . . . the participants may be held to have accepted risks which are inherent in that sport . . . but this does not eliminate all duty of care of the one participant to the other."

In the Canadian case of *Agar v. Canning*[13] it was said:

---

[9] *Clerk & Lindsell on Torts* (18th ed., Sweet and Maxwell, 2000), para. 7–04.
[10] See the cases referred to in this Chapter and also Beloff, Kerr and Demetriou (1st ed., Hart Publishing, 1999), para. 5.34.
[11] [1932] A.C. 562 at 580.
[12] [1968] A.L.R. 33.
[13] (1965) 54 W.W.R. 302 at 304.

"The conduct of a player in the heat of the game is instinctive and unpremeditated and should not be judged by standards suited to polite social intercourse."

The main debate with regard to the standard of care is whether it is the ordinary standard expected in the law of negligence or whether something more is required in order to establish liability. This would be to take account of the element of consent involved in participation in sports.

3.06   Those advocating a higher threshold for liability[14] suggest that the test which should be adopted is the one set out in the case of *Wooldridge v. Sumner*[15] in the context of the liability of participants to spectators (for which, see Chapter 4, below). In that case, the Court of Appeal held that liability would only be founded if it was shown that there had been a "reckless disregard" for the spectator's safety.

This test has been applied in foreign jurisdictions where negligence was alleged by one player against another, notably in the United States (see, for example, *Nabozny v. Barnhill*[16]). As Gardiner and Felix have stated[17]:

"In North Amercia, a test of reckless disregard has developed, which is regarded as providing a balance between the safety of players and the competitive edge of sport. We believe that British law should reflect this development. It should not be enough to merely show negligence on the part of the defendant. The effect of making the defendant liable only in these circumstances, should be to lower the standard of care owed by a defendant to a plaintiff thus making it more difficult for a plaintiff to establish liability on the part of the defendant. This it seems to us, is entirely appropriate given the element of consent involved in sporting situations. In the United States, Narol argues that a trend has emerged across a number of states or the need for reckless disregard to be established.[18] The test is seen as being that the player knows an act is harmful and intends to commit that act, but does not intend to harm his opponent by that act.[19] Thus it falls somewhere between an intentional trespass and negligence, and the issue of negligent trespass to the person will no longer arise."

Gardiner *et al.* state in *Sports Law*[20] that the reckless disregard test also provides a more subjectivist approach to liability for participator violence. By requiring the defendant to act with a reckless disregard for the opponent, it is in effect requiring him to consciously act outside of the accepted playing culture of the particular sport. To be liable, the defendant will have known of the risks of causing injury by his act, that the taking of such risks is unacceptable according to the playing culture of that sport, he will have

---

[14] See, for example, S. Gardiner and A. Felix, "Juridification of the Football Field: Strategies for Giving Law the Elbow", Marquette Sports Law Journal, Vol. 5, 189 at 205ff.

[15] [1963] 2 Q.B. 43.

[16] 334 NE 2d 259 (Illinois Appellate Court 1975).

[17] S. Gardiner and A. Felix, "Juridification of the Football Field: Strategies for Giving Law the Elbow", Marquette Sports Law Journal, Vol. 5, 189 at 207.

[18] M. Narol, "Sports Torts: Emerging Standard of Care", Trial, June 1990.

[19] *Nabozny v. Barnhill*, 334 NE 2d 259 (Illinois Appellate Court 1975).

[20] 2nd ed., Cavendish Publishing Ltd, 2000, Chap. 16.

gone on to do the act in spite of this and will have caused injury by the act. The test, they say, attempts to reflect more pragmatically the actual state of mind of the participant in judging whether liability should be imposed for the particular injury caused.

It should be noted that there are further distinctions which potentially   3.07 have yet to be drawn. For example, in Germany a distinction is made between team sports and sports performed individually with a higher duty of care attaching to the latter.[21]

There are two Court of Appeal authorities directly on the issue of the standard of care between participants, namely *Condon v. Basi*[22] and *Caldwell v. Fitzgerald & ors*[23] and a number of first instance decisions. Given the confusion which often arises in this area, it is worth looking at these judgments in some detail. It will be seen that the "reckless disregard" test has now been rejected by the Court of Appeal.

Condon v. Basi

The first major decision in this area came in *Condon v. Basi*[24] in which an amateur footballer was held liable for breaking his opponent's leg in a tackle during a local league match between the claimant's team Whittle Wanderers and the defendant's team Khalsa Football Club. The judgment is worth quoting in some detail. Lord Donaldson M.R.[25] commented on the apparent lack of authority and quoted from two Australian Judges:

> "It is said that there is no authority as to what is the standard of care which governs the conduct of players in competitive sports generally and, above all, in a competitive sport whose rules and general background contemplate that there will be physical contact between the players, but that appears to be the position. This is somewhat surprising, but appears to be correct. For my part I would completely accept the decision of the High Court of Australia in *Rootes v. Shelton* [1968] A.L.R. 33. I think it suffices, in order to see the law which has to be applied, to quote briefly from the judgment of Barwick C.J. and from the judgment of Kitto J. Barwick C.J. said, at 34:
>
> > 'By engaging in a sport or pastime the participants may be held to have accepted risks which are inherent in that sport or pastime: the tribunal of fact can make its own assessment of what the accepted risks are: but this does not eliminate all duty of care of the one participant to the other. Whether or not such a duty arises, and, if it does, its extent, must necessarily depend in each case upon its own circumstances. In this connection, the rules of the sport or game may constitute one of those circumstances: but, in my opinion, they are

---

[21] See M. Nolte, "An Introduction to (German) Sports Law", The International Sports Law Journal, October 2001, 14 at 17.
[22] [1985] 1 W.L.R. 866.
[23] [2001] E.W.C.A. Civ. 1054, Court of Appeal (Civil Division), Lord Woolf C.J., Tuckey L.J., June 27, 2001.
[24] [1985] 1 W.L.R. 866.
[25] With whom Stephen Brown L.J. and Glidewell J. agreed.

neither definitive of the existence nor of the extent of the duty; nor does their breach or non-observance necessarily constitute a breach of any duty found to exist.'

Kitto J. said, at 37:

'in a case such as the present, it must always be a question of fact, what exoneration from a duty of care otherwise incumbent upon the defendant was implied by the act of the plaintiff in joining in the activity. Unless the activity partakes of the nature of a war or of something else in which all is notoriously fair, the conclusion to be reached must necessarily depend, according to the concepts of the common law, upon the reasonableness, in relation to the special circumstances, of the conduct which caused the plaintiff's injury. That does not necessarily mean the compliance of that conduct with the rules, conventions or customs (if there are any) by which the correctness of conduct for the purpose of the carrying on of the activity as an organized affair is judged; for the tribunal of fact may think that in the situation in which the plaintiff's injury was caused a participant might do what the defendant did and still not be acting unreasonably, even though he infringed the "rules of the game." Non-compliance with such rules, conventions or customs (where they exist) is necessarily one consideration to be attended to upon the question of reasonableness; but it is only one, and it may be of much or little or even no weight in the circumstances.' "

3.08   Having quoted from these Judges, he noted the two differing approaches which as he saw it "produce precisely the same result". In summary, these two approaches were:

a. that of Barwick C.J. "to take a more generalised duty of care and to modify it on the basis that the participants in the sport or pastime impliedly consent to taking risks which otherwise would be a breach of the duty of care";

b. that "exemplified by the judgment of Kitto J." "where he is saying, in effect, that there is a general standard of care, namely the Lord Atkin approach in *Donoghue v. Stevenson* [1932] A.C. 562 that you are under a duty to take all reasonable care taking account of the circumstances in which you are placed, which, in a game of football, are quite different from those which affect you when you are going for a walk in the countryside."

He then went on to say:

"For my part I would prefer the approach of Kitto J., but I do not think it makes the slightest difference in the end if it is found by the tribunal of fact that the defendant failed to exercise that degree of care which was appropriate in all the circumstances, or that he acted in a way to which the plaintiff cannot be expected to have consented. In either event, there is liability."

As to the facts of the particular case, he quoted from the report of "the very experienced Class 1 referee, who officiated on this occasion" who said:

"After 62 minutes of play of the above game, a player from Whittle Wanderers received possession of the ball some 15 yards inside Khalsa Football Club's half of the field of play. This Whittle Wanderers' player upon realising that he was about to be challenged for the ball by an opponent pushed the ball away. As he did so, the opponent [the defendant] challenged, by sliding in from a distance of about three to four yards. The slide tackle came late, and was made in a reckless and dangerous manner, by lunging with his boot studs showing about a foot–18 inches from the ground. The result of this tackle was that [the plaintiff] sustained a broken right leg. In my opinion, the tackle constituted serious foul play and I sent [the defendant] from the field of play."

The Judge at first instance wholly accepted the referee's evidence, subject   **3.09** to a modification in that he thought the defendant's foot was probably nine inches off the ground. He said that he entirely accepted the "value judgments" of the referee and said:

"[The tackle] was made in a reckless and dangerous manner not with malicious intent towards the plaintiff but in an 'excitable manner without thought of the consequences.'"

The Judge's final conclusion was that:

"It is not for me in this court to attempt to define exhaustively the duty of care between players in a soccer football game. Nor, in my judgment, is there any need because there was here such an obvious breach of the defendant's duty of care towards the plaintiff. He was clearly guilty, as I find the facts, of serious and dangerous foul play which showed a reckless disregard of the plaintiff's safety and which fell far below the standards which might reasonably be expected in anyone pursuing the game."

Lord Donaldson M.R. agreed with the Judge and dismissed the appeal saying:

"For my part I cannot see how that conclusion can be faulted on its facts, and on the law I do not see how it can possibly be said that the defendant was not negligent."

Thus it was that Mr Basi was held liable for Mr Condon's broken leg, his sliding tackle having been adjudged to constitute "serious foul play", to have been made in a reckless and dangerous manner (albeit without malicious intent), and to have been worthy of a sending off.

First instance judgments after Condon v. Basi

Condon v. Basi was followed by a number of first instance decisions.   **3.10**

Chapter 3—Liability of participants to other participants

Elliott v. Saunders and Liverpool FC

In *Elliott v. Saunders and Liverpool FC*,[26] Paul Elliott, playing for Chelsea
Football Club, failed to establish that Dean Saunders, then of Liverpool,
had acted with such lack of care as to be in breach of his duty to exercise
reasonable care in all the circumstances, when the defendant's tackle had
severed the claimant's cruciate ligaments. In so holding, Drake J. appeared
to accept that the circumstances were such that the claimant would have to
have been able to establish that the defendant had been guilty of dangerous
and reckless play to get home. He went on to accept the evidence of the
defendant that he had raised his feet in the tackle at the last moment in an
instinctive attempt to avoid probable serious injury to himself. Such instinctive reactions were not such as, in the Judge's view, to give rise to liability in
law, occurring as they did in the heat of battle.

Drake J. concluded that a deliberate foul or an error of judgment might
be capable of giving rise to liability but, ultimately, each case turned on its
own particular facts.

McCord v. Swansea City Football Club

3.11　The significant breakthrough, in terms of a successful negligence claim by
one professional player against another, came in *McCord v. Swansea City
Football Club*,[27] when an award estimated to be in the region of £250,000
was made to a former Stockport County player, Brian McCord, whose
career ended when he broke his leg in a tackle. Kennedy J. found that the
Swansea City player, John Carnforth, had been negligent when he challenged McCord for a loose ball in a game in March 1993. The court ruled
that the tackle, in which Carnforth slid on one leg with his right foot over
the ball as the pair went for a 50–50 ball, was "an error which was
inconsistent with his taking reasonable care towards his opponent". He said
that he had adopted the stance that an "ordinary, reasonable"[27a] spectator
would take and concluded that the tackle was inconsistent with reasonable
care.

Watson v. City AFC v. Gray and Huddersfield Town FC

This case was followed by *Watson v. Bradford City AFC v. Gray and
Huddersfield Town FC*[28] in which the Bradford City player, Gordon Watson, succeeded in his negligence action against Kevin Gray and his club,

---

[26] Unreported, June 10, 1994; Halsbury's Laws of England 1994, Annual Abridgement, para.
2056.
[27] *The Times*, February 11, 1997; Q.B. Transcript, December 19, 1996.
[27a] See C. Moore, *Sports Law and Litigation* (2nd ed., CLT Professional Publishing, 2000)
p. 78.
[28] *The Times*, November 26, 1998.

Huddersfield Town, following an incident in a Nationwide League first division match in February 1997 in which Watson sustained a double fracture of his right leg. At trial, Hooper J. formulated the following test for negligence in player against player actions in the context of a professional football match:

"Had it been shown, on a balance of probabilities, that a player would have known there was a significant risk that if he tackled in the way he did, the other player would be seriously injured?"

This suggests a two-pronged approach:

(a) the risk must be significant;

(b) the risk must be of significant injury.

It is significant to note that in this case the court found that the tackle was negligent but not reckless and founded liability on this basis.

Specifically, Watson was chasing a loose ball when Gray launched himself **3.12** into the air at Watson from a distance of two to three yards away and at a right angle to him. Watson kicked the ball with a glancing blow and a split second later the sole of Gray's left boot, with his leg straight, struck Watson's right lower leg causing a double fracture.

The Judge said that such a forceful, high challenge, particularly when carried out when there was a good chance that the ball had been moved on, was one that a reasonable professional player would have known carried with it a significant risk of injury.[28a]

In addition to these cases, another was settled out of court for an undisclosed sum in 1997. It involved former Sheffield Wednesday defender Ian Knight and Chester City for whom Gary Bennett was playing when he made a tackle on Knight which ended Knight's career.

Pitcher v. Huddersfield Town Football Club Ltd

In *Pitcher v. Huddersfield Town Football Club Ltd*[29] the claimant was a professional footballer. He had started playing from a young age and was signed by Crystal Palace in 1994. He had a regular place in the first team and had played numerous league games and cup matches. Whilst playing against the defendant team he was injured by one of their players, Paul Reid, who, it was alleged, chased the claimant and lunged at him with his left leg and struck him with his boot on his right knee. This caused the claimant to suffer severe injury to his knee that was irreparable. The claimant immediately knew that something serious had happened and when he looked

---

[28a] See C. Moore, *Sports Law and Litigation* (2nd ed., CLT Professional Publishing, 2000) pp. 78–82.

[29] Queen's Bench Division, Hallett J., July 17, 2001.

down he saw that there was a stud mark imprint on his knee. The claimant argued that the defendant was negligent and that Paul Reid failed to exercise reasonable skill and care and that his standard of football fell below that expected of a professional footballer. The claim was for more than £1 million.[30]

3.13   Hallett J. held that the defendant was not in breach of its duty of care and could not be liable in negligence for this type of injury despite expert evidence in support of the claim from Sky Sports pundit Frank McLintock and [then] Crystal Palace manager David Bassett.[31] Paul Reid was guilty of a mis-timed tackle and an error of judgment. The expert evidence given by Jimmy Hill and Frank Clark on behalf of Huddersfield TFC, was that this type of tackle was seen many times every Saturday afternoon.

Further, there was no evidence to support the claimant's assertion that there were stud marks imprinted on his knee after the injury. The physio-therapist could not remember seeing such an injury on the claimant's knee and neither could his manager or his doctor. It was accepted that certain sports carried a risk of injury and that the level of care required was tailored to each set of circumstances.

Hallett J. concluded that it was for the claimant to establish on the balance of probabilities that the conduct of Paul Reid fell below the standard of a professional footballer. The claimant could not establish this and did not have enough evidence to support his claim in negligence. Specifically, she stated:

"The fact that he used his left foot was a mistake. In tactical terms he had a far better chance of intercepting the ball by using his right. He is on the evidence, however, not just a naturally left footed player but one who is reluctant to use his right. He would be a better player, no doubt, if he did use his right foot more often. Again there is nothing on the video or in the material before me to indicate to my satisfaction that he was doing anything other than instinctively using his strong foot. In the heat of the moment that is what many players may do.

I also accept the evidence that he was then committed in body and mind to continue the tackle. There may well be circumstances when a player committed as he was could and would still pull out of a tackle at the last minute or use some nifty footwork to avoid contact with the opposing player. Mistimed tackles do occur; players do make contact with other players without reaching the ball or before reaching the ball. If they do and the referee sees it, it will lead to a free kick. The rules are designed to discourage late tackles. They are, however, a common feature of the game and they do not lead automatically to a sending off.

There must be something more. I am satisfied that this was not something more; this was a misjudged attempt to get at the ball. It was the ball which was about to be passed which was a threat to Mr Reid's team, not Mr Pitcher. I am not prepared, therefore, to say on the balance of probabilities that this tackle was

---

[30] *The Guardian*, July 17, 2001. See also Legal news in brief, Xpress, July 2001, www.hextalls.com.
[31] Law Gazette, September 7, 2001.

anything more than an error of judgment, nor am I prepared to find that Mr Reid was guilty of negligence in failing to pull up, change direction or change his mind and bring his foot down in 0.2 of a second."

She went on to conclude:

"So, although I am satisfied that this was a late and no doubt a clumsy tackle in coaching terms, the claimant cannot establish that it went any further. It was a foul but I am not satisfied that it was more. It was an error of judgment in the context of a fast moving game where Paul Reid had to react to events in a matter of split seconds. Whatever their training and their skills, First Division footballers are far from infallible. This was the kind of tackle which, although against the rules of the game, occurs up and down the country every Saturday of the football season in Division One matches. As hard as he has tried, [Counsel for the Claimant] has not in my judgment succeeded in crossing the threshold, the high threshold that lay in his path to take this case from a simple late tackle, albeit one with tragic consequences to Mr Pitcher, to one actionable in negligence."

Caldwell v. Fitzgerald & ors[32]

Just before the judgment in *Pitcher v. Huddersfield Town Football Club Ltd* **3.14** came out the Court of Appeal gave judgment in the related case of *Caldwell v. Fitzgerald & ors*.[33] In that case the claimant was a jockey participating in a National Hunt race. The defendants were fellow competitors. The first defendant, riding a horse called Master Hyde, and the second defendant, on Mr Bean, crossed the path of Royal Citizen ridden by B on the inside rail of the racecourse and three quarters of a length behind. Royal Citizen shied from the closing gap, unseated B and hampered Fion Corn, ridden by the claimant, with the result that the horse fell, causing personal injury to the claimant.

Neither defendant had looked to the left before going for the rail and so crossing Royal Citizen's path, nor heard B shouting out a warning as they encroached. At a subsequent steward's inquiry the two defendants were found guilty of careless riding contrary to rule 153(iii) of the Jockey Club Rules in not having left B enough room to come round the inside rail.

Guidance issued to the stewards defines "careless riding" as:

"A rider is guilty of careless riding if he fails to take reasonable steps to avoid causing interference or causes interference by misjudgment or inattention."

Based on statistical evidence, the Judge concluded that careless riding was a relatively common offence (the statistics showed that in 1999 there were

---

[32] See C. Porter, "A Whole New Ball Game" and M. James and F. Deeley, "Sports Safety", Sports Law Bulletin, September/October 2001.

[33] [2001] E.W.C.A. Civ. 1054, Court of Appeal (Civil Division), Lord Woolf C.J., Tuckey L.J., June 27, 2001.

129 cases) and (as he described it) "low in terms of heinousness" by comparison with the other offences referred to in rule 153(iii).

3.15 The claimant subsequently brought an action in negligence claiming damages for personal injury. Two distinguished experts, John Francome and Carl Llewellyn, gave evidence at the trial. They agreed with the finding of the stewards because they thought that the defendants should not have taken the inside line unless and until they were one length clear of Royal Citizen and should have looked to their left to ensure that Royal Citizen was no longer in contention before changing course.

On February 1, 2001 Holland J. dismissed the claim, having found the defendants not liable in negligence, each of the defendants being guilty of a lapse of care which did not surmount the threshold of liability. In doing so he stated that in determining the standard of care required by one sporting participant to another the threshold for liability in practice was inevitably high and that in practice it might therefore be difficult to prove any such breach of duty in the absence of proof of conduct that in fact amounted to reckless disregard for the fellow contestant's safety. The claimant appealed. It was submitted on his behalf that the Judge had applied too low a test to the relevant standard of care, in effect equating breach with deliberate or reckless disregard for safety; in any event the Judge should have found the defendants liable.

3.16 As to the law, the Judge said that the "primary guidance" for him must come from the Court of Appeal. He noted that this court had never had to consider an entirely similar situation, but had considered analogous situations in five cases, which he reviewed. From these cases he extracted five propositions:

1. Each contestant in a lawful sporting contest (and in particular a race) owes a duty of care to each and all other contestants.

2. That duty is to exercise in the course of the contest all care that is objectively reasonable in the prevailing circumstances for the avoidance of infliction of injury to such fellow contestants.

3. The prevailing circumstances are all such properly attendant upon the contest and include its object, the demands inevitably made upon its contestants, its inherent dangers (if any), its rules, conventions and customs, and the standards, skills and judgment reasonably to be expected of a contestant. Thus in the particular case of a horse race the prevailing circumstances will include the contestant's obligation to ride a horse over a given course competing with the remaining contestants for the best possible placing, if not for a win. Such must further include the Rules of Racing and the standards, skills and judgment of a professional jockey, all as expected by fellow contestants.

4. Given the nature of such prevailing circumstances the threshold for liability is in practice inevitably high; the proof of a breach of duty will not flow from proof of no more than an error of judgment or from mere proof of a momentary lapse in skill (and thus care) respectively when subject to the stresses of a race. Such are no more than incidents inherent in the nature of the sport.

5. In practice it may therefore be difficult to prove any such breach of duty in the absence of proof of conduct that in point of fact amounts to reckless disregard for the fellow contestant's safety. I emphasise the distinction between the expression of legal principle and the practicalities of the evidential burden.

It was argued that the last two propositions were unduly restrictive and not supported by the Court of Appeal authorities, which the Judge considered.

In giving judgment, Tuckey L.J. then went on to look at those authorities. **3.17** The first was *Condon v. Basi*[34] which has been looked at above. He continued by saying that surprisingly, the court in *Condon* were not referred to three earlier Court of Appeal cases. The first two, *Wooldridge v. Sumner*,[35] and *Wilks v. Cheltenham Homeguard Motor Cycle Co. and Light Car Club*,[36] were spectator cases where the claimants were at a horse show (in *Wooldridge*) and a motorcycle scramble (in *Wilks*). These are dealt with in the next Chapter. Both cases in effect provided that the competitor needed to show a "reckless disregard" for the safety of the spectator for liability to attach.

In the third case, *Harrison v. Vincent*,[37] a sidecar passenger sued the motorcycle rider for injuries sustained during a race when he was unable to stop because he missed his gear and his brakes failed at the same time. Sir John Arnold approved the *Wooldridge* approach as the applicable standard so far as the claim was based on the rider missing his gear, but said the same did not apply to the brake failure because the fault had occurred before the race in the relative calm of the workshop.

The last, and in Tuckey L.J.'s view, most important of the cases considered by Holland J., was *Smoldon v. Whitworth*.[38] In that case the claimant sued another player and a referee at a rugby match in which he was badly injured when the scrum collapsed. The claim against the player was dismissed, but the referee was found liable and appealed. Lord Bingham C.J., giving the judgment of the court, recorded that the defendant had invited the Judge to say that nothing short of reckless disregard for the

---

[34] [1985] 1 W.L.R. 866.
[35] [1963] 2 Q.B. 43.
[36] [1971] 1 W.L.R. 668.
[37] [1982] R.T.R. 8.
[38] [1997] P.I.Q.R. P133.

claimant's safety would suffice to establish a breach of the duty which the referee admittedly owed to the player. The Judge, however, had adopted the test proposed by the claimant derived from *Condon* that the duty was to exercise such degree of care as was appropriate in all the circumstances. The court said that the Judge was right to accept the claimant's approach. This is dealt with in more detail in Chapter 12, below.

In *Smoldon*, Lord Bingham reconciled the differing approaches of the Judge in that case and of those in *Wooldridge and Wilks* with regard to spectators when he said:

> "There is in our judgment no inconsistency between this conclusion and that reached by the Court of Appeal in *Wooldridge v. Sumner and Wilks v. Cheltenham Homeguard Motor Cycle Co. and Light Car Cycle Club*. In these cases it was recognised that a sporting competitor, properly intent on winning the contest, was (and was entitled to be) all but oblivious of spectators. It therefore followed that he would have to be shown to have very blatantly disregarded the safety of spectators before he could be held to have failed to exercise such care as was reasonable in all the circumstances."

3.18   In *Caldwell*, Tuckey L.J. concluded that "The relevant principles to be applied to a case of this kind emerge clearly from the decision of this court in *Condon* and *Smoldon*, which are binding on us".

He explained away the Judge's mention of "reckless disregard" in the following way:

> "In his fourth and fifth propositions, the judge made it clear that he was referring to "the practicalities" of the evidential burden and not to legal principle. All he was saying was that, in practice, given the circumstances which he had identified, the threshold for liability was high. Lord Bingham C.J. said the same of a referee in *Smoldon*, even though, as he pointed out, the referee was not in the same position as a player because one of the referee's responsibilities was the safety of the players. Lord Brennan accepted that the threshold of liability as between participants must be at least as high as that between player and referee.
>
> The judge did not say that a claimant has to establish recklessness. That approach was specifically rejected by this court in *Smoldon*. As in *Smoldon*, there will be no liability for errors of judgment, oversights or lapses of which any participant might be guilty in the context of a fast-moving contest. Something more serious is required. I do not think it is helpful to say any more than this in setting the standard of care to be expected in cases of this kind.
>
> For these reasons I do not think that the judge applied the wrong standard of care in this case."

Judge L.J. agreed with Tuckey L.J. and stated:

> "In an action for damages by one participant in a sporting contest against another participant in the same game or event, the issue of negligence cannot be resolved in a vacuum. It is fact specific.

We are here concerned with a split-second, virtually instantaneous, decision made by professional sportsmen entrusted with powerful animals, paid and required by the rules of their sport to ride them, at speed, to victory or, failing victory, to the best possible placing: in other words, to beat all the other horses in the race, or endeavour to do so. The course has no lanes; nor is it straight. The horse, as this case demonstrated, has a will of its own. The demands on professional jockeys to ride at all are very heavy. They require skill and physical and mental courage. To win, beyond skill and courage, they need determination and concentration, the ability rapidly to assess and re-assess the constantly changing racing conditions, and to adjust their own riding and tactics accordingly—a quality that must depend in part on experience and in part on intuition or instinct.

Accidents and the risk of injury, sometimes catastrophic, both to horses and to riders, are an inevitable concomitant of every horse race—certainly over hurdles. All National Hunt jockeys know the risks. The rules of racing which bind them all, and the jockeys' own responsibilities to each other during the race, properly fulfilled, are intended to reduce the inevitable risks. But they cannot extinguish them. And, as a final ingredient, what is actually taking place on the real race-course is not nearly as sanitised as it can appear to be even to spectators in the stand or, more particularly, to those watching at home on television. Jockeys and horses are often in close proximity to the other runners. There is a good deal of noise and inevitable tension. Mistakes by riders and horses are inevitable; and fortune, good or bad, plays its part in each race, as it does in any other sporting event."

Judge L.J. referred to *Smoldon* and commented on the level of care required:

"The level of care required is that which is appropriate in all the circumstances, and the circumstances are of crucial importance. Full account must be taken of the factual context in which a referee exercises his functions, and he could not be properly held liable for errors of judgment, oversights or lapses of which any referee might be guilty in the context of a fast moving and vigorous context. The threshold of liability is a high one. It will not easily be crossed.

That case involved an action against a referee. Referees have specific responsibility for the safety of the participants in the sport. It is clear from the passage in Lord Bingham's judgment that a referee would be entitled to escape liability in negligence for what was no more than oversight or error of judgment. It seems to me to follow that a participant who has caused injury to another participant in the same game or contest should be similarly entitled.

Accordingly, for the reasons given by my Lord, and in this short judgment, Holland J. was entitled to find that negligence had not been established against the defendants."

Conclusion

From these cases and in particular *Condon* and *Caldwell*, the following **3.19** principles can be derived as to the standard of care:

1. there is a general standard of care, namely the Lord Atkin approach in *Donoghue v. Stevenson*[39] that a player is under a duty to take all reasonable care taking account of the circumstances;

2. the standard appears to be objective, but objective having regard to the particular set of circumstances;

3. the circumstances are of crucial importance to the level of care required;

4. liability will not attach for errors of judgment, oversights or lapses of which any player might be guilty in the context of a fast moving and vigorous context; something more serious is required;

5. the threshold of liability is a high one which is not easily crossed.

Perhaps another and more simple way of looking at this problem is to use a dictum of Lord Denning from a different context in the case of *Lane v. Holloway*.[40] In that case the claimant had challenged the defendant to a fight (after one of them had referred to the other's wife as a "monkey faced tart"), in the course of which, however, the claimant was injured by a severe punch in the eye. In holding the defendant liable, Lord Denning M.R. remarked that the defendant:

" . . . went much too far in striking a blow out of all proportion to the occasion."

Although that case was one where the cause of action was assault and the discussion centred on the issue of consent, it is suggested by David Griffith-Jones and Adrian Barr-Smith in *Law and the Business of Sport*[41] that the concept of acting "out of all proportion to the occasion" is a useful one when considering the nature and extent of a sportsman's liability to his opponents and fellow competitors.

3.20   What is absolutely clear is that the circumstances are of crucial importance. The following circumstances (among others) were taken into account in the three main cases:

1. *Condon*: that the circumstances in a game of football are quite different from those which affect you when you are going for a walk in the countryside.

2. *Smoldon*: that one of the referee's responsibilities was the safety of the players; that the context was fast moving and vigorous.

---

[39] [1932] A.C. 562.
[40] [1968] 1 Q.B. 379 at 388.
[41] Butterworths, 1997, p. 12.

3. *Caldwell*: that the decisions were split-second, virtually instantaneous; that the decisions were made by professional sportsmen entrusted with powerful animals, paid and required by the rules of their sport to ride them, at speed, to victory or, failing victory, to the best possible placing; the course had no lanes; nor was it straight; the horse had a will of its own; the demands on professional jockeys are very heavy; accidents and the risk of injury, sometimes catastrophic, both to horses and to riders, are an inevitable concomitant of every horse race, certainly over hurdles; all National Hunt jockeys know the risks; the rules of racing are intended to reduce the inevitable risks but cannot extinguish them; mistakes by riders and horses are inevitable and fortune, good or bad, plays its part in each race, as it does in any other sporting event.

In *Sports Law*,[42] Beloff, Kerr and Demetriou suggest that the following include the relevant circumstances to be taken into account:

1. whether the sport is a contact or a non-contact sport. Different standards apply to boxing (where the object is to engage in bodily contact) from rugby (where it is an incidental, but inevitable feature of the sport) to bowls (where such contact should not occur);

2. whether the accident is caused in the heat of the moment or in a quiet passage of play;

3. the level of risk necessarily accepted as inherent in the sport;

4. whether the rules of the game have been broken;

5. the cost and availability of precautions;

6. the level of risk involved.

Such a list is helpful and the factors speak for themselves. However, it is **3.21** not exhausative and other factors may be relevant to a specific context. Factors or circumstances which deserve further analysis in the present context are: specific factors or "circumstances" which have been considered to a limited extent and caused some debate are:

1. the cost and availability of precautions and the level of risk involved (points 5 and 6, above);

2. whether the standard of care required of professionals is the same as that required of amateurs;

---

[42] 1st ed., Hart Publishing, 1999, para. 5.38.

3. the significance of a breach of the rules of the game or lack of such a breach as the case may be.

These are briefly considered below.

Cost and availability of precautions and level of risk

3.22 The factors were relevant in *Lewis v. Bucknall Golf Club*[43] where a high handicap golfer was held to have been negligent in failing to wait before driving off the fifth tee. When he drove, he mis-hit the ball which struck and injured the pursuer, who was fully visible to him. The court stated that the mis-hit was something a reasonable man would have in contemplation as a risk that was reasonably likely to happen, *i.e.* more than merely possible, but less than probable, and it was negligent to run such a risk in a situation where it could be avoided without difficulty, disadvantage or expense.

This may be contrasted with *Feeney v. Lyall*[44] where the pursuer failed in a claim arising out of the circumstance that during a round of golf he was struck by a golf ball when he was in an unexpected fairway and invisible to the striker.

Professionals and amateurs

General principles

3.23 The question has arisen and become a matter of some debate as to whether professional footballers should be held to higher standards of care than amateurs.

From first principles it would seem logical that the answer to this question should be no. The standard is objective (as made clear in *Condon*) and therefore all should be held to the same standard.

Indeed, if it were otherwise, as Craig Moore has pointed out in *Sports Law and Litigation*,[45] the principles may lead to the anomalous situation that when a Premier League side plays a non-league side in an FA Cup match, the players of the former side owe a higher standard of care to their opponents than the corresponding obligation.

Such a conclusion would also be consistent with other analogous situations in the law of negligence. For example, in *Nettleship v. Weston*,[46] the Court of Appeal held that the duty of care owed by a learner driver was the same as that owed by every driver.

---

[43] [1993] C.L.T. (Sh. Ct.) 43.
[44] [1991] S.L.T. (Notes) 156.
[45] 2nd ed., CLT Professional Publishing, 2000.
[46] [1971] 3 W.L.R. 370.

Decided sports cases

However, despite these points, in *Condon*, Lord Donaldson controversially **3.24**
disagreed. In particular, he made the following comment (although on the
facts it was *obiter*):

> "The standard is objective, but objective in a different set of circumstances. Thus
> there will of course be a higher degree of care required of a player in a First
> Division football match than of a player in a local league football match."

However, in *Elliott v. Saunders and Liverpool FC*[47] which actually
involved professional footballers, whilst following *Condon v. Basi*, Drake J.
did not agree with these *obiter* comments. He said that the standard of care
in each case was the same, although, the nature and level of the match in
question (and accordingly, the standards of skill to be expected from the
players) would form part of the factual context within which such standard
fell to be applied.

However, in *Watson v. Bradford City AFC v. Gray and Huddersfield
Town FC*,[48] *Pitcher v. Huddersfield Town Football Club Ltd*[49] and *Caldwell
v. Fitzgerald & ors*,[50] the courts appear to have taken into account the fact
that the participants were professionals.

In *Watson v. Bradford City AFC v. Gray and Huddersfield Town FC*,[51]
the test used by the Judge (see above) was agreed on behalf of the claimants
subject to (among other things) that the standard must be that of a reasonable professional player.

In *Pitcher v. Huddersfield Town Football Club Ltd*,[52] it was held that it
was for the claimant to establish on the balance of probabilities that the
conduct of Paul Reid fell below the standard of a professional footballer.
Hallett J. found it relevant that the tackle was the type of challenge which
occurred up and down the country every Saturday in the First Division.[53]

In *Caldwell v. Fitzgerald & ors*,[54] the fact that the parties were pro- **3.25**
fessional jockeys was held to be a relevant circumstance. Ironically in this
case the fact that they were professionals almost mitigated their mistakes
due to the pressures on professional jockeys, "to beat all the other horses in
the race, or endeavour to do so".[55]

---

[47] Unreported, June 10, 1994; Halsbury's Laws of England 1994, Annual Abridgement, para.
2056.
[48] *The Times*, November 26, 1998.
[49] QBD, Hallett J., July 17, 2001.
[50] [2001] E.W.C.A. Civ. 1054, CA (Civil Division), Lord Woolf C.J., Tuckey L.J., June 27,
2001.
[51] *The Times*, November 26, 1998.
[52] QBD, Hallett J., July 17, 2001.
[53] *The Guardian*, July 17, 2001.
[54] [2001] E.W.C.A. Civ. 1054, CA (Civil Division), Lord Woolf C.J., Tuckey L.J., June 27,
2001.
[55] Judge L.J., above.

The conclusion in *Caldwell* is similar to that in *McComiskey v. McDermott*,[56] the duty owed by a rally driver to his navigator was held to be to exercise such care as was reasonably to be expected of a driver going all out to win the rally.

Conclusion

3.26 The answer to this may be that although the standard of care is objective and not variable, the fact that a particular participant is a professional may be a circumstance which can be taken into account among the many others. In particular, allowance can be made for the fact that different players at different levels within a sport will have different skill levels and expectations of risk. As Gardiner *et al.* put it in *Sports Law*[57]:

> "The same standard of play is not expected of a local league player and a national league player. However, the same standard of care in the circumstances is expected. The problem that has arisen is the clumsy means by which the courts have tried to reconcile these two concepts."

Breach of rules of game

3.27 In *Condon*, Lord Donaldson M.R. accepted the judgment of Kitto J. in *Rootes v. Shelton*.[58] In particular, Kitto J. stated:

> "Non-compliance with such rules, conventions or customs (where they exist) is necessarily one consideration to be attended to upon the question of reasonableness; but it is only one, and it may be of much or little or even no weight in the circumstances."

The clear implication is that, in the case of contact sports such as football and rugby, it will be almost impossible to establish liability unless the actions of the defendant are outside the rules of the game. Indeed, the Court of Appeal appear to have been saying that a breach of the rules is virtually a necessary, though not necessarily a sufficient, requirement for liability to attach.

In *Caldwell*, too, Tuckey L.J. stated:

> "The Jockey Club's rules and its findings are of course relevant matters to be taken into account, but, as the authorities make clear, the finding that the respondents were guilty of careless riding is not determinative of negligence. As the judge said, there is a difference between response by the regulatory authority and response by the courts in the shape of a finding of legal liability."

In the same case, Judge L.J. added in this regard:

---

[56] [1974] I.R. 75.
[57] 2nd ed., Cavendish Publishing Ltd, 2000, Chap. 16.
[58] [1968] A.L.R. 33 at 37.

"The rules of racing which bind them all, and the jockeys' own responsibilities to each other during the race, properly fulfilled, are intended to reduce the inevitable risks. But they cannot extinguish them."

Such an approach has also been applied in other sporting contexts. For example:

(a) In *Wright v. Cheshire County Council*,[59] the fact that certain gymnastic activities were being conducted in a manner which was generally accepted, caused the Court of Appeal to overturn a finding of liabilities in respect of injuries caused.

(b) In *Gilsenan v. Gunning*,[60] the "custom of the slopes" was one ingredient which went into determining the issue of liability in a skiing accident case.

(c) In *Leatherland v. Edwards*,[61] it was held that where a defendant breached a safety rule intrinsic to uni-hockey, he was negligent when the high follow through of his stick caused the claimant to lose the sight of one eye.

It should be noted in this context that just because a referee has failed to spot or to punish an action does not necessarily mean that liability must fail. Each case will depend upon its own facts but it is possible in theory to prove a breach of the rules in such a case in any event.   **3.28**

In the context of rules of the game, it is interesting to note that Simon Gardiner and Alexandra Felix in "Juridification of the Football Field: Strategies for Giving Law the Elbow"[62] suggest the possibility of changing the rules of football to widen the test of violent play and potentially giving the two linesman more powers as with rugby as better means of regulating play rather than ultimately through the courts.

One question which might arise in some cases is the status of various rules. For example, the British Surfing Association ("BSA") has the following Code of Conduct[62a]:

1. *All surfers must be able to swim at least 50 metres in open water.*

2. *Ensure that you are covered by Public Liability Insurance for surfing.*

3. *Keep your surfing equipment in good condition.*

---

[59] [1952] 2 All E.R. 789.
[60] (1982) 137 D.L.R. (3d) 252.
[61] Unreported, October 28, 1998; referred to by Beloff, Kerr and Demetriou in *Sports Law* (1st ed., Hart Publishing, 1999) para. 5.39, n. 41.
[62] Marquette Sports Law Journal, Vol. 5, 189 at 208–209.
[62a] See www.britsurf.co.uk/codeofconduct.html

4. *Always wear a surf leash to prevent you from losing your surfboard (or bodyboard). For you your board is a safety device, to others it may be a lethal weapon.*

5. *Have consideration for other water users including anglers.*

6. *Never surf alone or immediately after eating a meal.*

7. *Always return to the beach before nightfall.*

8. *Never mix surfing with alcohol or drugs.*

9. *Always wear a wetsuit when surfing in Britain.*

10. *If you are new to the sport never hire a surfboard without first having a surfing lesson. (Given by a BSA qualified instructor)*

11. *Be considerate of other beach users especially when carrying your board to and from the water.*

12. *When possible use a lifeguard patrolled breach. Obey the lifeguards' instructions and be prepared to assist them if required.*

13. *Where possible surf in a recognised surfing area (e.g. in between the black and white checked flags).*

14. *When paddling out avoid surfers who are riding waves.*

15. *When taking a wave see that you are clear of other surfers. Remember, if someone else is already riding the wave you must not take off.*

16. *Be environmentally friendly. Always leave the beach and other areas as you would wish to find them.*

The question might arise as to the significance of these rules in particular circumstances. For example, they may hold greater weight when an accident occurs in a competition governed by BSA Rules than when one occurs between two beginners visiting a particular beach for the first time and who have never even heard of the BSA.

Example
Champion surfer Nick Ridler is teaching his fiancée Ella Raleigh to surf at Saunton Sands in North Devon. Before starting he tells her that two of the most important rules of surfing are that you should not paddle out directly behind another surfer; and the surfer closest to the breaking of the wave has priority. Despite this, Ella Raleigh paddles for a wave and unfortunately fails to see that there is another surfer, Helene Piquion, on her inside and already paddling for it. Helene Piquion catches the wave. Spanish surfer and Salsa World Champion Nines tries to stop Ella Raleigh but unsuccessfully and very quickly thereafter Ella

Raleigh gets into the wave and "drops in" on Helene Piquion causing her to have a bad wipe out in which she injures her back.

Is Ella Raleigh liable for Helene Piquion's injuries?

Reaction of players, crowd and officials

The reaction of the players, crowd and officials may also be a circumstance **3.29** which may be taken into account. In *Pitcher*, in dismissing the case, Hallett J. said in this context:

> "I do find it significant that there was no reaction at the time from Mr Lewington, therefore, and also from five other Crystal Palace members in the dug-out, from the manager in the stand or his directors, and from the four Crystal Palace players within close range of Mr Pitcher plus of course the match officials. I accept that people, even the most experienced match officials, may miss a bad tackle because their eyes follow the ball and the play. I do, however, find it surprising that so many different people missed what is said to be a tackle obviously worthy of a red card. Not one of those with the best interests of Mr Pitcher and Crystal Palace at heart apparently saw anything to concern them unduly at the time.
>
> A large part of this case depends upon the video recording, interpreted by the witnesses as best they can. Despite the problems of the camera angles and the lack of definition, witnesses have attempted to assess body angles and the position of feet and legs and the timing of impact. In those circumstances the lack of contemporaneous reaction to a foot said to be far too high and a challenge said to be far, far too late is something to which I do pay attention. In my judgment the lack of reaction from so many people is by no means conclusive but it is a factor that I should take into account."

Proximity of officials

It is interesting to note that Hallett J. in *Pitcher* also pointed out a practical **3.30** reality when the referee was standing in a perfect position to judge:

> "There is nothing on that recording which came close to satisfying me that Paul Reid was doing anything other than going for the ball when he speeded up his run and when he launched his tackle. He would have been foolhardy in the extreme to go for the man, not the ball, with the referee directly behind him and in a perfect position to judge. I can see no evidence justifying the assertion that he was acting in that fashion."

Other cases

The main cases in this area have already been referred to earlier in this **3.31** Chapter. However, for reference purposes it is worth setting out a number of other cases in this context. A useful source is *Sport and the Law* by Edward Grayson.[63]

---

[63] Pp. 277–282.

Cleghorn v. Oldham[64]

Golfer not in the course of play swings club during demonstration and injures persons standing by. Player held liable. Principle: not in course of play. Defence rejected of consent to negligent act not unfair or vicious in recreation. Negligent misconduct actionable in recreation as in any other activity.

Pre-1962 unreported decision of Sellers L.J. on South Eastern Circuit[65]

Golfer in four-ball hit into rough, losing the ball. Said, "Out of it" and encouraged better players to proceed. Resumed after finding ball, causing injury as victim turned round at defendant's cry of "Fore". Player held liable. Principle: conduct outside the game; unnecessary for it; showed complete disregard for safety of those he knew were in line of danger from being an unskilled instead of lofted shot over their heads.

Brewer v. Delo[66]

The plaintiff, playing golf, was struck by a ball which had been accidentally "hooked" by the defendant and so gone off course. The plaintiff claimed damages, contending, *inter alia*, that the defendant was negligent in playing the ball while he was in range and in failing to give warning.

Held, on the facts, that the consequences were not foreseeable, alternatively the risk was so slight that it could be ignored; accordingly the defendant was not guilty of negligence.

Harrison v. Vincent[67]

3.32 The normal standard of care is expected of those who prepare vehicles for use in dangerous motor sports as opposed to the modified standard applicable to those acts done in the course of the sport. The organiser of such a sport has a duty to take reasonable steps to guard against contingencies which a carefree competitor might ignore. *Per curiam*: not every failure to comply with the rules governing a race is necessarily negligence. Their relevance is that if one does not comply with them, there must be a convincing reason for not doing so. The simple fact that no such accident has happened before is not such a convincing reason. A multiplier of 14 for a workman of 42 in employment is high, but by no means exceptional. The rider of a motor cycle and sidecar combination was racing in a race held

---

[64] (1927) 43 T.L.R. 465.
[65] See [1963] 1 Q.B. 43 at 55.
[66] (1967) 117 New L.J. 575, *per* Hinchcliffe J.
[67] [1982] R.T.R. 8.

under the provisions of an international code of practice. The standing
orders required that where there was a hairpin bend, a slip road should be
kept clear for at least 100 metres. In a race the organisers parked a recovery
vehicle some 30 to 40 metres from the course on a slip road, so that it
projected about two feet into the road. The rider in negotiating the bend at
this point found his rear brake had failed, was forced to leave the track, and
struck the recovery vehicle, injuring the passenger. The passenger sued the
rider and his employers and the organisers for negligence. It was held by the
trial judge that the rider and his employers were negligent in failing to install
or inspect the brake caliper properly which had caused the brake failure.

Held, that (1) since this was a matter done in the relative calm of the
workshop, and not in the flurry and excitement of the sport, the normal
standard of care applied, and not the modified standard applicable to acts
done in the course of violent sport where only reckless disregard for the
safety of the plaintiff or an intention to injure him would constitute a
breach; (2) the organisers were also guilty of negligence and the defence of
volenti non fit injuria did not avail them as the passenger was not aware of
the presence of the recovery vehicle; the organisers had a duty to take
account of contingencies which a carefree competitor might ignore and take
reasonable steps to guard against them: it should have been foreseeable that
this obstruction was a potential source of danger.

Bidwell v. Parks[68]

Golfer in tournament injured by ball hit from fellow competitor without
warning. Fellow competitor held liable. Principle: dangerous for 24 handicap golfer to take shots which could have gone anywhere without
warning.

3.33

Thomas v. Maguire and Queens Park Rangers[69]

Damaged ligaments to professional footballer (Tottenham Hotspur). Negligence claim based on illegal tackle. Agreed damages £130,000 settled out of
court.

Johnston v. Frazer[70]

The New South Wales Appeal Court upheld the trial judge's A$121,490
damages award for a broken thigh and back injuries caused by one horse
crossing in front of two other runners under the guidance of a jockey held

[68] Unreported except newspapers, Lewes Crown Court, French J., 1982. E. Grayson, *Sport and the Law* (3rd ed., Butterworths, 2000), p. 279.
[69] *Daily Mirror*, February 17, 1989, High Court, London.
[70] (1990) N.S.W.L.R. 89 (Australia).

to have failed to have taken reasonable care for the safety of a fellow jockey in the relevant circumstances.

O'Neill v. Fashanu and Wimbledon Football Club[71]

3.34   Negligence claims based on alleged illegal tackle. £70,000 agreed out-of-court settlement of claim without admission of liability after claimant's case and first defendant's disciplinary record admitted in evidence by Collins J.

Horton v. Jackson[72]

J appealed against a decision that the second defendants, B, a golf club, had not been negligent or in breach of their duty under the Occupiers' Liability Act 1957. J was ordered to pay £24,000 damages to H for personal injuries owing to J's negligence when playing a golf shot. H lost the sight of one eye when the golf ball hit him. J conceded that the finding against him was correct, but that B was more responsible for the accident. J argued that the Judge was wrong to find that if a screen between the ninth tee and the sixth green had been extended the accident would still have happened and that B's notice giving priority to those on the sixth green was a sufficient enough warning and they had not been negligent in failing to enforce the rule.

Held, dismissing the appeal, that the Judge was entitled to accept the expert evidence of an amateur golfer and past chairman of the Rules of Golf Committee of the Royal and Ancient Golf Club of St. Andrews, that the extension to the screen would have made no difference. Further, the Judge was also entitled to conclude that B had not breached their duty of care under section 2(2) of the 1957 Act as only two accidents had occurred in 800,000 rounds of golf played there and B could not have prevented the accident with a different sign and the one in existence was reasonable in the circumstances.

Stratton v. Hughes (Executrix of the Estate of Edward John Hughes) and Cumberland Sporting Car Club Ltd and RAC Motor Sports Association Ltd, Steele J.[73]

3.35   The claimant's claim for damages for personal injury sustained in a motor accident against his deceased co-driver who was killed in the National Rally Championship and the rally organisers. While the deceased was driving the Toyota car left the road, crossed a grass verge before colliding first with a lamp standard and then with a tree. The deceased co-driver was killed and the claimant sustained severe head and other injuries. The claimant had no

---

[71] *Independent*, October 14, 1994, High Court, London.
[72] [1996] C.L.Y. 4475, CA.
[73] Unreported, February 28, 1997.

recollection of the accident but alleged that the deceased was driving too fast, failed to keep any proper lookout and failed to take sufficient account of the bend at the final finish line or to so manage or control his vehicle so as to avoid a collision. He also alleged against the deceased defendant that a bias brake valve was illegally fitted in a manner likely to adversely affect the driver's ability to control the vehicle.

Steele J. held that tragic as the accident there was no basis upon which the court could find that the deceased had breached his duty of care he owed to the claimant either in relation to his driving or the fitting of the bias brake valve and this claim would be dismissed. The claim against the second and third defendants was also dismissed.[74] Further, in view of the findings that there had been no negligence by any of the defendants the court found it unnecessary to rule on the arguments raised on the application of the doctrine of *volenti non fit injuria*.

Pearson v. Lightning[75]

L was playing on the eighth hole of a golf course which ran parallel, but in 3.36 the opposite direction, to the ninth hole upon which P and two others were playing. The eighth was a dogleg to the right and the ninth a dogleg to the left and they were separated by about 15 metres of light rough which contained some bushes and trees. L, whose ball was lying in the rough between the fairways closer to the ninth hole than the eighth, decided to play a difficult shot over the top of a coppiced hazel. However, the shot failed to clear the bush and was deflected, hitting P who was 90 yards away, causing an injury to his eye and knocking him to the ground. Although L had shouted "fore", P had not heard him. L appealed against a decision that he was liable in negligence for P's injuries, contending that there had been no real risk, merely the possibility, of the shot resulting in injury.

Held, dismissing the appeal, that the shot which L had played had clearly been a difficult one and the likelihood of deflection from the bush towards the ninth fairway was foreseeable. A duty of care owed by L to P was thus established and L had been in breach of it. As L's ball had been lying closer to the fairway on which P was playing, L should have called to P before playing his shot out of courtesy and in order to alert P to the risk. Although the risk of causing injury was small, it was sufficient to render L liable.

Leatherland v. Edwards, Newman J.[76]

In an action before Newman J., the issue was whether a hockey player had 3.37 been negligent in taking a full follow-through which led to his stick causing the claimant a severe personal injury. The claimant claimed damages for damage to his eye and consequential loss arising out of an accident which

---

[74] For which, see Chap. 6.
[75] (1998) 95(20) L.S.G. 33; (1998) 142 S.J.L.B. 143, CA.
[76] Unreported, October 28, 1998.

occurred during a game of uni-hockey. The game was played on a tarmac surface, rather smaller in size than a conventional pitch, as part of a police officers' training course. The activity was intended to be a fast-moving non-contact sport. Speed was the essence of the game and the ball, which was soft, was not supposed to rise above the surface of the pitch. It was a clearly understood rule that the sticks should not go above waist height. The claimant had been a talented amateur sportsman but had not played uni-hockey before. He had recently left the Royal Navy and hoped to make a career as a police officer. A few minutes into the game the claimant, who had yet to strike the ball, was covering his goal. As he ran past the defendant, the defendant took a shot at goal. After hitting the ball, his stick continued with the follow-through in an arc and hit the claimant—whom the defendant had not seen—full in the eye. The claimant's eye imploded on impact and caused a terrible and painful injury resulting in the loss of sight of that eye. The defendant, who had played the game a few times before, admitted that had the follow-through been above shoulder height then it would have been dangerous but denied that he was negligent. The principle of there being a duty of care in games was not in dispute and it was accepted that the duty to take reasonable care for the safety of other participants stated in *Condon v. Basi*[77] applied.

Newman J. held that the defendant had breached the rules of the game by swinging his stick above shoulder height. It was a serious and dangerous breach. Such a breach, which followed an opportunity to shoot at goal when the defendant was unaware of the presence or run made by the claimant, had to be viewed with it in mind that in sport exuberance, enthusiasm and a lack of inhibition are really the "stuff and spirit of the game". However, the defendant broke a safety rule which, in effect, was at the heart of and itself central to the spirit and purpose of the game. Uni-hockey was a game where it must be readily foreseeable to anybody participating in it that, if he raises his stick with a forceful swing above shoulder height, he risks causing an injury to another player because the force and movement of the game is towards other players coming into proximity with each other in order to follow the ball. Having regard to all the circumstances of the case, the defendant, who was a commendably honest and candid witness, had been negligent. Judgment for the claimant and damages awarded accordingly.

Casson v. MOD[78]

3.38 Involving a teenager sustaining injuries whilst participating in a football match, the Judge was prepared to make a finding of negligence based on the

---

[77] [1985] 1 W.L.R. 866.
[78] Unreported, Bradford County Court, 1999. See speech of Andrew Deans to The Insurance Institute of London entitled "Implications of Professional Fouls" at www.iilondon.co.uk/pdf/Adeans17Jan01.pdf and E. Grayson, *Sport and the Law* (3rd ed., Butterworths, 2000).

concept of "reckless disregard". Thus adopting the terms used in the majority of football cases.

Poom v. Iron Maiden

Derby Football Club's Estonian goalkeeper Mart Poom bruised his penis playing in a charity football match against Iron Maiden early in 2002. Poom, playing as a striker in the match, collided awkwardly with the heavy metal band's keeper as he headed in a goal. No action was brought following the collision.

Dyck v. Laidlaw[79]

One skydiver was held liable for injuries caused to another in a mid-air collision during a free-fall formation; the defendant had been above the claimant and had made a turn in violation of established safety practices.

Conclusion

As the above makes clear, the law in this area is still developing and only time will tell how it will do so in the future. It remains uncertain whether a different standard of care should be applied to professionals compared to amateurs.   3.39

Further, the actual test remains open to debate. Is it, for example, "significant risk of serious injury" or is it "reckless disregard" or some other formulation? As Karen Greene of McGoldricks Solicitors[80] says:

> "Perhaps, ultimately, it comes down to a question of fact in the particular case: should this player be found to be liable for the injuries he has caused? Did he act unreasonably in all the circumstances?"

Perhaps the greatest difficulty is evidential although this may improve as video technology becomes both cheaper and more sophisticated. One suggestion to avoid the potential injustice of claims failing due to the paucity of evidence is mentioned by Simon Gardiner and Alexandra Felix in "Juridification of the Football Field: Strategies for Giving Law the Elbow".[81] They state that they support the development of a "no-fault" compensation scheme. This was suggested in *Elliott v. Saunders and Liverpool FC*.[82] Another possible development mentioned in that case was that clubs compulsorily insure players for potential claims in personal injury.

---

[79] [2000] 9 W.W.R. 517 (Alta. QB). See also Sports Law Bulletin, September/October 2001, World Digest.
[80] Contact: sfjc@ukgateway.net.
[81] Marquette Sports Law Journal, Vol. 5, 189 at 208–209.
[82] Unreported, June 10, 1994; Halsbury's Laws of England 1994, Annual Abridgement, para. 2056.

Certainly, in the light of the current authorities, one thing is clear: given the possibility of liability it would be advisable for all those taking part in sporting activities to make sure that they are adequately insured, certainly against third party liabilities. In the absence of this, players or clubs may find that they face bankruptcy in certain situations. With the recent developments in the law coupled with the rise of no win, no fee litigation, the number of cases in this area will inevitably increase in the next few years.

In *Smoldon v. Whitworth and Nolan*[83] Lord Bingham M.R. also made the following comment:

> "We are caused to wonder whether it would not be beneficial if all players were, as a matter of general practice, to be insured not against negligence but against the risk of catastrophic injury, but that is no doubt a matter to which those responsible for the administration of rugby football have given anxious attention."

The following examples highlight the risk:

Examples

The Mark Evans All Star XI is playing a friendly match against Manchester City which was organised at short notice. The Mark Evans team do not have liability insurance in place at the time of the match despite their manager Garry Wright's attempts to obtain it in time. Without such insurance, can the Mark Evans players afford to try and tackle the likes of Sean Wright-Philips and Nicky Weaver whose potential loss of earnings in the event of an injury could amount to millions of pounds?

Property tycoon and top Barrister Melanie Winter is playing in a Sunday morning hockey match for her Winter Wonderland XI against the Abigail Good XI in Porlock. Neither team has organised insurance. Melanie Winter earns £20 million per year from her property empire alone. Also on her team is Ali Cornish, the Chief Executive of Co-op Supermarkets PLC, who earns £5 million per year. Once again, without adequate insurance, can any of either Melanie Winter or Ali Cornishs' opponents afford to take the risk of tackling them?

---

[83] [1997] P.I.Q.R. P 133.

Chapter 4

Liability of participants to spectators

"When it comes to sports I am not particularly interested. Generally speaking, I look upon them as dangerous and tiring activities performed by people with whom I share nothing except the right to trial by jury".

Fran Lebowitz, *Metropolitan Life*, 1978.

Introduction

Whilst the previous Chapter dealt with the duty of care owed by partici- **4.01**
pants to participants, this Chapter deals with that owed by participants to
spectators.

The two leading cases in this area are *Wooldridge v. Sumner*[1] and *Wilks
v. Cheltenham Home Guard Motor Cycle and Light Car Club.*[2] Prior to
Wooldridge, there was as Diplock described in that case[3]:

> "an almost complete dearth of judicial authority as to the duty of care owed by the
> actual participants to the spectators."

At first blush one might wonder why the two situations should be considered separately. However, there is one significant difference which has led
to a distinction being made in the authorities. It is that whilst participants
are in the immediate contemplation of other participants, spectators are one
step removed.

This, it will be seen has led to a higher threshold being set for liability in
this area. Specifically, that a spectator must show that a participant showed
a "reckless disregard" for his safety.

Clear support for a different approach to be taken in this area was given **4.02**
by Bingham L.J. in *Smoldon v. Whitworth*[4] and approved more recently by
Tuckey L.J. in *Caldwell v. Fitzgerald & ors.*[5] In *Smoldon*, Bingham L.J.

---

[1] [1963] 2 Q.B. 43.
[2] [1971] 1 W.L.R. 668.
[3] At 65.
[4] [1997] P.I.Q.R. P133.
[5] [2001] E.W.C.A. Civ. 1054, CA (Civil Division), Lord Woolf C.J., Tuckey L.J., June 27,
2001.

reconciled the differing approaches of the Judge in that case and of those in *Wooldridge and Wilks* with regard to spectators when he said:

"There is in our judgment no inconsistency between this conclusion and that reached by the Court of Appeal in *Wooldridge v. Sumner* and *Wilks v. Cheltenham Homeguard Motor Cycle Co. and Light Car Cycle Club*. In these cases it was recognised that a sporting competitor, properly intent on winning the contest, was (and was entitled to be) all but oblivious of spectators. It therefore followed that he would have to be shown to have very blatantly disregarded the safety of spectators before he could be held to have failed to exercise such care as was reasonable in all the circumstances."

Given the paucity of authorities in this area, it is worth analysing the judgments in *Wooldridge* and *Wilks* in some detail.

Wooldridge v. Sumner

4.03 The leading case is *Wooldridge v. Sumner*[6] which involved an accident involving a horse rider, the facts of which led Dankwerts L.J.[7] to lament that the Judges were:

"unable to have the story from the horse's mouth."

The claimant was a photographer who was sitting close to the arena on an equestrian event when a horse ridden by the defendant went out of control and collided with him. The defendant was a skilled and experienced rider and although he was thrown in the accident he rode the horse again and it was judged to be champion of its class.

As mentioned above, the Court of Appeal held that in order to establish liability it had to be shown that the participant intended to injure the spectator deliberately, or that he displayed a reckless disregard for the safety of spectators.

A number of points arise from the judgments.

Limitation of Donoghue v. Stephenson

4.04 First, Diplock L.J.[8] analysed Lord Atkin's statement in *Donoghue v. Stephenson*[9] and said:

"To treat Lord Atkin's statement 'You must take reasonable care to avoid acts or omissions which you can reasonably foresee would be likely to injure your neighbour,'[10] as a complete exposition of the law of negligence is to mistake aphorism for exegesis. It does not purport to define what is reasonable care and

---

[6] [1963] 2 Q.B. 43.
[7] At 59.
[8] At 66–67.
[9] [1932] A.C. 562 at 580.
[10] [1932] A.C. 562 at 580.

was directed to identifying the persons to whom the duty to take reasonable care is owed. What is reasonable care in a particular circumstance is a jury question and where, as in a case like this, there is no direct guidance or hindrance from authority it may be answered by inquiring whether the ordinary reasonable man would say that in all the circumstances the defendant's conduct was blameworthy."

Standard of care: reckless disregard

He then went on to analyse what the standard of care should be for participants to spectators. He said[11]:

"A reasonable spectator attending voluntarily to witness any game or competition knows and presumably desires that a reasonable participant will concentrate his attention upon winning, and if the game or competition is a fast-moving one, will have to exercise his judgment and attempt to exert his skill in what, in the analogous context of contributory negligence, is sometimes called 'the agony of the moment.' If the participant does so concentrate his attention and consequently does exercise his judgment and attempt to exert his skill in circumstances of this kind which are inherent in the game or competition in which he is taking part, the question whether any mistake he makes amounts to a breach of duty to take reasonable care must take account of those circumstances . . .

The practical result of this analysis of the application of the common law of negligence to participant and spectator would, I think, be expressed by the common man in some such terms as these: 'A person attending a game or competition takes the risk of any damage caused to him by any act of a participant done in the course of and for the purposes of the game or competition notwith-standing that such act may involve an error of judgment or a lapse of skill, unless the participant's conduct is such as to evince a reckless disregard of the spectator's safety.' "

This was also the approach of Sellers L.J. who stated[12]:   **4.05**

"But provided the competition or game is being performed within the rules and the requirement of the sport and by a person of adequate skill and competence the spectator does not expect his safety to be regarded by the participant.

If the conduct is deliberately intended to injure someone whose presence is known, or is reckless and in disregard of all safety of others so that it is a departure from the standards which might reasonably be expected in anyone pursuing the competition or game, then the performer might well be held liable for any injury his act caused."

Distinction between injuries caused during play and at other times

Given that a participant may be expected to have more on his mind when   **4.06**
he is competing, Sellers L.J. took this to its logical conclusion and suggested

---

[11] At 67–68.
[12] At 56–57.

that the standard of care may be slightly different when he is not actually competing when he said[13]:

"There would, I think, be a difference, for instance, in assessing blame which is actionable between an injury caused by a tennis ball hit or a racket accidentally thrown in the course of play into the spectators at Wimbledon and a ball hit or a racket thrown into the stands in temper or annoyance when play was not in progress."

The distinction drawn between injury caused by actions during play and at other times, is simply a recognition that actions which are not part of the "heat of battle" and are outside the "flurry and excitement" of the competitive activity do not merit the same consideration.[14]

Thus, in the Canadian case of *Payne v. Maple Leaf,*[15] a spectator at an ice-hockey match recovered damages in respect of injuries sustained not due to an ordinary incident of the game of ice-hockey but as a result of a fight between two players.

Further examples abound, particularly in the context of injuries to fellow competitors. For example, in *Cleghorn v. Oldham*[16] the claimant was injured by the defendant demonstrating a golf swing otherwise than in the course of play.

So, too, in *Harrison v. Vincent*[17] in relation to the liability of the promoters of a motor cycle, in which however the rider of the motor cycle was held liable to his combination passenger for negligence not during the race itself but during the preparation of his machine beforehand.

Reasonable spectator

4.07 As well as emphasising that the standard of care involved looking at the reasonable participant in all the circumstances, Diplock L.J. also made it clear that the expectations of a reasonable spectator were also relevant when he said[18]:

"The matter has to be looked at from the point of view of the reasonable spectator as well as the reasonable participant; not because of the maxim *volenti non fit injuria,* but because what a reasonable spectator would expect a participant to do without regarding it as blameworthy is as relevant to what is reasonable care as what a reasonable participant would think was blameworthy conduct in himself."

---

[13] At 57.
[14] See D. Griffiths-Jones and A. Barr-Smith, *Law and the Business of Sport* (Butterworths, 1997), p. 8.
[15] [1949] 1 D.L.R. 369.
[16] (1927) 43 T.L.R. 465.
[17] [1982] R.T.R. 8.
[18] At 67.

As Diplock himself pointed out, the same idea was expressed by Scrutton L.J. in *Hall v. Brooklands*[19]:

"What is reasonable care would depend upon the perils which might be reasonably expected to occur, and the extent to which the ordinary spectator might be expected to appreciate and take the risk of such perils."

Volenti non fit injuria

However, in setting out the standard of care required and therefore the threshold for liability, Diplock L.J. was careful to articulate that he did not consider that the principle of *volenti non fit injuria*[20] had any application in this area of law. He said[21]:

"The spectator takes the risk because such an act involves no breach of the duty **4.08** of care owed by the participant to him. He does not take the risk by virtue of the doctrine expressed or obscured by the maxim *volenti non fit injuria*. That maxim states a principle of estoppel applicable originally to a Roman citizen who consented to being sold as a slave. Although pleaded and argued below it was only faintly relied upon by Mr Everett in this court. In my view, the maxim in the absence of expressed contract has no application to negligence simpliciter where the duty of care is based solely upon proximity or 'neighbourship' in the Atkinian sense. The maxim in English law presupposes a tortious act by the defendant. The consent that is relevant is not consent to the risk of injury but consent to the lack of reasonable care that may produce that risk (see *Kelly v. Farrans Ltd*,[22] *per* Lord MacDermott,[23] and requires on the part of the plaintiff at the time at which he gives his consent full knowledge of the nature and extent of the risk that he ran. (*Osborne v. London and North Western Railway Co.*,[24] *per* Wills J.,[25] approved in *Letang v. Ottawa Electric Railway Co.*[26] In *Dann v. Hamilton*[27] Asquith J. expressed doubts as to whether the maxim ever could apply to license in advance a subsequent act of negligence, for if the consent precedes the act of negligence the plaintiff cannot at that time have full knowledge of the extent as well as the nature of the risk which he will run. Asquith J., however, suggested that the maxim might nevertheless be applicable to cases where a dangerous physical condition had been brought about by the negligence of the defendant, and the plaintiff with full knowledge of the existing danger elected to run the risk thereof. With the development of the law of negligence in the last 20 years a more consistent explanation of this type of case is that the test of liability on the part of the person creating the dangerous physical condition is whether it was reasonably foreseeable by him that the defendant would so act in relation to it as to endanger himself. This is the

---

[19] [1933] 1 K.B. 205 at 214.
[20] For which, see Chap. 2.
[21] At 68–70.
[22] [1954] N.I. 41.
[23] At 45.
[24] (1888) 21 Q.B. 220; 4 T.L.R. 591, DC.
[25] At 220, 224.
[26] [1926] A.C. 725; 42 T.L.R. 596, HL.
[27] [1939] 1 K.B. 509; 55 T.L.R. 97; [1939] 1 All E.R. 59.

principle which has been applied in the rescue cases (see *Cutler v. United Dairies (London) Ltd*,[28] and contrast *Haynes v. Harwood*[29] and that part of Asquith J.'s judgment in *Dann v. Hamilton*[30] dealing with the possible application of the maxim to the law of negligence which was not approved by the Court of Appeal in *Baker v. T. E. Hopkins & Son*.[31] In the type of case envisaged by Asquith J., if I may adapt the words of Morris L.J. in *Baker v. T. E. Hopkins & Son*,[32] the plaintiff could not have agreed to run the risk that the defendant might be negligent for the plaintiff would only play his part after the defendant had been negligent."

4.09　　In making this clear, Diplock L.J. overcame the argument that since the claimant was ignorant of horses the defendant owed him a higher duty since he had not necessarily consented to the risks inherent in watching a competition involving horses. He therefore continued[33]:

"Since the maxim has in my view no application to this or any other case of negligence simpliciter, the fact that the plaintiff owing to his ignorance of horses did not fully appreciate the nature and extent of the risk he ran did not impose upon Mr Holladay any higher duty of care towards him than that which he owed to any ordinary reasonable spectator with such knowledge of horses and vigilance for his own safety as might be reasonably expected to be possessed by a person who chooses to watch a heavyweight hunter class in the actual arena where the class is being judged. He cannot rely upon his personal ignorance of the risk any more than the plaintiff in *Murray v. Harringay Arena*[34] could rely upon his ignorance of the risk involved in ice-hockey, excusable though such ignorance may have been in a six-year-old child."

Sellers L.J. confirmed this analysis when he said[35]:

"In my opinion a competitor or player cannot in the normal case at least of competition or game rely on the maxim *volenti non fit injuria* in answer to a spectator's claim, for there is no liability unless there is negligence and the spectator comes to witness skill and with the expectation that it will be exercised."

Dankwerts L.J. on the other hand seemed to take a slightly different approach from the other two and potentially allowed in the application of the principle of *volenti* when he said[36]:

---

[28] [1933] 2 K.B. 297, CA.
[29] [1935] 1 K.B. 146; 51 T.L.R. 100, CA.
[30] [1939] 1 K.B. 509 at 517.
[31] [1959] 1 W.L.R. 966; *sub nom. Ward v. Hopkins (T. E.) & Son Ltd* [1959] 3 All E.R. 225, CA.
[32] [1959] 1 W.L.R. 966 at 976.
[33] At 69.
[34] [1951] 2 K.B. 529.
[35] At 56.
[36] At 59–60.

"Further, in taking up his position in a place where spectators were not allowed in the afternoons and which must necessarily be in close proximity to horses proceeding at a gallop, in my opinion the plaintiff must be taken to accept the risk of something going wrong in the course of an event with resulting danger to persons so near to the line to be traversed by the competitors, even though he happened to be inexperienced in regard to competitions of this kind."

However, as he continued, he seemed to attribute such consent to the standard of care rather than the defence of *volenti*[37]:   **4.10**

"As Lord Oaksey said in *Bolton v. Stone*[38]: 'The standard of care in the law of negligence is the standard of an ordinarily careful man, but in my opinion an ordinarily careful man does not take precautions against every foreseeable risk. He can, of course, foresee the possibility of many risks, but life would be almost impossible if he were to attempt to take precautions against every risk which he can foresee. He takes precautions against risks which are reasonably likely to happen. Many foreseeable risks are extremely unlikely to happen and cannot be guarded against except by almost complete isolation.'
   Mr Holladay's duty to his employer was to utilise the qualities of the horse so as to show it to the best advantage. This involved the horse going at a fast gallop. Decisions have to be taken in a split second and it is impossible for a rider, as it seems to me, in such circumstances to calculate every possible result in his mind. He could not possibly be expected to foresee that someone would jump out from the line of the bench into the track of the horse. Persons who stand so close to the scene of such events must take the risk of something going wrong in the ordinary course of the sport, and which is a risk incidental to it. This clearly appears from the decision of this court in *Murray v. Harringay Arena Ltd*[39] I also would allow the appeal."

Rules of the game

In addition to the above, Sellers L.J. added a few extra comments as to the standard of care. In particular, he stated that the standard of care owed by a participant to a spectator depends upon which sport is being played. This is similar to the points made in the judgments quoted in the previous Chapter that the circumstances of each case are crucial. Specifically, he stated[40]:   **4.11**

"The relationship of spectator and competitor or player is a special one, as I see it, as the standard of conduct of the participant, as accepted and expected by the spectator, is that which the sport permits or involves. The different relationship involves its own standard of care."

---

[37] At 60.
[38] [1951] A.C. 850, 863; [1951] 1 T.L.R. 977; [1951] 1 All E.R. 1078, HL.
[39] [1951] 2 K.B. 529; [1951] 2 All E.R. 320n., CA.
[40] At 57.

On the facts of the case he went on to conclude[41]:

> "There can be no better evidence that Mr Holladay was riding within the rules than that he won, notwithstanding this unfortunate accident in the course of the event, and I do not think it can be said that he was riding recklessly and in disregard of all safety or even on this evidence without skill."

Wilks v. Cheltenham Home Guard Motor Cycle and Light Car Club

4.12   The other leading case in this area is *Wilks v. Cheltenham Home Guard Motor Cycle and Light Car Club*[42] which arose out of a motor-cycle "scramble" in a grass field at Withybridge off the Cheltenham to Gloucester Road. The claimants went to see the "scramble." They were in the spectators' enclosure. It was alongside a straight piece of the course and was fenced off with stakes and ropes. The spectators were lined against the "spectators' rope," which was designed to keep them in the enclosure. Then there was a 10-foot "no man's land" until you came to the "wrecking rope," which was designed to stop any motor-cycle from intruding.

During one of the races one of the competitors, Mr Ward, the second defendant, came up along the straight on his motor-cycle, parallel to the "wrecking rope." Suddenly he left the course and went into the spectators. Mr Wilks and his daughter were injured. They brought an action against the club which organised the scramble and against the rider of the motor-cycle.

At first instance, the judge exempted the club and condemned the rider to which the rider appealed.

Lord Denning commenced his analysis by saying that he thought that prima facie either the rider or the club was at fault since otherwise such an accident would not have happened[43]:

> "Let me say at once that this seems to me to be the sort of accident which ought not to occur if all those concerned use proper care. I should have thought that *prima facie* one or other was at fault—either the club in not taking proper safety precautions, or the rider in doing something foolhardy. At any rate, that is the inference which I should draw unless an adequate explanation was given."

Reasonable care going all out to win

4.13   The Judges looked at *Wooldridge* and refined the points made therein. In particular, it was emphasised that regard should be had to the fact that he is a competitor in a race in which he is expected to go all out to win.

---

[41] At 57.
[42] [1971] 1 W.L.R. 668.
[43] At 670.

Lord Denning stated[44]:

"Let me first try to state the duty which lies upon a competitor in a race. He must, of course, use reasonable care. But that means reasonable care having regard to the fact that he is a competitor in a race in which he is expected to go 'all out' to win. Take a batsman at the wicket. He is expected to hit six, if he can, even if it lands among the spectators. So also in a race, a competitor is expected to go as fast as he can, so long as he is not foolhardy. In seeing if a man is negligent, you ask what a reasonable man in his place would or would not do. In a race a reasonable man would do everything he could do to win, but he would not be foolhardy. That, I think, is the standard of care to be expected of him."

In this regard, Lord Denning sought to distinguish *Wooldridge* on the basis that in that case the rider was not involved in a race, in effect emphasising that part of the competition in that case was to control the horse. He stated[45]:

"We were referred to *Wooldridge v. Sumner* [1963] 2 Q.B. 43. It is, I think, different. It concerned a horse show where horses were to display their paces, but not to race. The riders ought not to give their horses their heads so as to go too fast. On that account the decision was criticised by Dr Goodhart in a note in the Law Quarterly Review, vol. 78 (1962), pp. 490–496. His criticism may be justified. But he points out, at 496, it is different in a race when a rider is expected to go 'all out' to win. In a race the rider is, I think, liable if his conduct is such as to evince a reckless disregard of the spectators' safety: in other words, if his conduct is foolhardy."

In this context, Edmund-Davies L.J. stated[46]:   **4.14**

"But, in all the perplexing circumstances of this case, was it right to hold Mr Ward guilty of negligence? Lord Denning M.R. has already referred to the decision of this court in *Wooldridge v. Sumner* [1963] 2 Q.B. 43 and I respectfully share his difficulty in accepting the view there expressed that a competitor in such events as this is to be held liable only if he acts in reckless disregard of the spectators' safety. For my part, I would with deference adopt the view of Dr Goodhart in 78 L.Q.R. at 496 that the proper test is whether injury to a spectator has been caused 'by an error of judgment that a reasonable competitor, being the reasonable man of the sporting world, would not have made'."

He concluded by stating that claimants should only be liable for errors of judgment or lapse of skill going beyond such as, in the stress of circumstances, may reasonably be regarded as excusable[47]:

"Nevertheless, although in the very nature of things the competitor is all out to win and that is exactly what the spectators expect of him, it is in my judgment still

---

[44] At 670.
[45] At 670.
[46] At 673.
[47] At 674.

incumbent upon him to exercise such degree of care as may reasonably be expected in all the circumstances. For my part, therefore, I would hold him liable only for damage caused by errors of judgment or lapse of skill going beyond such as, in the stress of circumstances, may reasonably be regarded as excusable."

Phillimore L.J. took an approach which whilst not differing in its result was less ready to criticise *Wooldridge*. He began by emphasising that spectators take on a certain amount of risk themselves[48]:

"In considering whether conduct by a competitor which leads to injury to a spectator is to be termed negligent it is obvious that the conduct must be looked at in all the circumstances. Anyone who attends a cricket match as a spectator must accept the risk of a batsman hitting a six into the crowd. There must always be a risk at a race meeting, whether the race is between horses or cars or motor-cycles, that a competitor who is riding or driving entirely properly may as a result of some unforeseen event be forced to leave the course, or at all events to collide with any barriers at the side of it."

4.15   He then went on to say[49] that he found himself attracted to the sort of test propounded by Sellers L.J., in *Wooldridge*, specifically,

"If the conduct is deliberately intended to injure someone whose presence is known, or is reckless and in disregard of all safety of others so that it is a departure from the standards which might reasonably be expected in anyone pursuing the competition or game, then the performer might well be held liable for any injury his act caused."

In addition, he cited with approval[50] the words of Diplock L.J., namely:

"A person attending a game or competition takes the risk of any damage caused to him by any act of a participant done in the course of and for the purposes of the game or competition notwithstanding that such act may involve an error of judgment or a lapse of skill, unless the participant's conduct is such as to evince a reckless disregard of the spectator's safety."

However, he emphasised that ultimately, the question boiled down to a question of fact over negligence[51]:

"It is, however, important to remember that the test remains simply that of 'negligence' and that whether or not the competitor was negligent must be viewed against all the circumstances—the tests mentioned in *Wooldridge v. Sumner* are only to be applied if the circumstances warrant them."

---

[48] At 675.
[49] At 676.
[50] At 676.
[51] At 676.

No evidence of excessive speed or recklessness

All of the Judges found that despite the findings of the Judge at first instance,   **4.16**
there had been no evidence of excessive speed or recklessness. It is clear
from the judgments that no adequate explanation had in fact been put
forward.

Lord Denning stated that[52]:

"The judge in this case found that the rider was reckless . . . I must say that I can
see no evidence to support those findings of the judge. There was no evidence
whatever of greatly excessive speed . . . There was no evidence of want of skill . . .
No doubt he 'lost control' of his motor-cycle, else he would not have gone over the
wreckingrope. But loss of control is just one of the things that may happen in a
[671] motor-cycle 'scramble.' It takes place over rough ground with undulations
and hazards liable to cause the most skilful rider to go out of control or to have
a spill. It is no more negligence than it is when a horse at a point-to-point runs out
at a jump."

Edmund-Davies L.J. emphasised how extraordinary the incident was[53]:

"Applying that test here, what follows? This was an extraordinary accident, none
of the witnesses called had ever known its like, and the defendant himself could
not explain it. Does that mean he is bound to fail? In my judgment, no. He gave
an account up to the moment when, he being then but 12–18 inches from the
wrecking rope and riding straight ahead, something caused his vehicle to veer left
and head straight for the rope. Nobody was able to challenge or criticise him up
to that moment. It is true that theories have been canvassed (for example, that he
may have hit something hard which caused him to lose control); but none can be
proved—either by the defendant or by anyone else."

Res ipsa loquitur

Given the lack of evidence of excessive speed or recklessness, the question   **4.17**
that arose as to whether the claimants could claim that the very fact that the
accident happened was evidence in itself that the defendant was negligent.
In other words, whether the claims could rely upon the maxim *res ipsa
loquitur*, the act speaks for itself.

In this regard, Edmund-Davies L.J. said[54]:

"Disaster suddenly arose without a tittle of evidence to indicate that he was then
driving in any way unusual even for a 'scramble,' and the mystery as to why he
lost control remains complete.

   To say that in these circumstances the doctrine of *res ipsa loquitur* (relied on by
the plaintiffs and held applicable by the judge) demands that the second defendant

---

[52] At 670.
[53] At 674.
[54] At 674.

must be held liable seems to me wrong. It is obvious that the doctrine should apply to a motorist who, for no apparent reason, leaves the highway and ends up by hitting someone on the pavement, as in *Ellor v. Selfridge and Co. Ltd* (1930) 46 T.L.R. 236. But the circumstances here are vastly different, and they give rise to the question whether *res ipsa loquitur* has any bearing. The point is important, for, as Sir Raymond Evershed M.R. said in *Moore v. R. Fox & Sons* [1956] 1 Q.B. 596, 614:

> 'It must, . . . always be a question whether, upon proof of the happening of a particular event, it can with truth be said that the thing speaks for itself. The event or "thing" may, or may not, produce that result. Not every accident has, without more, that effect. If, upon a closer analysis of the happening and its circumstances, it does not in truth appear fairly to follow that the proper inference is one of negligence, then the case is not one of *res ipsa loquitur* at all.'

Let us apply those words to the present case. As it happened, the defendant's vehicle veered to the left and landed amongst the spectators. But what if it had veered to its right and so became involved with and caused damage to one of the other competitors racing alongside the defendant? In those circumstances, it is virtually certain that no question of *res ipsa loquitur* would arise, and the plaintiff would just have to establish his case in negligence unaided by any such evidentiary rule. So also here. For my part, I cannot think that, in the difficult circumstances of the present case, it would be right to impute the defendant's loss of control to fault on his part. All happened in a split second, and (assuming the worst against him) even a slip or misjudgment too slight to be regarded as amounting to negligence could well account for this accident.

Accordingly, while one must feel particularly sorry for the male plaintiff, I do not think it would be just to hold the second defendant liable."

Phillimore L.J. also dismissed the argument that the claimants may rely upon the maxim *res ipsa loquitur* when he said[55]:

> "If, as the judge found, this fence was erected with complete efficiency, it is really impossible to see how this accident happened. There is no room for the application of the maxim *res ipsa loquitur*, since the fence was not under Ward's control."

Rules of the game

4.18 Finally, it is interesting to note that Edmund-Davies L.J. also cited[56] with approval Sellers L.J.'s judgment in *Wooldridge* when he said:

> "provided the competition or game is being performed within the rules and the requirement of the sport and by a person of adequate skill and competence the spectator does not expect his safety to be regarded by the participant."

---

[55] At 678.
[56] At 674.

Edmund-Davies L.J. stated[57] that this was:

"most valuable in pointing out those special features which are inherent in competitive events and which everyone takes for granted."

Conclusion

From these cases, a number of principles appear to emerge:

1. In determining the standard of care, the circumstances of each case are crucial.

2. In general, spectators will have to show that participants showed something akin to a reckless disregard for their safety in order to establish liability.

3. The matter should be looked at from the perspective of the reasonable spectator and what he would expect and not just from the perspective of the reasonable participant.

4. The maxim of *volenti no fit injuria* is not appropriate as a defence in itself but the reasonable expectations of the spectators are relevant to the standard of care which is to be applied.

5. In competitive sports, participants may reasonably be expected to be going all out to win and this is also to be taken into account in assessing the standard of care.

6. A distinction can be made between injuries caused during play and injuries at other times.

Ultimately, it will be a question of fact. Beloff, Kerr and Demetriou[58] summarise the position in the following way:

"There is in short a difference between a Carling colliding with a spectator and a Cantona kicking one."[59]

To which, may now be added :

" . . . or a Carragher throwing a coin at one."[60]

---

[57] At 674.
[58] *Sports Law* (1st ed., Hart Publishing, 1999), para. 5.44.
[59] Referring to Eric Cantona's infamous kung-fu kick on a spectator. See *R. v. Cantona, The Times*, March 24, 1995.
[60] Referring to the incident in which Jamie Carragher of Liverpool FC was sent off during his team's 1–0 defeat against Arsenal in the fourth round of the FA Cup at Highbury on January 27, 2002 after throwing a coin back into the crowd.

Chapter 5

Liability of organisers to spectators

"Some people think football is a matter of life and death . . . I can assure you that it is much more serious than that."

Bill Shankley, 1973.

Introduction

Organisers, promoters and occupiers may be liable for injuries caused to spectators at a sporting event. This Chapter looks briefly at the different potential causes of action and statutes in this area and then goes on to analyse some of the case law and principles which have developed.

5.01

Causes of action/statutes

Negligence and Occupiers' Liability Act 1957

The most likely cause of action is in negligence, and in addition under the Occupiers' Liability Act 1957 (as amended by the 1984 Act of the same name), which imposes a statutory common duty of care not differing materially, as to the standard of care, from that which obtains in common law negligence.

The most important provision of the 1957 Act is section 2 which provides:

"(1) An occupier of premises owes the same duty, the 'common duty of care', to all his visitors, except in so far as he is free to and does extend, restrict, modify or exclude his duty to any visitor or visitors by agreement or otherwise.

(2) The common duty of care is a duty to take such care as in all the circumstances of the case is reasonable to see that the visitor will be reasonably safe in using the premises for the purposes for which he is invited or permitted by the occupier to be there."

For a more detailed analysis of the particular provisions of the 1957 Act, the reader is referred to Chapter 10 of *Clerk & Lindsell on Torts*.[1]

---

[1] 18th ed., Sweet and Maxwell, 2000.

Breach of contract

5.02   Another potential cause of action may be for breach of contract. In particular, depending upon the facts, a paying spectator may be able to argue that there is an implied term that the grounds would be safe to use or free from any dangers.

In general this may not make any material difference when there is also a claim in negligence or under the Occupiers' Liability Act 1957. However, it may become important in certain circumstances due to the fact that damages are measured differently, in particular with regard to foreseeability, remoteness and economic loss.

Occupiers' Liability Act 1984

This deals with the liability of occupiers to trespassers and is dealt with in Chapter 15, below to which the reader is referred for more information.

Safety in sports grounds legislation

Whilst not necessarily giving rise to civil liability directly, also relevant in this area are the numerous pieces of legislation which have been introduced in the past 30 years with the aim of increasing safety in sports grounds. Sometimes these have been in reactions to tragedies such as that at Hillsborough, at others they have reflected a more general approach to dealing with public order in the country. Some of these are dealt with in Chapter 15, below and apply equally in this context. They include: the Fire Safety and Safety of Places of Sport Act 1987; the Public Order Act 1986; the Football Spectators Act 1989; the Football Offences Act 1991; the Criminal Justice and Public Order Act 1994; and the Football (Offences and Disorder) Act 1999. It is beyond the scope of this book to go into any further detail beyond that already taken in Chapter 15 and the reader is referred to the texts of the statutes themselves for more details.

Cases and principles

5.03   Whether or not the club or event organisers are liable for injury to spectators or others, such as officials, injured at the event naturally depends upon the facts. However, there have been a number of cases which have provided guidance on this issue.

Hall v. Brooklands Auto-Racing Club[2]

In this case, certain persons were the owners of a racing track for motor cars. The track was oval in shape and measured two miles or more in circumference. It contained a long straight stretch known as the finishing

---

[2] [1933] 1 K.B. 205.

straight, which was over 100 feet wide and was bounded on its outer side by a cement kerb six inches in height, beyond which was a strip of grass four feet five inches in width enclosed within an iron railing four feet six inches high.

Spectators were admitted on payment to view the races, and stands were provided in which they could do this in safety, but many persons preferred to stand along and outside the railing.

Among the competing cars in a long distance race on this track two cars 5.04
were running along the finishing straight at a pace of over 100 miles an hour and were approaching a sharp bend to the left; the car in front and more to the left turned to the right; the other car did the same, but in so doing touched the off side of the first mentioned car, with the strange result that the first mentioned car shot into the air over the kerb and the grass margin and into the railing, killing two spectators and injuring others. The course was opened in 1907. No accident like this had ever happened before.

In an action by one of the injured spectators against the owners of the racing track the jury found that the defendants were negligent in that having invited the public to witness a highly dangerous sport they had failed by notices or otherwise to give warning of, or protection from, the dangers incident thereto, and to keep spectators at a safe distance from the track.

On appeal, the Court of Appeal held that it was the duty of the appellants to see that the course was as free from danger as reasonable care and skill could make it, but that they were not insurers against accidents which no reasonable diligence could foresee or against dangers inherent in a sport which any reasonable spectator can foresee and of which he takes the risk, and consequently that there was no evidence to support the verdict of the jury.

The court drew a distinction between exposure to the ordinary risks 5.05
associated with presence at the event which the spectator must expect to run, and extraordinary perils to which he or she is additionally exposed in cases where the organisers or competitors act without proper regard to the safety of spectators. The latter, but not the former, will entail liability.

Scrutton L.J.[3] described the test as applying generally to cases:

> "where landowners admit for payment to their land persons who desire to witness sports or competitions carried on thereon, if those sports may involve risk of danger to persons witnessing them."

Thus he commented[4]:

> "A spectator at Lord's or the Oval runs the risk of being hit by a cricket ball, or coming into collision with a fielder running hard to stop a ball from going over the boundary, and himself tumbling over the boundary in doing so. Spectators at

---

[3] At 209.
[4] At 209.

football or hockey or polo matches run similar risks both from the ball and from collisions with players or polo ponies. Spectators who pay for admission to golf courses to witness important matches, though they keep beyond the boundaries required by the stewards, run the risk of the players slicing or pulling balls which may hit them with considerable velocity and damage. Those who pay for admission or seats in stands at a flying meeting run a risk of the performing aeroplanes falling on their heads."

Other cases

5.06 The principle enunciated in *Hall* has not changed, but has been applied on a number of occasions since. It is usually easy to predict the result of its application by using plain common sense. It is most unlikely that there will be liability unless the rules of the competition are breached, for compliance with them is the very thing which the claimant pays to watch. Such breach is a necessary but not a sufficient condition for liability.

However, it is another matter altogether if safety is compromised by malfunctioning equipment provided by the event organiser, such as a collapsing grandstand at the Cheltenham Races.[5] Indeed, the cases only very rarely reveal examples of liability being established where injury was caused through the actions of competitors.

The defendants have been successful in the following cases where spectators were injured by:

(a) a polo player on a pony running through a hedge[6];

(b) a racing car leaving the track[7];

(c) an ice hockey puck[8];

(d) the winning horse at a horse show which collided with a photographer[9];

(e) a motor-cycle at a scramble meeting[10]; and

(f) a discuss thrown at an athletics ground.[11]

5.07 An example of a recent case is *Thomas v. Osprey Leisure Ltd*[12] in which T had suffered injury when she slipped, fell and slid along the bowling lane

---

[5] *Francis v. Cockerell* (1820) 5 Q.B. 501; see also *Brown v. Lewis* (1896) 12 T.L.R. 455 (stand collapsed at Blackburn Rovers FC).

[6] *Piddington v. Hastings*, *The Times*, March 12, 1932.

[7] *Hall v. Brooklands* [1933] 1 K.B. 205.

[8] *Murray v. Harringay Arena* [1951] 2 K.B. 529.

[9] *Wooldridge v. Sumner* [1963] 2 Q.B. 43.

[10] *Wilkes v. Cheltenham Home Guard Motorcycle and Light Car Club* [1971] 3 All E.R. 369, CA.

[11] *Wilkins v. Smith* (1976) 73 Law Soc. Gaz. 938.

[12] December 8, 2000, District Judge James, Whitehaven County Court, Current Law, Case No. 213212.

at O's Superbowl premises. T, who had only been bowling once before and who was visiting O's premises for the first time, issued proceedings against O, contending that the premises were unsafe because there were no sufficiently obvious warnings of the dangerous nature of the slippery oiled lanes. O maintained that the written signs instructing bowlers not to cross the "foul line", together with audible announcements requesting bowlers not to cross those lines "in the interests of safety" were sufficient to discharge its duty under section 2(4) of the Occupiers Liability Act 1957.

The Judge held, giving judgment for the claimant, that as far as the written notices were concerned, the wording used was inadequate to convey the potential hazards of the game. The signs could easily be interpreted as indicating a rule of the game, since there was no mention of inherent danger such as the possibility of slipping. The audible announcements alone were insufficient to constitute a warning, especially as, on the evidence, there was uncertainty as to their regularity and their efficiency was entirely dependent on visitors listening to and concentrating upon them.

Duty of care not to cancel?

An example of a curious case in which the boundaries of the duty of care were highlighted is *MacDonald v. FIFA/SFA*[13] in which it was held that organisers of a football match do not owe a duty of care to a spectator for its cancellation.   5.08

Psychiatric damage

It is also theoretically possible that promoters and organisers may be liable to persons who suffer harm as a result of a sporting event even though they were not actually present at the ground. In *Alcock v. Chief Constable of South Yorkshire*,[14] a case arising out of the Hillsborough disaster where 96 football fans were crushed to death as a result of overcrowding in the stadium, the House of Lords considered whether a duty was owed to persons who suffered psychiatric injury as a result of the disaster. It was held that such a duty could be owed where a claimant fulfilled the following conditions: 5.09

(a) the claimant must have close ties of love and affection with the victim;

(b) the claimant must have been present at the accident or its immediate aftermath;

---

[13] Unreported, Court of Session, Outer House, 1999.
[14] [1992] 1 A.C. 310.

(c) the psychiatric injury must have been caused by direct perception of the accident or its immediate aftermath and not upon hearing about it from someone else.

This test does envisage the possibility of a duty to a person who was not at the scene at the time the disaster happened.

However, it is in practice extremely difficult for a bystander to recover damages for psychiatric injury. This is demonstrated by the fact that, in *Alcock*, the House of Lords dismissed all claims brought by relatives including the claim of a claimant who himself witnessed the scenes at the football ground where two of his brothers died.

Further, in *White v. Chief Constable of South Yorkshire*[15] the House of Lords dismissed the claims brought by police officers who suffered psychiatric injury as a result of witnessing the tragic scenes.

Conclusion

5.10   The importance of these cases is as much in their role in developing the law in relation to sporting activities as it is to the specific questions addressed. With the greater awareness of the need for safety at sporting events, it is probably likely that such cases will become rarer as time goes on. However, any safety procedures would struggle to deal with wholly unpredictable forms of behaviour such as that displayed by Eric Cantona when he made his infamous kung-fu kick on a spectator.[16]

Example

Marcus "the Boomer" is a big hitting golfing professional who is attending a longest drive competition at Sebastian's Driving Range. The competition organiser, Anouska, is in charge of safety arrangements. She knows that Marcus is capable of hitting the ball 375 yards. The driving range is 400 yards long and there is a spectators' gallery at the end. Anouska decides not to erect a 10 feet temporary fence (which she was offered for £500) since she regarded the chances of someone being hit as small. On the day of the event there is a strong tail wind and Marcus hit a ball out of the range into the spectators' gallery where it struck Tom who was out for a walk with his wife Maureen.

Can Tom sue either Anouska, Marcus or Sebastian?

---

[15] [1998] 3 W.L.R. 1509.
[16] *R. v. Cantona, The Times*, March 24, 1995.

Chapter 6

Liability of organisers to participants

"Maybe Napoleon was wrong when he said we were a nation of shopkeepers . . .
Today England looked like a nation of goalkeepers . . . "

Tom Stoppard, Professional Foul, BBC TV, 1977.

Introduction

The principles referred to in the previous Chapter apply equally to the   6.01
liability of organisers and occupiers to participants as they do to spectators.
Much of this is also covered in Chapter 15, below.

This Chapter elucidates how these principles would be applied to a
context involving participants through three examples of cases. It should be
noted that one issue which is more likely to be applicable to participants is
that of contributory negligence as compared with the more passive role of
spectators.

A separate Chapter is devoted to this topic since it is anticipated that in
future the number of cases in this area is likely to increase and with it
potentially the principles or the factors to be taken into account which may
distinguish them from the spectator cases.

Harrison v. Vincent

In *Harrison v. Vincent*,[1] the rider of a motor cycle and sidecar combination   6.02
was racing in a race held under the provisions of an international code of
practice. The standing orders required that where there was a hairpin bend,
a slip road should be kept clear for at least 100 metres.

In a race the organisers parked a recovery vehicle some 30 to 40 metres
from the course on a slip road, so that it projected about two feet into the
road. The rider in negotiating the bend at this point found his rear brake
had failed, was forced to leave the track, and struck the recovery vehicle,
injuring the passenger. The passenger sued the rider and his employers and
the organisers for negligence.

---

[1] [1982] R.T.R. 8; [1982] C.L.Y. 2159.

It was held by the trial judge that the rider and his employers were negligent in failing to install or inspect the brake caliper properly which had caused the brake failure.

As well as confirming the liability of the employers, the Court of Appeal also held that the organisers were guilty of negligence and the defence of *volenti non fit injuria* did not avail them as the passenger was not aware of the presence of the recovery vehicle.

The organisers had a duty to take account of contingencies which a carefree competitor might ignore and take reasonable steps to guard against them: it should have been foreseeable that this obstruction was a potential source of danger.

Glenie v. Slack and Barclay

6.03   The case of *Glenie v. Slack and Barclay*[2] also provides a good example of some of the issues which may arise with regard to the liability of organisers and occupiers to participants.

Facts

The claimant's case arose from an accident at a race track at Matchams Leisure Park, Hampshire. On March 13, 1993, the claimant was riding his motorcycle and side-car combination around the race track with a passenger in the side-car when it collided with a fence that ran around the inside of the race track. The passenger was killed and the claimant rendered paraplegic. He claimed damages for his personal injuries and losses. The first defendant ("S") was the owner of the race track and Matchams. The second defendant ("B") was the promoter and organiser of the race meeting. The claimant hoped to compete as a member of a team in races that evening. The accident happened in practice but it was disputed whether the practice was "official" practice.

6.04   The claimant alleged negligence and/or breach of the common duty of care under section 2 of the Occupiers Liability Act 1957. It was said that the racetrack was inherently dangerous by reason of the absence of an unobstructed central run-off area. The track was unusual as it was next to a stock car track and had the fatal fence in consequence. It was also alleged that the surface of the track was in an unsafe condition. Finally it was stated that B had failed to require the claimant to sign on so that he was covered by an insurance policy.

S argued that the claimant was not a lawful visitor to the track as far as S was concerned. Alternatively, S said that the claimant was *volens* as regards the risk of collision with the inner fence. It was also argued that,

---

[2] Unreported, April 19, 2000, CA (Kennedy L.J., Hale L.J., Harrison J.), Unreported, December 11, 1998, Q.B.D, H.H.J. Graham Jones.

insofar as a duty of care existed, reasonable care had to be considered in the context of a sport which was, by its nature, potentially and actually dangerous and the ambitious nature of the practice riding. There was evidence that S had followed the advice of the sport's governing body and there had been a previously good safety record. In any event, the claimant was contributorily negligent.

B denied that he was ever an occupier of the race track. The accident had taken place before the commencement of the race meeting and after the claimant had been refused permission to race at the meeting. In any event, it was suggested that the course was inherently safe and courts should not dictate the level of risk in a well run sport unless clear precautions were not taken to prevent a hazard becoming a certain risk of injury.

First instance

At first instance, H.H.J. Graham Jones sitting as a Deputy High Court Judge   **6.05** held that the width of the race track was substantial. It was equivalent to the width of a three lane motorway plus the hard shoulder. The evidence was that the surface of the track made a very good, fast, circuit for racing. But the course was unique, the only mini long track in the United Kingdom. It was also inherently unsafe.

The expert evidence made it clear that the inner fence was a danger and a hazard. Side-cars needed a safe run-off area on the infield because of their design and direction of travel when control was lost. The fence was a complete obstruction of this area. Side-cars in this sort of event were not fitted with brakes and the fence gave rise to a clearly foreseeable risk of injury. The race track ought not to have been constructed.

Riders attending the race track for the purposes of the evening event and   **6.06** authorised by B to ride on the track during the hours of the training school in the afternoon were lawful visitors *vis-à-vis* S. On the evidence and the facts, the claimant was a lawful visitor to the race track. A single simple notice referring to cars and not to any consequences of failing to sign on was not sufficient to alert the claimant to the fact that he might be an unlawful visitor.

S, as the owner and occupier of a track which was inherently unsafe, would still not be liable if he took such care as was, in the circumstances, reasonable. He had taken advice and the advisers knew, or ought to have known, of the dangers. The advisers were plainly at fault and should have advised that the location was wholly unsuitable for the construction of, or continued use of, motorcycle side-car racing. But S should also have appreciated the dangers for himself. He should not have constructed or allowed use of a race track where the infield was not clear but dangerously obstructed. He was, therefore, in breach of his duty of care.

As to B, it was clear that the practice was official race practice. The danger presented by the fence ought to have been obvious to B who was an experienced racer himself. He ought not to have promoted the event and was an occupier in common with S during the racing having sufficient control following the principles of *Wheat v. Lacon*.[3] B was in breach of his duty of care to the claimant.

6.07   The machine which the claimant was riding was not defective. The lack of brakes was in preparation for the race. The accident probably happened as a result of the claimant and his passenger not having ridden together before. The claimant could probably have done more to avoid the collision with the fence. Had there not been a fence, the clear infield would probably have allowed the claimant to recover. The presence of the fence was obviously causative.

    The defence of *volenti non fit injuria* was expressly preserved by section 2(5) of the Occupier's Liability Act 1957. The claimant had ridden freely and voluntarily on the track and knew the inner fence was there. No one pointed out its danger which was apparent to a more experienced competitor. Even if he had known of the risk for the defence to be active he must also have consented to the consequences of it. There was no satisfactory evidence of a track safety certificate being issued. The consequences would not have been apparent. The defence of *volenti* was not made out.

6.08   A large measure of contributory negligence was established. The claimant knew of the inexperience of his passenger and of the lack of brakes and of the bias towards their infield. He could have done more to avoid the collision. He was 50 per cent to blame for the accident.

    As between the defendants, S was two-thirds to blame for the dangers from the circuit and B one-third, for allowing the practice to go on.

    Judgment was therefore given for the claimant. There were also third party issues in the case but these were not determined by the court.

Court of Appeal

6.09   The case was then taken to the Court of Appeal by the first defendant where the issues were:

    (a) whether he, as the owner and occupier of a leisure park which included a racetrack, should have been exonerated of negligence in respect of an accident that happened there;

    (b) whether the claimant should bear a greater than 50 per cent degree of contributory negligence.

    By his respondent's notice, the claimant sought to reduce the degree of contributory negligence.

    The first defendant stressed that the sport of motorcycle sidecar racing was recognised but inherently very dangerous. The machines had no brakes

---

[3] [1966] A.C. 552.

and progressed in a powered skid. Some 80,000 laps had been completed at the racetrack without serious injury. The first defendant argued that he handed over control of the track to the second defendant for race meetings. He therefore disputed that he owed any duty of care to the claimant and, even if he did, then he was not in breach of any duty. He argued that the claimant was, at the time of the accident, a trespasser and had, additionally, voluntarily assumed the risk of injury implicit in racing at the track. Finally, the first defendant contended that the accident occurred because of the claimant's own poor control and driving and that, accordingly, the degree of contributory negligence should be much greater.

The Court of Appeal held that although the first defendant had handed over the organisation of the race meeting to the second defendant, and the reality was that so far as the claimant was concerned the second defendant was in charge, the first defendant had put the second defendant in charge. The claimant was a lawful visitor to the race track *vis-à-vis* the first defendant. It was impossible for the first defendant to maintain that the claimant was a trespasser so far as he was concerned. Accordingly, the first defendant owed the claimant the common duty of care.

As to breach of duty, the allegation was that because the run-off area was **6.10** obstructed the track was inherently dangerous and a prudent developer and operator would have discovered and reacted to this long before the accident. On the weight of evidence, the judge had correctly concluded that it must have been obvious that if any rider hit the fence in the run-off area at anything other than a shallow angle there was likely to be a serious injury. The track was therefore a hazard which was not properly to be regarded as acceptable for those participating in motorcycle and sidecar racing. In the language of the Occupiers' Liability Act 1957 it was foreseeable that the visitor would not be reasonably safe in using the premises for the purposes for which he was invited or permitted to be there.

But such a conclusion was not necessarily decisive. The duty of the first defendant was only to take such care as was reasonable to safeguard his visitors. The first defendant had sought advice but his advisor, whom he employed for the purpose, had been plainly at fault in failing to point out that the track was wholly unsuitable. If the servant was negligent the master must take the blame. There was evidence that concern had been expressed to the first defendant about the obstructed run-off area. The first defendant had not taken reasonable care to ensure that the track was safe.

It was no defence for the first defendant to say that the claimant had failed **6.11** to suggest to whom the first defendant should have turned for advice. The claimant merely had to show that the first defendant and/or those in his employment with whom he consulted, failed to exercise such care, as was in all the circumstances of the case reasonable, to see that the claimant would be reasonably safe in using the track.

On voluntary assumption of risk, the first defendant placed heavy reliance on section 2(5) of the 1957 Act but the Judge had correctly concluded that even if the claimant had appreciated the risk from the fence in the obstructed run-off area that would not have been enough to establish a defence. Consent to bear the consequences of risk must also be established. But in any event the claimant did not know that the track failed to comply with the safety standards laid down by the governing body of the sport. There was no voluntary assumption of risk.

The claimant's decision to ride with a passenger with whom he had never ridden before was culpable to a high degree and plainly causative, as was the fact that the claimant could have done more than he did to avoid the collision or lessen its impact by disconnecting the power. The claimant was properly judged to be at fault. But his contributory negligence was no greater than the negligence of the defendants in failing to ensure that there was a clear infield. There was no reason to interfere with the Judge's apportionment of contributory negligence.

Therefore the appeal and the cross appeal were dismissed.

Stratton v. Hughes, etc.

6.12 Another good example of a case in this context is that of *Stratton v. Hughes (Executrix of the Estate of Edward John Hughes) and Cumberland Sporting Car Club Ltd and RAC Motor Sports Association Ltd.*[4]

The claimant claimed damages for personal injury sustained in a motor accident against his deceased co-driver who was killed in the National Rally Championship and the rally organisers. While the deceased was driving the Toyota car left the road, crossed a grass verge before colliding first with a lamp standard and then with a tree. The deceased co-driver was killed and the claimant sustained severe head and other injuries. The claimant had no recollection of the accident but alleged that the deceased was driving too fast, failed to keep any proper lookout and failed to take sufficient account of the bend at the final finish line or to so manage or control his vehicle so as to avoid a collision. He also alleged against the deceased defendant that a bias brake valve was illegally fitted in a manner likely to adversely affect the driver's ability to control the vehicle.

Steele J. dismissed the claim against the first defendant.[5] In relation to the claims against the second and third defendants concerning the rally arrangements, he held that motor rallying is a sport which was known to all the participants to be inherently dangerous. The organisers of rallies owed a duty of care to the competitors and under the control of the RAC General Regulations they were required to provide for the safety of those who rally. The layout of the course was not unsafe.

The claimant's claim against all three defendants was therefore dismissed. In view of the findings that there had been no negligence by any of the

---

[4] Unreported, Steele J., February 28, 1997.
[5] For which, see Chap. 3.

defendants the court found it unnecessary to rule on the arguments raised on the application of the doctrine of *volenti non fit injuria*.

Other cases

The following examples, each decided on their facts, provide some further guidance[6]:

1. A rugby player was held to have accepted willingly the risk of playing the game on the defendant's pitch which, although it complied with the byelaws of the Rugby Football League, had a concrete wall running at a distance of seven feet three inches away from and along the touchline.[7]

2. However, this defence was not available where the driver of a racing car suffered injury in a crash caused by dangerous and inadequately protected flower bed running alongside the track, the driver being unaware of the nature and extent of the risk he was running.[8]

3. So, too, where the claimant slipped on the highly polished floor of a hall in which physical training classes were being conducted, since he had not agreed to take upon himself the risk of slipping on a floor not reasonably fit for the purpose.[9]

4. Also where a ballet dancer enrolled in a judo class and in the course of the first lesson had his arm broken, the instructor having allowed what should have been practice to turn into dangerous competition.

Conclusion

As mentioned above, the number of cases in this area is likely to increase. It **6.13** may be that as they do, the principles to be applied or the factors to be taken into account will be slightly distinguished from those relevant to spectators just as certain differences have emerged with regard to the liability of participants in different contexts.

Example

Hollywood hotshots Tom Waller and Jonathan Newman are producing and directing a film under their new collective label, "Brit Pack". During the filming of one of the stunts at the ski resort of Whistler, the locations director and romantic lead Fiona McKenzie organises a snowboarding competition for some of the crew.

---

[6] See *Charlesworth and Percy on Negligence* (10th ed., 2001, Sweet and Maxwell).
[7] *Simms v. Leigh Rugby Club* [1969] 2 All E.R. 923.
[8] *Latchford v. Spedeworth International, The Times*, October 11, 1983.
[9] *Gillmore v. L.C.C.* [1938] 4 All E.R. 331.

As a former snowboard world champion, she easily wins the competition. However, there is a tussle for second place between film stars Valerio Massimo and Tom Hampson culminating in a head to head in which Tom Hampson injures himself as a result of a defect in the course half-way down.

Are Brit Pack liable for Tom Hampson's injuries?

Chapter 7

Liability of participants and organisers to third parties

"My wife had an uncle who could never walk down the nave of his abbey without wondering whether it would take spin."

Lord Home, The Twentieth Century Revisited, BBC TV, 1982.

Introduction

In the previous Chapter we considered the liability of organisers to specta- **7.01** tors. There have been a number of cases involving injuries sustained by third parties—the innocent passer by. As Moore[1] recognises the liability is capable of arising in negligence or nuisance. The nuisance may arise in circumstances where people live in close proximity to sports grounds (*e.g.* cricket clubs). Many of the cases arise out of the common situation when a ball leaves the boundaries of the sporting venue. In both golf and cricket this is a frequent occurrence.

Balls being hit out of the ground

In cricket, a batsman may very well be attempting to hit the ball beyond the **7.02** perimeter of the ground. In golf, the player does not intend to hit the ball out of the ground. Does that mean that there are different standards to be applied? What degree of care must participants and organisers (within which we include the owners of sports grounds) exercise to escape liability as a result of the intended use of the sporting venue?

In *Bolton v. Stone*,[2] the claimant was on a side road of residential houses when he was injured by a ball hit by a player on a cricket ground abutting on that highway. The ground was enclosed on that side by a seven-feet fence, the top of which, owing to a slope, stood 17 feet above the level of the pitch. The wicket from which the ball was hit was about 78 yards from this fence and 100 yards from the place where the injury occurred. There was

---

[1] C. Moore, *Sports Law & Litigation* (2nd ed., CLT Professional Publishing Limited), Welwyn Garden City.
[2] [1951] A.C. 850.

evidence that over a period of years balls had been struck over the fence on very rare occasions.

7.03   However, the evidence was that the strike which had brought about the injury was exceptional. The House of Lords held that the members of the club were not liable in damages to the injured person, whether on the ground of negligence or nuisance. Although the possibility of the ball being hit onto the highway might reasonably have been foreseen, this was not sufficient to establish negligence, since the risk of injury to anyone in such a place was so remote that a reasonable person would not have anticipated it. Lord Porter stated[3]:

"Is it enough to make an action negligent to say that its performance may possibly cause injury, or must some greater probability exist of that result ensuing in order to make those responsible for its occurrence guilty of negligence? In the present case the appellants did not do the act themselves, but they are trustees of a field where cricket is played, are in control of it, and invite visiting teams to play there. They are, therefore, and are admitted to be responsible for the negligent action of those who use the field in the way intended that it should be used.

The question then arises: What degree of care must they exercise to escape liability for anything which may occur as a result of this intended use of the field?

Undoubtedly they knew that the hitting of a cricket ball out of the ground was an event which might occur and, therefore, that there was a conceivable possibility that someone would be hit by it. But so extreme an obligation of care cannot be imposed in all cases. If it were, no one could safely drive a motor car since the possibility of an accident could not be overlooked and if it occurred some stranger might well be injured however careful the driver might be. It is true that the driver desires to do everything possible to avoid an accident, whereas the hitting of a ball out of the ground is an incident in the game and, indeed, one which the batsman would wish to bring about; but in order that the act may be negligent there must not only be a reasonable possibility of its happening but also of injury being caused. In the words of Lord Thankerton in *Bourhill v. Young*[4] the duty is to exercise 'such reasonable care as will avoid the risk of injury to such persons as he can reasonably foresee might be injured by failure to exercise such reasonable care', and Lord Macmillan used words to the like effect.[5] So, also, Lord Wright in *Glasgow Corporation v. Muir*[6] quoted the well-known words of Lord Atkin in *Donoghue v. Stevenson*[7]: 'You must take reasonable care to avoid acts or omissions which you can reasonably foresee would be likely to injure your neighbour'. It is not enough that the event should be such as can reasonably be foreseen; the further result that injury is likely to follow must also be such as a reasonable man would contemplate, before he can be convicted of actionable negligence. Nor is the remote possibility of injury occurring enough; there must be sufficient proba-

---

[3] At 857.
[4] [1943] A.C. 92 at 98.
[5] *ibid*. at 104.
[6] [1943] A.C. 448 at 460.
[7] [1932] A.C. 562 at 580.

bility to lead a reasonable man to anticipate it. The existence of some risk is an ordinary incident of life, even when all due care has been, as it must be, taken."

Organisers and participants would be prudent to undertake some form of   **7.04**
assessment. If there are residential areas or public walkways within striking distance of the sporting venue the participant or, realistically, the organiser would be well advised to consider the measures in place to prevent projectiles injuring third parties.

The claimant was successful in *Lamond v. Glasgow Corporation.*[8] The defendant was the occupier of the golf course. As in the *Bolton* case, the claimant had been struck by a ball which was hit off the course. The claimant was positioned on a public lane close to the course. The evidence was that approximately 6,000 shots per year were hit over the fence. It was held that there was a reasonably foreseeable risk that someone would be struck by a ball. The occupiers had been negligent.

Limited assistance may be drawn from foreign jurisdictions.

In *Hennessey v. Pyne,*[9] the claimant's house was in close proximity to a golf-course and, in particular, a dog-leg hole. The house was hit regularly by stray balls. In view of the proximity of the house to the course, it was held that golfers owed a duty to exercise reasonable care for the safety of the people in the house.

In *Whitefield v. Barton,*[10] the claimant's car was damaged when it was hit   **7.05**
by a golf-ball. The defendant had checked before he hit the shot to see that the way was clear. However, the car was, at that time, out of sight. The claim against the player failed.

Other examples include, *Spray v. Manor & Ors,*[11] where the claim for damages failed as the court held that the golf club had taken all reasonable precaution short of closing the practice fairway to prevent golf-balls straying. See also *Castle v. St Augustine's Links Ltd*[12] where the evidence was that a considerable number of balls were hit onto the road and the claimant recovered.

The difficulty faced by occupiers and participants and, for that matter, insurers is determining when a risk of injury becomes sufficiently probable to require intervention or positive action. Of course, as technology improves and sports manufacturers continue their endless pursuit of the club that hits the ball further, it is likely that clubs will have to adopt new measures to eradicate the risk if it is real.

A fence which was adequate in 1975 to protect pedestrians from flying golf balls may be inadequate now. The introduction of graphite shafts and

---

[8] [1968] S.L.T. 291.
[9] [1997] 694 A2d 691.
[10] [1987] S.C.L.R. 259.
[11] Unreported, 1997.
[12] [1922] 38 T.L.R. 615.

titanium headed golf clubs mean that the average club golfer is more than capable of hitting drives in excess of 300 yards. In 1975, a top professional would have been unable to hit a drive 300 yards.

Example

Champion golfer Richard Hart is doing his finals at Magdalene College, Cambridge University. To take his mind off exams he goes into the second court and sets himself the challenge of hitting a golf ball up and over the Pepys library directly ahead of him and into the Fellows Garden beyond. His mind is focused solely on not smashing the windows of the library. To no-one's surprise, he succeeds in this primary objective. Unfortunately, however, the ball lands on the head of Mark Sefton who was having a quiet cigarette under a tree in the Fellows' Garden.

This is despite Richard Hart having sent his friend, Italian academic and fashion queen, Giorgia Bussolino to check that it was safe to hit the ball and despite Giorgia Bussolino having assured him that it was. Are either Richard Hart or Giorgia Bussolino liable for the injuries sustained by Mark Sefton?

Injunctive relief

7.06 An occupier of premises under attack from errant balls may attempt to restrain the sports club from continuing its activities until adequate measures are taken to prevent the nuisance. However, the courts' approach to such claims lacks clarity. Decisions appear to go both ways and it is difficult (perhaps impossible) to extract any consistent line of reasoning.

In *Lacey v. Parker and others*,[13] the court declined to grant a mandatory injunction to erect a 25-foot fence in front of the applicant's house to prevent cricket balls being hit into his garden. This approach is in line with the Court of Appeal's analysis in *Miller v. Jackson*.[14] Members of a village club played cricket in the evenings and at weekends in the summer months on a small ground where cricket had been played since about 1905, when it was surrounded by agricultural fields. The ground was leased to the club by the owners, the National Coal Board. In 1965 the NCB sold part of the adjacent pasture land to the local council who in 1970 sold it to developers. A line of houses was built so sited that it was inevitable that so long as cricket was played on the ground some balls hit beyond the boundary would fall into the rear gardens or on to or against the houses, despite a six-foot concrete boundary fence. In 1972 the claimant bought one of the houses. The rear garden of had a boundary with the cricket ground. Soon after taking possession they began to complain of incidents causing actual damage to their house and apprehension of personal injury which interfered with their enjoyment of their house and garden whenever cricket was being

---

[13] *The Times*, May 15, 1994.
[14] [1977] Q.B. 966.

played. In 1975 the club increased the height of the boundary fence to 15 feet. However, some balls continued to land in adjacent properties.

The claimants brought an action claiming damages for negligence and alternatively for nuisance. They also sought an injunction to restrain the club from playing cricket on the ground without first taking adequate steps to prevent balls being struck out of the ground on to their house or garden. Reeve J. awarded the claimants damages for personal inconvenience and interference with their past enjoyment of their property and granted them the injunction in the terms asked for.

By a majority of the Court of Appeal it was held that the defendants, so 7.07 long as they played cricket on that ground, were guilty of negligence every time a ball came over the fence and caused damage, for the risk of injury to person and property was continuous and no reasonable method of eliminating that risk had been produced. They were also guilty of nuisance since their use of their land involved an unreasonable interference with their neighbours' use and enjoyment of their house and garden. The claimants were under no duty to mitigate that risk.

Geoffrey Lane L.J. indicated that the court was bound by the rule in *Sturges v. Bridgman*,[15] which has never been questioned, that it is no answer to a claim in nuisance for the defendant to show that the claimant brought the trouble on his own head by coming to live so close to the defendant's premises that he would inevitably be affected by the defendant's activities where no one had been affected before. Lord Denning M.R. (dissenting) stated that the use of the ground for cricket was reasonable. It does not suddenly become a nuisance because a neighbour chooses to come to a house in a position where it might occasionally be hit by a cricket ball. He found that there was no negligence so as to give rise to a claim for damages.

The court in exercising its equitable jurisdiction to grant or refuse an 7.08 injunction was under a duty to have regard to the public interest. Where the effect of an injunction would prevent cricket being played on a ground where it had been played for over 70 years, the special circumstances were such that the greater interest of the public should prevail over the hardship to the individual householders by being deprived of their enjoyment of their house and garden while cricket was being played. The injunction was discharged and damages of £400 substituted for past and future inconvenience.

In *Kennaway v. Thompson*,[16] the claimant owned land next to a man-made lake on which a motor boat racing club had organised and carried on racing and water skiing activities since the early 1960s. Having obtained planning permission in 1969, she built a house, and went into occupation of it in 1972. From about 1969 there was a considerable increase in the club's

---

[15] (1879) 11 Ch.D. 852.
[16] [1981] Q.B. 88.

activities, and by 1977 there were race meetings most weekends between April and October with large, noisy boats taking part. Before each meeting there was a period of practice. In 1977 the claimant brought proceedings against the defendants as representatives of the club claiming damages for nuisance caused by the noise of the club's activities and an injunction to restrain further nuisance. She was awarded damages for past nuisance.

However, no injunction was granted on the ground that, because there was considerable public interest in the club it would be oppressive. She was awarded £15,000 damages in lieu, being the diminution in value of her property by reason of the nuisance. The Court of Appeal allowed the appeal. They held that in considering whether to award damages in lieu of an injunction the court was bound by the principles set out in *Shelfer v. City of London Electric Lighting Co.*[17]

7.09   In cases of continuing actionable nuisance the jurisdiction to award damages ought only to be exercised under very exceptional circumstances. The public interest in continuing the activity constituting the nuisance did not prevail over private interest in obtaining an injunction, and, accordingly, the claimant was entitled to an injunction to restrain future nuisance. The decision of the Court of Appeal marked a return to the position that damages will be awarded in lieu of nuisance only if the nuisance is trivial and occasional. Thus, *Miller* is open to criticism. It is difficult to see the rationale behind *Lacey* which post-dates *Kennaway*.

In the context of sports injury litigation two points can be extracted from the injunction authorities. First, it is a moot point as to whether erecting premises close to an arena from which balls are likely to be hit would constitute contributory negligence. It is noteworthy that the Court of Appeal in *Miller* stated that the claimant was under no duty to mitigate that nuisance. Secondly, the Court of Appeal found that the cricket club was negligent every time a ball was hit into the claimant's rear garden. So in the context of the earlier discussion of what constituted a sufficiently probable risk of injury, the facts of that case were sufficient.

Psychiatric injury

7.10   We considered in Chapter 5 the potential liability of organisers to spectators for psychiatric injury. A distinction must be drawn between claimants inside the ground and spectators outside.

The leading cases in this regard are *Alcock v. Chief Constable of South Yorkshire*[18] and *Page v. Smith*. In *Alcock*, the defendant was responsible for the policing of a football match at which, as a result of overcrowding in part of the stadium, 95 people died and many more sustained crushing injuries. As the disaster became apparent live pictures of the events at the stadium were

---

[17] [1895] 1 Ch. 287.
[18] [1992] 1 A.C. 310.

broadcast on television. The claimants were all related to, or friends of, spectators involved in the disaster. Some witnessed events from other parts of the stadium. One claimant, who was just outside the stadium, saw the events on television and went in to search for his missing son. Other claimants were at home and watched the events on live television broadcasts or heard of them from friends or through radio reports but only later saw recorded television pictures. All the claimants, alleging that the impact of what they had seen and heard had caused them severe shock resulting in psychiatric illness, claimed damages in negligence against the defendant.

On the issue of liability the judge held that the category of claimants entitled to claim damages for nervous shock included a sibling as well as a parent or spouse of a victim, and that those claimants present in or immediately outside the stadium at the time of the disaster or who watched it live on television were sufficiently close in time and place for it to be reasonably foreseeable that what they had seen would cause them to suffer psychiatric illness.

Accordingly, nine of the claimants, who were either parents, spouses or siblings of the victims and who were eye-witnesses of the disaster or who saw it live on television, were held to be entitled to claim damages for nervous shock. The remaining six claimants were excluded as claimants because they were in a more remote relationship or because they had heard about the disaster by some means other than live television broadcasts. The Court of Appeal allowed the defendant's appeal and dismissed the unsuccessful claimants' cross-appeal. **7.11**

The House of Lords held that in order to establish a claim in respect of psychiatric illness resulting from shock it was necessary to show not only that such injury was reasonably foreseeable, but also that the relationship between the claimant and the defendant was sufficiently proximate. The class of persons to whom a duty of care was owed as being sufficiently proximate was not limited by reference to particular relationships such as husband and wife or parent and child, but was based on ties of love and affection, the closeness of which would need to be proved in each case. The more remote the relationship would require careful scrutiny. The claimant must show propinquity in time and space to the accident or its immediate aftermath.

The House of Lords dismissed the appeal in the cases of the claimants who had been present at the football match. The mere fact of the relationship shown was insufficient to give rise to a duty of care. Furthermore, that the viewing of the disaster on television could not be said to be equivalent to being within sight and hearing of the event or its immediate aftermath; and, accordingly, the claimants' claims failed.

In *Page v. Smith*[19] the claimant while driving along the highway was involved in a collision with a car driven by the defendant. The claimant **7.12**

---

[19] [1996] 1 A.C. 155.

suffered no physical injury but three hours after the accident he felt exhausted and the exhaustion had continued. For 20 years prior to the accident the claimant had suffered from a condition variously described as myalgic encephalomyelitis, (aka. chronic fatigue syndrome or post viral fatigue syndrome) which manifested itself from time to time with different degrees of severity. The claimant brought an action claiming damages for personal injuries caused by the defendant's negligence in that as a result of the accident his condition had become chronic and permanent and that it was unlikely that he would be able to take full-time employment again.

The House of Lords held by a majority, that once it was established that the defendant was under a duty of care to avoid causing personal injury to the claimant, it mattered not whether the injury in fact sustained was physical, psychiatric or both. Applying that test, it sufficed to ask whether the defendant should have reasonably foreseen that the claimant might suffer personal injury as a result of the defendant's negligence, so as to bring him within the ambit of the defendant's duty of care. It was unnecessary to ask as a separate question, whether the defendant should reasonably have foreseen injury by shock. It was irrelevant that the claimant did not sustain external physical injury. In cases of nervous shock it is essential to distinguish between the primary victim and secondary victims. In claims by secondary victims the law insists on certain control mechanisms, in order to limit the number of potential claimants. These control mechanisms have no place where the claimant is the primary victim.

Conclusion

7.13 Many of the judgments in this Chapter are based upon public policy and are at the edge of the law of negligence. It is for this reason that they are not only interesting in their specific contexts but also in the direction in which they potentially point with regard to future developments in the law generally.

Chapter 8

Liability of organisers to members of rescue services

"Cricket is a game which the British, not being a spiritual people, had to invent in order to have some concept of eternity."

Lord Mancroft.

Introduction

We have seen in the previous two chapters that organisers may be liable to spectators and third parties. We now turn to members of the rescue services. Here we will concentrate primarily on psychiatric injuries sustained by those persons carrying out their function as rescuers. They will, by definition, only be called into action when accidents or disasters occur. In recent times, disasters have occurred in football stadiums (for example—Hillsborough which has already been considered in some detail, Bradford, and Ellis Park, Johannesburg).   **8.01**

Can rescuers recover damages for psychiatric injury suffered as a result of a rescue?

The answer is, as one might expect, a conditional, yes. The starting point with respect to the liability of to rescuers is that if a person by his negligence creates a dangerous situation whereby other people[1] are likely to suffer damage or if he puts himself in peril[2] he owes a duty of care to those altruistic people whom he ought reasonably to foresee may attempt to rescue that person at risk to their own safety.[3] Thus, the classes of claimant entitled to pursue damages for a psychiatric injury as a result of witnessing a catastrophic event is not limited to relatives.   **8.02**

---

[1] *Baker v. T.E. Hopkins Ltd* [1959] 1 W.L.R. 966.
[2] *Harrison v. British Railways Board* [1981] 3 All E.R. 679.
[3] See generally *Charlesworth & Percy on Negligence*, Sweet & Maxwell, London 2001, para. 2–134.

In *Chadwick v. British Railways Board*,[4] the claimant, as the administratrix of the estate of her late husband, Chadwick, brought an action for damages for personal injuries alleged to have been sustained by him as the result of his rescue activities at the scene of a serious railway accident which took place at Lewisham at about six p.m. on December 4, 1957, in which 90 persons were killed. The accident occurred about 200 yards from Mr Chadwick's home, and, on being informed of it, he immediately went to help. He remained at the scene until six o'clock the following morning.

There was evidence that because of his small stature he was able to render assistance by crawling into the wreckage to administer injections to injured persons and to aid persons to extricate themselves from the wreckage. Before the accident he was a cheerful, busy man carrying on a successful window-cleaning business and with many spare-time activities. After the accident, and, allegedly as a result of his experiences at the scene, he became psychoneurotic and had to spend six months in a mental hospital: his health deteriorated, he no longer took the interest in life which he had previously taken, and was unable to work. He died in 1962 of causes unconnected with the accident.

8.03   The defendants admitted that the accident was caused by their negligence, but denied liability to Mr Chadwick. In finding for the claimant Waller J. stated:

> "The second question I have to consider is whether foreseeability of injury by shock is necessary. The House of Lords in *Bourhill v. Young*[5] considered a number of matters in deciding whether or not the defendant owed a duty to the plaintiff and, in deciding that the plaintiff was outside the area of contemplation, one of the matters considered, particularly by Lord Wright,[6] was the foreseeability of injury by shock. In *King v. Phillips*[7] Denning L.J. said,[8] in the passage which was later quoted with approval by Viscount Simonds in *Overseas Tankship (United Kingdom) Limited v. Morts Dock & Engineering Co. Ltd (The Wagon Mound)*[9] that 'there can be no doubt since *Bourhill v. Young*[10] that the test for liability for shock is foreseeability of injury by shock.' I therefore must ask myself whether injury by shock was foreseeable in this case. The scene described by Mrs Taylor was the kind of thing to be expected if trains collided as these did and it was one which could, in my view, properly be called gruesome. In my opinion, if the defendants had asked themselves the hypothetical question 'If we run one train into another at Lewisham in such circumstances that a large number of people are killed, may some persons who are physically unhurt suffer injury from shock?' I think that the answer must have been 'Yes.'"

---

[4] [1967] 1 W.L.R. 912.
[5] [1943] A.C. 92.
[6] *ibid.* at 107.
[7] [1953] 1 Q.B. 429; [1953] 2 W.L.R. 526; [1953] 1 All E.R. 617, CA.
[8] [1953] 1 Q.B. 429 at 441.
[9] [1961] A.C. 388, 426; [1961] 2 W.L.R. 126; [1961] 1 All E.R. 404, PC.
[10] [1943] A.C. 92.

He went on: **8.04**

"The third question is: did the defendants owe a duty to the plaintiff, who was not their servant but who had come to their aid? The test is: what ought the defendants to have foreseen? In *Baker v. T.E. Hopkins & Son Ltd*[11] the Court of Appeal were considering the circumstances in which defendants owe a duty to rescuers. Morris L.J. said this[12]:

"The first stage in the proof of the claim involves proof that the defendant company was negligent towards their employees, the second that such negligence caused such employees to be in peril, the third that this could reasonably have been foreseen, and the fourth that it could also have been reasonably foreseen that someone would be likely to seek to rescue them from their peril and might either suffer injury or lose his life. In the classic words of Lord Atkin in *Donoghue v. Stevenson*[13]: 'You must take reasonable care to avoid acts or omissions which you can reasonably foresee would be likely to injure your neighbour.' Neighbours are those persons 'who are so closely and directly affected by my act that I ought reasonably to have them in contemplation as being so affected when I am directing my mind to the acts or omissions which are called in question.' So in this case it is said that, if the company negligently caused or permitted their servants to be placed in dire peril in a gas-filled well it ought reasonably to have been contemplated that some brave and stalwart man would attempt to save their lives. In the eloquent words of Cardozo J. in *Wagner v. International Railway Company*[14]: 'Danger invites rescue. The cry of distress is the summons to relief. The law does not ignore these reactions of the mind in tracing conduct to its consequences. It recognises them as normal. It places their effect within the range of the natural and probable. The wrong that imperils life is a wrong to the imperilled victim; it is a wrong also to his rescuer.' "

Does the concept of primary and secondary victims apply to rescuers?

We have seen that in *Alcock v. Chief Constable of South Yorkshire*,[15]   **8.05**
the concept of primary victim was introduced to apply to those cases where the claimant was involved mediately or immediately as a participant. The House of Lords included within that category rescue cases. As Lord Oliver stated[16]:

"Into the same category [as those personally threatened by a terrifying experience] as it seems to me, fall the so called 'rescue cases'. It is well established that the Defendant owes a duty of care not only to those who are directly threatened or

---

[11] [1959] 1 W.L.R. 966; [1959] 3 All E.R. 225.
[12] [1959] 1 W.L.R. 966 at 972.
[13] [1932] A.C. 562 at 580; 48 T.L.R. 494.
[14] (1921) 232 N.Y. Rep. 176, 180.
[15] [1992] 1 A.C. 310 at 407, 409.
[16] *ibid.* at 408.

injured by his careless acts but also to those, who, as a result are induced to go to their rescue and suffer injury in doing so."

This appears to be at odds with the decision of the House of Lords in *Page v. Smith*[17] where Lord Lloyd adopted a narrower construction of primary victim. In *Page*, the claimant was involved in a relatively minor road traffic accident. He was not physically injured but did suffer a recurrence of chronic fatigue syndrome brought about by the shock caused by the accident.

8.06   Lord Lloyd, giving the leading judgment, stated that in the case of a primary victim foreseeability of physical harm, in itself, was sufficient to enable the claimant to recover in respect of psychiatric illness. He went on to describe the claimant as a primary victim because:

" . . . he was himself directly involved in the accident, and well within the range of foreseeable physical injury."[18]

This approach was criticised by the Law Commission who argued that it should not be a condition of a rescuer's entitlement to recover damages for psychiatric illness that he or she is in physical danger.

The Law Commission's criticism of the decision in *Page* fell on deaf ears in *Frost & ors v. Chief Constable of South Yorkshire Police*.[19] In *Frost*, the House of Lords considered claims advanced by police officers who had suffered psychiatric injury following the Hillsborough disaster.

A large number of police officers brought proceedings against the Chief Constable. Liability was admitted and damages assessed in relation to those officers who were active in the immediate area where the deaths and injuries occurred. Five claimants were selected as representative of the various roles carried out by the remaining claimants. It was not in issue that those claimants had suffered post-traumatic stress disorder caused by their experiences arising from the tragedy. Four of them had been on duty at the stadium; the fifth had been responsible for stripping bodies and completing casualty forms at a hospital.

8.07   At first instance Waller J. dismissed the claims. He held that holding that although a relationship analogous to master and servant existed between the first defendant and the claimants, giving rise to a duty of care embracing psychiatric illness, that duty did not arise where the claimant was a secondary victim, unless he could succeed as a rescuer, and such a duty could not place a police officer in a better position than a bystander. Only one of the claimants was a rescuer in law and he could not recover since, being a professional rescuer not intimately participating in the incident itself, or in

---

[17] [1999] 2 A.C. 455.
[18] *ibid.* at 184.
[19] [1999] 2 A.C. 495.

the immediate aftermath, it would be both unattractive and unjust and unreasonable if he could recover whereas a bystander could not.

The Court of Appeal, by a majority, allowed appeals by the four claimants who had been on duty at the time of the disaster on the basis that a Chief Constable's duty of care to a police officer in relation to psychiatric injury caused in the course of employment arose irrespective of whether the employee would otherwise have been classified as a primary or a secondary victim. Likewise a tortfeasor owed a rescuer a duty of care in respect of psychiatric injury sustained during the rescue even if the rescuer would otherwise be classified as a secondary victim, so that each of the claimants who was present at the ground was owed a duty of care as a servant or as a rescuer or both.

The Court of Appeal's decision attracted much criticism from the press and families of the deceased. The thrust of the criticism was that it created an illogical situation whereby a family member of the deceased would be unable to recover compensation unless he satisfied the various criteria to be classified as a secondary victim whereas a police officer, who must expect to assist in circumstances such as Hillsborough, could recover.

The defendant appealed to the House of Lords. The claimant once again **8.08** advanced the "concept of a rescuer" as an exception to the limitations on recovery for pure psychiatric harm recognised by the House of Lords in *Alcock* and *Page*. Lord Steyn, who gave the leading judgment was not persuaded. He accepted that the law has long recognised the moral imperative of encouraging citizens to rescue persons in peril. He reiterated that a rescue attempt to save someone from danger would be regarded as foreseeable. A duty of care to a rescuer may arise even if the defendant owed no duty to the primary victim, for example, because the latter was a trespasser. If a rescuer is injured in a rescue attempt, a plea of *volenti non fit injuria*, contributory negligence, or *novus actus interveniens* will usually receive "short shrift".

He went on[20]

"The specific difficulty counsel faces is that it is common ground that none of the four police officers were at any time exposed to personal danger and none thought that they were so exposed. Counsel submitted that this is not a requirement. He sought comfort in the general observations in the *Alcock* case of Lord Oliver about the category of 'participants'. None of the other Law Lords in the *Alcock* case discussed this category. Moreover, the issue of rescuers' entitlement to recover for psychiatric harm was not before the House on that occasion and Lord Oliver was not considering the competing arguments presently before the House. The explanation of Lord Oliver's observations has been the subject of much debate. It was also vigorously contested at the bar . . . . Counsel was only able to cite one English decision in support of his argument namely the first instance judgment in

---

[20] *ibid.* at 499.

Chadwick. Mr Chadwick had entered a wrecked railway carriage to help and work among the injured. There was clearly a risk that the carriage might collapse. Waller J. said, at 918: 'although there was clearly an element of personal danger in what Mr Chadwick was doing, I think I must deal with this case on the basis that it was the horror of the whole experience which caused his reaction.'

On the judge's findings the rescuer had passed the threshold of being in personal danger but his psychiatric injury was caused by 'the full horror of his experience' when he was presumably not always in personal danger. This decision has been cited with approval.[21] I too would accept that the *Chadwick* case was correctly decided. But it is not authority for the proposition that a person who never exposed himself to any personal danger and never thought that he was in personal danger can recover pure psychiatric injury as a rescuer. In order to recover compensation for pure psychiatric harm as rescuer it is not necessary to establish that his psychiatric condition was caused by the perception of personal danger. And Waller J. rightly so held. But in order to contain the concept of rescuer in reasonable bounds for the purposes of the recovery of compensation for pure psychiatric harm the plaintiff must at least satisfy the threshold requirement that he objectively exposed himself to danger or reasonably believed that he was doing so. Without such limitation one would have the unedifying spectacle that, while bereaved relatives are not allowed to recover as in the *Alcock* case, ghoulishly curious spectators, who assisted in some peripheral way in the aftermath of a disaster, might recover. For my part the limitation of actual or apprehended dangers is what proximity in this special situation means. In my judgment it would be an unwarranted extension of the law to uphold the claims of the police officers. I would dismiss the argument under this heading."

8.09   So the House of Lords concluded that a Chief Constable owed police officers under his command a duty analogous to an employer's duty to care for the safety of his employees and to take reasonable steps to protect them from physical harm. However, that duty did not extend to protecting them from psychiatric injury when there was no breach of the duty to protect them from physical injury. The general rules restricting the recovery of damages for pure psychiatric harm applied to the claimants' claims as employees. There was no justification for regarding psychiatric injury sustained by police officers while on duty as being outside those restrictions. Accordingly, the employment relationship was insufficient to impose liability on the Chief Constable for psychiatric injury sustained by the claimants.

Lord Goff who dissented held that a police officer's role as a rescuer and as an employee with no choice but to become involved in events qualified them as primary victims.

In addition, the House went on to hold that a rescuer in relation to whom physical injury was not reasonably foreseeable could not recover damages

---

[21] See *McLoughlin v. O'Brian* [1983] 1 A.C. 410 *per* Lord Wilberforce, at 419 *per* Lord Edmund-Davies at 424, and *per* Lord Bridge of Harwich at 437–438; and in *Alcock* [1992] 1 A.C. 310 *per* Lord Oliver at 408.

for psychiatric injury sustained by witnessing, or participating in the after-math of, an accident which had caused death or injury to others. A rescuer who had not been exposed to the danger of physical injury or who did not reasonably believe himself to have been so exposed was accordingly to be classified as a secondary victim who, in common with spectators and bystanders, was required to satisfy additional conditions before he could recover damages for pure psychiatric injury.

It would be unfair as between different classes of claimants if police officers were regarded as a special category and were put in a more favour-able position in relation to damages than bereaved relatives of victims; and that, accordingly, since the claimants were not within the range of foresee-able physical injury, their claims based on their position as rescuers also failed.

The future

Lord Steyn described the law on the recovery of compensation for pure psychiatric harm as a "patchwork quilt of distinctions which are difficult to justify". There are, he argued, two theoretical solutions. The first was to wipe out recovery in tort for pure psychiatric injury. That would be contrary to precedent and, in any event, highly controversial. Only Parliament could take such a step. It is submitted that it is unlikely that they ever would.   **8.10**

The second solution is to abolish all the special limiting rules applicable to psychiatric harm. That appears to be the course advocated by Mullany and Handford, "Tort Liability for Psychiatric Damage". They would allow claims for pure psychiatric damage by mere bystanders.[22]

As Lord Steyn accepted, precedent rules out this course. In his view, the only sensible general strategy is for the courts is to say "thus far and no further". The categories as reflected in the decisions such as *Alcock* and *Page* should be treated as settled for the time being and for any expansion or development in this area of the law to be left to Parliament.

Example

PC Nicholas Helm is a police officer, on official duty, who attends a rugby match between the Marriott Marauders and the Briggs Wagons. Following a stunning try by the salmon hipped Richard Staveley for the Wagons there is a surge in the stand. As a result there is a crush in which spectators are killed. He knows that there are members of his family in the stand none of whom are injured. Nicholas performs heroically in the rescue operation but experiences shock. Can Nicholas claim as a rescuer? If he were rescuer, could he claim for shock suffered as a result of the fear that members of his family were imperilled.   **8.11**

---

[22] See (1997) 113 L.Q.R. 410 at 415.

Chapter 9

Liability of organisers for actions of spectators

*"Ernie: Excuse me, won't you—I'm a little stiff from badminton.
Eric: It doesn't matter where you're from."*

Eric Morecambe and Ernie Wise, The Morecambe and Wise Joke Book, 1979.

Introduction

Organisers are not just concerned about the behaviour of the participants.   **9.01**
They must also consider their potential liability for the actions of spectators.
Depressingly, that leads us to the subject of hooliganism. It has blighted
football for decades. The most appalling example occurred in 1985 before
the European Cup Final between Liverpool and Juventus at the Heysel
Stadium in Brussels. Rioting led to the deaths of 39, mainly Italian supporters. The behaviour of fans was a political issue. The Prime Minister, Mar-
garet Thatcher, indicated that English clubs should be banned from the
competition. UEFA imposed a five-year ban. Happily, concerted efforts by
the authorities, the increase in all-seater stadiums, more sophisticated policing and surveillance have resulted in a substantial reduction in crowd
violence. Nevertheless, the problem still exists. Certain clubs in the FA
Premier League and Football League still have a reputation for their fans
being involved with crowd disturbance. The England National Squad is
unable to travel to any international event without a massive security effort.
It is not always successful as events in Charleroi during the European
Championship 2000 demonstrated. Organisers must remain vigilant.

Cunningham & ors v. Reading Football Club

In *Cunningham & ors v. Reading Football Club*[1] a football club was held   **9.02**
liable for injuries caused to police officers on duty at a football match
because those injuries had resulted from the club's neglect to take precautions against clearly foreseeable acts of violent supporters. The claimants,

---

[1] [1991] P.I.Q.R. 141.

who included both police officers and spectators, had attended a football match between Reading and Bristol City. The claimants were struck by pieces of concrete loosened from the terraces and thrown at them by spectators.

The defendants had known in advance of the risk that there might be crowd violence. The match was considered to be a "local derby". The atmosphere was likely to be even more charged since the game would affect promotion hopes and Bristol City's supporters were known at the time to have a reputation for violent behaviour. The defendant was also aware that at a match about four months earlier, spectators had loosened concrete by kicking and jumping on it. They had then thrown the lumps of concrete at the police. The defendant, despite the serious consequences, took no action to prevent or even to make it harder for spectators to loosen the concrete. The claimants brought their actions for breach of duty under the Occupier's Liability Act 1957 and also in negligence. Mr Justice Drake held that the police and the spectators were visitors of the defendants and as such the defendant owed a duty to take such steps as were necessary to ensure that their visitors were safe. The stadium was variously described as being in an appalling dilapidated state. Drake J. considered the conduct of the spectators as being easily foreseeable and, as such, a reasonably prudent occupier would have realised that the concrete in the ground was dangerous, because it might supply a source of missiles, and would have taken steps to remove or minimise the risk. The Judge also commented that the exoneration by a Football Association Commission of Inquiry was irrelevant for the purposes of his consideration of whether or not there had been a breach of the common duty of care under the Act.

The facts in *Cunningham* were unattractive for the defendant. Every conceivable warning signal seems to have been present—it was a derby match, promotion/relegation issues, a club whose supporters had a reputation, a dilapidated ground which provided potential missiles, a history of concrete being used as missiles. It is submitted that the circumstances of any individual case need not necessarily be so damning to the organiser for liability to attach. Would the result have been any different if the offending supporters were from a club that was unassociated with violence/disturbance? Alternatively, would the result be different if the sport were different?

Hosie v. Arbroath Football Club

9.03 A further example of a football club being held liable for the actions of spectators arose in the case of *Hosie v. Arbroath Football Club*[2] where the claimant was injured as a rowdy crowd attempted to force open a gate. It

---

[2] [1978] S.L.T. 122.

was held that it was reasonably foreseeable that such a crowd might attempt to force the gate open. Consequently, the defendant was liable due to its failure to maintain the gate.

Conclusion

The principles enunciated in, for example, *Cunningham* may well be 9.04 extended to encompass other situations in the future. For example, if Monica Seles had been stabbed at Wimbledon rather than abroad by the Steffi Graf fan, the question may have been raised as to whether the All England Club would have been negligent in failing to provide adequate security.

If any theme may be drawn from the limited litigation in this field to date, it is that organisers need to have regard to the nature of the crowd they are expecting and to consider any physical features of the sports ground that they operate which may result in injury to other spectators.

Example

Coach Leaver takes his Newcastle "Geordies" Lacrosse team to play Coach Phillis' team the Sunderland "Lasses" in the local derby game. The match has always been played in a good spirit. Coaches Phillis and Leaver dislike each other intensely and have engaged in war of words in the local press and have requested that their supporters, who are mainly female, arrive in aggressive vocal mood. The match is played at the Catherine Campbell Recreational Ground where violence recently broke out due to poor crowd segregation at a netball game (also a predominantly female crowd). Butchart Merlot is on sale and can be taken into the stand. No crowd measures are taken. A crowd riot starts during the match during which Miss Charlotte Martin is hit on the head by a Butchart Merlot wine bottle which was thrown by an unknown spectator from within the stand.

Can Miss Martin recover damages from the organisers?

Chapter 10

Liability of governing bodies

"In boxing, the right cross-counter is distinctly one of those things it is more blessed to give than to receive."

P.G. Wodehouse, The Pothunters, 1902.

Introduction

Potentially, claimants may start pursuing governing bodies of sports in actions for negligence in the future. This possibility arises out of the case of *Watson v. British Board of Boxing*[1] in which the governing body of British boxing, the British Boxing Board of Control (BBBC) was held to have been negligent in failing to provide adequate emergency medical facilities at the world middleweight title fight between Chris Eubank and Michael Watson.

10.01

Like the case of *Smoldon v. Whitworth and Nolan*,[2] this case may well be used to extend liability into areas as yet not covered in the context of other sports' governing bodies. This Chapter therefore provides an analysis of the judgment in *Watson* followed by a look at what the future may hold in this area.

Summary of the facts in Watson

On September 21, 1991 Michael Watson fought Chris Eubank for the World Boxing Organisation super-middleweight title at Tottenham Hotspur Football Club in London. The referee stopped the fight in the final round when Watson appeared to be unable to defend himself. He had in fact sustained a brain haemorrhage and, after returning to his corner, he lapsed into unconsciousness on his stool. There was chaos in and outside the ring and seven minutes elapsed before he was examined by one of the doctors who were in attendance. He was taken on a stretcher to an ambulance which was standing by and which took him to North Middlesex Hospital. Nearly half an hour elapsed between the end of the fight and the time that he got there.

10.02

---

[1] [2001] Q.B. 1134; [2001] 2 W.L.R. 1256; I.L.R. January 11, 2001; *The Times*, October 12, 1999 (Kennedy J.).
[2] [1997] P.I.Q.R. P133. See Chap. 13 for more details.

At the North Middlesex Hospital he was intubated, that is an endo-tracheal tube was inserted, and he was given oxygen. He was also given an injection of mannitol, a diuretic that can have the effect of reducing swelling of the brain. The North Middlesex Hospital had no neurosurgical depart-ment, so Mr Watson was transferred by ambulance, still unconscious, to St Bartholomew's Hospital. There an operation was carried out to evacuate a subdural haematoma. By this time, however, he had sustained serious brain damage. This has left him paralysed down the left side and with other physical and mental disability.

The fight had taken place in accordance with the rules of the British Boxing Board of Control Ltd ("the board"). These rules included provisions for medical inspection of boxers and for the attendance of two doctors at a fight. In fact the board had required a third doctor to be present and that an ambulance should be in attendance.

10.03   Mr Watson brought an action against the board. He claimed that the board had been under a duty of care to see that all reasonable steps were taken to ensure that he received immediate and effective medical attention and treatment should he sustain injury in the fight. He contended that they were in breach of this duty with the consequence that he did not receive the immediate medical attention at the ringside that his condition required. In a nutshell, his case was that the resuscitation treatment that he received at the North Middlesex Hospital should have been available at the ringside, but was not. He further alleged that, had he received that treatment, he would not have sustained permanent brain damage. On September 24, 1999 Ian Kennedy J. gave judgment in favour of Mr Watson against the board.

The grounds of appeal

10.04   The board appealed against that judgment. The judgment was attacked root and branch. The board contended:

1. that it owed no duty of care to Mr Watson;

2. that, if it owed the duty alleged, it committed no breach; and

3. that the breach of duty alleged did not cause Mr Watson's injuries.

Duty of care

10.05   When considering whether the board owed Watson a duty of care, Ian Kennedy J. examined at some length the role played by the board in imposing, by rules and regulations, the safety standards to be observed by those involved in professional boxing in this country. His conclusions as to duty are to be found in the following passages from his judgment:

"The board does not create the danger. What it does do does at least reduce the dangers inherent in professional boxing. But at the same time it countenances and gives its blessing to contests where the safety arrangements are those of its making. The promoters and the boxers do not themselves address considerations of safety. Clearly, they look to the board's stipulations as providing the appropriate standard. It is not necessary for a supposed tortfeasor to have created the danger himself. In my view there is a quite sufficient nexus between the board and the professional boxer who fights in a contest to which its rules obtain to be capable of giving rise to a duty in the board to take reasonable steps to try to minimise or control whether by rules or other directions the risks inherent in the sport. To my mind it is difficult in such a situation to profess a concern for safety and to deny a duty such as I have described. Where there is a potential for physical injury, I do not believe that I have to go beyond the traditional concept of neighbourhood to find a duty where there is, as here, a clearly foreseeable danger. If authority is needed for this approach, it is to be found in the judgment of the Court of Appeal in *Perrett v. Collins* [1998] 2 Lloyd's Rep 255."

"There is always a risk, and the pool from which professional boxers tend to be recruited is unlikely to be one with an innate or well informed concern about safety, and one may ask why should the individual boxer not rely on the board's arrangements? The board professes—I do not for one moment question its sincerity—its lively interest in his safety. Its experience, contacts and resources exceed his own. It has the ability to require of promoters what it sees as good practice. I do not believe there is any difference in principle between giving advice about safety and laying down rules to provide for safety. Thus we find here a body with special knowledge which gives advice to a defined class of persons that it knows will rely upon that advice in a defined situation ... If, which I doubt, this conclusion represents any step beyond what is already settled law, I am fully persuaded it is a proper one to take."

The Judge's decision broke new ground in the law of negligence. In **10.06** *Caparo Industries plc v. Dickman*,[3] and in many subsequent cases, the House of Lords and the Court of Appeal have approved the approach to the development of the law of negligence recommended by Brennan J. in the High Court of Australia in *Sutherland Shire Council v. Heyman*,[4] where he said:

"It is preferable, in my view, that the law should develop novel categories of negligence incrementally and by analogy with established categories, rather than by a massive extension of a *prima facie* duty of care restrained only by indefinable 'considerations which ought to negative, or to reduce or limit the scope of the duty or the class of person to whom it is owed'."

The Judge referred to the question of whether to attach a duty of care to the facts of the present case would be an acceptable incremental extension of established liabilities or too long a step. He did not, however, identify any obvious stepping stones to his decision.

---

[3] [1990] 2 A.C. 605.
[4] (1985) 157 Crim.L.R. 424 at 481.

Lord Phillips M.R. in the Court of Appeal stated[5] that he did not find this surprising as there were features of this case which are extraordinary, if not unique. He went on to state that he would echo the comment of Lord Steyn in *Marc Rich & Co. AG v. Bishop Rock Marine Co. Ltd*[6]:

"none of the cases cited provided any realistic analogy to be used as a springboard for a decision one way or the other in this case. The present case can only be decided on the basis of an intense and particular focus on all its distinctive features, and then applying established legal principles to it."

Distinctive features of the Watson case

10.07   Lord Phillips M.R. then turned to the distinctive features of the *Watson* case.

1. *The sport of boxing itself.*
    Many sports involve a risk of physical injury to the participants. Boxing is the only sport where this is the object of the exercise.

2. *The British Boxing Board of Control.*
    No one can take part, in any capacity, in professional boxing in this country who is not licensed by the board and, at the same time, a member of it, for the two are essentially synonymous. Thus boxers, promoters, managers, referees, timekeepers, trainers, seconds, masters of ceremonies, match-makers, agents for overseas boxers, ringmasters and whips all have to be licensed by the board to perform their particular functions and become, when granted their licences, members of the board.

3. *The board's involvement in safety.*
    The physical safety of boxers has always been a prime concern of the board. The board set out by its rules, directions and guidance to make comprehensive provision for the services to be provided to safeguard the health of the boxer. All involved in a boxing contest were obliged to accept and comply with the board's requirements. So far as the promoter was concerned, these delimited his obligations.

4. *The regime applying to the contest between Watson and Eubank.*
    The contest was sponsored not by the board but by the World Boxing Organisation ("WBO"). This did not, however, affect the position so far as responsibility for the safety of the boxers was concerned. Rule 23 of the board's rules and regulations provided: "23.1 Commonwealth, European and World Championships when promoted in Great Britain and Northern Ireland must be organised and controlled

---

[5] [2001] Q.B. 1134 at 1142.
[6] [1996] A.C. 211 at 236.

in accordance with the regulations of the [board] except where such regulations may be at variance with those of any Commonwealth, European or World Boxing Authorities with whom the [board] may for the time being be affiliated, when the regulations of such authorities shall apply". The bout agreement, which was subject to the sanction of the board, provided: "The bout will be conducted in accordance with the rules and regulations of the WBO and [the board]". Mr Block, the secretary of the board's southern area council, reported to the board that the arrangements in place were satisfactory and that the tournament could receive the board's approval. He gave evidence that the WBO imposed no medical requirements in respect of the fight and that, in these circumstances, the ordinary board rules and policy would and did apply. In accordance with normal practice, the medical officers for the contest were nominated by the southern area council.

5. *Reliance.*

In 1990 Mr Watson had been involved in litigation with his manager, in which the board had filed an affidavit. This stated that the board was accepted as being the sole controlling body regulating professional boxing in the United Kingdom and stressed the importance that the board place on ensuring the safety of boxers. In a witness statement in the present proceedings, Mr Watson stated that this accorded with his understanding as a boxer that the board undertook responsibility for all the medical aspects of boxing, including the medical supervision of boxing contests, in the United Kingdom.

The law

Caparo Industries plc v. Dickman

Lord Phillips then went on to analyse the law. He pointed to the case of   **10.08** *Caparo Industries plc v. Dickman*[7] in which Lord Bridge of Harwich considered a series of decisions of the Privy Council and the House of Lords in relation to the duty of care in negligence and summarised their effect:

> "What emerges is that, in addition to the foreseeability of damage, necessary ingredients in any situation giving rise to a duty of care are that there should exist between the party owing the duty and the party to whom it is owed a relationship characterised by the law as one of 'proximity' or 'neighbourhood' and that the situation should be one in which the court considers it fair, just and reasonable that the law should impose a duty of a given scope upon the one party for the benefit of the other."

---

[7] [1990] 2 A.C. 605 at 617–618.

Lord Bridge went on to state that these ingredients were insufficiently precise to be used as practical tests and to commend the desirability of proceeding by analogy with established categories of negligence. Lord Oliver of Aylmerton[8], also emphasised the difficulty of using the three requirements as a practical guide to the existence of a duty of care:

> "the postulate of a simple duty to avoid any harm that is, with hindsight, reasonably capable of being foreseen becomes untenable without the imposition of some intelligible limits to keep the law of negligence within the bounds of common sense and practicality. Those limits have been found by the requirement of what has been called a 'relationship of proximity' between plaintiff and defendant and by the imposition of a further requirement that the attachment of liability for harm which has occurred be 'just and reasonable'. But although the cases in which the courts have imposed or withheld liability are capable of an approximate categorisation, one looks in vain for some common denominator by which the existence of the essential relationship can be tested. Indeed it is difficult to resist a conclusion that what have been treated as three separate requirements are, at least in most cases, in fact merely facets of the same thing, for in some cases the degree of foreseeability is such that it is from that alone that the requisite proximity can be deduced, whilst in others the absence of that essential relationship can most rationally be attributed simply to the court's view that it would not be fair and reasonable to hold the defendant responsible. 'Proximity' is, no doubt, a convenient expression so long as it is realised that it is no more than a label which embraces not a definable concept but merely a description of circumstances from which, pragmatically, the courts conclude that a duty of care exists."

Marc Rich & Co. AG v. Bishop Rock Marine Co. Ltd

10.09 Saville L.J. expressed a similar view in *Marc Rich & Co. AG v. Bishop Rock Marine Co. Ltd*[9]:

> "whatever the nature of the harm sustained by the plaintiff, it is necessary to consider the matter not only by inquiring about foreseeability but also by considering the nature of the relationship between the parties; and to be satisfied that in all the circumstances it is fair, just and reasonable to impose a duty of care. Of course . . . these three matters overlap with each other and are really facets of the same thing. For example, the relationship between the parties may be such that it is obvious that a lack of care will create a risk of harm and that as a matter of common sense and justice a duty should be imposed ... Again in most cases of the direct infliction of physical loss or injury through carelessness, it is self-evident that a civilised system of law should hold that a duty of care has been broken, whereas the infliction of financial harm may well pose a more difficult problem. Thus the . . . so-called requirements for a duty of care are not to be treated as wholly separate and distinct requirements but rather as convenient and helpful

---

[8] At 633.
[9] [1994] 1 W.L.R. 1071 at 1077.

approaches to the pragmatic question whether a duty should be imposed in any given case."

This passage was approved by Lord Steyn when the case reached the   **10.10**
House of Lords.[10] Lord Steyn stated:

"since the decision in *Dorset Yacht Co. Ltd v. Home Office* [1970] A.C. 1004 it has been settled law that the elements of foreseeability and proximity as well as considerations of fairness, justice and reasonableness are relevant to all cases whatever the nature of the harm sustained by the plaintiff."

Perrett v. Collins

One case which it was said on behalf of Mr Watson was analogous was   **10.11**
Perrett v. Collins,[11] the only case referred to by Ian Kennedy J. when considering the question of duty of care. The background to this case was described by Hobhouse L.J.[12]:

"The third defendants are a trading company incorporated under the Companies Acts. The precise nature of the company's constitution is not covered by the evidence. It has limited liability. It trades under the name of the 'Popular Flying Association' and it appears that either its main role or one of its main roles is to run that association. That association exists to facilitate amateurs to enjoy facilities for flying light aircraft. Thus, it has members who pay membership fees or subscriptions in return for which it provides them with facilities. These facilities include a scheme which enables members to construct and fly their own light aircraft. The Kit Fox aircraft is an aircraft which is designed for this purpose. It is supplied to amateur flyers in a kit form which they can then assemble for themselves. In order that, when complete, the aircraft can obtain first a provisional and then a full certificate of airworthiness, the assembly of the aircraft has to be supervised and checked by an inspector. Mr Usherwood was the person who was carrying out this role in relation to Mr Collins's assembly of this aircraft. The plaintiff's allegation is that during this process an alternative gearbox was fitted without the appropriate and corresponding substitution of a propeller which matched the substituted gearbox. The company, as the Popular Flying Association, appoint inspectors for the purpose of, among other things, inspecting aircraft during the course of their construction by members of the association and certifying whether the relevant work has been done to his 'entire satisfaction' and the aircraft is in an airworthy condition. Any such inspector has to be approved by the association . . . "

Mr Usherwood had authority, under an order made pursuant to the Civil   **10.12**
Aviation Act 1982, to certify that the aircraft was fit to fly. He did so, notwithstanding, so it was alleged, that the mismatch between gearbox and propeller made the aircraft unairworthy. The owner of the aircraft took off,

---

[10] [1996] A.C. 211 at 235.
[11] [1998] 2 Lloyd's Rep. 255.
[12] At 258–259.

with the claimant on board as a passenger. The aircraft crashed and the plaintiff sustained personal injuries. He sued the owner, Mr Usherwood and the Popular Flying Association ("the PFA").

A preliminary issue was tried as to whether Mr Usherwood and the PFA owed the claimant a duty of care. They argued that, if they had failed to exercise reasonable care, this was not the direct cause of the claimant's injuries—the direct cause being that the aircraft had been designed in a manner that made it unairworthy. Thus the necessary "proximity" was not made out. They also argued that it was not fair, just and reasonable that the PFA should be liable to negligence. The PFA was not a commercial undertaking. If it was held liable it might withdraw from its work, or have to pass on the cost of increased insurance to the detriment of small aircraft operators.

10.13   In the leading judgment Hobhouse L.J. rejected the submission that any negligence on the part of Mr Usherwood was only an indirect cause of the crash. The role of Mr Usherwood was distinct and independent from the role of the constructor of the plane. Mr Usherwood, who alone of those involved had technical expertise, might be the only person who had been negligent. In these circumstances the claim against Mr Usherwood was a conventional claim for carelessness causing direct and foreseeable personal injury. Questions of what was fair and reasonable did not arise. Hobhouse L.J. expounded the relevant principles of law in the following passages:

"A minimum requirement of particularity and contemplation is required. But it has never been a requirement of the law of the tort of negligence that there be a particular antecedent relationship between the defendant and the plaintiff other than one that the plaintiff belongs to a class which the defendant contemplates or should contemplate would be affected by his conduct. Nor has it been a requirement that the defendant should inflict the injury upon the plaintiff. Such a concept belongs to the law of trespass not to the law of negligence:".[13]

"Where the plaintiff belongs to a class which either is or ought to be within the contemplation of the defendant and the defendant by reason of his involvement in an activity which gives him a measure of control over and responsibility for a situation which, if dangerous, will be liable to injure the plaintiff, the defendant is liable if as a result of his unreasonable lack of care he causes a situation to exist which does in fact cause the plaintiff injury. Once this proximity exists, it ceases to be material what form the unreasonable conduct takes. The distinction between negligent mis-statement and other forms of conduct ceases to be legally relevant, although it may have a factual relevance to foresight or causation. Thus a person may be liable for directing someone into a dangerous location (*e g* the Hillsborough cases; *e g Sharp v. Avery and Kerwood* [1938] 4 All E.R. 85) or a producer may be liable for the absence of an adequate warning on the labelling of his product (*e g Heaven v. Pender* (1883) 11 QBD 503, 517 *per* Cotton L.J.). Once the defendant has become involved in the activity which gives rise to the risk, he

---

[13] At 261.

comes under the duty to act reasonably in all respects relevant to that risk. Similarly none of the particular difficulties which arise in relation to economic loss arise in relation to the causing of personal injury. Once proximity is established by reference to the test which I have identified, none of the more sophisticated criteria which have to be used in relation to allegations of liability for mere economic loss need to be applied in relation to personal injury, nor have they been in the decided cases:".[14]

While Buxton L.J. agreed with Hobhouse L.J. that the negligence alleged **10.14** fell into the category of directly causing foreseeable personal injury, both he and Swinton Thomas L.J. considered the question of whether it was fair and reasonable to impose a duty of care. Each emphatically concluded that it was. The statutory obligations in relation to certifying airworthiness was designed, at least in substantial part, for the protection of those who might be injured if an aircraft was certified as being fit to fly when it was not. If the PFA was not liable in negligence, the plaintiff might be left without a remedy against anyone. Dealing with the arguments of policy advanced on behalf of the PFA, Buxton L.J. observed that there was no evidence of any of the asserted potential effects of a finding of negligence against the PFA. He added[15]:

"If the plaintiff has been negligently injured by a failing by the PFA, I cannot see that it would be right to withhold relief from him simply on the ground that to grant that relief might cause a rise in the PFA's insurance premiums, or even cause a more expensive system of inspection to be substituted for that of the PFA."

Lord Phillips M.R. commented on this case as follows[16]:

"While I do not agree with Mr Mackay's submission that *Perrett v. Collins* [1998] 2 Lloyd's Rep. 255 provides a close analogy to the present case, I do find helpful the formulation of legal principle by Hobhouse L.J., at p. 262, which I have set out above. Mr Watson belonged to a class which was within the contemplation of the board. The board was involved in an activity which gave it, not merely a measure of control, but complete control over and a responsibility for a situation which would be liable to result in injury to Mr Watson if reasonable care was not exercised by the board. Thus the criteria identified by Hobhouse L.J. for the existence of a duty of care were present."

Conclusion

Having reviewed the authorities in *Watson*, Lord Phillips M.R. stated[17]: **10.15**

"These cases establish that, where A advises B as to action to be taken which will directly and foreseeably affect the safety or well-being of C, a situation of

---

[14] At 262.
[15] At 277.
[16] At 1162.
[17] At 1159.

sufficient proximity exists to found a duty of care on the part of A towards C. Whether in fact such a duty arises will depend upon the facts of the individual case and, in particular, upon whether such a duty of care would cut across any statutory scheme pursuant to which the advice was given."

Proximity

10.16 On the issue of proximity, Lord Phillips M.R.[18] pointed to the special features of the case. In particular, the principles alleged to give rise to a duty of care in the case were those of assumption of responsibility and reliance. In effect, Mr Watson's case could be summarised as follows:

1. The board assumed responsibility for the control of an activity the essence of which was that personal injuries should be sustained by those participating.

2. The board assumed responsibility for determining the details of the medical care and facilities which would be provided by way of immediate treatment of those who received personal injuries while taking part in the activity.

3. Those taking part in the activity, and Mr Watson in particular, relied upon the board to ensure that all reasonable steps were taken to provide immediate and effective medical attention and treatment to those injured in the course of the activity.

The peculiar features of the duty of care alleged are as follows:

1. The duty alleged is not to take reasonable care to avoid causing personal injury. It is a duty to take reasonable care to ensure that personal injuries already sustained are properly treated.

2. The duty alleged is not directly, through the servants or agents of the board, to provide proper facilities and administer proper treatment to those injured. It is to make regulations imposing on others the duty to achieve these results.

Fair, just and reasonable

10.17 Lord Phillips M.R. then went on[19] to analyse whether the imposition of a duty of care would be fair, just and reasonable. He stated[20]:

"Many of the matters considered under the heading of proximity are also relevant to the question of whether it is fair, just and reasonable to impose a duty of care

---

[18] At 1149.
[19] At 1162.
[20] At 1162.

in this case. Because the facts of this case are so unusual, there is no category in which a duty of care has been established from which one can advance to this case by a small incremental step. In these circumstances the task is to look at the circumstances in which specific factors have given rise to the duty of care and to consider whether, on the facts of this case, they should also give rise to such a duty. While it is difficult, or perhaps impossible, to avoid a degree of subjectivity when considering what is fair, just and reasonable, the approach must be to apply established principles and standards."

He then went on[21] to point to matters which he considered particularly material. These were:

1. Mr Watson was one of a defined number of boxing members of the board.

2. A primary stated object of the board was to look after its boxing member's physical safety.

3. The board encouraged and supported its boxing members in the pursuit of an activity which involved inevitable physical injury and the need for medical precautions against the consequences of such injury.

4. The board controlled every aspect of that activity.

5. In particular, the board controlled the medical assistance that would be provided.

6. The board had, or had access to, specialist expertise in relation to appropriate standards of medical care.

7. The board's assumption of responsibility in relation to medical care probably relieved the promoter of such responsibility. If Mr Watson has no remedy against the board, he has no remedy at all.

8. Boxing members of the board, including Mr Watson, could reasonably rely upon the board to look after their safety.

He then concluded[22]:

"All these matters lead me to conclude that the judge was right to find that the board was under a duty of care to Mr Watson."

Policy considerations

Finally, Lord Phillips looked at whether there were any policy considera- **10.18** tions which needed to be take into account. In particular, it was argued that

---

[21] At 1162–1163.
[22] At 1163.

a duty of care should not be imposed upon the board because it was a non-profit-making organisation and did not carry insurance.

Lord Phillips remarked on this[23]:

> "Considerations of insurance are not relevant. Nor do I see why the fact that the board is a non-profit-making organisation should provide it with an immunity from liability in negligence."

It was also argued that a finding in favour of Mr Watson in this case would involve postulating that other sporting regulatory bodies, such as the Rugby Football Union, owed duties of care to the participants in their sports in relation to their rules and regulations. In answer, Lord Phillips stated[24]:

> "It does not follow that the decision in this case is the thin end of a wedge. The facts of this case are not common to other sports. In any event it would be quite wrong to determine the result of the individual facts of this case by formulating a principle of general policy that sporting regulatory bodies should owe no duty of care in respect of the formulation of their rules and regulations. I conclude that the judge correctly found that the board owed Mr Watson a duty of care."

Volenti non fit injuria

10.19 As to the issue of *volenti non fit injuria*,[25] Ian Kennedy J. at first instance held that although the claimant clearly consented to the risk of injury at the hands of his opponent, he did not consent to the risk of injury flowing from the board's failure to ensure that its safety arrangements were as carefully worked out as they might have been.

This was not directly at issue before the Court of Appeal.

Breach of duty of care

10.20 The next question to answer was whether the board breached the duty of care which it owed.

The relevant allegations of negligence can be summarised as follows. The board failed to inform itself adequately about the risks inherent in a blow to the head. The board failed to require the provision of resuscitation equipment at the venue, together with the presence of persons capable of operating such equipment. The board failed to require a medical examination of Mr Watson immediately following the conclusion of the contest. The board failed to ensure that those running the contest knew which hospitals in the vicinity had a neurosurgical capability.

---

[23] At 1163.
[24] At 1163.
[25] For which see Chap. 2, above, for more details.

On this issue, the Judge at first instance stated the following:

"The standard response where the presence of subdural bleeding is known or suspected has been agreed since at least 1980, which is to intubate, ventilate, sedate, paralyse, and, in Britain at least, to administer mannitol. The patient can then be taken straight to the nearest neurosurgical unit. Mr Hamlyn said, and I accept, that there would have been very few British neurosurgeons who at this time would have questioned the need to put up a line and administer this diuretic in a case such as the present. Professor Teasdale had some reservations about the effectiveness of some of this, but he accepted that this was standard practice. I have not heard evidence to the effect that the board or its medical advisers had before this incident considered, and for some reason decided not to follow, what may not unfairly be called this protocol. I can only conclude that for some reason no thought was given to the practicality of introducing this standard response . . .

Nothing that I have heard persuades me that there was any impracticality, whether in terms of manpower or in cost to the promoters, in the board having included such a requirement in their rules. I have had no evidence to suggest that a doctor of suitable grade and with the necessary skills would command a fee substantially in excess of that payable to the board's doctors under its system, nor that there would be any significant cost in having the necessary equipment to hand . . .

I am left with the clear impression that the board's medical advisers have not looked outside their personal expertise. The board has argued that until this accident no one had suggested that they should institute this protocol. That is true as a fact. The duty of the board and of those advising it on medical matters was to be prospective in their thinking and seek competent advice as to how a recognised danger could be combated. In some circumstances it can be very relevant to show that no criticism had been received about this or that practice but I have seen nothing to suggest that that is a point in this context . . .

Accordingly, I am left in no doubt that the board was in breach of its duty in that it did not institute some such system or protocol as Mr Hamlyn was to propose. There is no question but that anyone with the appropriate expertise would have advised such a system whatever reservations they may have had, as had Professor Teasdale, about its ultimate utility."

10.21 Later in the judgment the Judge suggested, by implication, that the board's rules should have included a requirement that a boxer who was knocked out, or seemed unfit to defend himself, should be immediately seen by a doctor.

The Judge's reference to Mr Hamlyn was to a neurosurgeon who operated on Mr Watson at St Bartholomew's Hospital and who gave evidence on his behalf at the trial. Mr Watson was the third boxer on whom Mr Hamlyn had operated for similar injuries. His belief was that the brain damage that occurred in each case could probably have been avoided in whole or in a large part if the boxer had received immediate resuscitation at the ringside. On his initiative a meeting took place with the Minister for Sport, two of Mr Hamlyn's colleagues, the board's chief medical officer, Dr Whiteson, and other board officials on October 16, 1991. At this meeting Mr Hamlyn expressed the view that it was vital that at the ringside there should be the right doctors with the right equipment. This meant doctors able to intubate and put up a drip to treat the injured boxer immediately with mannitol. It was also important to have a prior arrangement with the hospital with a neurological unit, and with that unit placed on standby.

At first instance, the Judge concluded that for some reason no thought was given to the practicality of introducing at the ringside what he found had been a standard response, where the presence of subdural bleeding was known or suspected, since at least 1980. The judge went on to review such statistical evidence as there was in relation to the frequency of occurrence of head injuries in boxing and observed that there had been no evidence to suggest that the board considered and balanced the difficulty of providing the adequate response to the risks of head injury against their frequency of occurrence and severity of outcome.

10.22   The board called to give evidence Mr Peter Richards, a consultant neurosurgeon with Charing Cross Hospital between 1987 and 1995. He had particular experience of brain injuries caused by sporting activities. He was present at the meeting held with the Minister for Sport after Mr Watson's injuries. He gave evidence that he agreed with Mr Hamlyn's views. Had he been asked in the period before the Eubank/Watson fight to advise on precautions in relation to the risk of serious head injury, he said that he would have given the same advice as Mr Hamlyn.

The judge held that it was the duty of the board, and of those advising it on medical matters, to be prospective in their thinking and to seek competent advice as to how a recognised danger could best be combatted. He held that he was left in no doubt that the board was in breach of its duty in that it did not institute some such system or protocol as that which Mr Hamlyn was later to propose. He held that anyone with the appropriate expertise would have advised the adoption of such a system.

Lord Phillips M.R. concluded[26]:

"I consider that these were proper findings on the evidence and that Mr Watson's case on breach of duty was made out."

Causation

10.23   The final question was whether the board's breach of its duty of care caused the injuries upon which the claim was based.

At first instance, the relevant findings of the Judge were:

"If the protocol had been in place, and Dr Shapiro had been required to go straight to the ring, he would have begun the necessary procedures within a minute or two of the collapse and so by 23.00. It would only have added three minutes or so if

---

[26] At 1170.

he had waited until he was summoned. In the event those same procedures could not have been begun before 23.25 at the earliest, to allow some time for an examination after the claimant's recorded time of arrival at the North Middlesex. At least 20 minutes, and probably nearer 30 minutes, could have been saved. Any necessary discussion with a neurosurgeon could as easily have been done from the venue . . . In my view the claimant makes his case on causation when he shows, as he has done, that with the protocol in place he would have been attended from the outset by a doctor skilled in resuscitation, who would have made any necessary inquiries of the neurosurgeons at St Bartholomew's, who would themselves have been on notice. The claimant would have been resuscitated within a few minutes of 23.00 and in St Bartholomew's by 23.45 at the latest. In effect, Dr Cartlidge's ideal world would have been in being, and the claimant's outcome would have been materially improved . . . On the evidence earlier treatment would have made a significant difference to the outcome . . . The final question is: to what extent? I do not believe that the evidence admits of any accurate answer to this question but that is by no means an uncommon situation in cases of this sort. Medical knowledge does not enable one to say what, on the balance of probabilities, would have been the outcome if the protocol had been in place and followed."

The Judge held that on these facts Mr Watson was entitled to recover for **10.24** his injuries in full, relying on the authorities of *McGhee v. National Coal Board*[27]; *Wilsher v. Essex Area Health Authority*[28] and *Hotson v. East Berkshire Area Health Authority*.[29] He summarised his findings on the facts:

"1. Here all that is clear is that on the balance of probabilities the claimant's present state would have been materially better than it actually is. It is not possible to measure even on the balance of probabilities where the damage would have stopped if the protocol had been followed. The occurrence of a haematoma could not have been prevented but its effects could have been mitigated. So the tortious damage may be seen as consecutive to, and aggravating, that which was inevitable . . . On the facts of the present case the claimant suffered only a minor primary injury. He would thus have developed the subdural haemorrhage in the most favourable circumstances possible, short of doing so in hospital with staff around him. The probability must therefore have been that he could have been among those patients who would have had a favourable outcome, or no circumstance peculiar to his physical make-up has been identified to suggest why that should not be so."

Lord Phillips M.R. concluded on the appeal of this point that[30]:

"A defendant seeking to disturb the findings of fact of a trial judge in relation to causation undertakes a hard task. I consider that the judge was entitled to find on the evidence that, had the Hamlyn protocol been in place, the outcome of Mr

---

[27] [1973] 1 W.L.R. 1.
[28] [1988] A.C. 1074 at 1090.
[29] [1987] A.C. 750 at 783.
[30] At 1173.

Watson's injuries would have been significantly better. On the law relied upon by the judge, this was all that Mr Watson needed to succeed."

Appeal dismissed

10.25 For all of these reasons, Lord Phillips M.R. dismissed the appeal. May and Laws L.JJ. agreed with the judgment of Lord Phillips M.R.

On June 7, 2001, leave to appeal was granted by the Appeal Committee of the House of Lords. However, the petition of the British Boxing Board of Control was withdrawn on terms agreed between the parties on January 9, 2002.

The way forward in boxing

10.26 The *Watson* case highlighted the need for safety controls in the sport of boxing. This is particularly so as tragic injuries have been sustained in recent years not only by Michael Watson but also by, for example, Gerald McClellan, Carl Wright, Rod Douglas and Paul Ingle.

Barry McGuigan, the former featherweight boxing world champion and the founder and president of the Professional Boxers' Association has made a number of proposals aimed at making boxing safer. In particular, he has stated[31]:

> "Boxing is one of the least dangerous contact sports we have. There are so many other sports where contestants are killed and injured. You hear of jockeys breaking their necks falling off horses, only recently for example the captain of the Welsh rugby team was paralysed—a young man tragically cut down in his prime. All you have to do is ring up St. John's Ambulance or any emergency unit on any given week, and you'll find that a rugby player had their neck broken or their collarbone broken or have cerebral damage. My point is that boxing shouldn't be singled out. We all have a right to take part in whatever sport we want, even if there is a risk attached.
>
> As administrators of boxing however, we have an obligation to protect professional boxers as much as we can. Now, how can we make boxing safer? We can make boxing safer by first of all setting a very high standard for referees. Secondly, we need to have anaesthetists ringside rather than just paramedics. This is something we have been fighting for for a very long time, and it hasn't been set in place by the British Boxing Board of Control as yet. It's compulsory in Wales because Wales is a smaller area and the doctor over there, a guy called Ray Moncell, is absolutely fantastic. He has boxing safety down to a fine art: He has anaesthetists there in case anything goes wrong The experts are there to administer a general anaesthetic, the boxer is put into a controlled coma, he is brought to hospital, they get the job done—bang! This should be made mandatory throughout the country.

---

[31] Based on an interview with Derek Cusack of the Cyber Boxing Zone Journal which appeared in the July 1998 issue and a conversation with Tim Kevan on May 3, 2002. See http://cyberboxingzone.com/boxing/box7–98.htm.

They should have anaesthetists at every single one of the 350–odd shows we have per year, and the Board of Control should pay for that. MRI scans have now become compulsory thanks to our hounding the Board of Control, which is a great thing. Monitoring of MRI scans has already been shown to be effective in Robbie Regan's case [Note: Then WBO bantamweight champion Regan was forced to retire in 1998 when he failed an MRI scan] . . . There's now talk about introducing what's called psychometric testing. It's an IQ test which they carry out on you each year making sure there is no psychological damage or depreciation.

Thanks to the P.B.A. hounding the Board of Control, they have accepted that MRI scans are a necessity and they've accepted psychometric testing. But a regulation which should be imposed also is that no professional boxing should be staged more than 30 minutes away from a neurosurgical hospital. Not all hospitals are neurosurgical, and any neurosurgeon will tell you that the fighter, the athlete, the accident victim, whatever, must get to them within what they call 'the golden hour.' If they don't get there within that hour, they have different degrees of brain damage . . .

In general terms, we need to make the gloves shock absorbent. We need to put more focus on the gloves . . .

In a recent survey, we put a headguard on a computerised head which was able to mimic how a head reacted and how a brain reacted when struck by a punch. We used heavier, 10oz. gloves which ironically created more reverberation to the base of the brain whereas the smaller gloves without the headguard, created more initial shock but didn't shake the head or create as much deep trauma. We have to concentrate more on the trauma and energy that the head absorbs when struck by various types of boxing glove to discover which glove should be used and which is the safest."

Wider implications of the judgment in Watson

The finding that a governing body had imposed upon it a duty of care to ensure that participants in its sport are not exposed to unnecessary risks to their health and safety potentially has wide-ranging ramifications for the governing bodies of other sports such as rugby and certain martial-arts where the risk of serious injury is present.   **10.27**

The duty would vary from sport to sport. In *Watson*, the BBBC failed to provide the necessary post-match care to a boxer who had suffered brain injury. This type of injury is a foreseeable result of boxing and it is further foreseeable that if it is not treated sufficiently quickly the injuries will be exacerbated, as they were found to have been in *Watson*.

The question is whether this rule is to apply to other sports. As Grayson says in *Sport and the Law*[32]:

"Should all rugby games have doctors, stretchers and neck braces available in case of a damaged spine from a collapsed scrum? Should all football matches have splints available in the case of broken legs? Should hockey games have eye or

---

[32] 3rd ed., Butterworths, 2000, Chap. 16.

dental treatment available in case of the ball or stick causing facial injury? These would certainly seem to be natural extensions of the *Watson* decision."

10.28   These potential extensions refer only to the provision of associated medical treatment for relatively commonly occurring or foreseeable injuries. A governing body might be able to insulate itself from liability by the provision of adequate guidelines to leagues and clubs but only if they were in some way policed. It is one thing to give guidance but another to have those supposedly guided completely ignore the advice with impunity.

As Grayson continues, potentially more dramatic for sport would be the possibility that liability could be imposed on a governing body for the inadequacy of its in-game safety rules. Where a specific injury, or injury from a specific act was a common occurrence in a sport, it is now possible that a governing body will be liable for such inquiries as are so caused. The court in *Watson* held that one of the reasons why governing bodies exist is to provide guidance conduct and disseminate research and educate all those involved in its sport about safety issues. If it is known that stamping in rugby, or elbowing in football, or bouncers in cricket are dangerous and can cause injury unless the rules are either changed or more rigorously enforced, an incremental development of the law from *Watson* would see governing bodies liable for their failure to ensure the safety of their sport's participants.

Another question which arises is whether the same obligations would exist in, for example, amateur as opposed to professional boxing. As Moore states in *Sports Law and Litigation*[33]:

"It ought to make no difference if the contest is run under the auspices of the BBBC, but to impose such a duty in all contests, at whatever level, is unlikely to satisfy any reasonable cost/benefit analysis."

10.29   In any event, he goes on to suggest that following *Watson*, a governing body should:

1. undertake a risk assessment with a view to determining whether medical cover is required for a sporting event;

2. if there is a need for such cover, only persons with requisite skill and experience should be engaged; and

3. if there is deemed not to be a need for medical cover, then advise participants why not so as to enable them to make their own arrangements, if necessary.

Finally, it will be interesting to see if the introduction of the European Convention of Human Rights ("ECHR") has any effect on the approach

---

[33] 2nd ed., CLT Professional Publishing, 2000, pp. 88–89.

taken on such cases. In particular, Article 2 concerns the right to life and might apply, for example, to the provision of adequate medical facilities in a boxing contest.

Section 6 of the Human Rights Act 1998 imposes compliance with the Convention upon "public authorities". It remains to be seen whether this will include, for example, governing bodies.

If it did and the facts in *Watson* were repeated, then a boxer in Watson's position would no doubt argue that, in order to comply with Article 2 of the Convention, the governing body ought to have provided adequate emergency medical facilities because of the known risk of potentially fatal head injuries. A cause of action under the Convention would be in addition to those in contract and tort.

The question then would be whether it would be open to the governing body to argue that such measures would have been too costly or that other priorities were more important. It would probably not be since Article 2 bestows an absolute right. It seems likely that Article 2 will be frequently deployed against those respondents who seek to argue that a particular cause of action was not justified on a cost/benefit analysis. Since such an argument did not prevail in *Watson*, it is difficult to see how a governing body in the BBBC's position would be any better placed defending a claim brought under the Convention. **10.30**

It is also no answer to say that Article 2 is restricted to those cases where actual loss of life occurred. It has been interpreted so as to cover cases where injury has been sustained, so long as loss of life was a possible consequence of the act or omission complained of.[34]

Perhaps the most significant long term issue to arise from the case of *Watson* is the fact that it highlighted the need for bodies such as the BBBC to be insured against the risks of such liability. This is dealt with in more detail in Chapter 25, below.

---

[34] See C. Moore, *Sports Law and Litigation* (2nd ed., CLT Professional Publishing, 2000), pp. 224–227.

Chapter 11

Negligent medical care

"A minor operation: one performed on somebody else."

Anonymous.

Introduction

This Chapter provides a brief introduction to the principles associated with **11.01** medical negligence. It is slightly peripheral to the main subject of sporting injuries covered by this book although given the figures quoted in the Introduction, above, and specifically that there are between six million and nineteen million new sporting injuries each year,[1] it is likely that in future sports-related medical negligence claims may become more common.

The context of such claims may arise not only from medical treatment in hospitals but also potentially in relation to inappropriate medical advice, treatment or medication given by clubs, coaches or team doctors. Potentially, claims may also arise through a failure to advise as to possible side effects of (legal) drugs which then cause injury. Whilst not directly relevant to this Chapter, the background of the human rights legislation should also be borne in mind and specifically Article 2 of the European Convention of Human Rights and the right to life and the provision of adequate medical facilities.

The Bolam test

The classic test for the standard of care required of a doctor or any other **11.02** person professing some skill or competence is the direction to the jury given by McNair J. in *Bolam v. Friern Hospital Management Committee*[2]:

> "I myself would prefer to put it this way, that he is not guilty of negligence if he has acted in accordance with a practice accepted as proper by a responsible body of medical men skilled in that particular art . . . Putting it the other way round, a

---

[1] British Sports Council Survey, *Epidemiology of Exercise*, 1991; C. Moore, *Sports Law and Litigation* (2nd ed., CLT Professional Publishing, 2000), p. 145.
[2] [1957] 1 W.L.R. 583 at 587.

man is not negligent, if he is acting in accordance with such a practice, merely because there is a body of opinion who would take a contrary view."

Specifically in that case it was held that in deciding whether a doctor is negligent in failing to warn a patient of the risks involved in a particular treatment, it is appropriate to consider firstly whether good medical practice required that a warning should have been given to the patient before he submitted to the treatment, and, secondly, if a warning had been given, what difference it would have made.

11.03   The claimant sustained fractures of the acetabula during the course of electro-conclusive therapy treatment given to him while he was a voluntary patient at the defendants' mental hospital. He claimed damages against the hospital alleging that the defendants were negligent:

(a) in failing to administer any relaxant drug prior to the passing of the current through his brain;

(b) since they had not administered such drug, in failing to provide at least some form of manual restraint or control beyond that given;

(c) in failing to warn him of the risks involved in the treatment.

Expert witnesses all agreed that there was a firm body of medical opinion opposed to the use of relaxant drugs, and also that a number of competent practitioners considered that the less manual restraint there was, the less was the risk of fracture. It was the practice of the defendants' doctors not to warn their patients of the risks of the treatment (which they believed to be small) unless asked. Following the direction quoted above, the jury returned a verdict for the defendants.

Sidaway and Maynard

11.04   The *Bolam* test was re-affirmed by two House of Lords' cases in the 1980s.

Sidaway v. Board of Governors of the Bethlem Royal Hospital, etc.

11.05   In *Sidaway v. Board of Governors of the Bethlem Royal Hospital and Maudsley Hospital*,[3] it was held that where a claim is made arising out of an alleged failure on the part of a surgeon to warn his patient of risks inherent in the operation the proper test is that used in *Bolam*, namely the standard

---

[3] [1985] A.C. 871.

of the ordinary skilled man exercising and professing to have the skill of the surgeon concerned.

They also stated *per curiam* that whilst it is primarily a matter for the surgeon concerned to exercise his own clinical judgment when weighing just how much disclosure of risk is advisable in the case of a particular patient, there could exist circumstances where the degree of risk was such that, whatever responsible medical opinion might say to the contrary, a judge could be justified in holding the patient's right to decide to outweigh that body of opinion, and concluding that no reasonable medical man would have failed to disclose the particular risk under consideration.

In that case, S underwent surgery for persistent pain which carried an inherent risk of damage to the spinal cord, even if performed properly and skilfully, put at between one and two per cent. In the event the operation was performed with all proper skill and care, but S nevertheless suffered very severe injuries. She claimed that she had not been warned of the intrinsic risk of the operation, and that had she been so warned she would not have consented to the surgery.

11.06 The judge found that by the accepted standards of 1974 (when the operation had been carried out) the surgeon had followed a practice accepted as proper by a responsible body of medical opinion in not warning S in detail of the risk of damage to the spinal cord. Accordingly he acquitted the surgeon of negligence and his decision was upheld by the Court of Appeal.

The House of Lords dismissed the appeal and held that the judge had been correct in applying the *Bolam* test and had been entitled to find that the surgeon had acted in accordance with a standard accepted as proper by a responsible body of medical opinion, and that he had not thereby departed from the standard of an ordinary skilled man professing to have those skills as a surgeon.

11.07 Whilst ordinarily it would be impossible to hold a doctor negligent who had conformed to a view held by a respected body of medical opinion, the case could arise, where the degree of risk was substantial or the consequences particularly grave, that the patient's right to make the decision himself outweighed even the respected body of medical opinion. On the facts of the present case S had failed to prove the surgeon in breach of any duty of care and the appeal had to be dismissed.

In his speech, Lord Scarman stated[4]:

> "The *Bolam* principle may be formulated as a rule that a doctor is not negligent if he acts in accordance with a practice accepted at the time as proper by a responsible body of medical opinion even though other doctors adopt a different practice. In short, the law imposes the duty of care: but the standard of care is a matter of medical judgment."

---

[4] At 881.

Maynard v. West Midlands Regional Health Authority

11.08 In *Maynard v. West Midlands Regional Health Authority*,[5] the House of Lords held that in the medical profession, as in others, there is room for differences of opinion and practice, and a court's preference for one body of opinion over another is no basis for a conclusion of negligence.

In that case, M brought an action against the health authority for damages for negligence alleging that the decision to carry out an exploratory operation based on a mistaken diagnosis had been negligent.

At trial a distinguished body of expert medical opinion was called approving the health authority's action, but the judge said that he preferred the evidence of an expert called for M who said that a correct diagnosis should have been made at the outset and that it had been wrong and dangerous to undertake the operation. The Court of Appeal reversed the decision of the trial judge.

11.09 The House of Lords dismissed the appeal holding that in the medical profession, as in others, there was room for differences of opinion and practice, and a court's preference of one body of opinion to another was no basis for a conclusion of negligence.

When it was alleged that a fully considered decision by two consultants in their own special field had been negligent, it was not sufficient to establish negligence for the claimant to show that there was a body of competent professional opinion that considered that the decision had been wrong if there was also a body of professional opinion, equally competent, that supported the decision as having been reasonable in the circumstances.

In his speech, Lord Scarman stated[6]:

"I do not think that the words of Lord President Clyde in *Hunter v. Hanley*,[7] can be bettered:

'In the realm of diagnosis and treatment there is ample scope for genuine difference of opinion and one man clearly is not negligent merely because his conclusion differs from that of other professional men . . . The true test for establishing negligence in diagnosis or treatment on the part of a doctor is whether he has been proved to be guilty of such failure as no doctor of ordinary skill would be guilty of if acting with ordinary care . . . ' "

Bolitho v. City and Hackney H.A.

11.10 Following these cases, claims often foundered when defendants called evidence to show that the defendant acted in accordance with a practice which

---

[5] [1985] 1 W.L.R. 634.
[6] At 638.
[7] 1955 S.L.T. 213 at 217.

was accepted at the time as appropriate by a responsible body of professional medical opinion skilled in the particular form of treatment (which might be as small as 10 per cent).

This came under further challenge in the House of Lords in the case of *Bolitho v. City and Hackney H.A.*[8] In that case, B, the administratrix of the estate of a child, P, who suffered catastrophic brain damage when respiratory failure resulted in cardiac arrest, appealed against a Court of Appeal ruling[9] dismissing her appeal against the dismissal of her claim for damages for medical negligence.

The trial judge had found that P's doctor had breached her duty of care by failing to attend P, but that the breach had not caused P's death since, had the doctor attended, she would not have performed the intubation needed to save P's life and, on the basis of the expert medical evidence presented, she would not have been negligent in failing to do so.

In reaching the latter conclusion, the judge had applied the test established in *Bolam* and B contended that this test had no application to issues of causation and the judge had misdirected himself in referring to it.

The House of Lords held, dismissing the appeal, that the *Bolam* test was of central importance in determining whether the doctor would have been negligent in failing to intubate. **11.11**

However, they went on to hold that the court was not obliged to hold that a doctor was not liable for negligent treatment or diagnosis simply because evidence had been called from medical experts who genuinely believed that the doctor's actions conformed with accepted medical practice.

The reference in *Bolam* to a "responsible body of medical men" meant that the court had to satisfy itself that the medical experts could point to a logical basis for the opinion they were supporting. Where cases concerned the balancing of risks against benefits, the court had to be sure that, in forming their opinion, the medical experts had considered the issue of comparative risks and benefits and had reached a view which could be defended.

However they went on to say that it would only be in rare cases that the court would reject the medical experts' view as unreasonable and the evidence did not support such a conclusion in the instant case. **11.12**

Specifically, Lord Browne-Wilkinson stated[10]:

"Mr Brennan . . . submitted that the judge had wrongly treated the *Bolam* test as requiring him to accept the views of one truthful body of expert professional advice even though he was unpersuaded of its logical force. He submitted that the judge was wrong in law in adopting that approach and that ultimately it was for

---

[8] [1998] A.C. 232; [1997] 3 W.L.R. 1151; [1997] 4 All E.R. 771; [1998] P.N.L.R. 1; [1998] P.I.Q.R. P10; [1998] Lloyd's Rep. Med. 26; (1998) 39 B.M.L.R. 1; (1997) 94(47) L.S.G. 30; (1997) 141 S.J.L.B. 238; *The Times*, November 27, 1997.
[9] [1993] P.I.Q.R. P334; [1994] C.L.Y. 3368.
[10] At 241–243.

the court, not for medical opinion, to decide what was the standard of care required of a professional in the circumstances of each particular case.

My Lords, I agree with these submissions to the extent that, in my view, the court is not bound to hold that a defendant doctor escapes liability for negligent treatment or diagnosis just because he leads evidence from a number of medical experts who are genuinely of opinion that the defendant's treatment or diagnosis accorded with sound medical practice. In the *Bolam* case itself, McNair J.[11] stated that the defendant had to have acted in accordance with the practice accepted as proper by a 'responsible body of medical men.' Later,[12] he referred to 'a standard of practice recognised as proper by a competent reasonable body of opinion.' Again, in . . . *Maynard's* case,[13] Lord Scarman refers to a 'respectable' body of professional opinion. The use of these adjectives—responsible, reasonable and respectable—all show that the court has to be satisfied that the exponents of the body of opinion relied upon can demonstrate that such opinion has a logical basis. In particular in cases involving, as they so often do, the weighing of risks against benefits, the judge before accepting a body of opinion as being responsible, reasonable or respectable, will need to be satisfied that, in forming their views, the experts have directed their minds to the question of comparative risks and benefits and have reached a defensible conclusion on the matter."

11.13   There are decisions which demonstrate that the judge is entitled to approach expert professional opinion on this basis. For example, in *Hucks v. Cole*,[14] a doctor failed to treat with penicillin a patient who was suffering from septic spots on her skin though he knew them to contain organisms capable of leading to puerperal fever. A number of distinguished doctors gave evidence that they would not, in the circumstances, have treated with penicillin. The Court of Appeal found the defendant to have been negligent. Sachs L.J. said[15]:

> 'When the evidence shows that a lacuna *in professional practice exists by which risks of grave danger are knowingly taken, then, however small the risk, the court must anxiously examine that lacuna*—particularly if the risk can be easily and inexpensively avoided. If the court finds, on an analysis of the reasons given for not taking those precautions that, in the light of current professional knowledge, there is no proper basis for the *lacuna*, and that it is definitely not reasonable that those risks should have been taken, its function is to state that fact and where necessary to state that it constitutes negligence. In such a case the practice will no doubt thereafter be altered to the benefit of patients. On such occasions the fact that other practitioners would have done the same thing as the defendant practitioner is a very weighty matter to be put on the scales on his behalf; but it is not, as Mr Webster readily conceded, conclusive. The court must be vigilant to see whether the reasons given for putting a patient at risk are valid in the light of any well-known advance in medical knowledge, or whether they stem from a residual adherence to out-of-date ideas.'

---

[11] [1957] 1 W.L.R. 583 at 587.
[12] At 588.
[13] [1984] 1 W.L.R. 634 at 639.
[14] [1993] 4 Med.L.R. 393 (a case from 1968).
[15] At 397.

Again, in *Edward Wong Finance Co. Ltd v. Johnson Stokes & Master*,[16] the **11.14**
defendant's solicitors had conducted the completion of a mortgage transaction in
Hong Kong style rather than in the old fashioned English style. Completion in
Hong Kong style provides for money to be paid over against an undertaking by
the solicitors for the borrowers subsequently to hand over the executed documents. This practice opened the gateway through which a dishonest solicitor for
the borrower absconded with the loan money without providing the security
documents for such loan. The Privy Council held that even though completion in
Hong Kong style was almost universally adopted in Hong Kong and was therefore
in accordance with a body of professional opinion there, the defendant's solicitors
were liable for negligence because there was an obvious risk which could have
been guarded against. Thus, the body of professional opinion, though almost
universally held, was not reasonable or responsible.

These decisions demonstrate that in cases of diagnosis and treatment there are
cases where, despite a body of professional opinion sanctioning the defendant's
conduct, the defendant can properly be held liable for negligence (I am not here
considering questions of disclosure of risk). In my judgment that is because, in
some cases, it cannot be demonstrated to the judge's satisfaction that the body of
opinion relied upon is reasonable or responsible. In the vast majority of cases the
fact that distinguished experts in the field are of a particular opinion will demonstrate the reasonableness of that opinion. In particular, where there are questions
of assessment of the relative risks and benefits of adopting a particular medical
practice, a reasonable view necessarily presupposes that the relative risks and
benefits have been weighed by the experts in forming their opinions. But if, in a
rare case, it can be demonstrated that the professional opinion is not capable of
withstanding logical analysis, the judge is entitled to hold that the body of opinion
is not reasonable or responsible.

I emphasise that in my view it will very seldom be right for a judge to reach the **11.15**
conclusion that views genuinely held by a competent medical expert are unreasonable. The assessment of medical risks and benefits is a matter of clinical judgment
which a judge would not normally be able to make without expert evidence. As
the quotation from Lord Scarman makes clear, it would be wrong to allow such
assessment to deteriorate into seeking to persuade the judge to prefer one of two
views both of which are capable of being logically supported. It is only where a
judge can be satisfied that the body of expert opinion cannot be logically supported at all that such opinion will not provide the benchmark by reference to
which the defendant's conduct falls to be assessed."

Application to sporting cases

The case of *Bolitho* potentially opens the door to an increase in medical **11.16**
negligence claims. However, Lord Browne-Wilkinson was careful to limit
the extent of what he was saying.

As mentioned above, potentially medical negligence claims may arise not
only from medical treatment in hospitals but also potentially in relation to

---

[16] [1984] A.C. 296.

inappropriate medical advice, treatment or medication given by clubs, coaches or team doctors.

Potentially, claims may also arise through a failure to advise as to possible side effects of (legal) drugs which then cause injury.

Conclusion

11.17 It remains likely that medical negligence cases will remain rare and difficult and often expensive to prove. Craig Moore in *Sports Law and Litigation*[17] states:

> "Perhaps the first question which a seriously injured player will ask a doctor or a surgeon is: 'will I ever play again?' In the absence of an express and unequivocal promise to that effect (or any other promise for that matter), a court would be reluctant to find that an implied undertaking had been given (see *Thrake v. Maurice*.[18] In any case, except for the most straightforward of surgical procedures, it is most unlikely that a doctor or a surgeon would give anything approximating a definitive promise that a particular outcome will be achieved. Perhaps Jose-Maria Olazabal had those considerations in mind when he took the view that the delay in overcoming his injury was simply the rub of the green."

Example

Professional golfers Bruce Wilson and Bob Chambers are taking part in a head to head golf match at Sedbergh Golf Course. During the match, Bob Chambers injures his shoulder and Lorna Wilson asks the crowd whether anyone is a doctor. As it transpires, Dr Tim Rose and his wife Helena are watching and he treats Bob Chambers on the spot. In particular, he diagnoses the injury as a dislocated shoulder and manages to jolt it back into place. Unfortunately, Bob Chambers suffers further problems with his shoulder which he is later told by Consultant Orthopaedic Surgeons Simon Nixon and Simon Darling is due to the treatment he received from Dr Tim Rose.

Did Dr Tim Rose owe Bob Chambers a duty of care?

---

[17] 2nd ed., CLT Professional Publishing, 2000.
[18] [1986] Q.B. 644.

Chapter 12

Negligent coaching

"Look, if you're in the penalty area and aren't quite sure what to do with the ball, just stick it in the net and we'll discuss all your options afterwards."

Bill Shankley to a player (attrib.)

Introduction

It is important to realise that the term "coach" describes many different **12.01** roles within the world of sport—from the person who selects players for an international football team, to the person who works with a multiple grand-slam tennis champion to improve the fitness and technical game of the champion, to a P.E. teacher who explains to a seven-year-old girl how to hold a cricket bat.

It seems clear and obvious that in certain circumstances a coach will owe *some* duty of care to his subjects. The precise ambit of that duty will, it is submitted vary greatly depending upon various factors. It is not possible to formulate a "one size fits all" duty that all coaches owe to all those that they coach. It is submitted that the relative experience or expertise of the coach and the subject, as well as their respective ages and the nature of their relationship will be highly relevant in determining the scope of any duty of care, whether the coach was negligent and whether there was contributory negligence. In some circumstances, there may be a contractual relationship between the injured claimant and his coach (or the employer of the coach). It is submitted that the same factors will be relevant in determining the existence and potential breach of an implied term as in deciding on a duty of care, breach and apportionment in negligence.

In this chapter the term "coach" will be used broadly to cover all those who provide instruction or education to participants in sport (and therefore covers situations in which the term "instructor" might be more appropriate in common parlance, such as to describe the person who teaches a paying customer how to use a paraglider or kitesurf). In some such circumstances, a coach may have contractual duties to supply equipment that do not arise out of his role as a coach. There are very few reported cases about the liability of coaches for injuries to participants, but principle may be gleaned by reference to other areas of the law (both the general law of negligence and sports law).

The basis and extent of a duty of care

12.02 It is submitted that the essential feature of a coaching role that gives rise to a duty of care owed by the coach to his subject is reliance by the subject upon the expertise and/or experience of the coach. This will be most obvious when the subject is a child and/or a novice to the sport in question[1] and the coach is an experienced specialist. In some circumstances the coach may have actual disciplinary authority over the participant (for example, a teacher and a child or a football manager and a player), or the power to alter the course of the career of a player. When an injury occurs to a participant in respect of which the coach may be vulnerable to an action for damages, it will usually be because the coach has told the participant to undertake a particular task in a way or to an extent that is unsafe in the circumstances. The power that a coach typically has in such a relationship —whether it exudes from disciplinary authority, the ability to exclude the participant from a team or event, or merely because the participant trusts the judgment of the coach—might explain why the participant is willing to undertake an activity that might otherwise appear foolhardy. This "power dynamic" in the relationship needs to be taken into account by a court in considering a defence of *volenti non fit injuria* or contributory negligence.

Bearing this in mind, it seems that the liability of a coach in negligence is theoretically based upon an assumption of responsibility.[2] The coach holds himself out as a competent individual qualified to instruct the participant who, by reason of his use of the coach, implies that he requires further instruction or assistance in some areas of his technique, temperament or fitness. The coach can be said to assume responsibility for the safe instruction and assistance of the participant in those areas and the participant relies upon the experience and expertise of the coach not only to make the required improvement to the ability of the participant but also to do so safely. The principles for establishing a duty of care are therefore derived from authorities such as *Hedley Byrne v. Heller and Partners*[3] and *Chaudhry v. Prabhakar.*[4]

Where there is a contract under which the coach is retained by the potential claimant, it is submitted that the preferred route is an action for breach of contract. Examples of terms of general application that might be

---

[1] Chap. 14 deals with the liability of schools and this Chapter will encroach as little as possible on that territory.

[2] This seems to make more sense, in theory, than to simply say that there is "sufficient proximity" between a coach and a participant. By using an "assumption of responsibility" analysis, one can decide whether and to what extent a coach has assumed responsibility for each aspect of the safety of the participant.

[3] [1964] A.C. 465.

[4] [1989] 1 W.L.R. 29.

implied would, it is submitted, include terms that the coach will not instruct the participant to do any act that is likely to cause injury to the participant without warning the participant of the risk of such injury, that he will not instruct the participant to do any act in any way that is likely to cause injury to the participant without warning the participant of the risk of such injury, that he will satisfy himself that the participant is competent to perform any act he instructs the participant to undertake.[5]

The more experienced the participant, the less onerous will be the role of **12.03** the coach. To take cricket as an example, one would not expect Duncan Fletcher, the England Coach, to have to tell Graham Thorpe to wear a helmet when facing a fast bowler such as Darren Gough in the nets.[6] On the other hand, the England and Wales Cricket Board (ECB) has recently published "Guidance on Wearing of Helmets"[7] which requires the use of helmets for all "young players" (those under the age of 18) while batting or keeping wicket close to the stumps. It specifically directs coaches and instructors to require young players to wear their helmets before allowing them to bat or keep wicket standing up.[8] The guidance is not "mandatory", in the sense that the ECB has no power to enforce the compliance, but is designed to avoid actions for negligence. The existence of the guidelines is, however, powerful evidence of negligence against a coach who fails to follow them. Young persons may be allowed to bat without helmets where they have obtained written consent from their parents. If a young person refuses to wear a helmet then the coach should not allow him to participate and will be likely to be found to have been negligent if he does allow him to bat. It is, however, inconceivable that a coach could be sued successfully in similar circumstances by a 30-year-old international cricketer.

It is not inconceivable that a coach might be held liable in negligence **12.04** merely for allowing a participant to take part in an activity at all where it should have been obvious to the coach that the participant was not competent to participate either because of some feature of the participant or because of the inherent danger involved in the activity in question. If a primary school teacher does not teach a seven-year-old the proper way to perform a high jump but merely expects him to make the jump he may be liable for any ensuing injury—with very young pupils the likelihood is that

---

[5] All such terms could be subject to a proviso such as "so far as is reasonably practicable in accordance with the proper performance of his duties under the contract", so as prevent a coach being liable for injuries arising out of risks that are essential to the sport or activity undertaken—for instance, parachuting or paragliding.

[6] Although, interestingly, television footage of international teams netting often seems to show players batting in nets without helmets—while their team-mates are unlikely to hurl down bouncers at 90mph in the nets, and batsmen are unlikely to play the sorts of stroke (*e.g.* the sweep where the batsman goes down on one knee) that are likely to bring the ball close to the face, this hardly sends out the correct message to young cricketers and coaches at the lower levels of the game.

[7] www.ecb.co.uk.

[8] As the guidance points out, umpires and captains of adult sides also have a potential liability if they allow young players to play without wearing helmets.

they will not have had previous coaching outside of school. Similarly, a parachute instructor cannot assume that a participant knows what to do before telling him to jump out of the plane.

Physical instruction

12.05 Where the sport in question is overtly physical rather than technical (*e.g.* athletics, weight lifting, gym-floor exercises) the basis of liability is more clear-cut (although still based upon reliance). Clearly a coach will be liable if he negligently instructs a gym member to lift a weight greater than the gym member could reasonably be expected to bear.[9] A coach who tells an inexperienced 10-year-old boy to run five laps of the track and thus pushes him too hard may be negligent.[10] One reported case dealing with the liability of a coach in very straightforward circumstances is *Affutu-Nartoy v. Clarke & anor*[11] in which the claimant was awarded damages following a high tackle by the teacher who was supposed to be demonstrating how to tackle in rugby.

Example

Pop and movie star Kirsty Duffy is filming for her new pop video. Dance choreographers Fay Sizer and Veronique Backhouse teach her a dance routine which is both technically and physically challenging. In the course of filming at the glamorous new London club Elysium which is owned by club mogul Mark Young and is below the historic Café Royale, Kirsty Duffy injures her back and is unable to complete the video in time for the single to be able to compete for a Christmas number one. Fay Sizer and Veronique Backhouse had told Kirsty Duffy that she should not try anything that she did not feel up to.

Are Fay Sizer and Veronique Backhouse liable for Kirsty Duffy's injuries and the losses flowing therefrom?

Qualification

12.06 While the vast majority of sports have schemes whereby coaches may be trained and officially recognised, not all instruction will be carried out by qualified coaches. It is natural (particularly in team games such as cricket,

---

[9] In this situation liability will depend upon the amount of information that the coach has about the capabilities of the participant, but it is submitted that the principle that the coach should satisfy himself as to the competence of the participant before instructing him to lift any weight at all places the onus on the coach to ask basic questions about the experience, strength and (perhaps) medical history of the participant.

[10] A useful example of guidance for this sort of situation is once more found on the ECB's excellent website. It relates to fast bowling and, under the heading "Injury Prevention for Fast Bowlers" sets out the maximum number of balls that any person of any given age (up to Under 19s) during any net session and the number of sessions allowed per week. The guidance also includes information about the action that a young bowler should be taught, warming up and the surface that should be used, as well as footwear. The aim of all of this guidance is to prevent injuries (particularly to the back) and thereby to prevent litigation.

[11] *The Times*, February 9, 1984.

football or hockey) for the Captain or "manager" (who may not necessarily have a role in formal coaching) or other senior players to pass on tips to less experienced players. Young participants may naturally rely upon such advice. This may lead to difficult situations in terms of liability—for instance it would be a question of fact whether a senior player at a small amateur cricket club was in any way "holding himself out" as a person on whom a young player could rely, and where that senior player wrongly and repeatedly told the youngster to adjust his bowling action in a certain way.

On the other hand, if a person has the title of coach, it must be that he holds himself out as a person on whom a participant can rely, even if that participant knows that the coach is not accredited. Clearly a coach would be liable in negligence if he wrongly claimed to have certificates and experience and due to his incompetence a participant was injured.

Psychiatric damage

Thus far this Chapter has concentrated exclusively on physical injuries such **12.07** as muscle tears and broken bones. However, given the proliferation of sports psychologists and the controversial employment of faith-healers and the like in certain circumstances, it is not too fanciful to imagine that a coach might potentially be liable for psychiatric harm to a participant caused during hypnosis or inappropriate psychotherapy,[12] particularly in light of the case of *Lynn Elizabeth Howarth v. Phillip Green*[13] in which the claimant was awarded damages for the negligence of a stage hypnotist whose act—which included age regression—caused her to suffer psychiatric illness.

Conclusion

Although there is very little authority on the duties to be expected of **12.08** coaches, the principles upon which they will be held liable for breach of contract or negligence ought to be clear. The relevant factors to be taken into account in assessing liability will include the following (which is not intended to be an exhaustive list):

- the relative age of the coach and participant;

- the relative experience of the coach and the participant;

- any other features of the relationship that lend the coach particular power or influence over the participant;

---

[12] Although football players who have been traumatised by the sight of an angry manager throwing teacups around the dressing room at half time do not have a legal remedy.
[13] May 25, 2001, QBD Leveson J.; L.T.L. August 7, 2001—unreported elsewhere.

- the extent to which the coach holds himself out as being suitably experienced or qualified;
- the knowledge of the coach as to the experience, features and capabilities of the participant (and the extent to which the coach has attempted to obtain such information);
- the nature of the activity in question and in particular the extent to which risk of injury is inevitable;
- any published guidance of which the coach was or ought to have been aware.

Finally, it is worth emphasising the immense benefit to participants and coaches of full-time coaches ensuring that they have adequate insurance cover in place before embarking upon instruction. This may be arranged individually or through a club or school.

Chapter 13

Liability of referees

"We're supposed to be perfect our first day on the job and then show constant improvement."

Ed Vargo, major league baseball umpire.

The potential liability of referees may at first blush seem surprising to some **13.01** but when one considers that players may be liable to each other it may be said that this should be all the more so for referees since they often have positive responsibilities to ensure safety.

The position was put beyond doubt with the judgment in *Smoldon v. Whitworth and Nolan*[1] in which a referee of a colts rugby union match was found liable for very serious injuries suffered by the claimant as a consequence of a collapsed scrum.

This Chapter analyses the reasons for that judgment in order that the potential liability of referees in other contexts may better be assessed. At the end of the Chapter a brief examination is then made of a novel claim made by supporters against a referee.

Facts in Smoldon

In *Smoldon*, the second defendant had been refereeing a rugby match **13.02** between Burton Colts and Sutton Coldfield Colts on October 19, 1991. The claimant was the Captain and hooker of the Sutton Coldfield team who, then aged $17\frac{1}{2}$, was catastrophically injured during the match when a scrum collapsed and his neck was broken.

The circumstances were that the referee had allowed numerous scrums to collapse in what was, by all accounts, an ill-tempered match. The case itself was an extreme one on the facts which included the following set of circumstances:

1. the game was a Colts (Under 19) game;

2. the laws of the game as applied to Colts had been specifically revised by the International Rugby Football Board to reduce the risk of such

---

[1] [1997] P.I.Q.R. P133.

injuries, in particular by requiring that scrums should be required to form a defined sequence of crouch-touch-pause-engage;

3. the International Board and the defendant's own Society of Referees had issued directives and minutes emphasising the importance of the above rule;

4. prior to the accident, the defendant had failed to enforce those rules and allowed the scrums to "come in hard" which had lead to more than 20 collapsed scrums;

5. the referee had failed to take appropriate steps to enforce the laws, even in the face of a warning from one of his touch judges that someone would get hurt if he did not step in and also in the face of shouts from spectators and complaints from certain players.

Function of referee

13.03 In approaching the case, Lord Bingham L.C.J. analysed the function of the referee. Effectively, these amount to some of the crucial "circumstances" relevant to the standard of care as explained in some detail in Chapter 3 (above) in relation to the liability between participants.

Lord Bingham said that the referee's function was:

"to supervise the playing of the match between the opposing teams, endeavouring to apply the rules of the game fairly and judiciously so as to ensure that the flow of play is not unnecessarily interrupted, that points awarded are fairly scored and that foul or dangerous play is discouraged and where appropriate penalised or prevented.

This function, has often to be performed (as in the present case) in the context of a fast-moving, competitive and vigorous game, calling for many split-second judgments and decisions. The referee cannot be in all parts of the field at the same time. He cannot hope to see everything which goes on. It is a demanding and difficult job, usually (as here) performed out of goodwill by a devotee of the game."

Duty of care

13.04 The second defendant pleaded that in order to establish liability the claimant would have had to have shown a deliberate or reckless disregard for the safety of the person injured, in circumstances where, without such deliberate or reckless disregard, he should have intervened and where such intervention would have prevented the occurrence of the injury.

This was founded on observations of Sellers and Diplock L.JJ. in *Wooldridge v. Sumner*[2] (for which see Chapters 3 and 4, above), a case in which

---

[2] [1963] 2 Q.B. 43.

a photographer attending an equestrian competition was injured by one of the competitors. Sellers L.J. said[3]:

"If the conduct is deliberately intended to injure someone whose presence is known, or is reckless and in disregard of all safety of others so that it is a departure from the standards which might reasonably be expected in anyone pursuing the competition or game, then the performer might well be held liable for any injury his act caused."

Diplock L.J., having recognised[4] "that the standard of care which a reasonable man will exercise depends upon the conditions under which the decision to avoid the act or omission relied upon as negligence has to be taken", went on to say[5]:

"The practical result of this analysis of the application of the common law of negligence to participant and spectator would, I think, be expressed by the common man in some such terms as these:

'A person attending a game or competition takes the risk of any damage caused to him by any act of a participant done in the course of and for the purposes of the game or competition notwithstanding that such act may involve an error of judgment or a lapse of skill, unless the participant's conduct is such as to evince a reckless disregard of the spectator's safety'."

Drawing an analogy between the duty owed by participant to spectator and that owed by referee to player, counsel for the second defendant accordingly argued that while the second defendant owed the claimant a duty of care and skill, nothing short of reckless disregard of the claimant's safety would suffice to establish a breach of that duty. **13.05**

The claimant relied on the judgment of Sir John Donaldson M.R. in *Condon v. Basi*[6] and submitted that the second defendant owed a duty to the claimant to exercise such degree of care as was appropriate in all the circumstances. This test Sir John derived from the judgment of the High Court of Australia in *Rootes v. Shelton*,[7] and it was adopted by Drake J. in *Elliott v. Saunders*.[8]

In *Smoldon*, the Judge adopted the test proposed by the claimant and Lord Bingham stated that in the court's judgment he was right to do so. The second defendant had accepted that he owed a duty to the claimant, so that there was no issue whether any duty of care arose at all or whether any such duty was owed to the claimant. The issue of policy (or of what is just and **13.06**

---

[3] At 57.
[4] At 67.
[5] At 68.
[6] [1985] 1 W.L.R. 866 at 868.
[7] [1968] A.L.R. 33.
[8] Unreported, June 10, 1994; Halsbury's Laws of England 1994, Annual Abridgement, para. 2056.

reasonable) which has to be resolved where these questions arise did not here fall for decision. The only question was what duty was owed. The second defendant feared that if the test proposed by the claimant and upheld by the judge were held to be correct, the threshold of liability would be too low and those in the position of the second defendant would be too vulnerable to suits by injured players. In response to this, Lord Bingham M.R. stated:

> "We do not accept this fear as well-founded. The level of care required is that which is appropriate in all the circumstances, and the circumstances are of crucial importance. Full account must be taken of the factual context in which a referee exercises his functions, and he could not be properly held liable for errors of judgment, oversights or lapses of which any referee might be guilty in the context of a fast-moving and vigorous contest. The threshold of liability is a high one. It will not easily be crossed.
>
> There is in our judgment no inconsistency between this conclusion and that reached by the Court of Appeal in *Wooldridge v. Sumner* and *Wilks v. Cheltenham Cycle Club*. In these cases it was recognised that a sporting competitor, properly intent on winning the contest, was (and was entitled to be) all but oblivious of spectators. It therefore followed that he would have to be shown to have very blatantly disregarded the safety of spectators before he could be held to have failed to exercise such care as was reasonable in all the circumstances. The position of a referee vis-à-vis the players is not the same as that of a participant in a contest vis-à-vis a spectator. One of his responsibilities is to safeguard the safety of the players. So although the legal duty is the same in the two cases, the practical content of the duty differs according to the quite different circumstances."

Level of skill required by referee

13.07   There was a narrow argument in the case concerning the level of skill required of a referee such as the second defendant. The second defendant contended that the court should consider whether he had fallen below the level of skill reasonably to be expected of a referee of his grade refereeing an Under 19 Colts match in October 1991. The claimant contended that the level of skill required was determined by the function a referee was performing and not by his grade: accordingly, it was suggested that the level of skill required was that reasonably to be expected of a referee refereeing an Under 19 Colts match in October 1991, irrespective of the grade of the referee. In answer to this debate, Lord Bingham M.R. stated:

> "In the present case, this difference of approach is academic, since the grade which the second defendant held (C1) was entirely appropriate to the match which he was refereeing. This is not a case of a referee taking charge of a match above his professed level of competence. We prefer the plaintiff's formulation, but we do not think it matters."

Acts and omissions

The second defendant placed great reliance on the facts that he had not **13.08**
himself directly caused any injury to the claimant, and that any such injury
was the result of acts and omissions on the part of third parties (namely, the
other members of the scrum).

He relied on observations of Lord Mackay of Clashfern in *Smith v.
Littlewoods Organisation Ltd*[9] to support the submission that the second
defendant could not be held liable unless the court found that there was a
high level of probability of injury of a kind which the Laws were designed
to prevent as a result of a collapse of the scrum. It was not enough to show
a high probability that the scrum would collapse; it had to be shown that if
it did collapse serious injury of the kind specified was not merely a possible
but a highly probable consequence.

In reply to this argument, Lord Bingham M.R. stated:

"We are quite unable to accept that submission. There can be no doubt that the
scrummaging rules set out above were designed to minimise the risk of spinal
injuries caused in collapsing scrums, this being a risk of which those managing or
coaching rugby teams or refereeing or playing in matches were by October well
aware. It is accepted that the second defendant owed the plaintiff a duty of care
and skill. It is further accepted that serious spinal injury was a foreseeable
consequence of a collapse of the scrum and of failure to prevent collapse of the
scrum. If the second defendant were properly found to be in breach of his duty of
care owed to the plaintiff by failing to take appropriate steps to prevent a collapse
of the scrum, and if as a result of his failure a scrum did collapse and a player such
as the plaintiff thereby suffered spinal injuries of the kind which the rules were
designed to prevent, then in our judgment the second defendant would be liable
in law for that foreseeable result of his breach of duty, despite the fact that
(quantified statistically) it was a result which was very unlikely to eventuate."

Volenti non fit injuria

The second defendant's first and main defence was that he had not com- **13.09**
mitted any actionable breach of duty. But he pleaded that if, contrary to that
main defence, he had committed such an actionable breach of duty, then the
claimant had consented to the risk of injury of the type sustained by him by
voluntarily playing as a member of the front row of his team's pack of
forwards and/or by voluntarily participating in the practice of collapsing,
thereby also increasing the risk that the opposing front row might seek to do
the same.

However, at first instance, in the course of his judgment, the Judge
acquitted the claimant of accusations made against him personally and
found that the claimant had done nothing in the course of the game, and

---

[9] [1987] A.C. 241 at 261.

particularly in the last three set scrums, which amounted to improper play and that he had not by his own negligence contributed to his own injury. The Judge also rejected the second defendant's reliance on the defence *volenti non fit injuria*, observing that although the claimant had consented to the risk of injury in this game of rugby, he could not by inference be held to have consented to the second defendant's breach of duty as found by the Judge.

The second defendant argued on appeal that the Judge was wrong to have rejected his defence of *volenti*. He argued that since the claimant himself had known of the rules and of the dangers of collapse, he had impliedly consented to the risk of injury.

Lord Bingham M.R. dismissed this argument stating:

> "In our judgment this argument is unsustainable. The plaintiff had of course consented to the ordinary incidents of a game of rugby football of the kind in which he was taking part. Given, however, that the rules were framed for the protection of him and other players in the same position, he cannot possibly be said to have consented to a breach of duty on the part of the official whose duty it was to apply the rules and ensure so far as possible that they were observed. If the plaintiff were identified as a prime culprit in causing the collapse of the scrums, then this defence (and contributory negligence) might call for consideration. But that is not the case.

Factual grounds of appeal

13.10 The second defendant did not challenge the Judge's finding on the approximate number of collapsed scrums and the reasons for those collapses. He did, however, make a number of factual criticisms of other features of the judgment. It is helpful to set them out here in order better to understand the circumstances or factual matrix within which the judgment was made.

It should be noted that the second defendant asked that the following criticisms of the Judge's approach should be considered cumulatively and not as individual items. However, even on this approach Lord Bingham stated that:

> "we are not persuaded that grounds exist for disturbing the judge's conclusion."

Immaturity of colts

13.11 Counsel for the second defendant criticised the significance attached by the judge to the physical immaturity of Colts. Lord Bingham M.R. dismissed this saying:

> "We cannot accept this criticism as sound. It is not in doubt that the authorities responsible for the government of rugby football introduced a number of new rules specifically designed to protect young players against the risk of spinal

injuries caused by excessive impact on engagement and by collapsed scrums. It would seem clear that one of the reasons for affording this special protection was the belief that younger players were particularly susceptible to injuries sustained in this way. Whether or not there were other reasons for giving this protection, it seems very unlikely that the physical differences between teenagers and grown men was not a prominent reason."

Absence of complaint

The second defendant relied very heavily on the fact that although this match was watched by a number of adults, including parents, former players and club officials, no one during the match or at half time remonstrated with the second defendant or in any way complained at his failure to referee the scrummaging in the game in a proper manner. Even the players, who could be assumed to be familiar with the rules, did not complain at the time. This showed, so it was argued, that the complaint made against the second defendant was one made with the benefit of hindsight and in knowledge of the claimant's catastrophic injury. If in truth the second defendant's refereeing was as incompetent and ineffective as was suggested, then it was inconceivable that no contemporary complaint was made. **13.12**

In responding to this point, the claimant drew attention to the evidence of Mr Shingles, the Sutton touch judge: if the front row forwards were exchanging punches, as he suggested, they could not be binding properly, and lack of binding is a recipe for collapse. Attention was also drawn to evidence that the Burton captain had complained to the referee at the time about the collapsing of the scrums, to evidence from the replaced Sutton hooker that he had protested to the referee about the behaviour of the opposing front row, to evidence that other spectators had shouted to the referee to keep the front rows apart, to evidence from a witness (whom the Judge accepted) that he had at the time found the frequency of collapsed scrums very worrying and to the reports critical of the number of collapsed scrums written shortly after the match.

Lord Bingham M.R. stated in this regard: **13.13**

"It is perhaps a little unfortunate that the judge did not expressly address the second defendant's submission on this matter, but he must have had it in mind and it clearly did not weigh with him. This may be because of evidence given by the second defendant himself, which (on the judge's unchallenged finding on the number of collapsed scrums) virtually amounted to an admission.

The judge was also no doubt mindful of the evidence of Mr Johnson, the second defendant's expert witness, whom the judge accepted:

'Q. With the 1991/92 phased engagement of the crouch-touch-pause-engage, if that is being enforced and the sides are evenly matched, as I understand your evidence you would not expect more than five or six collapsed scrums at most during the game?

A. I would be surprised if I saw that many if that actually was happening.

Q. So five or six would in fact cause you surprise?

A. It would indeed.

Q. Twenty five in the course of a game of under 19, 1991/92 rules being enforced, would be quite remarkable, would it not?

A. We would spend an awful long time, my Lord, afterwards discussing his performance in the bar. The answer is yes.'

In the light of this evidence, it is not altogether surprising that the judge was not swayed by the absence of contemporary complaint."

The advice from the touchline

13.14 Complaint was made of the significance attached by the Judge to the warning given to him by Mr Shingles, the touch judge. However, Lord Bingham M.R. stated:

> "It is true that the judge did attach significance to this evidence, but only because of the light it threw on the second defendant's failure to stamp his authority and discipline on these two packs. The judge did not relate the evidence directly to the collapse of the scrums. We cannot accept that the judge misunderstood or improperly relied on this evidence."

Enforcement of C-T-P-E

13.15 The second defendant attacked the Judge's conclusion that the second defendant did not enforce the particular "C-T-P-E scrummaging sequence", and drew attention to the evidence of witnesses who testified that he did. The Judge's conclusion on this point was crucial to his decision against the second defendant, and it was understandable that the second defendant recognised the need to undermine it.

However, Lord Bingham M.R. stated that:

> "the judge did not lack evidence on which to base his conclusion. We can see no basis upon which this court could properly prefer the evidence of witnesses whom we have not seen to that of witnesses whom the judge did see and hear and whose evidence he accepted. The judge's conclusion is also strengthened by the expert evidence that if the C-T-P-E scrummaging sequence had been enforced, there would not have been the number of collapsed scrums which the judge found to have occurred.
>
> In our judgment this court cannot not properly disturb the judge's conclusion."

Reports of other matches

13.16 The judge placed no reliance on reports of the second defendant's refereeing of other matches, most of which were favourable but one of which was critical of his failure to control the scrummaging. The second defendant accepted that such reports would be unhelpful if the complaint in this case were of a momentary lapse or failure, but submitted that since the complaint was of an overall failure to control the match and impose his authority it was relevant to take account of other matches in which he was reported to have shown proper control and authority. In answer, Lord Bingham M.R. stated:

> "In our judgment the trial judge was entitled to take the view he did. The evidence was that this was the first Under 19 match which the second defendant had refereed since new rule changes had come into force. The judge was in our opinion right to concentrate his attention on the evidence of what happened during this match, and to regard evidence of what had happened in other matches as unhelpful."

Failure to call "no-side"

Although the second defendant accepted that a power to call "no-side" was   **13.17** conferred by the rules, he criticised the Judge's conclusion that this course should have been followed as unrealistic in the circumstances. It was a course so extreme and so rarely followed that the second defendant could not be fairly criticised for having failed to adopt it.

Lord Bingham M.R. stated in this regard:

> "We see some force in this criticism. Although the power to call no-side prematurely exists, it is plainly a power to be exercised as a last resort, when and only when all other measures have failed. But the judge placed little reliance on this conclusion in his judgment, and rightly so because, on his findings, the second defendant certainly had not adopted all the measures which he could have adopted to impose his authority on the two packs and insist on observance of correct scrummaging procedures, nor did he suggest that the players were in any way resisting or defying his authority. The gravamen of the charge against the second defendant is that he failed to take the prescribed steps to ensure that proper procedures were followed, and that is a charge which on the evidence the second defendant failed to rebut."

Opening of the floodgates

In answer to the worry that the judgment in favour of the claimant would   **13.18** open the floodgates for claims against referees, Lord Bingham M.R. stated:

> "The judge was at pains to emphasise that his judgment in favour of the plaintiff was reached on the very special facts of this case, having regard in particular to the rules designed to afford protection to players aged under 19 and to the evidence that the number of collapsed scrums which was permitted to occur in the course of this match was well in excess of what any informed observer considered to be acceptable. He did not intend to open the door to a plethora of claims by players against referees, and it would be deplorable if that were the result. In our view that result should not follow provided all concerned appreciate how difficult it is for any plaintiff to establish that a referee failed to exercise such care and skill as was reasonably to be expected in the circumstances of a hotly-contested game of rugby football. We are caused to wonder whether it would not be beneficial if all players were, as a matter of general practice, to be insured not against negligence but

against the risk of catastrophic injury, but that is no doubt a matter to which those responsible for the administration of rugby football have given anxious attention."

Overall, the Court of Appeal had emphasised that the threshold of liability is a high one and further that all the circumstances had to be taken into consideration. The referee could not be properly held liable for errors of judgment, oversight or lapses of which any referee might be guilty in the context of a fast-moving and vigorous context.

However, they had also distinguished the duty owed by referees to players from that owed by players to spectators and concluded that a referee owes a higher duty to the players under his control than a player does to a spectator.

13.19   As the personal injury Barrister Perrin Gibbons[10] says:

"Whilst this case does not necessarily open the floodgates for litigation against referees, it will no doubt lead to other actions over the course of the next few years."

Example

Rhiannon Jones has just qualified as a netball referee and is refereeing a match between Tivington and Carhampton. During the match she is criticised by supporters of both teams for failing to keep her eyes on the ball. Indeed, video evidence later shows that during the course of the first half she had failed to award fouls on 44 occasions. Mindful of this, the manager of Tivington, Lara Hawketts, suggests at half-time that she get a grip on the match. However, 10 minutes into the second half, discipline has already broken down again and a fight breaks out between Tivington player Paula Williams and Carhampton player Nancy Fernee in which Nancy Fernee sustains a black eye.

Along with any potential liability of Paula Williams, is Rhiannon Jones liable for the injuries sustained by Nancy Fernee?

Liability to supporters

13.20   A novel cause of action was pleaded a few years ago against the football referee Mike Read.[11] He refereed the Chelsea-Leicester FA Cup Fifth round replay at Stamford Bridge in February 1997. He awarded a penalty to the home side which led to the winning goal and which gave rise to much controversy.

Proceedings were issued against Mr Reed and the Football Association by some Leicester supporters who claimed compensation for the severe distress and anxiety which they allegedly suffered as a consequence of his decision, compelling them to take time off work to recover from the physical trauma.

---

[10] Of 9 Gough Square.
[11] See C. Moore, *Sports Law and Litigation* (CLT Professional Publishing, 2nd ed., 2000).

The claim was struck out as an abuse of the process of the Court. No doubt issues of duty of care, breach, foreseeability and causation formed part of the reasoning for this decision. However, as Craig Moore points out,[12] it does not necessarily mean that clubs themselves may consider some form of claim in the future for the actions and decisions of match officials.

Example

Premier league referee Lee Baker is refereeing a football match between Porlock and Exmoor Rangers. Property tycoon Matthew Waddams has money riding upon the outcome of the match and makes a contract with Lee Baker that he will give Exmoor Rangers at least four penalties in the match and will send off at least two of the Porlock players in return for which he will give Lee Baker a barrel of scrumpy cider. During the match Lee Baker sends off Mark Atwood and Joe King who were playing for Porlock but only awarded Exmoor Rangers three penalties.

Can Matthew Waddams sue Lee Baker for breach of contract?

---

[12] *Sports Law and Litigation* (CLT Professional Publishing, 2nd ed., 2000).

Chapter 14

Liability of schools

"[Italian defender] Tardelli's been responsible for more scar tissue than the sur-geons of Harefield Hospital."

Jimmy Greaves, ITV World Cup Panel, 1982.

Introduction

Until recently, there has been very little specific guidance to school teachers   **14.01**
as to how their roles should be performed during sporting activities. This
has lead to difficulties in determining whether they have breached any duty
they owe. Sport is now a fundamental part of schooling and education.
Physical education now forms part of the National Curriculum.[1] The attainment target in PE sets out the knowledge, skills and understanding that
pupils of different abilities and maturities are expected to have by the end of
each key stage. Attainment targets consist of eight level descriptions of
increasing difficulty, plus a description of exceptional performance above
level 8. Each level description describes the type and range of performance
that pupils working at that level should characteristically achieve. Further
guidance is provided in the Physical Education in the National Curriculum
publication.[2] It adopts an approach mirroring the health and safety regulations introduced under European Law for the management of health and
safety at work.

The strategy of the European framework directive (89/391) was to
impose upon employers the duties of avoiding risks to health and safety,
evaluating risks which cannot be avoided, combating risks to health and
safety at their source, adapting to the individual and technical progress and
developing a coherent prevention strategy. There followed six daughter
directives known as the "six pack". The United Kingdom's response was to
introduce regulations supplemented by Approved Codes of Practice and

---

[1] See Education (National Curriculum) (Attainment of Targets and Programmes of Study in
Physical Education) Order 1995 (S.I. 1995 No. 60) and the Education (National Curriculum) (Attainment of Targets and Programmes of Study in Physical Education) (England)
Order 2000 (S.I. 2000 No. 1607). For an analysis of this area of the law, see C. Moore,
Sports Law and Litigation, ante and E. Grayson *Schools, Sports and the Law, ante*, which
have been of considerable assistance.
[2] HMSO.

guidance notes. These include, the Workplace (Health Safety and Welfare) Regulations 1992 and the Management of Health and Safety at Work Regulations 1992. It is worth bearing in mind the obligations placed upon employers given that the guidance provided in the Physical Education in the National Curriculum adopts a similar methodology.

When guidance is provided to schools and teachers alike, it is much easier to identify specific breaches of the standard of care in particular cases. As Mike Waters of Lucas & Co. Solicitors says "In the light of the 1995 Order and the other grounds for making criticisms of bad practice, claimants have more grounds for bringing claims in this area than they ever did before".

14.02 It is quite clear from recent developments that the obligations and duties placed on schools and local authorities (which we consider further in the next chapter[3]) are greater now than they have been. This is no more clearly demonstrated than in the decision handed down by the House of Lords in four conjoined appeals which raised the question as to whether those engaged in the education of young persons could be held liable for negligent acts and omissions which caused loss, injury or damage to their students. We will consider only two (although the following cases are unrelated to sports injuries they provide helpful guidance).

In *Phelps v. Hillingdon London Borough Council*[4] the claimant, was referred by her school to the defendant local education authority's school psychological service. An educational psychologist employed by the authority reported that testing had revealed no specific weaknesses. Shortly before the claimant left school she was privately diagnosed as dyslexic. She brought an action against the authority claiming that they were vicariously liable for the psychologist's negligent assessment. The judge held that the psychologist had owed a duty of care to the claimant. The adverse consequences of the claimant's dyslexia could have been mitigated by early diagnosis and appropriate treatment or educational provision. The psychologist's negligence had caused the damage in respect of which the claimant's claim was made. The Court of Appeal allowed an appeal by the authority. The claimant appealed.

14.03 The claimant in the fourth case (*Jarvis*) was born in 1979. He had learning difficulties and his special educational needs were assessed. An educational psychologist's report did not refer to dyslexia. His mother felt that he should be placed in a unit specialising in dyslexia, but he was placed elsewhere. He issued a writ alleging, *inter alia*, negligence and breach of duty both by the psychologist for whom the local education authority was vicariously liable and by the authority itself for failing to provide competent advice through its educational psychology service. The Judge, on application by the authority, refused to strike out the claimant's claim in negligence,

---

[3] There is considerable overlap in this context between schools and local authorities since pursuing one in damages will often involve pursuing the other.

[4] [1999] 1 W.L.R. 500.

but the Court of Appeal allowed an appeal by the authority. The claimant appealed.

The House of Lords allowed each of the claimant's appeals. A person exercising a particular skill or profession might owe a duty of care in its performance to those who might foreseeably be injured if due care and skill were not exercised. Such a duty did not depend on the existence of a contractual relationship between the person causing and the person suffering the damage. Where an educational psychologist was specifically asked to advise as to the assessment of and future provision for a child and it was clear that the child's parents and teachers would follow that advice, a duty of care arose. The local education authority was vicariously liable for a breach of that duty notwithstanding that the breach had occurred in the course of the performance of a statutory duty and a breach of the authority's duties under the Education Acts 1944 and 1981 did not itself sound in damages. In the relationship between the claimant and the educational psychologist employed by the defendant authority in the first case and the task the psychologist had been performing had created the necessary nexus for a duty of care to arise. That the Judge had been entitled to hold her in breach of that duty and the authority vicariously liable for her breach. There was no wider interest of the law which would require that no remedy in damages be available. The recognition of a liability upon employees of the education authority for damages for negligence in education would not lead to a flood of claims, or even vexatious claims, which would overwhelm the school authorities, nor would it add burdens and distractions to the already intensive life of teachers. A very useful book on this subject is *School Sports and the Law* by Edward Grayson.[4a]

Training and supervision

Teachers taking physical education classes will be expected to be familiar **14.04** with the rules of the sport and the safe use of any equipment involved. This is unlikely to present a problem with common sports such as football whereby a maintenance of discipline is likely to prevent any serious accidents. However, in other sports, such as gymnastics essential technique will be required in order to instruct pupils safely. The dicta of Millett L.J. in *Fowles v. Bedforshire County Council*[5] (although not a case involving a school) provides considerable assistance. The claimant injured himself whilst performing a forward somersault. *Per* Millett L.J.:

"Anyone who assumes the task of teaching the forward somersault [a difficult manoeuvre] is under a duty not only to teach the technique involved in the

---

[4a] Craven. CCH Group Limited, 2001.
[5] *The Times*, May 22, 1995, CA.

exercise and the dangers involved in its performance but to teach the steps which must be taken to prepare for it, including laying of the crash mat, and to explain the dangers of performing the exercise in an inappropriate environment. It matters not how obvious a danger may be, it should be pointed out. This is particularly the case where the danger of a minor accident (such as hitting an obstruction) may be obvious, but the risk of really serious injury is unlikely to be appreciated by the inexpert."

It is widely accepted that the duty of care owed by a teacher to a pupil is similar to that of a reasonable and prudent parent in the same position as a teacher. One must be careful to distinguish between a genuine accident and breach of duty. In *Van Oppen v. Clerk to the Trustees of the Bedford Charity (Harpur) Trust*,[6] the claimant suffered a spinal injury whilst playing rugby at school. The parties agreed that the school was under a duty to take reasonable care for the health and safety of the pupils in its charge, the standard being that of the reasonable parent. It was eventually conceded that the school had taken reasonable care for his safety on the rugby field. One must compare and contrast that with the case of *Smoldon v. Whitworth and Nolan*,[7] where the referee was found liable for injuries suffered by the claimant following the collapse of the scrum. However, in that case there was evidence that the scrum had collapsed consistently. The court held that if the referee were found to be in breach of his duty of care by failing to take appropriate steps to prevent a collapse and if as a result of his failure a scrum did collapse and a player thereby suffered spinal injuries of a kind the rules were designed to prevent, then the referee would be liable in law for that foreseeable result of his breach of duty, despite the fact that, quantified statistically, it was a result which was very unlikely to eventuate. The referee's function was to supervise the playing of the match, endeavouring to apply the rules of the game fairly and judiciously so as to ensure that the flow of play was not unnecessarily interrupted, that points awarded were fairly scored and that foul or dangerous play was discouraged and, where appropriate, penalised or prevented. Arguably the duty of a teacher who is *in loco parentis*, is higher than that of a referee.

14.05   Other examples of a teacher being found liable for failure to adequately instruct and train include that of a teacher who failed to provide adequate training to a boy diving into the shallow end of a pool. Whereas, in *Hill v. Durham County Council*[8] the claimant failed to establish negligence against the local authority when she suffered an rupture of the Achilles tendon in a hopscotch type game arranged by her school. The claimant alleged that there had been a failure to perform warm-up exercises. The Judge, at first instance, held that the hopscotch type game was not an inappropriate way in which to have started. The Court of Appeal, whilst criticising the absence

---

[6] [1990] 1 W.L.R. 235.
[7] *The Times*, December 18, 1996.
[8] Unreported, January 31, 2000. CA.

of reasoning, upheld the decision. They noted that there was evidence that warm-up exercises could not always prevent injury.

In *Affutu-Nartoy v. Clarke and Inner London Educatoin Authority*[9] a teacher was held to be responsible for an accident which occurred during a rugby lesson. The teacher held demonstrating tackling. He made a high tackle as a result of which one of his pupils was injured. The court held that he should not have made the tackle at all. He could have demonstrated the skills required or not required without having to engage in physical contact.

The teacher must supervise sports activities. The most recent and controversial decision in this area was in the case of *Chittock v. Woodbridge*.[10] The defendant school was held liable to a claimant who had suffered a serious spinal injury whilst in a school skiing holiday in Austria. The background to this claim is unusual. The claimant who was 17 and a keen sportsman, was left wheelchair-bound after falling on his back while skiing off-piste. The claimant, who was an intermediate skier, and two contemporaries, had joined the trip, which was aimed mainly at junior boys, with their parents' written consent to them skiing unsupervised. He was travelling too fast and out of control and failed to pay attention to the topography, the presence of the warning sign and the fact that slower moving skiers were in front of him. The Judge, in finding the school responsible (he also made a finding of 50 per cent contributory negligence on the part of the claimant) said that the school was to blame because of its failure the day before to adequately respond to a second occasion when the claimant had skied off-piste in circumstances when he knew he should not have done so. On that occasion the teacher who had already reprimanded the claimant and his friends for skiing off-piste on the first occasion, told him and another boy off but did not remove their ski passes "because the staff were trying to treat them as adults". The Judge rejected argument that merely to tell the boys off was within the reasonable range of decisions that a teacher acting in the place of a parent should have reached. This was a deliberate breach of instruction and, as the teacher had accepted in evidence, demonstrated the boys could not be trusted.

In *Chittock* it was accepted that a reasonable and prudent parent would **14.06** have allowed the claimant and his two friends to ski on their own on such a trip. The decision has considerable significance for school trips and the level of instruction and supervision which is required on those trips. Doug McAvoy, the general secretary of the National Union of Teachers, said the union would be reviewing its guidelines to members on school trips in the light of the *Chittock* case. He claimed that a precedent has been set by this ruling stating that "even though the teacher gave instructions to pupils and all necessary steps were taken by the school, they were not enough". He

---

[9] *The Times*, February 9, 1984.
[10] *The Times*, April 5, 2001.

went on to say that "as a result of this ruling there was a greater chance that a court will find some negligence on the part of a school or teacher." Time will tell whether or nor he is right.[11] The defendant school appealed.[11a] On the appeal, the school argued that the Judge had erred in that he gave insufficient weight to claimant's age and skiing experience and to the agreement that he should be allowed to ski unsupervised. They further contended that he wrongly relied on the evidence of claimant's skiing expert on the sanction that should have been given in response to the second off-piste excursion when the test was what a reasonable teacher or parent might have done.

The Court of Appeal allowed the appeal. They held that the Judge had erred by finding that the teacher's decision not to sanction the claimant was not within a range of reasonable responses for a teacher in his position. The teacher's reaction to the second off-piste incident, giving a severe reprimand and accepting the assurances from the 17-year-olds that they would not ski off-piste again, was not outside the range of reasonable responses in the circumstances. The decision in this case was not one on which expert evidence could sensibly be determinative. It was a matter of judgment for the teacher in charge. They went on to state that if, contrary to the view of the court, the school had been negligent, the breach of duty could not on a balance of probabilities be said to have caused the accident. It is a sad fact that cases of this type are likely to discourage schools from organising such trips.

In *Gibbs v. Barking Health Authority*,[12] the claimant, in the course of gymnastic training, was required to vault over a horse. For some reason the boy landed in a stumble and was injured. The master who had been in charge of the lesson did nothing to assist the boy in landing. It was held that the master had not taken reasonable care and the education authority was liable in damages to the injured boy. The Court of Appeal judgment, which is brief, handed down by Slesser L.J., states no more than that the Judge at first instance had found that there was inadequate care. In the circumstances they would not interfere with that decision.

14.07 The decisions in *Chittock* and *Gibbs* can be contrasted with the result in *Wright v. Cheshire County Council*.[13] The claimant was taking part in gymnastic exercises in a school run by the defendant. He was in a party of 10 boys who were vaulting the buck. It was the duty of the boy last over the buck to wait at the receiving end of the buck to assist as necessary the next boy coming over. As the claimant was vaulting the bell rang to signal the end of the class and the boy at the receiving end of the buck ran off without waiting to receive the claimant. He fell and was injured. There was evidence

---

[11] In Chap. 15 further consideration will be given to out of school activities arranged by schools and local authorities.
[11a] *The Times*, July 15, 2002.
[12] [1936] All E.R. 115.
[13] [1952] 2 All E.R. 789.

given that this procedure (allowing the boys to carry out the practice themselves) was an approved procedure by the school designed to give the boys confidence. A physical training instructor also gave evidence that the practice was dangerous. The Court of Appeal held that the test of what was reasonable in ordinary and everyday affairs could be answered by experience arising from practices adopted generally and followed successfully. The evidence in this case had been that the procedure had been used and approved for many years and given the nature of the activity in question the defendant had not been negligent. In his judgment Singleton L.J. stated[14]:

> "The bell was an indication of break for play-time. In the ordinary course the boys, on the sound of the bell, would receive an order to go to the corner at which their squad paraded before being dismissed. Why should the defendants apprehend that on this, or any other, occasion the boy would run away when the claimant was in the act vaulting? So far as we know, that sort of thing had never happened before. The boys all had experience, seven months in the school and the plaintiff (and no doubt the other boys) had been in junior school before and had taken part in physical exercise and drill".

However, intellectually this analysis seems inconsistent with the character of the guidance provided in the HMSO publication on physical education in the National Curriculum—namely ongoing evaluation of risks to safety, assessing risks which cannot be avoided, combating risks to safety at source and adapting to the individual and technical progress. It is a moot point as to whether *Wright*, if heard now, would have a different result. In light of *Chittock*, perhaps not. However, it does seem a little naive not to anticipate the possibility that a child might run off upon hearing the bell for break-time.

However, a similar legal and factual analysis to that adopted in *Gibbs* can **14.08** be seen in *Wilson v. Governors of The Sacred Heart Roman Catholic School*.[15] Although not a sporting injury case it is of assistance. The claimant suffered injury to his eye caused by a fellow pupil as the children were leaving school. The judge found that the appellant school was in breach of duty in failing to provide at least one adult to supervise children as they made their way from the school building to the school gate, and awarded the claimant limited damages. The defendant school appealed successfully. They argued that the judge erred in his application of the test of the reasonably careful father and had failed to have any or sufficient regard to the authorities cited to him with regard to application of that test. There was evidence that care assistants were on duty at lunchtime but there was no particular history showing the necessity for the presence of such assistants at going-home time. The claimant had been going home unaccompanied

---

[14] At 792.
[15] [1998] 1 F.L.R. 663.

from the school from the age of six and no one suggested that his mother was failing in her duty by not meeting him at the school. The very short period in which pupils ran or walked from the door to the exit gate was quite different from the lunch period when supervision was provided.

14.09 The difficulty of eliciting a consistent approach is further demonstrated by *Alexander (a minor) v. King Edward School Bath Governors*.[16] In a trial on liability only in an action for damages for personal injury the claimant succeeded. She suffered personal injuries when a pupil at the defendant's school hit her in the mouth with a hockey stick. The accident occurred at the end of a boys' practice session when a boy was performing a practice shot. As he followed his shot through with his stick over his left shoulder, he hit the claimant in the mouth causing damage to her teeth and lips, and psychological trauma. The claimant alleged that the defendant had failed to supervise the pupils adequately whilst on the hockey pitch, and not at all as they left the pitch; and that a number of pupils were swinging their hockey sticks after leaving the pitch. It was accepted that there was a duty to supervise, but the adequacy of supervision was in dispute. The Circuit Judge found as a fact that the boys had been unruly at the end of the practice session and that they had continued to be unruly as they left the hockey pitch and started to disperse through the gate. The three teachers who were supervising were concentrating on the collection of kit and not on the boys. He found that if a teacher had been standing at the side of the gate as the pupils left, it would have deterred their unruly behaviour, wherever the children were going thereafter. A teacher could not be expected to insure children against injury from ordinary play. However it was their duty to supervise children in the playground, although the supervision need not be continuous. In addition, the claimant was not a pupil at the school, but was a visitor for the purposes of the Occupiers' Liability Act 1957, and accordingly the defendant owed her the common duty of care under that Act. On the basis of all the evidence, there was a breach of the accepted duty to supervise, and the defendant fell below the appropriate standard of care.

14.10 The appropriate level of training and supervision will differ from case to case. The standard of supervision and instruction expected will be higher where participants are disabled. For example, see *Morrell v. Owen*[17] where the claimant was injured following the misthrow of a discus at a disabled sporting event. It was the kind of throw which was entirely foreseeable, and so too was the accident in question. The Judge added that the coaches in the event owed a greater duty of care to the participants than would be owed by the coaches had the participants been able bodied.

The particular responsibility of the coaches where the participants were disabled includes instructing the disabled participants in appropriate safety procedures and practice and providing for the safe passage of participants/

---

[16] Unreported, May 9, 2000.
[17] *The Times*, December 14, 1993.

spectators moving into and out of the a relevant area. There can be little doubt that a school would be required to meet the same standards.

Defective/inappropriate/inadequate equipment

Where an injury arises out of defective sports equipment the likelihood is **14.11** that liability will attach to the school who provided that equipment. Good practice dictates that gymnasium equipment (and the like) should be checked regularly. It is probably not sufficient that a teacher inspect the equipment prior to each lesson. It would be advisable for schools to insure that equipment is independently tested on a regular basis to ensure that the apparatus is in a suitable condition. Pursuant to the Workplace (Health Safety and Welfare) Regulations 1992 an employer and persons who are in charge of work premises are required to keep the premises in an efficient state. Regulation 5 prescribes that the workplace, equipment, devices and systems shall be maintained in an efficient working order, an efficient state and in good repair. The regulations also prescribe standards for the temperature in indoor workplaces (reg. 7), room dimensions and space (reg. 10) and the conditions of floors and traffic routes (reg. 12))—all of which may have some relevance in a sports injury context.

It will be necessary to consider whether the equipment being provided is suitable for the purpose for which it is being used. For example, see *Kershaw v. Hampshire County Council*.[18] The facts, are similar to *Wright*, considered above. The claimant was in a physical education class doing gymnastics. The girls were vaulting over a box using a trampette rather than a springboard. As in *Wright*, girls who had vaulted over the box were required to assist the girls who came over next. The teacher in charge of the class had left the gym. The claimant injured herself. The judge held that the defendant knew or ought to have known that a trampette was more dangerous than a springboard. In addition, the teacher should not have allowed activities to continue in her absence.

Litigants will wish to consider any literature which may exist and be **14.12** available to those providing physical education. For example, the ECB published guidance on the equipment which should be provided to junior cricketers. It is recommended that batsmen wear helmets. The practice of the wicket-keeper "standing-up" to the wicket (*i.e.* just behind the stumps) is to be discouraged unless the wicket-keeper is also wearing a helmet. The ECB recommends that young players should not be allowed to bat or to stand up to the stumps when keeping wicket without a helmet against a hard ball except with written parental consent.

It is worth bearing in mind that not all helmets provide a faceguard. The ECB suggest that a helmet with a faceguard should be regarded as a normal item of protective equipment when batting against a hard ball, together with

---

[18] Unreported, 1982.

pads, gloves and, for boys, an abdominal protector (box). There is a British Standard (BS7928:1998) for cricket helmets and organisers should ensure that their helmet conforms to this standard.

The ECB in their advice indicated that anyone failing to follow the new guidelines would lay itself open to legal repercussions in the event of serious head injury to pupils playing cricket with a hard ball. Moreover, it is the responsibility of heads and those in charge of cricket to ensure that those who coach cricket in schools are aware of the new guidance.

The guidance applies until a young player reaches the age of 18, at which point he can make his own decisions as to whether he wears a helmet or not. If a younger player receives a head injury in a situation where the guidance has not been followed, it is likely that the person responsible for the player at the time of the injury would have a potential civil liability in common law under a claim for damages for negligence.

In the cricketing sphere, the ECB also provides a "Fast Bowling Directive" for junior cricket. There are strict guidelines for fielding. Umpires, teachers and coaches need to know the age group of all the players in the team, particularly if there are younger players playing in a higher age group.

Defective/inadequate premises

14.13   As one might expect, if there is a potential liability for defective equipment, then there is a potential liability for defective premises. It is possible that the courts may be able to draw assistance from the substantial body of cases on defective work premises. Within a sporting context there are few cases reported.

In *Ralph v. London County Council*[19] the claimant was injured after he put his hand through a glass partition playing a game in an assembly hall. The hall was too small. The claimant succeeded. The court took more lenient approach in *Comer v. Governor of St Patricks RC Primary School*.[20] The claimant was a father who took part in the father's race at the school sports day. Close to the finishing line there was a brick wall about six feet high. In an attempt to stop himself after the race the appellant put out his hands and broke both his arms on the wall. The case was dismissed on the basis that the school owed him no duty of care and on the basis of the principal of *volenti non fit injuria*. The appellant claimed that the respondent had been negligent in arranging and laying out the race with a brick wall close to the finish line. The Judge accepted that the race arrangement was unsafe and that a substantially longer run out at the end was required but that this was a fun race and that the appellant could not reasonably have been expected to be at the risk of "falling victim to the hazards of the

---

[19] [1946] T.L.R. 63.
[20] Unreported, November 13, 1997, CA.

proximity of the wall". The Court of Appeal held that the race could not be characterised as "arranged and laid out" as if it was a professional meeting at a sports centre. The appellant knew the layout of the race even though he had not turned his mind to it before or during the race and it was apparent to him that he was running towards a brick wall. The respondent was fully entitled to expect him to look after himself and adjust his actions accordingly even if he was trying to win the race. It was foreseeable that he would try to win the race but it was not foreseeable that he would try to do so at the expense of all other considerations, namely, his personal safety. Whilst *Comer* is probably correct on its facts, the result might, and probably would, have been different if the race involved pupils.

Not all schools have a wide range of sport facilities. In the circumstances, **14.14** they make do with what they have. For example, it is not uncommon when the weather is poor, for assembly halls to be used as 5-a-side football pitches or indoor uni-hockey pitches (a game involving plastic light hockey sticks and a light plastic puck). Potential claimants may wish to consider whether the dimensions of the hall are suitable for games of that type (consider finding out the required size of, say, a netball court if that was the activity being carried out). Further claims may arise if the floor was of an unsuitable construction for any or a particular type of sporting activity. There are minimum requirements for the size of playing fields in any school.[21] They must also be suitable for playing team games. Sport England provides guidance on different surfaces for sports activity. The Sports Council and the Hockey Association in conjunction with the all England Women's Hockey Association prepared a paper on the planning design, construction and management of artificial grass pitches. By examining such material, litigants will be able to consider with greater certainty whether appropriate safety measures were taken.

The Health and Safety Executive/Local Authorities Enforcement Liaison Committee (HELA) produced revised guidelines for the management of health and safety in swimming pools. These followed the HSC publication in 1999 of the Management of Health and Safety in Swimming Pools (HSG179). Schools and local authorities are subject to these guidelines. Schools and local authorities will need to give consideration to whether or not their swimming pool meets the required standard which include gradients in the pool. HSG179 does not, of itself, require any retrospective physical alterations to swimming pools. A risk assessment may identify that there is a significant risk of harm to a person arising from the physical environment of their pool. Consideration should be given to physical alterations as one of the possible solutions to the problem. Additional risk reduction measures, such as increased supervision, barriers, signage, etc. will also need to be considered.

---

[21] Education (School Premises) Regulations 1999, see also Chap. 5 of *School Sports and the Law* by Edward Grayson (Craven. CCH Group Limited, 2001).

Conclusion

14.15 So what can we draw from the cases referred to above. It is clear that schools have to give considerable thought to the abilities of those teaching physical education. Proper instruction in the rules of the game being played and frequent (and, in certain circumstance, constant) supervision is almost always going to be required. Where a pupil disobeys a direct instruction such as to create a risk to himself or others, the teacher must ensure that appropriate punishment/re-instruction is provided. Such punishment may necessarily involve exclusion from the activity being performed. Contact sports create a higher risk and allowing a teacher who was unfamiliar with the methods adopted to train and officiate such games is likely to increase the risk of a finding of negligence. Schools will also need to consider whether, in the light of the National Curriculum the proposed sporting activity is suitable for the class or classes of persons for whom it is intended. This includes considering whether an individual pupil, unlike his classmates, is capable of the task in hand.

Example

Penny, a physical education teacher, is taking a gymnastics lesson. Katie, a physiotherapist, is training to be a physical education teacher and so shadows Penny and helps out by carrying Penny's clipboard. In the class of 20 there are three very able gymnasts—Zib, Helen and Stas—all of whom have a reputation for mischief. Penny leaves Katie in charge when she receives a telephone call from a friend about where they are going to meet for lunch. Zib, Helen and Stas, whilst Katie is not looking, decide to get on a trampoline together. Penny told all class members at the beginning of the year that no more than one person at a time is allowed on the trampoline. Although mischievous, Zib, Helen and Stas have never broken those rules. Zib is injured in a collision with Helen and Stas. Is the school liable?

Would the result be different if Katie was qualified?

Chapter 15

Liability of local authorities

"Many continentals think life is a game, the English think cricket is a game."

George Mikes, How to be an Alien, 1946.

Introduction

We saw in Chapter 14 that there is a considerable overlap between the **15.01**
liability of schools and local authorities. Local authorities are creatures of
statute. Their responsibilities are often created and defined by statute (some
more clearly than others). The existence of a statutory duty does not
extinguish any common law duty. In a sports context, local authorities
provide for the general public many sports facilities—gyms, swimming
pools, tennis courts, municipal golf courses—the list is endless.

Liability of public authorities exercising statutory powers

We should touch briefly on the liability of public authorities for actions or **15.02**
omissions which arise in the exercise of its statutory powers. There are
peculiar difficulties that arise when considering the liability of a public body
when it is alleged to have been negligent in the performance of its functions
as a public authority as opposed to its status as an occupier (which is
considered later). In order to establish a duty of care the claimant will need
to satisfy the test laid down in *Caparo Industries Plc v. Dickman*[1] by Lord
Bridge:

> "What emerges is that, in addition to the foreseeability of damage, necessary
> ingredients in any situation giving rise to a duty of care are that there should exist
> between the party owing the duty and the party to whom it is owed a relationship
> characterised by the law as one of 'proximity' or 'neighbourhood' and that the
> situation should be one in which the court considers it fair, just and reasonable
> that the law should impose a duty of a given scope upon the one party for the
> benefit of the other."

Given that they have obligations to a wide community the court will
consider whether it is realistic that the relationship of sufficient proximity

---

[1] [1990] 2 A.C. 605 *per* Lord Bridge at 617–618.

can exist between the body and the individual.[2] Where damage is caused by the action of a public body, that action will often have been taken in the exercise of a power vested in it by Parliament. However, it is not a defence to an action in negligence for that public body to state that it was carrying out such a function. There could be no liability in respect of anything done within the ambit of a discretion conferred by statute. It is less likely that a duty of care would be imposed on a person exercising his public duty if a potential conflict could arise between the carrying out of the public duty and acting defensively for fear of an action in negligence being brought.[3]

15.03   There are a number of considerations in deciding whether it is fair, just and reasonable that a duty of care should be imposed when a public body is carrying out statutory powers. It would normally be unnecessary to embark on any further inquiry whether it was fair, just and reasonable if a person had assumed responsibility to another in respect of services. So, where sports facilities are provided, the authority assumes a responsibility. The more straightforward approach is to consider the local authority's responsibility as an occupier or at common law.

A useful case for defendants in actions relating to the exercise of a power is *Stovin v. Wise*.[4] In that case, N, in its capacity as highway authority, appealed from a finding that, in failing to propose the expeditious removal of a dangerous obstruction near a road it was in breach of a common law duty of care to road users. N had become aware of a visibility problem caused by a bank of land at a road junction where three accidents had previously occurred in the past 12 years. The matter had been discussed with the land owners, and it had been agreed that N would carry out the necessary work. However, no action had been taken to remove the obstruction by the date on which S was seriously injured as a result of a collision with a car driven by W, who joined N as second defendant to S's claim for damages.

15.04   The House of Lords held, allowing the appeal, that under section 79 of the Highways Act 1980 a highway authority had discretionary powers to require the removal of such obstructions. However, a statutory power did not give rise to a common law duty of care and N had not acted unreasonably in failing to proceed under that power. Even if the work ought to have been carried out, it could not be found that a public law duty gave rise to an obligation to compensate those suffering loss due to its non-performance. The creation of a duty of care in the circumstances posed an unacceptable risk to local authority budgetary decision making in an area where road users themselves were subject to compulsory insurance requirements.

---

[2] See *Charlesworth & Percy on Negligence* (10th ed., Sweet & Maxwell, 2001), para. 2–31.
[3] *W v. Home Office*, The Times, March 14, 1997.
[4] [1996] A.C. 923; [1996] 3 W.L.R. 388; [1996] 3 All E.R. 801; [1996] R.T.R. 354; (1996) 146 N.L.J. Rep. 1185; (1996) 93(35) L.S.G. 33; (1996) 140 S.J.L.B. 201; *The Times*, July 26, 1996; *Independent*, July 31, 1996.

Occupiers' Liability Act 1957

In Chapter 5 we considered the obligations placed upon the occupier of **15.05** premises arising out of the 1957 Act. Under section 2(2) the occupier is under a duty to take such care as in all the circumstances of the case is reasonable to see that the visitor will be reasonably safe in using the premises for the purpose for which he is invited by the occupier to be there. This is known as the common duty of care.

Defective premises

There are many examples of defective premises. We shall consider a few **15.06** examples. We saw in the previous Chapter that where an accident occurs claimants would be well advised to approach the appropriate sporting governing body to see whether or not basic requirements have been satisfied. In addition, an occupier does not necessarily escape liability for dangerous hazards on his premises simply by handing over control of the premises to another. So where in *Glenie v. Slack & anor*[5] the owner and occupier of a race track handed over control of the circuit to a promoter for a race meeting, the occupier and operator did not escape liability for dangerous hazards in the construction of the race track which breached the sport's governing body's safety standards.

Motor cross/scrambling

In *Davis v. Feasey & anor*,[6] the central issue was whether, as the claimant/ **15.07** respondent contended, a track laid out for a motorcycle race was in breach of the rules for such races. The meeting was organised by the defendants/ appellants. The track was designed by the defendant. It consisted of a series of bends and jumps. At part of the track were two banks. The claimant lost control crossing these banks, fell and suffered a grave spinal injury. The claimant alleged that the two banks consisted of a double jump. Double jumps were not permitted under the rules of the sport's governing body as they were accepted as being dangerous. The defendants admitted that they had owed a duty of care. They argued that the banks were not a double jump but a roll-over and it should have been obvious to the claimant that a certain line through the bends was dangerous. It was also argued that the sport was inherently dangerous and that to find against the defendants would place the future of the sport in jeopardy. The defendants, however, elected to call no evidence. The Judge had been entitled to come to the conclusion that the banks were double jumps on the evidence before him. It was foreseeable that some riders would fall into the dead ground at the

---

[5] Unreported, April 9, 2000, CA.
[6] Unreported, May 14, 1998, CA.

double jump. Simple steps could have prevented this hazard. In the circumstances the track layout, even for a dangerous sport, was unduly hazardous. These conclusions must be seen in the context of the prohibition in the rules of double jumps. Had the defendants conformed to the rules for track layout the accident and the action would not have followed.

Gymnasia

15.08   The more common examples of injury will involve slipping and tripping accidents. Personal injury practitioners will have much experience of such claims through accidents at work (usually arising from alleged breaches of the Workplace (Health Safety and Welfare) Regulations 1992). In *Gillmore v. London County Council*[7] the claimant had joined a class in physical training organised by the defendant council and paid a fee upon joining. The hall where the exercises were performed was fairly highly polished. One of the exercises involved hopping on one leg and lunging at another member of the class. The claimant slipped and suffered injury. The duty of the Council was to provide a floor which was reasonably safe in the circumstances, and this they had failed to do. The accident did not result from a risk which the claimant agreed to take, and a *volenti* defence was not available. Today these proceedings would be pursued on the basis of, *inter alia*, liability under the 1957 Act.

Swimming pools

15.09   Most local authorities are likely to provide one or more swimming pools. A significant amount of litigation arises out of accidents in swimming pools. Any public body providing a swimming pool for public use should ensure that the pool is of appropriate dimensions.[8] The depth of the pool should be clearly marked and identifiable. The pool and the surrounding area should be the subject of a regular, thorough cleaning regime which meets the manufacturer's standards (guidance will usually be provided by those who build the pool—failing which the HSE provide appropriate guidelines). Failure to comply with these minimum requirements will also certainly result in an adverse finding on liability in the event of an accident.

So, in *Taylor v. Bath and North East Somerset District Council*[9] the claimant successfully sued the local authority for a failure to operate an adequate cleaning regime. The claimant had just delivered her daughter to a swimming instructor at the side of the pool. She fell on the tiled flooring, which she claimed was very slippery. She suggested that this was as a result of an accumulation of body fats on the surface of the tiling. This problem

---

[7] [1938] 4 All E.R. 331.
[8] See Chap. 14.
[9] Unreported, January 27, 1999.

was aggravated by a lack of special systematic and chemical cleaning. The manufacturers had given clear instructions on the routine for cleaning the tiles. Only ordinary cleaning had taken place despite previous complaints. The Judge held that slippery tiles caused the accident. Body fat had accumulated on the tiles. The claimant was wearing suitable shoes and was walking in a sensible manner. The defendant owed the claimant a duty to take such care as was reasonable to see that she was reasonably safe in her use of the premises under section 2 of the Occupiers' Liability Act 1957. It was foreseeable that if the defendant failed to arrange for the tiles to be cleaned in accordance with the routine prescribed by the manufacturers someone would fall. Since the tiles had not been cleaned in that prescribed manner the defendant was liable.

In *Greening v. Stockton-on-Tees Borough Council*[10] the defendant coun-   **15.10** cil was the owner of a swimming pool where the level of the water was at the same level as the edge of the pool. The claimant was injured when he swam into the edge of the pool. The sides of the pool comprised light blue coloured tiles, the top edge of which had been tiled with a 20mm dark blue finger tile. The judge found that the water had been murky and that the narrow top band of finger tiles had been insufficiently wide to have alerted swimmers to the edge of the pool. The defendant appealed on the grounds that it had not been so murky so as to have created a foreseeable risk and that the Judge should have found that the finger tiles had been of sufficient width. If unsuccessful then the defendant contended that the Judge should have found contributory negligence. The Court of Appeal held that although expert evidence had been presented on behalf of both sides the Judge was entitled to prefer the evidence presented on behalf of the claimant that the top band of tiles should have been wider. Given the murkiness of the water which the claimant had noticed and the difficulty the Judge had found to exist in seeing the edge the Judge should have found that the claimant ought to have been exercising greater care than he had been. The court found the claimant 50 per cent contributorily negligent—arguably a harsh decision.

In *Banks v. Bury Borough Council*[11] the defendants were liable where they had not displayed the depth of the shallow end of the pool with sufficient prominence to give warning of it.[12]

Finally, in *O'Shea v. Royal Borough of Kingston-upon Thames Council*[13] the defendant appealed against finding of negligence where rules and regulations at their public swimming pool stated that diving was inadvisable because of the pool's shallowness. The lifeguards were instructed to prohibit diving at the shallow end and to advise all bathers to use a shallow dive. The

[10] Unreported, November 6, 1998, CA.
[11] [1990] C.L.Y. 3284.
[12] See Chap. 13 regarding the structural and dimensional requirements of swimming pool prescribed by the Health and Safety Executive.
[13] [1995] P.I.Q.R. 208.

claimant had dived in at the deep end, struck his head on the bottom and was seriously injured. The Judge had found the council liable in negligence and that the claimant was contributorily negligent in failing to notice the depths which were indicated along the side of the pool. The Court of Appeal rejected the appeal. The only safe system which the defendants should have adopted was to prohibit diving altogether.

Sports pitches

15.11 In *Dibble v. Carmarthern Town Council*[14] a goalkeeper settled a claim for £20,000 damages after suffering "horrific" burns from pitch markings when he dived to make a save. The claimant did not realise how badly he was hurt until he took his shirt off after the game and discovered a four-inch wide strip of flesh had been burnt off from his shoulder to his hip. He was scarred for life by pitch markings drawn with hydrated lime. At the time of the incident, in December 1998, he was playing for Barry Town in the League of Wales, against Carmarthen Town at their council-maintained ground.

Another example similar to those relating to sports pitches is that of *Cook, Cochrane and Hampson v. Doncaster Borough Council*[15] in which competitors recovered damages for injuries resulting from a defect in a race track controlled by a local authority, which caused horses and jockeys to stumble and fall.

Occupiers' Liability Act 1984

15.12 The 1957 Act deals with the duty of the occupier to lawful visitors. What is the position in relation to trespassers? Those who provide sports facilities must consider their obligations to unlawful visitors. Pursuant to section 1(3) of the Occupier's Liability Act 1984 an occupier owes a duty to another (not being his visitor) if he is aware of a danger or has reasonable grounds to believe it exists, he knows or has reasonable grounds to believe that the other is in the vicinity of the danger and the risk is one against which, in all the circumstances of the case, he may reasonably be expected to offer some protection. The duty is to take such care as is reasonable in all the circumstances to ensure that the trespasser does not suffer injury. Guidance, predating the Act, but which remains good, is provided in *British Railways Board v. Herrington*[16] *per* Lord Bridge:

> "The relevant likelihood to be considered is of the trespasser's presence at the actual time and place of danger to him. The degree of likelihood needed to give rise to the duty cannot, I think, be more closely defined than as being such as would impel a man of ordinary humane feelings to take some steps to mitigate the

---

[14] Unreported, 2001.
[15] *The Sporting Life*, July 16, 1993.
[16] [1972] A.C. 844 at 941–942.

risk of injury to the trespasser to which the particular danger exposes him. It will thus depend on all the circumstances of the case: the permanent or intermittent character of the danger; the severity of the injuries which it is likely to cause; in the case of children, the attractiveness to them of that which constitutes the dangerous object or condition of the land; the expense involved in giving effective warning of it to the kind of trespasser likely to be injured, in relation to the occupier's resources in money or in labour."

In *Ratcliffe v. McConnell & anor,*[17] Stuart Smith L.J. noted that the nature and extent of what is reasonable to expect of the occupier depended on whether the trespasser was very young or very old and so might not appreciate the nature and danger which was or ought to be apparent to an adult. In *Radcliffe*, the claimant, a university student, climbed over a fence surrounding a swimming pool on college grounds. The pool was marked with signs indicating the shallow and deep ends. He dived into the pool at the shallow end and struck his head on the bottom. He suffered tetraplegic injuries. The Court of Appeal held that the defendant college was not liable.

It is thus not possible to dismiss obligations to trespassers. There are still **15.13** derelict stadia in existence (some are still in use!). Facilities such as for example, a Lido may provide a great attraction to youths. Local authorities would be well advised to consider their security arrangements for such venues. The facts of *Radcliffe* were quite extreme. Other cases may not be.

Example

Top club promoter and fashion guru Andrew Clancy has organised a themed football night at trendy nightclub the Attic in the West End of Minehead in association with rock-DJ Etienne Abrahams and the girl band duo, 'Giggle', of Anna Kevan and Rhiannon Jones. The owner of the Attic, Rich and Famous Pam Sharrock, has given strict instructions that entry is to be strictly on payment of £10. Despite this, football heroes Dean Norton and Nick Ridler arrive at the party and naturally, Andrew Clancy lets them enter the club for free. They are both later injured on the steps whilst kicking a football around.

Are Dean Norton and Nick Ridler trespassers within the meaning of the 1984 Act?

Are either Pam Sharrock or Andrew Clancy liable for the injuries?

Contributory negligence

Defendants will wish to consider whether or not the claimant has been **15.14** guilty of contributory negligence. Assistance may be drawn from cases involving accidents at work. For example, it is now settled (see *John Summers & Sons v. Frost*[18]) that where an accident was just the type that

---

[17] *The Times*, December 3, 1998.
[18] [1955] A.C. 740.

statutory regulation was designed to avoid and where the workman was injured as a result of momentary inadvertence and not disobedience or reckless disregard then no contributory negligence will be found. In *Ryan v. Manbre Sugars Ltd*[19] the Court of Appeal indicated that in the circumstances of that case pure inadvertence was not negligence and excusable inadvertence was not contributory negligence.

A finding of contributory negligence is likely, where a claim is made under the 1984 Act, save in the case of young children.

Supervision and instruction

15.15   We saw in the previous Chapter a number of cases where liability arose following inadequate supervision. Outside school, the local authority, through its employees, may not be in *loco parentis* (it almost certainly is for pupils in school). Nevertheless, inadequate supervision will place an authority at risk. So where council staff, present at a gymnasium, were aware that young persons were regularly performing gymnastics without any supervision the council's negligence was held to be a causative factor of the claimant's injuries. A proper system of instruction would have included an express prohibition against practising such an exercise in the absence of a supervisor and directions for the safe placing of crash mats, which at the time of the accident, were wrongly positioned. Similarly, in *Conrad v. Inner London Education Authority*[20] the instructor of a council run judo-lesson failed adequately to supervise a class.

Where a clear and unambiguous warning of particular dangers is given and where there is appropriate instruction as to the manner in which any hazards should be approached, the defendant will avoid liability. The court will consider the medium of the warning. In *R and R v. Ski Llandudno Limited*[21] the claimants were descending a toboggan run owned by the defendant. They entered a bend at excessive speed and lost control. Each was injured. Notices were displayed which demonstrated the use of the handbrake and informed drivers to descend at moderate speed. At first instance the Judge held that the defendant owed a duty to clearly and unambiguously warn the claimant of the dangers of excessive speed and the need to apply the brake before entering a bend. The defendant had not done this. However, the breach of duty was not causative of the accident because the first claimant would not have heeded an oral warning. There was a small element of risk in a toboggan ride. It was not an inherently dangerous sport. Nor was there anything inherently dangerous in the run itself provided that there was a system to warn users not to take bends too fast and informing them of the importance of breaking prior to the bend. It was not possible to

---

[19] [1970] 114 Sol. J. 492.
[20] [1966] 116 N.L.J. 1630.
[21] Unreported, July 31, 2001, CA.

ensure that toboggan drivers complied with instructions received and the Judge had found that a warning in this case to brake at the bends would not have made any difference.

Local education authorities and out/after school activities

Games clubs, adventure activities and holidays, and after school clubs are **15.16** commonly arranged and implemented by schools. We considered the recent case of *Chittock v. Woodbridge School*[22] in the previous Chapter.

The Activity Centres (Young Persons Safety) Act 1995 was introduced following the Lyme Bay tragedy where the organisers of an ill-fated canoeing expedition were prosecuted for manslaughter. The managing director of the company was convicted. The company itself was also convicted of health and safety offences. The Act makes provision for the regulation of centres and providers of facilities where children and young persons under the age of 18 engage in adventure activities, including provision for the imposition of requirements relating to safety. The Secretary of State designates a licensing authority to exercise such functions as may be prescribed by regulations relating to the licensing of persons providing facilities for adventure activities. The Activities (Licensing) Designation Order 1996[23] designated the licensing authority. The Adventure Activities Licensing Regulations 1996[24] provide for the licensing of persons providing relevant activities. Relevant activities include[25]:

CLIMBING	WATERSPORTS	TREKKING	CAVING
(on natural outdoor features)	(on most lakes, fast flowing rivers & the sea)	(in remote moreland or mountain areas)	Caving Pot-holing Mine exploration
Rock climbing	Canoeing	Hillwalking	
Abseiling	Kayaking	Mountaineering	
Ice climbing	Dragon boating	Fell running	
Gorge walking	Wave skiing	Orienteering	
Ghyll scrambling	White-water rafting	Pony trekking	
Sea level traversing	Improvised rafting	Mountain biking	
	Sailing	Off-piste skiing	
	Sailboarding		
	Windsurfing		

[22] *ibid.*
[23] S.I. 1996 No. 771.
[24] S.I. 1996 No. 772.
[25] The information in the table was extracted from the AALA's website.

The Act creates a criminal offence of carrying out any activity for which a license is required. If a local authority maintains responsibility for and control over the safety management of activities taking place then effectively they are the provider and would require a licence. Thus they must obtain a licence. Schools and colleges are exempt for activities they offer to their own students or pupils but require a licence to offer licensable activities to pupils of another school if payment is involved.[26] Where the local authority provides facilities to an education establishment a licence will be required. The Adventure Activities Licensing Authority (AALA) has no statutory enforcement powers and cannot investigate accidents or dangerous occurrences. However, it is responsible for dealing with complaints involving licensed activities and for taking the appropriate action. This may include imposing extra conditions in licences and informing the appropriate enforcement authority (HSE/local authority) of concerns that cannot be resolved by AALA.

Highways Act 1980

15.17 The Highways Act will be well known to personal injury practitioners from tripping cases. The highway authorities are given powers and obligations to construct, maintain and improve highways under the Highways Act 1980 (the 1980 Act). Section 41 imposes a duty to maintain the highways. Maintenance includes repair for the purposes of the Act. The duty to maintain the highway is absolute.[27] However, this does not mean that the highway has to be perfect. A claimant must prove that the highway was in such a condition that it was dangerous to traffic or pedestrians. The court will ask itself whether it can be said that the danger may reasonably have been anticipated by continued use by the public. The Act has significance since many sports take place on highways. For example, cycling, horse-riding and road running.

The highway authority will avoid liability if it can establish the statutory defence set out in section 58 of the Act. It provides that if the authority can prove that they had taken all such care as in all the circumstances was reasonably required to ensure that the part of the highway to which the action relates was not dangerous to traffic. The Court will be invited to consider, amongst other things, the character of the highway and the traffic which was reasonably expected to use it, the standard of maintenance appropriate to that highway, the state of repair one would reasonably expect to find that highway, whether the highway authority knew or ought to have known that the highway was likely to cause damage to users and any relevant warning notices.

---

[26] For a greater explanation of the Regulations, it is recommended that you read the HSE publication entitled "Guidance to The Licensing Authority on The Adventure Activities Licensing Regulations 1996" (Ref L77). HSE Books.

[27] *Griffiths v. Liverpool Corporation* [1967] Q.B. 374.

The Court of Appeal has discouraged comparison between cases since **15.18** each will be decided on its own facts. Nevertheless, we include a few examples for your consideration. In *Byrne v. The Welsh Office*[28] the claimant was riding his cycle as close to the verge of the road as possible because he heard the sound of a vehicle behind him. His front wheel passed across the mouth of a drainage grip destabilizing the bicycle and throwing him into the road causing the injuries. It was held that man-made drainage provisions must not constitute concealed hazards for any road user. The highway authority was under a statutory duty to maintain and repair the highway under section 41(1) and that the injury to a cyclist was readily and easily foreseeable. The defendant's statutory defence under section 58 of the Highways Act 1980 was rejected. The defendant well knew about the offending feature but failed to appreciate the potential danger (s.58(2)(d)) because it was not assessed in relation to cyclists.

In *Papworth v. Battersea Corporation (No.2)*[29] the claimant fell off her bicycle when she cycled over a sewer grating inserted below road level. The sewer grating and framework were laid so as to cause a considerable depression in the road but the work was done with due care and skill in accordance with current road construction practice. It was held that although there was a defect in that the depression in which the grating was situated was excessive, which was dangerous to a careful cyclist, the local authority were not negligent in not having discovered the defect. The local authority had exercised due care and skill in the original construction of the grating. Thus, they were not liable through the work having subsequently turned out to be dangerous.

Example

Nicky Bailey and Laura Collins are going to a drinks party they have been invited to hosted by Christopher Walken on the King's Road. They are late, having been delayed at another party hosted by Jeremy Irons in Lots Road, Chelsea. They have had a couple of drinks at that party but are not drunk. They set off walking at speed. As they are going along Cheyne Walk, Nicky trips over a hole in the road which is two inches deep and injures herself. The hole had been caused by a monster truck being driven by rugby superstar Richard Pool-Jones who was with his wife Hannalie the day before.

Are the local authority liable for Nicky Bailey's injuries?

Safety in sports grounds legislation

The Safety at Sports Ground Act 1975 came into operation on September 1, **15.19** 1975. The Act was implemented following the Report of the inquiry into Crowd Safety at Sports Grounds ("the Wheatley Report"). The Two main provisions of the Act are:

---

[28] Unreported, September 29, 1995, CA.
[29] [1916] 1 K.B. 583.

   (a) A power exercisable by the Secretary of State, to designate sports stadiums with a capacity for more than 10,000 spectators. Once designated, a stadium will require a Safety Certificate from the local authority.

   (b) It places a duty and a responsibility upon the local authority for the issue of a General Safety Certificate to all stadiums as designated. They may include in the Certificate such terms and conditions as they deem necessary to ensure spectator safety within the stadium.

The designating order, made by the Secretary of State was on July 31, 1976.[30] This brought within the scope of the Act all stadiums that can accommodate more than 10,000 spectators. The Fire Safety and Safety at Places of Sport Act 1987 (amending the 1975 Act by removing the distinction between sports ground and sports stadium and giving the Secretary of State the power to vary by Order the minimum spectator capacity for designated grounds depending upon the class of sports ground). By virtue of the Safety of Sports Ground (Accommodation of Spectators) Order 1996,[31] which came into force on March 25, 1996 the figure of 10,000 was reduced to 5,000 for certain classes of ground. The class of sports ground to which this reduction was to apply consisted of sports grounds in England and Wales at which association football was played and which were occupied by a club which is a member of the Football League Limited or the Football Association Premier League Limited.

15.20   The 1987 Act strengthened the local authorities' duty to enforce the 1975 Act and regulations made under it. It also requires authorities to inspect designated sports grounds at least once every 12 months in accordance with guidance given by the Secretary of State. Guidance on the safety of spectators at sports grounds first became available when the Wheatley Report on Crowd Safety at Sports Grounds was published in 1972. That publication has been updated on several occasions following the fire at Valley Parade, Bradford, in 1985, and after the Hillsborough tragedy. The most recent edition was published in 1997 which has been extended to include the findings of recent studies into the behaviour of spectators and the knowledge of design and management issues. The Guide has no statutory force but many of its recommendations will be given force of law at individual grounds by their inclusion in Safety Certificates issued under the 1975 Act or the 1987 Act.

The Sporting Events (Control of Alcohol, etc.) Act 1985 prohibits the possession of alcohol on public transport to designated sporting matches. It is also an offence to be drunk on coaches and trains to those matches. It is an offence to attempt to enter a ground when drunk or in possession of alcohol. It is also an offence to possess or consume alcohol within view

---

[30] The Safety of Sports Grounds (Designation) Order 1976 (S.I. 1976 No. 1264).
[31] S.I. 1996 No. 499.

of the pitch during the period of the match or to be drunk during the period of the match. The police have a power to search someone reasonably suspected of committing an offence under the Act, and to arrest such a person. This can include searching coaches or trains carrying passengers to or from matches or on arrival as well as searching fans waiting to enter a ground or inside a ground.

Conclusion

The local authority has a wide range of responsibilities. Their liability in respect of accidents occurring within a sporting arena has the potential to be enormous given the huge number of accidents which occur each year. The local authority will avoid that liability by ensuring that the facilities they provide are of high quality and that they follow the advice provided to them by manufacturers, the Health and Safety Executive and sports governing bodies. **15.21**

Example

Michael Snr. and Derek, two local authority sport's liaison officers, organise a road cycle race under the aegis of the authority's "Get Sporty 2002" programme. They proposed route includes a gentle off-road section with bumps of up to 50mm. The cyclists will also travel down Fry-Trent Boulevard where the finish line is situated. There is a 15mm lip across the boulevard before the finish line. Michael Snr and Derek are aware of the lip. It is not yet the financial year-end. Consequently, Rosemary and Jeanette, in the finance department, will not release funds from their road maintenance budget to repair the road. A sign is erected at the entrance to the boulevard to warn participants of the lip. On the day of the race Michael Jnr, Jonathon, Katrina and Christopher are in a sprint for the finish line. Christopher falls when he hits the lip.

Are the Council liable?

Introduction to Chapters 16, 17 and 18: dangerous sports, field sports and watersports

"I do not participate in any sport with ambulances at the bottom of a hill."

Erma Bombeck.

The following three Chapters deal, broadly speaking, with liabilities arising from sports that are inherently dangerous and that take place "outdoors" —that is to say outside the confines of a small, well-defined and privately owned arena. Such activities share many of the legal characteristics of "spectator" sports such as football, cricket and tennis but there are important distinctions too. In sports where the nature of the activity produces an inevitable and obvious danger to the life and limb of participants, third parties and animals, and where those activities are conducted on land to which the public may have unrestricted access,[1] governments have been more willing to intervene and to require minimum standards relating to equipment, training, etc. In some instances, most obviously target shooting and hunting with guns, there is an essential overlap with general criminal and tort law. A further difference from sports such as football or cricket is that the element of competition may be less fundamental to the activity being carried out and therefore there may be more scope for individuals to participate without being part of any organised group or club. Further, due to the logistics involved (*e.g.* the lack of a discernible "arena", the long time-scale involved) the viewing—and therefore the commercial—potential may be less obvious. It follows that the need for safeguards is high but the ability for rules and regulations to be enforced is low due to the lack of coherent structures or universal governing bodies, and the lack of revenue from spectators, viewers or advertisers.

Chapter 16 deals with the liability of the organisers of "adventure activities" and sporting holidays while Chapter 17 examines the specific liability of water authorities to those participating in sport or leisure activities within their waters, and Chapter 18 addresses liability arising out of country sports.

---

[1] As opposed to dangerous sports in private arenas such as motor racing.

173

Chapter 16

Liability of organisers of sporting holidays and adventure activities

"I went skiing last week and broke a leg. Fortunately, it wasn't mine."

Anonymous.

This Chapter deals with the remedies for claimants injured undertaking adventure activities. As many "extreme sports" are undertaken in the context of a trip away from home (such as a surf trip), the Chapter also deals with liability of the organisers of holidays. There is not a great deal of specific law dealing with these areas, most liability issues being resolved in contract or tort, and with most safety requirements left to self-regulation. This area is likely to become increasingly important as new sports such as kitesurfing, mountain boarding and canyoning push forward the extreme frontiers ever further.

Adventure activities

Every year hundreds of thousands of people within England and Wales **16.01** participate in outdoor activities such as hill walking, caving, canoeing, potholing and mountaineering. The enormous social and physical benefits of encouraging widespread participation in such activities is obvious, yet the potential for serious injury and the associated costs (NHS treatment, mountain rescue operations, etc.) is great. Until recently, governments had not intervened by way of legislation in such pursuits, but in recent years Parliament has recognised the need for special measures to be put in place to ensure the safety of certain classes of participant in certain outdoor activities that involve an obvious threat to life and limb. In particular, the Adventure Activities Licensing Regulations 1996, made pursuant to the Activity Centres (Young Persons Safety) Act 1995, ensure that only licensed bodies may commercially provide certain outdoor activities to persons under the age of 18. The difficulty facing the government and licensing bodies is to ensure that legitimate public concerns about the safety of participants (particularly children) in activities such as skiing, water sports and mountaineering are met without severely limiting the opportunity for widespread enjoyment of such activities. The catalyst for this legislation was the tragedy that occurred in Lyme Bay in 1993.

Four sixth-form students were drowned when their canoes capsized in Lyme Bay, Dorset. The director of the activity centre responsible for their safety had been warned several months earlier by a member of staff that a serious accident was likely unless safety features were improved. He took no action, and was sentenced to four years' imprisonment as a result. The Lyme Bay tragedy provided a legal milestone in that it marked the first occasion on which a charge of corporate manslaughter was successfully brought in the United Kingdom. As well as being the first time that a director of a company had been jailed for manslaughter in such a capacity, this case sounded the death knell for unlimited self-regulation of the leisure industry. A private members' bill was introduced, leading to the legislation set out below, which effectively requires any body providing caving, climbing, trekking or watersports facilities for profit to young persons to be licensed.

The Activity Centres (Young Persons Safety) Act 1995[1]

16.02   The Act itself merely empowers (and indeed requires) the Secretary of State to make regulations in relation to Activity Centres. The preamble to the Act reads,

> "An Act to make provision for the regulation of centres and providers of facilities where children and young persons under the age of 18 engage in adventure activities, including provision for the imposition of requirements relating to safety."

Section 1(1) requires the Secretary of State to designate a licensing authority to create "such functions as may be prescribed by regulations relating to the licensing of persons providing facilities for adventure activities." Section 1(2) requires the body designated as the licensing authority to have been nominated by the Health and Safety Commission.

Section 1(3) provides that the definition of "facilities for adventure activities" is to be fixed by regulations, but that it does *not* include

(a) "facilities which are provided exclusively for persons who have attained the age of 18"; or

(b) "facilities which do not consist of, or include some element of, instruction or leadership."

Section 1(4) lists the matters as to which regulations may make provision, including the circumstances in which licences are required for the provision

---

[1] Ch. 15.

of adventure activities, requirements to be satisfied on an application for a licence, the conditions for the grant of a licence, a complaints procedure against the licensing authority and appeals against decisions of the licensing authority.

Section 2 authorises regulations to provide for offences and punishment. Section 3(3) requires the Secretary of State to consult the Health and Safety Commission and any other persons as he considers appropriate before making regulations under Section 1 and 2. In turn, section 3(4) authorises the Health and Safety Commission from time to time to submit to the Secretary of State proposals for making regulations.

The Adventure Activities Licensing Regulations 1996

Regulations were subsequently laid before Parliament in 1996. The Adven- **16.03**
ture Activities (Licensing) (Designation) Order 1996 (S.I. 1996 No. 771) designated a body (Tourism Quality Services Limited) as the licensing authority. The principal regulations, however, are the Adventure Activities Licensing Regulations 1996 (S.I. 1996 No. 772]. These introduce the scheme of licensing and inspection foreseen by the Act.

Regulation 3(1) states:

"3.—(1) Subject to paragraph (2) and regulations 15(1) and 19 a person is required to hold a licence in respect of the provision of facilities for adventure activities if that person—

(a) provides such facilities in return for payment; or
(b) is a local authority and the facilities are provided to an educational establishment in respect of the pupils of such an establishment;

and where such facilities are so provided by a person at or from more than one activity centre, and those activity centres are being operated by that person at the same time throughout any period of 28 days or more, a separate licence shall be required in respect of the facilities provided at or from each such centre."

Four broad exceptions are created by Regulation 3(2), These allow genuine members' clubs[2] and other voluntary associations, and "educational establishments"[3] to provide facilities for children and young persons who are their members or pupils. They also allow the unlicensed provision of

---

[2] Reg. 3(2)(a). This exception covers the members of other voluntary associations where there is an agreement between the organisations. Non-members may also have facilities provided to them for a maximum total of three days within any period of 12 months per person "for the purpose only of encouraging interest in its activities or attracting new members". Guests and trial memberships need not therefore lead to an application by a voluntary association for a licence. "voluntary association" is defined in regulation 2.

[3] Reg. 3(2)(b). "educational establishment" is defined in Regulation 2. Significantly, it does not include "an establishment engaged primarily in the provision of sporting, recreational or outdoor activities". This would seem to require a commercial sporting academy to apply for a licence.

activities and facilities to young persons who are accompanied by a parent or guardian during their participation in the relevant activities,[4] and the delegation of authority from one person or organisation to another under the authority of the same licence.[5]

16.04   It is to be noted that the regulations require a licence to be held for the provision of facilities for adventure activities, and not merely for the provision of the whole "activity" itself. "Adventure activity" is defined in regulation 2 as "caving, climbing, trekking or watersports"[6] (each of which terms is separately defined) and "facilities for adventure activities" is defined as facilities which consist of, or include some element of, "instruction or leadership given to one or more young persons in connection with their engagement in an adventure activity (other than instructions given solely in connection with the supply of equipment for use in such an activity)".

It is important to realise that a licence must be specific as to the facilities and activities that it covers. That is not to say that a separate application need be made by one company in respect of each activity it wishes to offer, but regulation 6(b) requires the licence to state "the facilities for adventure activities which may be provided pursuant to the licence". It would clearly fly in the face of the scheme if, for example, an application by a company specialising in the provision of canoeing facilities automatically allowed that company to offer trekking or potholing facilities. The licence must also specify the date of commencement and cessation of the licence. The duration of the licence must be no greater than three years.[7]

Applications

16.05   Once an application for a licence has been made (pursuant to regulation 4), the licensing authority is required to consider the following matters, and shall not grant a licence unless it is satisfied that the applicant has[8]—

"(i)   made a suitable and sufficient assessment of the risks to the safety of the young persons and other persons who will be engaged in the adventure activities in respect of which the application is made or whose safety may be affected thereby;

---

[4] Reg. 3(2)(c).
[5] Reg. 3(2)(d).
[6] Each of these terms is defined separately in reg. 2. Further information about licensable activities and in general is to be found at the Adventure Activities Licensing Authority's website, www.aala.org.
[7] Reg. 6(d).
[8] Reg. 5(1)(a).

(ii) identified the measures he needs to take in consequence of that assessment to ensure, so far as is reasonably practicable, the safety of those persons;

(iii) made the arrangements referred to in regulation 7(1)(a) and (b)[9];

(iv) appointed competent persons to advise him on safety matters or has competence in such matters himself."

Further, an inspection fee must be paid.[10] If the licensing authority is satisfied that the above stipulations have been met, and once it has considered a report to it by an expert appointed by the authority,[11] it then has a discretion whether to grant a licence, pursuant to regulation 5(1).

Regulation 7(1) requires the licensing authority to attach certain compulsory conditions to all licences. The key requirements are that the licence-holder should maintain facilities to review the risk assessment required by regulation 5(1),[12] and that he should maintain suitable and sufficient arrangements for the appointment of a sufficient number of qualified instructors, for the giving of safety information to instructors and participants, for the provision and maintenance in good repair of such equipment as is needed to ensure the safe performance of the activities, and for the provision of first aid and the summoning of rescue services in the event of an emergency.[13] The licence-holder must also be advised by a competent safety advisor unless he has competence in safety matters himself, ensure that the licensing authority is permitted to inspect equipment and documents, give information on request about the provision of facilities to the licensing authority, and display a copy of the licence at the activity centre. Any advertisement in which the licence-holder refers to his licence must specify the adventure activities covered.[14] Regulation 7(2) empowers the licensing authority to attach to the licence such other conditions relating to safety as it considers necessary.

Regulation 8 makes provision for revocation of a license. Regulation 14 **16.06** deals with appeals to the Secretary of State, and regulation 16 creates offences. It is an offence to do anything for which a licence is required otherwise than in accordance with a licence,[15] or to make a false statement (either deliberately or recklessly) to the licensing authority in order to obtain a licence.[16]

---

[9] See below.
[10] Reg. 5(1)(b). The amount is set out in Sched. 1 to the Regulations.
[11] Reg. 5(2) and reg. 10. Regs 5(3)–(5) require an inspection to be made before such a report is completed except where the application is for renewal of a licence and there has been an inspection in the previous year.
[12] Reg. 7(1)(a).
[13] Reg. 7(1)(b).
[14] Reg. 7(1)(c)–(g).
[15] Reg. 16(1).
[16] Reg. 16(2).

As well as exercising its statutory functions in considering applications for licences, the licensing authority issues advice and guidance to local authorities, companies and the public at large. The licensing authority is not charged with the enforcement of the regulations—this role is shared between local authorities and the Health and Safety Executive.[17]

The legislative regime is subject to a triennial review, and at the time of writing, the Department For Education and Skills website carried the following announcement (dated June 15, 2001), "The DfES reviewed the scheme during 1999 and announced that the scheme would continue subject to another triennial review in 2002. Before then, the Department will amend the Adventure Activities Licensing Regulations 1996 to simplify the operation of the scheme, to lighten the burden on small companies and to widen the scope of the scheme to include canyoning".

Detailed definitions of much of the terminology, and exceptions from the scheme are contained in the regulations.

16.07   The scheme of the legislation is aimed at the prevention of tragedies through proactive steps. That is not to say that the regulations do not have a role to play in determining civil liability when things go wrong. Although they do not apparently create any specific new cause of action, failure to attain the standards required by the regulations would be strong evidence of negligence or breach of contract, and could be pleaded as such in an action for personal injury by a participant in adventure activities against an activity centre that failed to provide a sufficient number of qualified instructors, for example. Arguably, the licensing authority could be held liable for negligently issuing a licence where it ought to have been obvious that one or more of the conditions specified in regulation 5 or regulation 7 had not been complied with, yet a licence was granted or renewed.

Outdoor activities not regulated by Parliament

16.08   Despite the existence of these regulations it would be wrong to suppose that the majority of outdoor activities that involve an obvious risk of injury are now subject to statutory control. In fact, the opposite is true. Adventure activity providers may be covered by the requirements of general health and safety legislation but the 1995 Act and 1996 regulations remain the only example of legislation that specifically regulates a class of outdoor sports in the U.K.

Many obviously dangerous pursuits such as kitesurfing,[18] canyoning, hang-gliding or paragliding may be undertaken by any person who has the means to participate in them, and organisations may provide equipment and facilities without being monitored by any regulatory regime. Although

---

[17] Reg. 17 and The Adventure Activities (Enforcing Authority and Licensing Amendment) Regulations (S.I. 1996 No. 1647).
[18] For which see www.ukkiteboardingcentre.com.

organising bodies do exist to provide information, training and assistance in activities such as paragliding, broadly speaking these are private bodies (either limited companies, or unincorporated associations such as members' clubs) and they are not charged with duties of inspection, licensing or supervision of those members of the public who participate in the relevant sport or activity.

There is therefore no requirement that any person who flies a para-glider should have received any training, registered with any regulatory body or acquired insurance to cover the risks that might arise to himself or any third parties. That is not to say that bodies offering training and providing equipment do not owe a duty of care to participants with whom they have contact. If a company or unincorporated association hires a defective canoe, hang-glider or safety harness to a person who is injured as a result, or negligently instructs him in the use of such equip-ment then the company or unincorporated association may be liable to him under the common law of contract and/or negligence, or by reference to general health and safety, sale of goods, supply of goods and services, and other related legislation.

Further, there is no limitation upon private individuals participating in any of the activities covered by the 1996 Regulations, and even involving their children in such activities. Generally, safety in the outdoor activity industry relies upon a mixture of self-regulation through clubs, voluntary associations and the like, and best practice from individuals. **16.09**

It is interesting to compare obviously dangerous and unregulated activ-ities such as hang-gliding and paragliding with similar activities that are subject to very strict regulatory regimes. The case of *Disley v. Levine (trading as Airtrack Levine Paragliding)*[19] illustrates the potential practical effect of the lack of regulation. The claimant was under instruction on a tandem paraglider when she was injured. The Court of Appeal unanimously held that a tandem paraglider was not an aircraft governed by the Carriage by Air Acts (Application of Provisions) Order 1967. The claimant's claim was therefore not statute-barred by the provisions of the Order and she was entitled to claim damages in contract and negligence. The operation and maintenance of aircraft (including microlights) are strictly regulated. Licens-ing schemes exist whereby certain institutions run training courses and issue licences for paragliding, hang-gliding and the like, but these organisations do not discharge statutory functions and they represent an example of self-regulation of an inherently dangerous sphere of activities.

In general, then, the law applicable to accidents arising out of most outdoor activities will be the common law of contract and tort. Suppliers of equipment and providers of training may have liabilities under the Sale of Goods Act 1979 and the Supply of Goods and Services Act 1995, and in the common law of negligence, if a person is injured as a result of their defective

---

[19] Unreported, July 11, 2001, CA.

gear or incompetent instruction. The Unfair Contract Terms Act 1977 and the Unfair Terms in Consumer Contracts Regulations 1999 severely restrict the ability of suppliers of goods and services to exclude or limit liability for death and personal injury.

16.10   An example of a situation in which self-regulation has led to a coherent and well publicised set of rules that are internationally accepted is alpine skiing. The International Skiing Federation (FIS)[20] has a 10-point safety code to which all skiers are expected to adhere. Rather similar in legal effect to the Highway Code in road traffic cases, it gives guidance as to the steps that a skier should take to avoid accidents and contains rules and guidance on matters such as overtaking and entering marked ski runs. In this way it is a useful guide in determining liability between participants for accidents caused on the slopes.

His Honour Judge Bowsher Q.C. considered the FIS rules in analysing liability for a skiing accident in the recent case of *Lyon v. Maidment*,[21] in which it was found as a matter of fact that the defendant who was skiing downhill behind the claimant did not cause the claimant to fall and injure himself.

An interesting recent case involving a skiing accident (but not the FIS rules) was *Chittock v. Woodbridge School I*[22] in which the court decided that a school was liable to a pupil injured when he disobeyed clear instructions not to ski off-piste, resulting in his suffering serious injuries. Although the court acknowledged the claimant's negligence in disobeying these safety instruction, and reduced his damages by 50 per cent, it nonetheless found the school liable in negligence for failing to prevent the pupil from skiing following earlier breaches of discipline. This decision was reversed by the Court of Appeal in a decision that has important implications for those responsible for the well-being of children engaged in any activities that involve an element of risk. The court held that the teacher had not been negligent in issuing a severe reprimand and accepting assurances from his 17-year-old pupils as to their future conduct. In so holding, the court considered that this course of action fell within a reasonable range of responses from a teacher in that situation. This approach recognises the need for teachers to have a discretion and to be able to exercise that discretion in disciplinary matters with reference to their own professional experience and expertise, particularly when dealing with older pupils. Further it strikes a balance between the need to protect children under the care of a school and the daily reality of having to deal with young people in potentially dangerous situations. The court went on to find, in any event, that any negligence of which the teacher may have been culpable could not properly be said to have caused the accident.

---

[20] www.fis-ski.com.
[21] [2002] EWHC 1227.
[22] *The Times*, July 15, 2002.

Holiday law

One further avenue of recourse for claimants injured in adventure activities on an overnight trip or holiday might be the Package Travel, Package Holiday, and Package Tours Regulations 1992 (S.I. 1992 No. 3288). Pursuant to these regulations, any business selling a package tour or holiday to a consumer has a potential liability to that consumer arising out of improper performance of that contract. This can include liability for the acts and/or omissions of third parties (*i.e.* those retained by a tour operator or travel agent to provide services and facilities to the consumer). In this regard, see the decision of the Court of Appeal in *Hone v. Going Places Leisure Travel Limited*[23] in which the travel agent was held to be a party to the contract, not merely the agent of the tour operator.

16.11

Liability is not strict, but the effect of the regulations is to give the holidaymaker a remedy against a vendor who may have little or no direct control over the act or omission that causes the injury or loss to the consumer. Holidaymakers therefore have remedies against the negligent act and/or breach of contract of the organisers, retailers and suppliers of package holidays.

The remedy for vendors, of course, is to put in place proper arrangements for indemnity and insurance with their suppliers, and to use only reputable suppliers. In the case of a foreign holiday booked in the U.K., the holidaymaker is given the added advantage of being able to bring an action against a company in the U.K. rather than pursuing a Turkish airline or a Spanish hotel. A "package" means:

> "the pre-arranged combination of at least two of [accommodation, travel and other tourist services] offered at an inclusive price and when the service covers a period of more than twenty four hours or includes overnight accommodation."[24]

The onus is on the claimant to prove that there has been improper performance.

Of course, tour operators owe duties to customers under the general law of contract independently of the regulations[25] and there is scope for the courts to award general damages for disappointment, distress and the like to the customer and to members of his family[26] (and, presumably, any other travelling companions on whose behalf he contracts).

16.12

---

[23] *The Times*, August 6, 2001.
[24] Reg. 2.
[25] *Jarvis v. Swan Tours Ltd* [1973] QB 233.
[26] *Jarvis v. Swan Tours Ltd* (above); *Jackson v. Horizon Holidays Ltd* [1975] 1 W.L.R. 1468.

Example

Adventurer Richard Waddams organised a package tour to Portugal for surfers Lawrence and Elizabeth Dick in which he guaranteed them "awesome and consistent waves". He organised their flights on the low cost Michael Pritchett Airlines, their accommodation at the James Roccelli Hotel in Sagres and their food at the German bar near the coast, run by top vegetarian chef Katie Langdon who lives there with her daughter Hannah. The waves were to be served up at the "secret spot" known to locals as "Punta Puiva". Unfortunately, during their week long stay, whilst the weather was beautiful the high pressures which caused it meant that there were no waves.

Could Lawrence and Elizabeth Dick sue Richard Waddams under the Package Travel, Package Holiday, and Package Tours Regulations 1992?

Volenti non fit injuria

16.13　The comments earlier in this book relating to the defence of *volenti non fit injuria* also apply in the field of extreme sports and adventure activities. When a man takes off on a hang-glider he consents to the risk of falling if the wind is too strong or if he fails to control the contraption in accordance with his training and instruction, but he cannot be taken to consent to the hang-glider falling apart because of negligent maintenance, or to the risk of injury because he has been incompetently instructed.

Similarly, a participant in paintballing consents to being painfully hit by paint-pellets hitting him at high velocity. He does not consent to being blinded by such a pellet because the goggles provided to him were not sufficiently strong to absorb a direct hit.

It should be noted that the much-publicised death of Kenneth Costin in January 2001 was found by the coroner to have occurred after Mr Costin, who had a pre-disposition to debilitating migraines, "undertook a sudden and unexpected manoeuvre which on the balance of probabilities set off a train of unexpected and unforeseen events which on the balance of probabilities exacerbated his underlying migraine . . . ". The coroner allowed his findings to be published. He did not specifically find that the sudden and unexpected manoeuvre was being hit by a paintball, although he did record a verdict of misadventure.[27]

Generally, paintballing is regulated only by British Standards relating to the weapons themselves, although rapid-fire or particularly high velocity weapons are capable of falling foul of the Firearms Act.[28]

---

[27] For more information, visit the United Kingdom Paintball Sports Federation Website, www.ukpsf.com.

[28] For further information about the impact of this Act upon sporting activity see Chapter 18.

Chapter 17

Liability of public authorities for water-related injuries and illness

"If I say it's safe to surf, it's safe to surf."

Robert Duvall, Apocalypse Now.

Introduction

This Chapter discusses the potential liabilities that may arise in the context **17.01** of watersports with an emphasis on the liability of water authorities and other bodies that are involved in waste management. Injuries caused by negligent management and control of motor boats, jet-skis and the like fall to be considered under the general law of tort, considered earlier in this book. Maritime law may apply in some circumstances, but that is beyond the scope of this work.

Just as an occupier of land may be responsible for injuries caused in consequence of the condition of his land,[1] so too the organisation responsible for a body of water may be liable for injury or illness caused by the condition of the water. Further, the law imposes duties upon potential polluters to ensure that bodies of water are not excessively contaminated. Participants in watersports such as surfing are inevitably in close contact with the water itself, and therefore at risk of illness if that water is contaminated by hazardous substances.

The reader is specifically referred to the web-site of Surfers Against Sewage,[2] an organisation which has done more than any other in this country to help clean up our coastline.

While there is no specific legislation to protect surfers, swimmers and sailors, in recent years the courts have applied general environmental protection legislation in a way that may serve the interests of participants in other watersports. The emphasis in the case law has been on the "public law" duties owed by water authorities and potential polluters rather than the right to compensation of participants. There exists a clear social need to dispose of waste in some way, and arguably in the sea in particular.

---

[1] Occupier's Liability Act 1957, see Chap. 5 above.
[2] At www.sas.org.uk.

The problem and potential solutions

17.02   There is much circumstantial evidence that bathers and surfers have fallen gravely ill as a result of pollution in the sea. In 1999 Heather Preen died having contracted the E.coli bacteria having been bathing off the coast at Dawlish. Other children bathing at the same time also contracted the bacteria. For many years there has been concern about the health of surfers, with some surveys suggesting that surfers are three times as likely to contract the hepatitis A virus as the ordinary population.

On their web-site, Surfers Against Sewage describe the problem in the following way[3]:

> "The aquatic environment has traditionally been viewed as a bottomless pit for human derived waste and bodies of water have been (and in some places still are) rated for their ability to dilute and disperse this waste. Many different types of waste enter the water from numerous sources. SAS focus on the 300 million gallons of raw or partially treated sewage discharged around the UK coastline each day and the two million tonnes of toxic waste dumped into the sea every year.
>
> It is an unavoidable fact of nature that humans produce waste, so there will always be a continuous supply of sewage requiring disposal. Similarly, toxic chemicals that are by-products of industrial processes also require disposal. The amounts of these chemicals can be minimised, and in some cases alternatives found, but the reality is that these substances will continue to be a problem until the general public use their power as consumers to create a demand for change.

> *Sewage*

> In many countries, sewage treatment and disposal is primitive and whatever goes down the toilet washes up on the beach or along the banks of rivers. This was the situation in the UK before the Surfers against Sewage campaign. Now it is changing, but there is more work still to be done.
>
> Treating the sewage, as is becoming more widespread, adds another factor. Treatment separates the solids from the liquid (which will be further treated), but the solid component, the sludge, still requires disposal. A large amount of UK-produced sludge used to be dumped at sea, but since December 1998 this disposal route has been legally closed.

> *The Problem Simplified*

> The majority of homes in the UK are linked to mains sewers. Everything that goes into the drains, bleach, chemicals from domestic products, paint and solvents, oils and fats and everything that is flushed down the loo will end up in the sewerage system.
>
> The result is a complex mixture of liquids and solids, a "faecal soup", which could end up in the seas and rivers if it isn't adequately treated before being discharged.

---

[3] See www.sas.org.uk/campaign/theproblem.asp.

Faecal Soup: the Ingredients

sewage related debris (SRD)
bacteria and viruses found in the human intestine
chemicals and heavy metals from household and beauty products
nutrients (nitrates and phosphates)
endocrine disrupting substances
oils, fats and greases

Chemicals

It isn't widely known, but sewage treatment processes (with the possible exception of microfiltration) are not designed to remove chemicals from sewage discharges. These substances enter the sewage system from households, offices, public places, light and heavy industry and medical establishments.

Products in every day use in the home can contain a vast array of chemicals and organic compounds that are flushed, washed away after bathing or showering, or disposed of directly into the drains. Industrial discharges are limited by consents that allow controlled amounts of specified substances into the sewerage system. All are perfectly legal discharges.

Once in the system these contaminants combine together, making it even harder to predict their effects when they enter the environment. Many of these substances are persistant and have a tendency to bioaccumulate. This means that they will remain in the environment indefinitely, either in the water column itself or in the flesh and fat of organisms."

They also suggest what is the solution to the problem[4]:

"In 1990 when the campaign began, SAS believed that it was vital not simply to protest, but also to provide answers to the problem of sewage pollution. The organization aimed to be 'solution-based' providing solutions that were both environmentally friendly and cost effective.

To provide impetus for the improvements that were required at sites all around the UK, SAS had to focus on three key areas. The first was to make the general public aware of the problems and so create a demand for improvements.

Once the Government became aware of the strength of the nation's desire for clean, safe beaches, SAS' next task was to ensure that those in power were provided with accurate information.

Finally, as the legislation that determines the quality of UK rivers and beaches originates in Europe, it was essential to assess the effectiveness of this legislation and to inform key E.U. decision makers of errors and inadequacies.

Irrespective of legislative demands and water company promises, full treatment (in line with recommendations of the House of Commons Select Committee 1999) is the only solution. SAS call for 'end of pipe' standards, which means that sewage must be fully treated before it is discharged making the effluent in the outfall pipe (and the aquatic environment) clean and safe."

---

[4] See www.sas.org.uk/campaign/solution.asp.

As well as these changes, there are remedies which can be sought through the courts. In particular, there are three sources of public law duties on authorities in respect of the quality of water: domestic legislation, Community Law and the European Convention on Human Rights.

Domestic public law duties

17.03   The relevant authorities are not merely water authorities, but can also include local authorities, private bodies that process waste and sewage and the government. There is a complex web of statutory liabilities that can be roughly summarised as follows:

1. Sewage treatment plants have duties relating to the effective treatment of that sewage and are potentially liable for any escape of that sewage;

2. A water authority has a duty to monitor/control sewage and take appropriate steps to treat it. It may have permission (or "consent") to discharge sewage into the sea subject to conditions.

3. Local authorities have duties in relation to waters owned/controlled by them to take steps against polluters if the pollution causes a statutory nuisance;

4. Government agencies may have duties to make regulations about means in which discharge is controlled/released, issue "consents" to water authorities and attach conditions to those consents.

Two leading cases demonstrate the inter-relation of these duties and deal in particular with the duty on a local authority under sections 79 and 80 of the Environmental Protection Act 1990 ("EPA") to inspect its land for statutory nuisances, as defined by section 79, and to serve an abatement notice on the person responsible for the nuisance once that nuisance is detected. In both of the cases set out below, the party allegedly responsible for the creation of the statutory nuisance was a water authority discharging sewage into open waters pursuant to a consent granted by the National Rivers Authority (NRA). The only provisions of section 79 that would appear capable of defining statutory nuisances that might arise in the context of bodies of water are section 79(1)(e) that specifies that "any accumulation or deposit which is prejudicial to health or a nuisance", and section 79(1)(h) that refers to "any other matter declared by any statute to be a statutory nuisance".

R. v. Carrick D.C., ex p. Shelley

17.04   In the case of *R. v. Carrick D.C., ex p. Shelley*[5] the decision of the local authority not to serve an abatement notice on the water authority under

---

[5] *The Times*, April 15, 1996; [1996] Env.L.R. 273 at 277–278.

section 80 of the Environmental Protection Act 1990 ("EPA") was challenged on judicial review on behalf of two mothers of young children in the area. The local authority had a duty, pursuant to section 80, to serve an abatement notice on a person responsible for causing a "statutory nuisance", defined as including: "any accumulation or deposit which is prejudicial to health or a nuisance" (s.79(1)(e)). The question of who is responsible for causing the statutory nuisance is a question of fact, as is the question whether a statutory nuisance exists. In each case this will be a question of expert evidence based upon the monitoring of the relevant beach or waterway.

It appears that it was accepted by the parties in *Carrick DC, ex p. Shelley* that condoms and sanitary products would fall within this definition. It was certainly accepted by the Judge. The difficulty facing the local council was that it was reluctant to serve an abatement notice on the water authority when the water authority could have challenged that decision in the magistrates' court (a statutory avenue of appeal). The local council decided that it would not be "appropriate" to serve a notice on the water authority. It seems that it took into account the fact that the water authority had complied with the conditions attached to its consent from the NRA, and the fact that the deposit of condoms and sanitary products was affected by tidal conditions that were beyond the control of the water authority.

That is not to suggest that the local council did not take the pollution problem seriously; it merely weighed up competing factors and decided against the service of an abatement notice. This decision-making process was the nub of the case. Carnwarth J. decided (correctly, it is submitted) that the local council had no discretion to exercise. Once it had determined that there was a statutory nuisance and had identified the person responsible for it, it had no option but to serve an abatement notice. He stated,

"the issue under s.80 is one of fact, not discretion. So far as the decision to serve an abatement notice is concerned, if the authority are satisfied on the balance of probabilities that there is a statutory nuisance, they have a duty to serve a notice.

(2) that duty is not affected by any action of the NRA under the Acts relating to them. They are separate duties. If there is a statutory nuisance on the beach that is a matter for the District Council, even if it is caused by discharges from outfalls within the jurisdiction of the NRA."

The factual question whether the local authority's decision that there was a statutory nuisance was correct would fall to be decided on any appeal by the water authority. It was irrelevant that the water authority was acting in compliance with the conditions attached to its consent. The local authority had asked itself the wrong question and the application for judicial review was allowed.

This decision is a potentially powerful weapon for pressure groups such as Surfers Against Sewage. If they can collate information about pollution in an area, so as to show that a statutory nuisance exists then the local authority, once satisfied that the statutory nuisance does in fact exist, has no option but to serve an abatement notice on the water authority. For this reason, the decision places an onerous duty upon water authorities to take steps to ensure that items such as condoms and sanitary towels are not discharged into waters from which they are likely to be washed onto beaches.

Regina v. Falmouth and Truro Port Health Authority, ex p. South West Water Ltd

17.05   The scope of *Carrick D.C., ex p. Shelley* is limited by the decision of the Court of Appeal in *Regina v. Falmouth and Truro Port Health Authority, ex p. South West Water Ltd.*[6] In this case the Court of Appeal decided that an area of the river Fal known as the "Carrick Roads" did not constitute a "watercourse" for the purposes of section 79(h) of the EPA and section 259(1)(a) of the Public Health Act 1936. The public health authority had served an abatement notice on the water authority under section 80 of the Act on the basis, as explained by Simon Brown L.J., that,

> "Section 79(1) of the 1990 Act, as amended by section 2 of the Noise and Statutory Nuisance Act 1993, specifies matters which constitute 'statutory nuisances'. They include, under paragraph (h), 'any other matter declared by any enactment to be a statutory nuisance'. That brings in section 259(1)(a) of the Public Health Act 1936, as amended by the 1990 Act, which provides:
>
> > 'The following matters shall be statutory nuisances for the purposes of Part III of the Environmental Protection Act 1990, that is to say—(a) any pond, pool, ditch, gutter or watercourse which is so foul or in such a state as to be prejudicial to health or a nuisance . . . '

The judgment of Hale L.J., with which the court unanimously agreed, was that, after consideration of the legislative history of section 259(1) of the 1936 Act a watercourse could not be said to include a body of water as wide as the Carrick Roads. Hale L.J. stated specifically,

> "by no linguistic contortions can a 'watercourse' be made to include the open sea."

The effect of this decision means that the only relevant "statutory nuisance" under section 79 applicable to the open sea would be section 79(1)(e). The requirement for a "deposit" tends to suggest that the relevant area would be land, not the water itself. However, it must be arguable that an "accumulation" of a particular sort of waste or chemical within a given area of water could constitute a nuisance under section 79(1)(e).

---

[6] [2000] Q.B. 445.

Carrrick D.C., ex p. Shelly was also distinguished in the *Falmouth and Truro Port Health Authority* case on the basis that consultation and resultant delay by the local authority before serving an abatement notice would not of themselves place the authority in breach of its duties under section 80 of the EPA.

Potential civil liability of public authorities

It is submitted that the decision in *Carrick D.C., ex p. Shelley* is unlikely to   **17.06** give rise to actions for damages against local authorities for failing to serve an abatement notice. The duty under section 80 of the EPA does not specifically create any civil liability and therefore a surfer contracting a disease as a result of such a failure would be unable to found an action upon that section of the Act. The burden of proving that a local authority had been negligent in deciding that a sewage outlet did not cause a statutory nuisance would necessarily be high.

Further, there are strong policy reasons (the need to dispose of waste in an effective way, the financial constraints on public bodies, the existence of a statutory regime for regulation) why neither the NRA nor the relevant water authority is likely to be found to owe a duty of care to ensure that water in which bathers swim or surf is not so contaminated as to be likely to cause disease. This is reflected in the sympathy Carnwath J. had with the local authority's predicament. Alternatively, if a duty of care does exist, it would be difficult to prove breach of that duty where the water authority had complied with the conditions of its consent, and the NRA had carried out a proper assessment of the proposed outlet before granting or renewing any consent and conditions. Following the decision of the House of Lords in *Hunter v. Canary Wharf*[7] it is highly unlikely that a bather or surfer would be able to sue for damages in nuisance, having no proprietary interest in the water. A local authority owning a beach may lack motivation to sue for nuisance for reasons of cost and policy. However, it is possible to envisage the owners of a private beach or of a house with land backing onto a body of water bringing a successful action in nuisance if condoms, sanitary products, etc. were being washed up onto its land. Further, in the case of a disastrous spillage or a complete disregard by the relevant public authority it might be possible to bring an action in negligence. In extreme circumstances an action for misfeasance in public office might also arise.

European Community law

Directive 76/160/EEC

There are two directives that are particularly relevant in determining water   **17.07** quality. Directive 76/160, incorporated into U.K. law by The Bathing Waters

---

[7] [1997] 2 W.L.R. 684.

(Classification) Regulations 1991,[8] set out minimum mandatory standards of water cleanliness where an area has been designated as bathing waters. There is a duty upon the government (exercised by the National Rivers Authority) to test such waters for compliance with the prescribed standards between May and September each year. The European Commission is currently reviewing Directive 76/160, according to its website.[9]

Directive 91/217/EEC (amended by Directive 98/15/EEC)

17.08   Directive 91/217 (amended by Directive 98/15) requires Member States to put in place systems of waste water collection from domestic and light industrial premises in any urban area (where the population is in excess of 2000), to provide treatment facilities and to regulate the discharge of all urban waste water and industrial waste. Generally, waste has to be subject to "secondary treatment" (biological treatment) but the requirements are to be more stringent in designated "sensitive areas".

R. v. National Rivers Authority, ex p. Moreton

17.09   In the case of *R. v. National Rivers Authority, ex p. Moreton*[10] the applicant, a frequent swimmer in the Tenby region, sought to challenge the decision of the NRA to allow the water authority to discharge sewage from its works in Tenby. She alleged that the water authority had wrongly taken into account the water authority's budget, had failed to have regard to Directive 76/160 and had misunderstood Directive 91/271. In dismissing her application for judicial review, Harrison J. decided that the applicant had failed to demonstrate that the NRA had failed to follow Directive 76/160 or that it had misunderstood Directive 91/271. Further, the NRA was entitled to have regard to the water authority's budget. Nonetheless, the case demonstrates that the NRA has a duty to comply with the directives, that swimmers have sufficient standing to bring a claim for judicial review of its decisions and that a water authority (along with the NRA) may have to reconsider its plans if it can be shown that it has not acted in accordance with E.U. law.

European Convention of Human Rights ("ECHR")

Article 8 of the ECHR

17.10   The European Convention on Human Rights, to which the courts in the U.K. must now have regards pursuant to the Human Rights Act 1998, may

---

[8] S.I. 1991 No. 1597.
[9] http://europa.eu.int/water.
[10] [1996] Env. L.R. 234.

assist those directly affected by pollution. Article 8 of the Convention provides:

> "1. Everyone has the right to respect for his private and family life, his home and his correspondence.
>
> 2. There shall be no interference by a public authority with the exercise of this right except such as is in accordance with the law and is necessary in a democratic society in the interests of national security, public safety or the economic well-being of the country, for the prevention of disorder or crime, for the protection of health or morals, or for the protection of the rights and freedoms of others."

Guerra & ors v. Italy

It has been held by the European Court of Human Rights in *Guerra & ors*   **17.11**
v. Italy[11] that, where the applicants lived a kilometre away from a factory that produced fertilisers and other chemical compounds and in the course of its production cycle the factory released large quantities of inflammable gas—a process which could have led to explosive chemical reactions, releasing highly toxic substances—and sulphur dioxide, nitric oxide, sodium, ammonia, metal hydrides, benzoic acid and above all, arsenic trioxide,

> "The direct effect of the toxic emissions on the applicants' right to respect for their private and family life means that Article 8 is applicable."[12]

In that case 150 people had been hospitalised on account of acute arsenic poisoning. following an explosion at the factory in 1976. The Court went on to hold that

> "Italy cannot be said to have 'interfered' with the applicants' private or family life; they complained not of an act by the State but of its failure to act. However, although the object of Article 8 is essentially that of protecting the individual against arbitrary interference by the public authorities, it does not merely compel the State to abstain from such interference: in addition to this primarily negative undertaking, there may be positive obligations inherent in effective respect for private or family life (see the *Airey v. Ireland* judgment of October 9, 1979, Series A no. 32, p. 17, § 32)."

This is an important point, as it renders public bodies liable for breaches of Article 8 where they have not caused the breach but have failed to prevent it.

---

[11] (1998) 26 E.H.R.R. 357; see also *Lopez-Ostra v. Spain* (1995) 20 E.H.R.R. 277.
[12] *Guerra & ors v. Italy* (1998) 26 E.H.R.R. 357.

Article 8.2

17.12 Contracting States to the ECHR are protected by Art 8.2 where a breach by them of an individual's rights pursuant to Article 8 cab be justified by reference to one of the factors set out in Article 8.2. The question is whether an interference is lawful *and* proportionate. This requires a "balancing" exercise to be carried out by the relevant public authority. The public authority is given the additional protection of a "margin of appreciation" in conducting this balancing exercise. In the case of *Lopez-Ostra v. Spain*[13] the European Court of Human Rights held that, while the existence of a tannery in a Spanish town was beneficial to the economic well-being of the town (a relevant factor under Article 8.2) this did not outweigh the right to private life. The Court held,

> "Naturally, severe environmental pollution may affect individuals' well-being and prevent them from enjoying their homes in such a way as to affect their private and family life adversely, without, however, seriously endangering their health.
>
> Whether the question is analysed in terms of a positive duty on the State—to take reasonable and appropriate measures to secure the applicant's rights under paragraph 1 of Article 8 (art. 8.1)—, as the applicant wishes in her case, or in terms of an 'interference by a public authority' to be justified in accordance with paragraph 2 (art. 8.2), the applicable principles are broadly similar. In both contexts regard must be had to the fair balance that has to be struck between the competing interests of the individual and of the community as a whole, and in any case the State enjoys a certain margin of appreciation. The State did not succeed in striking a fair balance between the interest of the town's economic well-being—that of having a waste-treatment plant—and the applicant's effective enjoyment of her right to respect for her home and her private and family life."

Other relevant principles

17.13 There are three questions to be answered in deciding whether an individual has a good Article 8 claim;

(1) Applicability—is Article 8 engaged? That is to say, can the individual identify which rights may be contravened and bring these within the scope of Article 8?

(2) Is there a breach of Article 8—have those rights been contravened?

(3) Can that breach by justified under Article 8.2 by the public authority—balancing and the margin of appreciation are relevant. The public body may well seek to argue that it is necessary in the interests of public health/economic well-being to dump waste at sea.

---

[13] (1995) 20 E.H.R.R. 277.

Other relevant articles

In *Lopez-Ostra* the Court rejected the contention that the applicant's right   **17.14**
under Article 3 (protection from inhumane or degrading treatment) had
been violated. The threshold for treatment to contravene Article 3 is a high
one. That is not to say that in some circumstances (*e.g.* where a person
becomes severely ill as a result of exposure to pollution) Article 3 will not
be engaged. It is important to note that, whereas a public authority may
justify a breach under Article 8, the protection afforded to individuals by
Article 3 is absolute, and cannot be justified.

In *Guerra v. Italy* it was held that Article 10 (which "basically prohibits
a government from restricting a person from receiving information that
others wish or may be willing to impart to him", according to the Court) did
not apply so as to render the state liable for withholding information
pertaining to the factory.

Conclusion

The law in this area has developed only relatively recently with an increased
awareness of the need to look after the health of our seas and coastline.
With the work of organisations such as Surfers Against Sewage it looks
likely that it is set to develop further in the future both through legislation
from Europe and in the U.K. as well as through the courts.

Chapter 18

Liability involving country sports

"We'll be talking to a gunsmith who's invented a sage-and-onion bullet that shoots the goose and stuffs it at the same time."

The Two Ronnies, BBC TV.

Introduction

Even the most casual observer of current affairs will be aware of the continuing controversy surrounding the question whether fox hunting ought to be made illegal. While this issue undoubtedly has a legal aspect, it is better characterised as a political dispute. As will be seen throughout this Chapter, decisions by local authorities with regard to the legality of hunting on their land have formed the subject of much litigation over recent years. However, the purpose of this Chapter is to examine the circumstances in which liability for personal injuries is likely to arise out of field sports, and the relationship between such situations and situations giving rise to liability that have been discussed earlier in this book. Clearly, different legal principles apply when deciding the liability of a hunt for personal injury caused by the dogs of the hunt than apply in the case of a professional footballer involved in an over-zealous tackle on an opponent. In may ways, liability arising out of country sports is less of a distinct subject than liability arising out of competitive professional sports. However, the potential for serious injury is likely to be just as great.

18.01

Shooting

The use of firearms is—for obvious reasons—heavily regulated by statute. The principal source of prohibition on firearms is to be found in the Firearms Act 1968. This has been amended by the Firearms Act 1982 and, rather more controversially, by the two Firearms (Amendment) Acts of 1997. The 1997 legislation was enacted in response to the Dunblane massacre and its purpose was to drastically restrict the availability of handguns. The first of the two Acts[1] was one of the last statutes enacted by John

18.02

---

[1] Ch. 5.

Major's Conservative government. While it added handguns (any gun with a barrel length of less than 30 centimetres or a total length of less than 60 centimetres) to a list of weapons for which an absolute prohibition existed (along with automatic weapons), it left open the possibility of special permits for target shooting with small calibre pistols. The Labour Government took power in May 1997 and subsequently enacted the Firearms (Amendment) (No. 2) Act 1997[2] which removed the exemption for small calibre pistols. The effect of this was a total ban on handguns in the U.K.[3] One drastic sporting consequence was the closure of pistol shooting clubs. This has had the unfortunate effect of preventing British sportsmen and women from practising target shooting in the U.K. Shooting will be allowed at the Commonwealth Games in 2002, but the British team has had to train abroad.[4] As for shotguns and rifles, a firearms certificate is required for the legal ownership of such a weapon. Such certificates are granted by the Police. An applicant has to show necessity for such a weapon. Use for sport (such as clay pigeon shooting) may be a good reason.

Once a certificate has been obtained there is no requirement for a shooter to register with any governing body in order to carry out competitive shooting. Anyone with a licence can, it seems, organise a clay pigeon shot on his own land. Other competitors may use guns owned by the person with the certificate without any requirement of registration. Clearly, if a shooter injures a third party as a result of his own negligence he will be personally liable to that third party in damages. It is possible to envisage circumstances where the owner would be liable to the third party for injury caused by a person using the owner's gun (for instance if the shooter was known to be a bad shot, irresponsible or visually impaired, or if the gun has a defect of which the owner was or ought to have been aware). Owners are therefore well advised to enter into insurance policies covering loss or damage to third parties (as are their guests). The general law of negligence is to be applied to injuries caused in this way, as is the law on vicarious liability and employers' liability.

Hunting

18.03   In Britain this usually refers to hunting with dogs rather than shooting. Hare coursing, fox hunting and stag hunting are some of the most popular activities. It currently seems likely that a "middle way" licensing scheme will be introduced in respect of hunting with dogs. While this area is ripe for political and philosophical debate about freedom of the individual and the rights of animals, these are not particularly germane to personal injury law.

---

[2] Ch. 67.
[3] With the exception of Northern Ireland.
[4] See the article by Kate Hoey, Labour MP for Vauxhall and former Minister for Sport, "Why David Blunkett is shooting himself in the foot", *The Guardian*, December 17, 2001.

There is plenty of judicial authority relating to the use of land for hunting[5] and to what constitutes cruelty to animals in particular situations.[6] This, however, is not particularly relevant to the issue of liability for personal injuries. Once again, the general common law of negligence will apply. However, it is worth examining two particular areas in particular—liability for injuries caused by animals (such as horses and hounds) and liability of and to trespassers.

Animals

As a general proposition, the owner or keeper of an animal has a potential liability in negligence or nuisance for the actions of that animal. However, the common law position is supplemented by the provisions of the Animals Act 1971. The Act imposes strict liability (*i.e.* liability without the need for evidence of negligence) in respect of damage caused by certain types of animal. It also sets up specific defences.[7] Section 2(1) of the Act provides,   **18.04**

> "Where any damage is caused by an animal which belongs to a dangerous species, any person who is a keeper of the animal is liable for the damage, except as otherwise provided by this Act."

The phrase "dangerous species" is defined in section 6(1) as follows,

> "A dangerous species is a species—
>
> (a) which is not commonly domesticated in the British Islands; and
> (b) whose fully grown animals normally have such characteristics that they are likely, unless restrained, to cause severe damage or that any damage they may cause is likely to be severe."

This is unlikely to apply in hunting cases. Of more practical importance is section 2(2) which provides that,

> "(2) Where damage is caused by an animal which does not belong to a dangerous species, a keeper of the animal is liable for the damage, except as otherwise provided by this Act, if—
>
> (a) the damage is of a kind which the animal, unless restrained, was likely to cause or which, if caused by the animal, was likely to be severe; and
> (b) the likelihood of the damage or of its being severe was due to characteristics of the animal which are not normally found in animals of the same species

---

[5] For example, *Scott v. National Trust* [1998] 2 All E.R. 705; *R v. Somerset County Council ex parte Fewings* [1995] 1 W.L.R. 1037; [1995] 3 All E.R. 20.

[6] *Bandeira v. RSPCA* (Administrative Court, February 28, 2000, LTL, unreported elsewhere).

[7] It must be remembered that the Act is not the only avenue of recourse open to claimants and that the defences to actions under the Act will not necessarily be defences to actions brought in negligence.

or are not normally so found except at particular times or in particular circumstances; and

(c) those characteristics were known to that keeper or were at any time known to a person who at that time had charge of the animal as that keeper's servant or, where that keeper is the head of a household, were known to another keeper of the animal who is a member of that household and under the age of sixteen."

18.05 An important point in relation to this section is that the definition of species includes sub-species.[8] Therefore, an animal's propensity to bite or chase should be judged by reference to other animals within the subspecies. Although a horse cannot be defined as a dangerous animal for the purposes of section 2(1), strict liability will attach if its keeper knows that it is liable to bolt or to rear more often than others and in a dangerous manner, and such bolting or rearing causes damage.

Section 4 provides the following general defences,

"(1) A person is not liable under sections 2 to 4 of this Act for any damage which is due wholly to the fault of the person suffering it.

(2) A person is not liable under section 2 of this Act for any damage suffered by a person who has voluntarily accepted the risk thereof.

(3) A person is not liable under section 2 of this Act for any damage caused by an animal kept on any premises or structure to a person trespassing there, if it is proved either—

(a) that the animal was not kept there for the protection of persons or property; or

(b) (if the animal was kept there far the protection of persons or property) that keeping it there for that purpose was not unreasonable."

As trespass provides a complete risk under the Act in most circumstances, a trespasser injured by an animal may be better advised to bring an action in negligence.

Trespass

18.06 Huntsmen may be guilty of trespass if their animals wander onto land owned by another person and they negligently fail to prevent this.[9] In such circumstances they would be liable for any damage caused. They may injure hunt saboteurs who happen to be trespassers (whether on land owned by the hunt or by others). Alternatively, they may be injured when trespassing. One of the more controversial areas of personal injury law concerns liability to trespassers on private land. As regards occupier's liability, the position is as set out in the Occupier's Liability Act 1984, which makes it clear that a defendant will not be able to escape liability merely because the claimant is

---

[8] s.11.
[9] *League of Cruel Sports Ltd v. Scott* [1985] 3 W.L.R. 400; [1985] 2 All E.R. 489.

a trespasser where there exists *"any risk of [the trespasser] suffering injury on the premises by reason of any danger due to the state of the premises or to things done or omitted to be done on them"*[10] and (section 1(3)),

> "(3) An occupier of premises owes a duty to another (not being his visitor) in respect of any such risk as is referred to in subsection (1) above if—
>
> (a) he is aware of the danger or has reasonable grounds to believe that it exists;
> (b) he knows or has reasonable grounds to believe that the other is in the vicinity of the danger concerned or that he may come into the vicinity of the danger (in either case, whether the other has lawful authority for being in that vicinity or not); and
> (c) the risk is one against which, in all the circumstances of the case, he may reasonably be expected to offer the other some protection."

The key provision is, it is submitted, section 1(3)(c) which requires the court to take account of all the circumstances of the case. In *Revill v. Newbery*[11] the Court of Appeal held that the owner of a shed on an allotment who shot through a hole in a closed door with a shotgun, thus injuring a burglar who was attempting to break in, could properly be held to be liable for the injuries to that burglar. Their Lordships held that it was not a case in which the fact of occupation was determinative of the outcome—so the case was decided on basis of negligence rather than the Occupier's Liability Acts—but they used section 1 of the Act to assist their analysis of the duties owed by the Defendant in negligence.[12]

As regards hunt saboteurs, irrespective of whether they commit any criminal offence[13] (which will depend on the circumstances and their precise actions) they may be liable in negligence (or, indeed, the tort of trespass itself) for any injury or damage caused to horses, riders or property. They may find that any damages they would otherwise have received in negligence for injuries they might suffer in the course of their protests will be disallowed or reduced in line with the reasoning applied in *Revill v. Newbery*,[14] or indeed by reference to the defence of *volenti non fit injuria* (where they are injured by putting themselves in the path of a galloping horse). **18.07**

Conclusion

Although country sports are subject to restriction by legislation to a much greater extent than is the case with most sports, the reasons for such legislation tends to be political and not based upon any view of the activities **18.08**

---

[10] s.1(1)(a).
[11] [1996] Q.B. 567.
[12] The burglar was held to be two thirds liable and his damages were reduced accordingly..
[13] See, for example, *R v. Morpeth Ward Justices, ex p. Joseland, Ward and others, The Times,* March 4, 1992; (1992) 95 Cr.App.R. 215.
[14] Above.

in question as sports, or the importance of sport. The intervention is typically based upon feelings of moral outrage or very obvious safety concerns. Beyond such powerful legislation, and away from the corridors of power, there is in fact less structured competition in field sports than in many other sports. Legal principles involved in assessing liability for personal injuries will often be drawn from the general law of tort, although the fact that an injury or damage occurs in the course of a sport may be a relevant circumstance in determining the existence and scope of any duty of care or in apportioning liability.

Chapter 19

Liability of manufacturers/designers

"Contract: an agreement that is binding on the weaker party."

Frederick Sawyer.

Introduction

Much of this book has been concerned with liability of persons or organisa-   **19.01**
tions for acts and omissions that fit the legal definition of negligence. While
the vast majority of personal injuries suffered by participants will need to
have been caused by the negligence of another in order to attract damages,
there are other avenues of recourse in some circumstances. In particular,
when a competitor is injured (or suffers certain other loss or damage) as a
result of a defect in a piece of equipment he is using then he may have a
remedy against the manufacturer (or, potentially, against the supplier or
distributor) of that piece of equipment, even if it is not possible to show that
the manufacturer (or other person) was in any way negligent. If the injured
party has a contract with the supplier or manufacturer of the equipment
there may be an implied term on which he can rely. Relatively recent
Consumer Protection Legislation—in particular the Consumer Protection
Act 1987—(enacted primarily to give effect to European law) has supplemented the common law remedies available under general principles of
negligence (as discussed in Chapter 2, above) and the law of contract so as
to give extensive protection to consumers. A rock-climber who falls due to
a defective rope, or a goalkeeper in a hockey match who is injured because
the protective armour fails to absorb the impact of the ball may be able to
succeed in an action for damages against the manufacturer of the rope or
armour.

It is perhaps easier to envisage such situations in relation to adventure
activities and extreme sports rather than more traditional games, but as
technological advances continue to make an impact on all sports, the
importance of having the right kit increases. Bold claims are made for what
could be considered the most basic of products—such as training shoes with
"shock absorbers" and ventilation. While some such advertisements may be
aimed as much at the fashion victim as at the serious runner, it is undoubtedly important for a marathon runner to have shoes that are comfortable

and light and that absorb as much impact as possible. If such a runner pays for trainers that make such bold claims but suffers injury because the shoes do not last the distance, he may have a remedy. At the other end of the sporting spectrum, a grand prix team or driver should have a remedy in a situation where the car crashes because a component used in the gearbox or steering system fails. Proving negligence in such situations may be difficult but it is clearly in the interest of sporting participants to have a remedy.

The principles of liability for negligence will not be repeated here, having been discussed earlier in Chapter 2.

Contract

19.02 The most obvious way in which liability may arise in the absence of a finding of negligence at common law is under the law of contract. The Sale of Goods Act 1979 in itself encodes the common law as to implied terms. By section 13 of the Sale of Goods Act 1979 there is a term implied into any contract for the sale of goods that the goods will comply with the description applied to them. If a breach of this term leads to personal injury then a claimant will be able to rely upon it in an action for damages against the vendor. The description in question needs to be essential to the quality of the goods for a breach to be actionable. For instance, if a climber orders a rope of such thickness as to be able to support his weight, and the product supplied is too thin and he falls as a result, he may sue for breach of contract, relying upon an implied terms under section 13. A groundsman supplied with the incorrect type of turf or seed may sue the vendor if his football pitch "cuts up" and deteriorates rapidly as a result. However, it is worth pointing out that most sporting equipment, particularly of a sort that might lead to personal injury if defective, is of such a nature that it will generally be obvious to the purchaser if it does not meet the description.

Of more practical importance in matters relating to personal injuries are the implied terms imported by virtue of section 14 of the 1979 Act (as amended by the Sale and Supply of Goods Act 1994). Subsection 14(2) requires goods to be of "satisfactory quality" when they are sold in the course of a business. Whether this requirement has been met is a matter to be decided by reference to what a reasonable person would regard as satisfactory by reference to specific factors listed, taking into account the price, the description of the goods and "all the other relevant circumstances."

There may well be an overlap in many situations between the term requiring "satisfactory quality" and the term implied by subsection 14(3), requiring that the goods are fit for any particular purpose that the buyer may have made known to the seller. The knowledge of the buyer is relevant to liability under subsections 14(3) and 14(2). Obviously, the buyer cannot claim under either of these sections if he knew (or ought to have discovered, having had the opportunity for inspection) of the defects of which he subsequently seeks to complain. Further, if the seller can prove that the buyer did not rely on the skill and judgment of the vendor, or that it was unreasonable for him to have done so, he may have a defence to an action based upon subsection 14(3). The ambit of subsections 14(2) and 14(3) is generally limited to goods put to normal use (unless the buyer notifies the seller of an unusual use for the goods).

Consumers are also protected by statutory implied terms in respect of **19.03** goods that they hire. Therefore, a skier who cannot afford his own equipment but rather hires it from a supplier is afforded similar protection to that enjoyed by a person who buys such equipment, and if the bindings on his ski boot fail to release him in the event of a fall, causing him to break his leg, he may be able to base an action on section 4 of the Supply of Goods and Services Act 1982, which contains stipulations as to fitness for purpose and satisfactory quality in terms almost identical to those found in the Sale of Goods Act 1979.

The potential difficulty with remedies based upon the law of contract is, of course, that they are only open to parties to the contract. While this will be the case in many situations (*e.g.* a gym member injured by a defective treadmill), it will not cover all such situations (although it is feasible that the Contracts (Rights of Third Parties) Act 1999 might assist in some situations). Protection for consumers has therefore been extended by specifically designed consumer protection legislation.

Consumer Protection Act 1987

This legislation was enacted in order to give effect to the Council Directive **19.04** on the approximation of the laws, regulations and administrative provisions the member States concerning liability for defective products, Directive 85/374. Essentially, it provides for strict liability (*i.e.* liability without proof of negligence or breach of contract) against manufacturers (and certain other parties in the supply-line) in cases where damage occurs as a result of a defect in a product. The class of potential claimants is not limited to private individuals, but it may be difficult for professional sportsmen or sporting clubs to rely upon the Act in relation to damage to commercial property.[1]

The scheme of the Act

Section 2(1) of the Act provides that, **19.05**

> "Subject to the following provisions of this part, where any damage is caused wholly or partly by a defect in a product, every person to whom subsection (2) below applies shall be liable for the damage."

---

[1] s.5(3).

The scope of the Act is explicitly stated to be wide, by the reference to "any damage," although it is restricted somewhat by section 5(1), which defines damage thus,

> "Subject to the following provisions of this section, in this Part 'damage' means death or personal injury or any loss of or damage to any property (including land)."

Further, section 5(2) provides that damage to the product itself is not actionable under the Act (although, if a contract exists, the purchase price could be recovered). This is also the position in negligence. Pursuant to section 5(4), a claimant may only found an action for damage to property upon the Consumer Protection Act if the value of the damages claimed (excluding interest) exceeds £275. There is no "lower limit" in personal injury cases (in respect of general or special damages). Pure economic loss is not recoverable.

Perhaps the most significant limitation upon the loss recoverable is that found in section 5(3), which states,

> "(3) A person shall not be liable under section 2 above for any loss of or damage to any property which, at the time it is lost or damaged, is not—
>
> (a) of a description of property ordinarily intended for private use, occupation or consumption; and
>
> (b) intended by the person suffering the loss or damage mainly for his own private use, occupation or consumption."

19.06 The effect of section 5(3) is to prevent an action for loss or damage to commercial property from being brought under the Act. This seriously restricts the usefulness of the Act in professional sport. The owner of a competing racehorse that is injured and has to be put down because of defective shoes, or blinkers that come loose during a race, will be unable to sue for any loss in respect of the horse as it falls outside the stipulations of section 5(3), being in reality a chattel bred or bought for potential profit. However, the jockey injured when falling from the same horse in the same circumstances would be able to rely upon the Act, as the restriction in section 5(3) applies only to "damage to any property"—not to personal injury.

The exclusion of liability for loss or damage to commercial property reflects the fact that the Act (as its title obviously suggests) is designed primarily for the protection of consumers who use goods that have been supplied to them by a commercial undertaking. This aspect of the Act is also reflected by the requirement that the defendant should be dealing in the course of a business in order for liability to attach. Pursuant to section 4(1)(c), it is a defence for a defendant to show that,

> "(c) that the following conditions are satisfied, that is to say—

(i) that the only supply of the product to another by the person proceeded against was otherwise than in the course of a business of that person's; and

(ii) that section 2(2) above does not apply to that person or applies to him by virtue only of things done otherwise than with a view to profit;"

Subject to this important restriction, the class of potential defendants is set out at section 2(2):—

"(2) This subsection applies to—

(a) the producer of the product;

(b) any person who, by putting his name on the product or using a trade mark or other distinguishing mark in relation to the product, has held himself out to be the producer of the product;

(c) any person who has imported the product into a member State from a place outside the member States in order, in the course of any business of his, to supply it to another."

The term supplier is defined in detail at section 1(2). Section 2(3) creates a further class of potential defendant—the supplier (at any point in the supply chain—not merely the person who supplied goods to the claimant personally) who refuses to identify, "one or more of the persons (whether still in existence or not) to whom subsection (2) above applies in relation to the product" after a request has been made within a reasonable period of time.

Proving a "product" is "defective"

Although liability is strict, the claimant still must prove that the product in question was defective and that the defect caused ("wholly or partly") the damage complained of to the ordinary civil standard. **19.07**

A product is defined[2] as "any goods or electricity" and is expressed to include a product which is comprised in another product, such as a raw material. A product will be found to be defective for the purposes of the Act when,

"the safety of the product is not such as persons generally are entitled to expect."

"Safety" is not limited to personal safety, but also includes "safety in the context of risks of damage to property." Section 3(2) states,

"(2) In determining for the purposes of subsection (1) above what persons generally are entitled to expect in relation to a product all the circumstances shall be taken into account, including—

---

[2] s.1(2).

    (a) the manner in which, and purposes for which, the product has been marketed, its get-up, the use of any mark in relation to the product and any instructions for, or warnings with respect to, doing or refraining from doing anything with or in relation to the product;

    (b) what might reasonably be expected to be done with or in relation to the product; and

    (c) the time when the product was supplied by its producer to another;

and nothing in this section shall require a defect to be inferred from the fact alone that the safety of a product which is supplied after that time is greater than the safety of the product in question."

Clearly, this list of relevant factors is not intended to be exhaustive. It is comparable with the list of factors found in section 14 of the Sale of Goods Act 1979 and the Sale and Supply of Goods Act 1982.

Prohibition on exclusion of liability

19.08 Section 7 imposes an absolute prohibition on the exclusion of liability under the Act in the following terms,

"The liability of a person by virtue of this Part to a person who has suffered damage caused wholly or partly by a defect in a product, or to a dependant or relative of such a person, shall not be limited or excluded by any contract term, by any notice or by any other provision."

This is much broader than the prohibitions found in the Unfair Contract Terms Act 1977 and the Unfair Terms in Consumer Contracts Regulations 1999; the provision is absolute, whereas in general contractual situations an exclusion will be allowed unless it fails to meet tests as to its reasonableness. Contributory negligence is, however, a defence.

Conclusion

19.09 There are three potential avenues of recourse for sporting participants injured (or suffering other loss) because of defective equipment. The first is an action in negligence, the second a claim under any contract that might subsist and the third a claim against a manufacturer or supplier under the Consumer Protection Act 1987. If a claim for damage to property is brought under the latter legislation, it may only be in respect of property that is intended to be used for non-profit making activities. However, there is no such limitation upon claims for personal injuries under the Act, so that a professional basketball player injured when a net and its support fall on him because of a defect may sue for damages for pain, suffering and loss of amenity but may also claim loss of earnings. In this sense the Act protects persons other than consumers who suffer personal injury. The great benefit of the Consumer Protection Act is that there is no need to show negligence or for the claimant to be in a contractual relationship with the defendant.

Part III

Criminal and Other Disciplinary Jurisdictions

Criminal and Other Disciplinary Punishations

Chapter 20

Criminal law

"Don't take that, 'Judge not lest ye shall be judged' line with me, young man."

Gahan Wilson, "The Weird World of Gahan Wilson", cartoon, 1975.

Introduction

The criminal law can cover most aspects of sporting life both on and off the 20.01
field. From Duncan Ferguson's conviction for assault to Tonya Harding's
conviction for obstructing justice by failing to report her ex-husband's
involvement to the Police in the attack on Nancy Kerrigan just before the
1994 Winter Olympics.

This Chapter analyses a few of the principles most commonly associated
with sporting life. However, given that the potential size of the subject and
the fact that it is merely peripheral to that of sports injury law, it is not dealt
with in any depth and the reader is referred to other texts such as *Archbold*
for further help.

The authors have found *Sports Law*, by Gardiner *et al.*[1] and *Law and the
Business of Sport* by David Griffith-Jones and Adrian Barr-Smith[2] partic-
ularly helpful. The reader is also referred to *Sport and the Law* by Edward
Grayson,[3] in particular for a summary of numerous prosecutions.[4]

Offences

Homicide

Homicide is the unlawful killing of a living person under the Queen's peace. 20.02
It can be subdivided into two distinct offences, murder and manslaughter.
The distinction between the two offences is in the *mens rea*.

The *mens rea* for murder is either the intent to kill or intent to cause
grievous bodily harm to a person who then dies. The authors are unaware

---

[1] 1st ed., Cavendish Publishing Ltd, 1998.
[2] Butterworths, 1997.
[3] 3rd ed., Butterworths, 2000.
[4] At pp. 259–264.

of any sports related cases which have resulted in a conviction for murder, unless something really out of the ordinary has occurred.

There are several ways in which manslaughter can be committed. However, the only one which is relevant to sport is constructive or unlawful act manslaughter.

Example
R. v. Moore[5]

> The goalkeeper in a football match was in the process of clearing the ball when the defendant jumped, with his knees up against the back of the victim, which threw him violently forward against the knee of the goalkeeper. The victim died a few days later from internal injuries. In summing up the judge said that the rules of the game were quite immaterial and it did not matter whether the defendant broke the rules of the game or not. Football was a lawful game but it was a rough one and persons who played it must be careful not to do bodily harm to any other person. No one had the right to use such force and when death resulted the crime of manslaughter had been committed. A verdict of guilty was returned.

Section 18 of the Offences Against the Person Act 1861

20.03 This states:

> "Whosoever shall unlawfully and maliciously by any means whatsoever wound or cause any grievous bodily harm to any person, with intent . . . to do some grievous bodily harm to any person . . . shall be guilty of an offence."

For the purposes of this Chapter, only this part of section 18 is relevant. The wounding or grievous bodily harm must be caused with intent to wound or cause grievous bodily harm. Again, the main requirement is that there be an assault or a battery. As this is the most serious of the offences, there is a further requirement that the defendant actually intends that the result of his action will be either a wound or grievous bodily harm, not just the initial touching.

Example
R. v. Lloyd[6]

> In the course of a rugby union game, the victim was tackled. As he lay on the ground, the defendant kicked him in the face with such force that he had to spend four days in hospital with a fractured cheekbone. Held that although forceful contact within the rules was allowed, the game was not a licence for thuggery. The victim had not provoked the defendant and as on-field violence needs as much

---

[5] [1898] 14 T.L.R. 229.
[6] [1989] Crim.L.R. 513.

discouragement as violence on the terraces a sentence of 18 months was appropriate.

Section 20 of the Offences Against the Person Act 1861

This states: **20.04**

> "Whosoever shall unlawfully and maliciously wound or inflict any grievous bodily harm upon any other person—shall be guilty of . . . an offence."

The *mens rea* is that there must be intention or recklessness as to whether force is inflicted on the victim plus at the time that the act is committed the defendant must foresee some harm as the result of his action. He need not foresee either a wound or grievous bodily harm, just some harm. The result of the infliction of the force must be either a wound or grievous bodily harm. A wound is where the continuity of the skin is broken.

Example
R. v. Billinghurst[7]

> In an off the ball incident during a rugby union match, the defendant punched the victim, fracturing his jaw. The only issue at trial was whether there was consent. Held, that players are deemed to consent only to force of a kind which could be reasonably expected to happen during a game. There is no unlimited licence to use force in the game. In directing the jury the judge said that they may consider decisive whether the force used was in the course of play or outside the course of play. As a man of good character, the defendant was sentenced to nine months, suspended for two years.

Section 47 of the Offences Against the Person Act 1861

This states that: **20.05**

> "Whosoever shall be convicted . . . of any assault occasioning actual bodily harm shall be liable . . . to be imprisoned."

The *mens rea* is either an intention that force is applied or recklessness as to whether force will be applied to the person of another.

Example
R. v. Birkin[8]

> Following a late tackle in a football game, the defendant struck the tackler in the face breaking his jaw in two places. The defendant pleaded guilty and in mitigation stated that it was a spur of the moment action, with the degree of injury

---

[7] [1978] Crim.L.R. 553.
[8] [1988] Crim.L.R. 854.

caused neither intended or expected. Held that incidents such as this could not be tolerated on or off the field. The original sentence of eight months was reduced to six months in custody.

Common assault

20.06   This can be committed by either a technical assault or a battery. Assault is an act which causes the victim to apprehend the immediate infliction of unlawful person force. Battery is the actual infliction of unlawful force upon the body of another. The *mens rea* or intention element for the offence is intention or recklessness as to the touching.

Example
Baker v. Bridger[9]

> In 1985 a woman footballer who broke an opponent's jaw in a women's friendly [*sic*!] match on May Day was convicted of assault and ordered to pay £250 compensation by Clacton Magistrates.

Breach of the peace

20.07   This occurs where there is a threat to a person or his property. The powers arise under section 115 of the Magistrates' Court Act 1980 and the Justices of the Peace Act 1361.

Example
Butcher v. Jessop[10]

> Several professional footballers became involved in a goal mouth fight during a Glasgow Rangers FC v. Glasgow Celtic FC Scottish Premier Division match.
>   Held, *inter alia*, that because of the history of sectarian violence between the rival fans (Rangers and Celtic are traditionally Glasgow's Protestant and Catholic teams respectively), the players' behaviour was likely to cause a serious breach of the peace in the form of crowd disturbance. Two of the players were bound over.

Other offences

20.08   It would not be appropriate to list all of the offences which may potentially be associated with sport. These would range from public order offences and specific crowd control offences to health and safety offences committed by clubs. It should also be borne in mind that as well as primary responsibility, secondary liability can also rest with accomplices.

---

[9] *Daily Express*, May 1985; E. Grayson, *Sport and the Law* (Butterworths, 2000), p. 345.
[10] [1989] S.L.T. 593.

An example from another jurisdiction is provided by Grayson in *Sport and the Law*[11]:

Calder Race Course, Miami[12]

In 1986, reported from America in circumstances which would have been treated similarly in the U.K., namely a fight between two women jockeys. One bit the arm of another who then required a tetanus injection. The Stewards imposed a £30 fine for "causing a disturbance in the jockey's quarters", a TV room.

Defences

The two most common defences to charges of violence in a sporting context are consent and self-defence.　20.09

Consent

The concept of consent is used to ensure that many minor assaults and batteries in sports are never considered for prosecution. Although there are no cases involving participants which give direct and detailed guidance on this issue, a number of cases do provide some guidance.　20.10

R. v. Brown[13]

This case involved a group of sado-masochists who participated in con-　20.11
sensual acts of violence against each other for sexual gratification. They were charged with various offences under sections 20 and 47 of the Offences Against the Person Act 1861. On a ruling by the trial Judge that the prosecution did not have to prove lack of consent by the victim, the group pleaded guilty and were convicted. They appealed against conviction on the ground that the judge had erred in his ruling. The Court of Appeal (Criminal Division) dismissed the appeal.

The House of Lords held, dismissing the appeal (Lord Mustill and Lord Slynn of Hadley dissenting), that although a prosecutor had to prove lack of consent in order to secure a conviction for mere assault, it was not in the public interest that a person should wound or cause actual bodily harm to another for no good reason and, without such a reason, the victim's consent afforded no defence to a charge under sections 20 or 47. The satisfying of sado-masochistic desires did not constitute such a good reason. Since the defendants had admitted the charges against them and since the injuries

---

[11] Butterworths, 2000, p. 345.
[12] *Daily Express*, July 1, 1986.
[13] [1994] 1 A.C. 212; [1993] 2 W.L.R. 556; [1993] 2 All E.R. 75; *The Times*, March 12, 1993; *Independent*, March 12, 1993; *The Guardian*, March 12, 1993.

inflicted were neither transient nor trifling, the question of consent was immaterial and the Judge's ruling had, accordingly, been correct.

In his speech, Lord Mustill stated[14]:

"Some sports, such as the various codes of football, have deliberate bodily contact as an essential element. They lie at a mid-point between fighting, where the participant knows that his opponent will try to harm him, and the milder sports where there is at most an acknowledgement that someone may be accidentally hurt. In the contact sports each player knows and by taking part agrees that an opponent may from time to time inflict upon his body (for example by a rugby tackle) what would otherwise be a painful battery. By taking part he also assumes the risk that the deliberate contact may have unintended effects, conceivably of sufficient severity to amount to grievous bodily harm. But he does not agree that this more serious kind of injury may be inflicted deliberately. This simple analysis conceals a number of difficult problems, which are discussed in a series of Canadian decisions, culminating in *Reg. v. Ciccarelli*,[15] on the subject of ice hockey, a sport in which an ethos of physical contact is deeply entrenched. The courts appear to have started with the proposition that some level of violence is lawful if the recipient agrees to it, and have dealt with the question of excessive violence by enquiring whether the recipient could really have tacitly accepted a risk of violence at the level which actually occurred. These decisions do not help us in the present appeal, where the consent of the recipients was express, and where it is known that they gladly agreed, not simply to some degree of harm but to everything that was done. What we need to know is whether, notwithstanding the recipient's implied consent, there comes a point at which it is too severe for the law to tolerate. Whilst common sense suggests that this must be so, and that the law will not license brutality under the name of sport, one of the very few reported indications of the point at which tolerable harm becomes intolerable violence is in the direction to the jury given by Bramwell L.J. in *Reg. v. Bradshaw*[16] that the act (in this case a charge at football) would be unlawful if intended to cause 'serious hurt.'"

A-G's Reference (No. 6 of 1980)[17]

20.12 In this case, the respondent and the victim had a fistfight in a public street which resulted in actual bodily harm to the victim. The respondent was charged with assault causing actual bodily harm and was acquitted. The question referred to the Court of Appeal was[18]:

"Where two persons fight (otherwise than in the course of sport) in a public place can it be a defence for one of those persons to a charge of assault arising out of the fight that the other consented to fight?"

---

[14] [1994] 1 A.C. 212 at 265–266.
[15] (1989) 54 C.C.C. (3d) 121.
[16] 14 Cox C.C. 83.
[17] [1981] Q.B. 715.
[18] At 717.

The court answered the question in the negative. Lord Lane C.J. said[19]:

> "Bearing in mind the various cases and the views of the text book writers cited to us, and starting with the proposition that ordinarily an act consented to will not constitute an assault, the question is: at what point does the public interest require the court to hold otherwise?"

He later said[20]:

> "The answer to this question, in our judgment, is that it is not in the public interest that people should try to cause, or should cause, each other actual bodily harm for no good reason. Minor struggles are another matter. So, in our judgment, it is immaterial whether the act occurs in private or in public; it is an assault if actual bodily harm is intended and/or caused. This means that most fights will be unlawful regardless of consent. Nothing which we have said is intended to cast doubt upon the accepted legality of properly conducted games and sports, lawful chastisement or correction, reasonable surgical interference, dangerous exhibitions, etc. These apparent exceptions can be justified as involving the exercise of a legal right, in the case of chastisement or correction, or as needed in the public interest, in the other cases."

R. v. Donovan[21]

In this case the appellant was charged with indecent and common assault   **20.13** upon a girl whom he had beaten with her consent for his own sexual gratification. In delivering the judgment of the Court of Criminal Appeal, Swift J. said[22]:

> "If an act is unlawful in the sense of being in itself a criminal act, it is plain that it cannot be rendered lawful because the person to whose detriment it is done consents to it. No person can license another to commit a crime. So far as the criminal law is concerned, therefore, where the act charged is in itself unlawful, it can never be necessary to prove absence of consent on the part of the person wronged in order to obtain the conviction of the wrongdoer. There are, however, many acts in themselves harmless and lawful which become unlawful only if they are done without the consent of the person affected. What is, in one case, an innocent act of familiarity or affection, may, in another, be an assault, for no other reason than that, in the one case there is consent, and in the other consent is absent. As a general rule, although it is a rule to which there are well established exceptions, it is an unlawful act to beat another person with such a degree of violence that the infliction of bodily harm is a probable consequence, and when such an act is proved, consent is immaterial."

He went on to point to the exceptions[23]:

---

[19] At 718–719.
[20] At 719.
[21] [1934] 2 K.B. 498.
[22] At 507.
[23] [1934] 2 K.B. 498 at 508–509.

"There are, as we have said, well established exceptions to the general rule that an act likely or intended to cause bodily harm is an unlawful act. One of them is dealt with by Sir Michael Foster in the chapter just cited, where he refers to the case of persons who in perfect friendship engage by mutual consent in contests, such as 'cudgels, foils, or wrestling,' which are capable of causing bodily harm. The learned author emphasizes two points about such contests: (1.) that bodily harm is not the motive on either side, and (2.) that they are 'manly diversions, they intend to give strength, skill and activity, and may fit people for defence, public as well as personal, in time of need.' For these reasons, he says that he cannot call these exercises unlawful."

R. v. Coney[24]

20.14 In this case, the 11 judges who heard it held that a prize-fight was unlawful, that all persons aiding and abetting therein were guilty of assault, and that consent of the persons actually engaged in fighting to the interchange of blows did not afford any answer to the criminal charge of common assault.

The appellants were spectators at an organised fight between two men near a public road. Cave J. said[25]:

"The true view is, I think, that a blow struck in anger, or which is likely or is intended to do corporal hurt, is an assault, but that a blow struck in sport, and not likely, nor intended to cause bodily harm, is not an assault, and that, an assault being a breach of the peace and unlawful, the consent of the person struck is immaterial. If this view is correct a blow struck in a prize-fight is clearly an assault; but playing with single-sticks or wrestling do not involve an assault; nor does boxing with gloves in the ordinary way, and not with the ferocity and severe punishment to the boxers deposed to in *R. v. Orton.*[26]"

Stephen J. said[27]:

"The principle as to consent seems to me to be this: When one person is indicted for inflicting personal injury upon another, the consent of the person who sustains the injury is no defence to the person who inflicts the injury, if the injury is of such a nature, or is inflicted under such circumstances, that its infliction is injurious to the public as well as to the person injured. But the injuries given and received in prize-fights are injurious to the public, both because it is against the public interest that the lives and the health of the combatants should be endangered by blows, and because prize-fights are disorderly exhibitions, mischievous on many obvious grounds. Therefore the consent of the parties to the blows which they mutually receive does not prevent those blows from being assaults."

---

[24] [1882] 8 Q.B.D. 534.
[25] At 539.
[26] (1878) 39 L.T. 293.
[27] At 549.

In this passage Stephen J. clearly considered that prize-fights were likely to   20.15
cause breaches of the peace and that no consent could render fights with
such a result lawful. In a later passage on the same page he said:

> "In cases where life and limb are exposed to no serious danger in the common
> course of things, I think that consent is a defence to a charge of assault, even when
> considerable force is used, as, for instance, in cases of wrestling, single-stick,
> sparring with gloves, football, and the like; but in all cases the question whether
> consent does or does not take from the application of force to another its illegal
> character, is a question of degree depending upon circumstances."

In this passage he appears to be considering organised sports where danger
to life and limb is merely incidental to the main purpose of the activity.
Hawkins J. said[28]:

> "As a general proposition it is undoubtedly true that there can be no assault unless
> the act charged as such be done without the consent of the person alleged to be
> assaulted, for want of consent is an essential element in every assault, and that
> which is done by consent is no assault at all."

He later said:

> "it is not in the power of any man to give an effectual consent to that which
> amounts to, or has a direct tendency to create, a breach of the peace; so as to bar
> a criminal prosecution."

Hawkins J. concluded that every fight in which the object and intent of each
of the combatants was to subdue the other by violent blows tending to a
breach of the peace was illegal and he distinguished friendly encounters in
the following passage[29]:

> "The cases in which it has been held that persons may lawfully engage in friendly
> encounters not calculated to produce real injury to or to rouse angry passions in
> either, do not in the least militate against the view I have expressed; for such
> encounters are neither breaches of the peace nor are they calculated to be pro-
> ductive thereof . . . "

In concluding that prize-fights were unlawful he was influenced mainly, if
not entirely, by the fact that they were likely to be productive of breaches of
the peace.

It would seem to be wrong to treat the first cited dictum of Hawkins J. as   20.16
referring to all assaults irrespective of the gravity thereof. The court was

---

[28] At 553.
[29] At 554.

considering a charge of common assault and it does not seem that the judge was intending to lay down a general principle which was applicable also to assaults charged under section 47 of the Act of 1861 or to offences under section 20 thereof.

Lord Coleridge C.J.,[30] similarly concluded that the combatants in a prize-fight could not consent to commit a breach of the peace.

Although there was unanimity among the judges in *Coney* as to consent in the particular circumstances affording no answer to a charge of assault, there were differing reasons advanced for reaching that conclusion. However, Cave, Stephen and Hawkins JJ. and Lord Coleridge C.J. all considered that effectual consent could not be given to blows producing or likely to produce a breach of the peace. Stephen J. specifically referred to prize-fights being injurious to the public as disorderly exhibitions and it may be assumed that the other three judges also had in mind the public interest in preventing breaches of the peace. Given the fact that the fight took place before a crowd of more than 100 persons the likelihood of a breach of the peace would by itself have been sufficient to negative consent without considering the nature and effect of the blows struck.

Nevertheless, Stephen J. also considered that it was against the public interest that blows should endanger the health of the combatants. Whether he had in mind only blows which produced "a maim" is not stated although in the editions of his *Digest of the Criminal Law* published before and after *Coney* he stated[31]:

"Everyone has a right to consent to the infliction upon himself of bodily harm not amounting to a maim".

20.17 *Coney* therefore seems to be authority for the proposition that the public interest limits the extent to which an individual may consent to infliction upon himself by another of bodily harm and that such public interest does not intervene in the case of sports where any infliction of injury is merely incidental to the purpose of the main activity.

R. v. Bradshaw[32]

20.18 On the subject of duels, Bramwell L.J. said in this case[33]:

"No persons can by agreement go out to fight with deadly weapons, doing by agreement what the law says shall not be done, and thus shelter themselves from the consequences of their acts."

---

[30] At 567.
[31] 3rd ed., 1883, art. 206.
[32] (1878) 14 Cox C.C. 83.
[33] At 84–85.

East's Pleas of the Crown[34]

The Judge in this case famously made the following comments on the issue **20.19** under discussion[35]:

> "if death ensue from such [sports] as are innocent and allowable, the case will fall within the rule of excusable homicide; but if the sport be unlawful in itself, or productive of danger, riot, or disorder, from the occasion, so as to endanger the peace, and death ensue; the party killing is guilty of manslaughter. . . . manly sports and exercises which tend to give strength, activity and skill in the use of arms, and are entered into merely as private recreations among friends, are not unlawful; and therefore persons playing by consent at cudgels, or foils, or wrestling, are excusable if death ensue. For though doubtless it cannot be said that such exercises are altogether free from danger; yet they are very rarely attended with fatal consequences; and each party has friendly warning to be on his guard. And if the possibility of danger were the criterion by which the lawfulness of sports and recreations was to be decided, many exercises must be proscribed which are in common use, and were never heretofore deemed unlawful. . . . But the latitude given to manly exercises of the nature above described, when conducted merely as diversions among friends, must not be extended to legalise prize-fighting, public boxing matches, and the like, which are exhibited for the sake of lucre, and are calculated to draw together a number of idle disorderly people. . . . And again, such meetings have a strong tendency in their nature to a breach of the peace."

Crown Law by Sir Michael Foster[36]

One of the oldest quotes still referred to in recent times on this issue comes **20.20** from Sir Michael Foster's work on *Crown Law*. In particular, he distinguished[37] beneficial recreations such as single-stick fighting from:

> "prize-fighting and . . . other exertions of courage, strength and activity . . . which are exhibited for lucre, and can serve no valuable purpose, but on the contrary encourage a spirit of idleness and debauchery . . . "

Self-defence

A person who is being, or who believes that they are about to be, attacked **20.21** can use reasonable force to repel the attacker. This can be used by either the victim or somebody who is using force to protect the victim. The use of force must be reasonable in the circumstances. The victim is judged on the facts as he honestly believes them to exist.

Self-defence is a complete defence to a crime resulting in the victim receiving no punishment for his actions, as it operates to legalise the act.

---

[34] (1803), Vol. 1, Chap. V, pp. 268.
[35] At 268–270, paras. 41 and 42.
[36] 3rd ed. 1792.
[37] At 260.

In sport, this is most likely to be an issue in off the ball incidents. If the incident is on the ball, the defence of consent or a claim of accident will usually be more appropriate.

Example
R. v. Hardy[38]

Following a neck injury in a rugby union match, there was a brawl between the players of both sides. During the course of this brawl, the defendant punched the deceased on the jaw. The deceased fell and hit his head on the ground, which was still very hard from a recent frost. The deceased died two days later.

The defendant was acquitted of manslaughter on the grounds of self-defence. He claimed that he was receiving repeated blows to the back of the head and neck and that the only way that he believed that he could prevent further blows was to hit his assailant. The unforeseen consequences of the act did not affect the operation of the defence.

Conclusion

20.22 This Chapter has provided only a very brief introduction to this subject. However, this is not to underestimate its relevance on sporting life. Indeed, such behaviour is never out of the headlines for very long. These range from, for example, the cases of Everton's Duncan Ferguson[39] and Manchester United's Eric Cantona[40] in 1995, to the more recent incident involving the Liverpool player Jamie Carragher where the police issued him with a formal warning after he was sent off after throwing a coin back into the crowd during Liverpool's FA Cup defeat against Arsenal. There is no doubt that the criminal law will continue to provide the extreme boundaries for sporting behaviour in the future.

---

[38] *The Guardian*, July 27, 1994.
[39] *R. v. Ferguson*, *The Times*, October 12, 1995.
[40] *R. v. Cantona*, *The Times*, March 24, 1995.

Chapter 21

Compensation for criminal injuries

"I think crime pays. The hours are good, you travel a lot."

Woody Allen, Take the Money and Run, screenplay, 1969.

In the previous Chapter we saw that indiscretions on the sports field can **21.01** result in criminal prosecution. But where does that leave the victim? Compensation for the aggrieved party may be recovered in one of two ways. First, the criminal court sentencing the protagonist may order compensation to be paid. Secondly, a remedy may sought under the Criminal Injuries Compensation Scheme. Each has its drawbacks.

Compensation orders

A compensation order may be made in respect of any personal injury **21.02** suffered as a result of a criminal offence, following the conviction of the offender. Section 130 of the Powers of Criminal Courts (Sentencing) Act 2000 provides:

"(1) A court by or before which a person is convicted of an offence, instead of or in addition to dealing with him in any other way, may, on application or otherwise, make an order (in this Act referred to as a 'compensation order') requiring him—

  (a) to pay compensation for any personal injury, loss or damage resulting from that offence or any other offence which is taken into consideration by the court in determining sentence; or
  (b) to make payments for funeral expenses or bereavement in respect of a death resulting from any such offence, other than a death due to an accident arising out of the presence of a motor vehicle on a road but this is subject to the following provisions of this section and to section 131 below

  . . .

(11) In determining whether to make a compensation order against any person, and in determining the amount to be paid by any person under such an

order, the court shall have regard to his means so far as they appear or are known to the court."

Three important points are taken from section 130.

21.03　　The first and perhaps the most obvious observation is that before the court can make an award of compensation to the injured party there must be a conviction. If the offender is acquitted of the offence out of which injury is said to have arisen but convicted of some other offence arising out of the same subject matter a compensation order cannot be made.[1] As the author of *Archbold* identifies, the question is:

> "not whether the loss results solely from the offence, but whether it can fairly be said to result from the offence".[2]

The courts have considered their power to make compensation orders where the injury has been caused by a person other than the offender. In a sporting context, one can easily imagine circumstances where an individual may be injured by someone other than the offender. For example, brawls during rugby and ice hockey matches are all too common (although significant injuries in the case of the latter example would be unusual). *Archbold*[3] submits that the criminal courts have tended to take the view that:

> "where the offender has instigated the incident by an initial act of violence or abuse, or joined in after the incident has started but before the loss, damage or personal injury has been caused, the loss, damage or personal injury can be said to have resulted from the offence of which he has been convicted. If the actions which cause the injuries go beyond the expected scope of the fracas, the offender will not be responsible for the injuries so inflicted"[4]

The second point to be drawn from sub-section 11 is that the court must have regard to the means of the defendant. It does not follow that all professional sportsmen are well paid. In the vast majority of cases they will not be. In the case of amateur sport, this will almost certainly be the case. It is probable that any award made by a court will be payable in small weekly or monthly instalments. The criminal courts have consistently sought to avoid excessively long periods of repayment. Nevertheless, a court may, in an appropriate case, allow two or, perhaps, three[5] –years to pay.

21.04　　Pursuant to section 133, the Act allows a magistrates' court to discharge or reduce the amount payable under a compensation order in particular

---

[1] See Archbold, *Pleadings and Procedure* (Sweet & Maxwell, 2002), s.5–415 citing *R. v. Halliwell* 12 Cr.App.R.(S) 692.

[2] See *Rowlston v. Kenny* 4 Cr.App.R.(S) 85, CA.

[3] *Ibid.*

[4] See *R. v. Derby* 12 Cr.App.R.(S) 502, CA, *R. v. Taylor* 14 Cr.App.R.(S) 276, CA, *R. v. Geurtjens* 14 Cr.App.R.(S) 280, CA, *R. v. Deary* 14 Cr.App.R.(S) 648, CA.

[5] A three year period would be regarded as appropriate only in an exceptional case: see *R. v. Olliver and Olliver* 11 Cr.App.R.(S) 10, CA.

circumstances. These include where the offender has suffered a substantial reduction in his means since the time when the compensation order was made.

In principle any order made by the court would have regard to the Judicial Studies Board, *Guidelines for the Assessment of Damages in Personal Injury Cases.*[6] However, in reality, the award is likely to be drastically reduced from that which would be payable in a civil court or under the Criminal Injuries Compensation Scheme because the award is means tested.

Thirdly, a court must make a compensation award. This is a matter for the court's discretion. If the court chooses not to make such an award, the injured party is left without a remedy in the criminal court.

How much can the criminal court award and what information does it require?

We saw above that the court will consider both the offender's means and the **21.05** Judicial Studies Board Guidelines (JSB's). The guidelines are used by the judiciary in civil courts for the assessment of general damages in personal injury cases. However, section 131 of the Powers of Criminal Courts (Sentencing) Act 2000 provides:

"(1) The compensation to be paid under a compensation order made by a magistrates' court in respect of any offence of which the court has convicted the offender shall not exceed £5,000.

(2) The compensation or total compensation to be paid under a compensation order or compensation orders made by a magistrates' court in respect of any offence or offences taken into consideration in determining sentence shall not exceed the difference (if any) between—

(a) the amount or total amount which under subsection (1) above is the maximum for the offence or offences of which the offender has been convicted; and

(b) the amount or total amounts(if any) which are in fact ordered to be paid in respect of that offence or those offences."

So, the court is limited to a statutory maximum of £5,000. In addition, before the court will make a compensation order it will require detailed information about the nature of the precise injuries suffered.[7]

In conclusion, a compensation order is unlikely to provide the injured party with adequate recompense save in the case of the most modest injury. The principal drawbacks can be summarised as (1) a conviction must be secured, (2) the awards, if made, are likely to be significantly below that

---

[6] Published by Blackstone Press Ltd, London, currently in its 5th Edition.
[7] *R. v. Cooper* 4 Cr.App.R.(S) 55, CA.

which would be recovered in civil proceedings, and (3) they are means tested.

The Criminal Injuries Compensation Scheme (CICS)

21.06   The CICS has as its purpose the compensation of innocent victims of crimes of violence. From the victim's point of view, it has two distinct advantages to the compensation order considered above. First, it is not a precondition to an award under the CICS that the offender has been convicted. There may be insufficient evidence to bring a criminal prosecution. Secondly, they are not means tested and are intended to provide a victim with appropriate compensation.

In 1964 the government established a non departmental public body —the Criminal Injuries Compensation Board (CICB)—to administer compensation throughout Great Britain on the basis of common law damages to victims of violence. The scheme was introduced to provide an acknowledgement of society's sympathy for such victims. In 1996 the Criminal Injuries Compensation Authority was established to administer a tariff based scheme which came into effect for all applications received on or after April 1, 1996. From April 1, 2001, all new applications received will be considered under the revised Criminal Injuries Compensation Scheme 2001. The 2001 Scheme will be considered in greater detail. The following is not intended to be a complete guide to the scheme.[8]

The 2001 scheme

21.07   The purpose of this guide is to explain the main provisions of the scheme and to give you information about how the scheme works. It is not, however, a substitute for the scheme itself and cannot cover every situation. One of the drawbacks of the scheme is that if an injured party decides to seek legal or other advice to assist in making an application, the costs of that advice are not recoverable under the scheme.

Eligibility for compensation?

21.08   To be considered for an award under the scheme an applicant must have been:

   (a) a victim of a crime of violence, or injured in some other way covered by the scheme;

   (b) physically and/or mentally injured as a result;

---

[8] For a detailed review of the 1996 scheme see D. Foster, *Claiming Compensation for Criminal Injuries* (2nd ed., Tolley Publishing Co Ltd, 1997). For a guide to the 2001 scheme see the CICA website at www.cica.gov.uk.

(c) in England, Scotland or Wales at the time when the injury was sustained; and

(d) injured seriously enough to qualify for at least the minimum award available under the scheme; or

(e) a dependant or relative of a victim of a crime of violence who has since died.

Unless there are good reasons the applicant should also:

(a) have reported the incident personally to the police as soon as possible after it happened;

(b) send his application so that the authority receives it within two years from the date of the incident causing the injury.[9]

This time limit may, however, be waived if the authority considers that there is a good reason for the delay and it is in the interests of justice to do so.

Upon receipt of the application form, the claim will be dealt with a by a claims officer. He will then normally make enquiries of the Police, medical authorities and other relevant bodies to enable the claim to be assessed. The claims officer is responsible for deciding in accordance with the scheme what awards (if any) should be made in individual cases, and how they should be paid.

Where did the incident happen?

The injury must have been sustained in Great Britain or one of the other places set out in paragraph 8 of the scheme. Injuries sustained elsewhere, for example on a sporting trip abroad, are not eligible although there could be a remedy under a similar scheme in force in the country concerned. If the injury was sustained in Northern Ireland the applicant is not eligible to apply under this scheme. Northern Ireland has its own scheme.   21.09

Directly attributable

An applicant will only be compensated for injuries directly resulting from a crime of violence or threat of violence. This means that the authority must satisfy itself, on the basis of all the available facts, that not only was the incident in which you were injured a crime of violence, but also that the incident was the substantial cause of your injury.   21.10

---

[9] Para. 17 of the scheme.

Crime of violence

21.11   There is no legal definition of the term but "crimes of violence" usually involve a physical attack on the person, for example assaults or wounding. This is not always so, however, and every case is considered on the basis of its circumstances. For example the threat of violence may, in some circumstances, be considered a crime of violence.

Accidental injury

21.12   As a general rule, you will not be entitled to compensation if you were injured accidentally. There are some exceptions. If your injuries were sustained as a result of your involvement (whether intentional or not) in the prevention of an offence you may be eligible. So within a sporting context it may be that an individual who was injured during an attempt to prevent or halt a sports field brawl could be entitled to an award. Similarly, an individual may also be entitled to an award if he was injured during the course of such an action even though he was not himself taking part in it. If you were, for example, an innocent bystander and you were knocked over and injured by the offender or the pursuer, you could be entitled to an award. These conditions apply even if the suspected offence was not a crime of violence.

Eligibility and the power to withhold or reduce awards

21.13   The original scheme, introduced in 1964, envisaged that it would be inappropriate for those with significant criminal records or those whose own conduct led to their being injured, to receive compensation from public funds. It was also felt that people who failed to co-operate in bringing the offender to justice should not benefit from such payments. These provisions continue in this scheme. Accordingly, the authority has within its power the discretion to withhold or reduce an award which might otherwise be granted if one or more of the reasons which are set out in paragraph 13 of the scheme apply to a claim.

Informing the police

21.14   It is not necessary for an offender to have been convicted before an award can be made. Some offenders are never found. However, it is submitted that this is unlikely to present a problem within the context of sporting injuries. More likely, is that a conviction is never secured. However, the authority attaches great importance to the duty of every victim of crime to inform the Police of all the circumstances without delay and to co-operate with their enquiries and any subsequent prosecution. It is particularly important that the incident should have been reported since it is the authority's main safeguard against fraud. If the circumstances have not been reported to the Police, and the applicant can offer no reasonable explanation for not doing so, it is likely that any application for compensation will be rejected.

Failure to inform the Police is unlikely to be excused on the grounds of feared reprisals, or failure to recognise the assailant, or that he saw no point in reporting it. It is not sufficient to assume that the incident will have been reported by someone else. Reports by team mates will not be sufficient unless there was a good reason for the applicant not informing the Police as well. All the relevant circumstances should be reported to the Police. If important information is deliberately left out or the Police were otherwise mislead, an application for compensation will normally be rejected.

Helping the Police to prosecute

If the incident has been promptly reported to the Police there remains a   **21.15** discretion to reduce or withhold compensation if you subsequently fail to co-operate in bringing the offender to justice. For example, where an applicant refuses to co-operate with the Police by, for example, refusing to make a statement, attend court, or makes a statement that is later withdrawn, an award will normally be refused. Whereas, where the applicant was willing to co-operate but in the particular circumstances, it was decided by the Police or the prosecuting authority that no further action should be taken or prosecution brought, an award may be made, assuming that no other issues of eligibility are in question. As with non-reporting, fear of reprisals will not generally be an excuse. If an applicant first refused to cooperate with the Police but subsequently changed his mind and assisted them in all respects then the authority may consider whether a reduction of the award in respect of the initial failure or refusal to cooperate is appropriate.

Failure to co-operate with the CICA

The authority may withhold or reduce payment of an award if the applicant   **21.16** persistently fails to comply with requests for information or otherwise fails to give all reasonable assistance to the authority or any other relevant authority in connection with the application.

Conduct before, during or after the event

In this context "conduct" means something which can fairly be described as   **21.17** bad conduct or misconduct and includes provocative behaviour and offensive language. So in cases of fighting, an award may be reduced or withheld if, for example, without reasonable cause the applicant struck the first blow, or if the incident in which the applicant was injured formed part of a pattern of violence in which he was a voluntary participant, or where the applicant was injured whilst attempting to obtain revenge against the assailant, or if the applicant used offensive language or behaved in an aggressive or threatening manner which led to the attack which caused the injuries.

Criminal convictions

21.18   Paragraph 13(e) of the scheme provides that an award may be withheld or reduced on account of an applicant's character as shown by his criminal convictions (excluding convictions which are spent). The rationale behind this reduction is that a person who has committed criminal offences has probably caused distress and loss and injury to other persons, and/or caused expense to society by reason of court appearances and the cost of supervising sentences, even when they have been non-custodial, and the victims may themselves have sought compensation, which is another charge on society. Even though an applicant may be blameless in the incident in which the injury was sustained, Parliament has nevertheless provided in the scheme that convictions which are not spent under the Rehabilitation of Offenders Act 1974 should be taken into account.

Assuming an award is made—what is recoverable?

General damages awards

21.19   If the application is acceptable the authority will assess whether or not the injury is serious enough to qualify for at least the minimum award payable under the tariff. The minimum award is £1,000.[10] If it does, the claims officer will then identify the tariff level into which your injury falls. The applicant may be required to attend a medical examination by a doctor nominated by the authority.[11] Where the victim suffers more that one injury, the tariff award will be that for the highest rated injury plus, where the other injuries are separate from the highest rated injury and from one another, 10 per cent of the tariff value of the second most serious injury and, where appropriate, 5 per cent of the tariff value of the third most serious injury. This means, for example, that where the injuries are a depressed fracture of the skull (single tariff payment £6,000), loss of two front teeth (£2,000) and a broken nose (£1,500), the combined award would be £6,000 + £200 + £75 totalling £6,275.

   An award will be reduced by the full amount of any payment of compensation or damages received in respect of the same injuries.[12] If the authority makes an award and the applicant subsequently receives compensation or damages, the applicant will be required to pay back the full

---

[10] Para. 25–29 of the scheme. The scheme has 25 levels of compensation ranging from £1,000 to £250,000.

[11] Para. 20 of the scheme.

[12] Para. 48 of the scheme.

amount of the other payment up to the level of the authority's award of compensation.

Recovery of other losses under the 1996 scheme

If the injury has caused the applicant to lose or is likely to cause that person **21.20** to lose earnings or earning capacity for longer than 28 full weeks, the applicant may be eligible for additional compensation for this loss. However, note that compensation is not payable for the first 28 full weeks of lost earnings or earning capacity.

An applicant may be compensated for "special expenses"[13] if, as a direct result of the injury he has been incapacitated or is likely to be incapacitated for longer than 28 full weeks and have incurred special expenses for medical, dental, optical treatment, related equipment and care.

Reviewing decisions

The Claims Officer will reach a conclusion as to the appropriate award. The **21.21** applicant may disagree with the decision reached by the claims officer and seek a review. The applicant may apply in writing within 90 days from the date of the letter giving notice of the original decision, giving reasons. The case will then be considered afresh by a claims officer more senior than the one who made the original decision. Both eligibility for and the amount of any award will be reviewed and a fresh decision, with reasons, will be sent to the applicant. On a review of the decision a claims officer may increase, reduce or withhold an award.

Appeals to the Criminal Injuries Compensation Appeals Panel

If, after review, the applicant considers that there are grounds for contesting **21.22** the result of the review he may appeal, within 30 days from the date of the letter giving notice of the reviewed decision, to the Criminal Injuries Compensation Appeals Panel. The members and staff of this panel are entirely independent from the authority and have wide powers within the terms of the scheme to consider afresh the original application and any further information the applicant may wish to provide. On consideration of an appeal the Panel may increase, reduce or withhold an award. A decision made by the Panel, whether at an oral hearing of your case or otherwise, is final.

The 1996 scheme

The Criminal Injuries Compensation Scheme (2001) applies to all applica- **21.23** tions received by the Criminal Injuries Compensation Authority on or after

---

[13] Paras 35–36 of the scheme.

April 1, 1996. In truth, the 2001 scheme does not differ in substance (or indeed in paragraph numbers within the scheme) to merit any further consideration.

Conclusion

21.24 At the beginning of this Chapter, we indicated that there were drawbacks with respect to each of the schemes for the recovery of compensation. There are two. Firstly, the duty to report to and co-operate with the Police. Of course, in day to day life this is a duty which would be of no concern. However, with regard to criminal acts perpetrated on the sports field victims it is likely that many will be ignored or put down to over-exuberance by the victim and not reported to the police. As a result any claim is likely to fail. Secondly, a claim for loss of earnings (usually the most substantial aspect of any claim) will only be considered after 28 weeks absence.

In the circumstances, although the compensation order and/or the criminal injuries compensation scheme are alternative means of obtaining compensation, if the a proposed defendant is not impecunious a civil action is, by far, the preferred option.

Chapter 22

Sporting disciplinary hearings

"LAWYER (to judge): And as a precedent, your honor, I offer a Perry Mason case first televised four years ago which . . . "

Chon Day, "DAC News" cartoon, 1969.

Introduction

So far this book has concentrated on the relationship between sporting injuries and national or international law, as recognised by the courts. However, it is far more common for a participant in competitive sports to find herself appearing before a disciplinary panel of some sort than in a court of law. The rules of any given sport or game will be designed to ensure fair play and proper competition, and it has been argued in the highest jurisprudential circles, that no game can properly exist without rules.[1] In many sports one of the objectives of such rules of play[2] will also be to minimise the risk of injury to participants. Such rules emanate in general from within the sport and are unlikely to be the result of lobbying from outside pressure groups. The prohibition on two-footed tackles in football is clearly designed to lessen the likelihood of serious injuries to players (some would argue that it is also intended to make the game more attractive to watch), and the limitation on the number of "bouncers" to be bowled in any one over in cricket also has a safety aspect (although, once again, it is supposed to make the game a better spectacle). The ban on the use of performance-enhancing drugs in sport is no doubt primarily designed to provide fair competition, but it also has a health aspect.

22.01

In the case of each of the above examples, breach of the rules (if detected) will have an immediate effect on the course of the game itself in the awarding of a free kick (and perhaps a yellow or red card), extra runs or disqualification from the event in question. It may carry with it an automatic ban or fine. Such a breach may also have less immediate consequences. It may form the basis of disciplinary proceedings before a tribunal.

---

[1] H.L.A. Hart, *The Concept of Law*, OUP.
[2] It is interesting that in many sports, notably cricket, the primary rules are in fact known as the *laws* of the game.

The tribunal may have power to fine a competitor or his club or suspend him for a specified number of games or amount of time. In some cases, a disciplinary tribunal may also have a second role as an appellate body to review the decisions of referees or umpires made at the time of the offence.

There is an inherent problem in many sporting disciplinary decisions taken at the time of the offence—the primary decision-maker (with or without video technology) has to try to make the correct decision within a short time frame. The game has to carry on reasonably quickly. There is an inevitable trade off of accuracy for expediency. While video adjudication might be put to good use in a sport such as cricket or American football, where long pauses are part of the rhythm of the game, even the most bitterly aggrieved Premier League manager would be likely to agree that video adjudication during the course of a football match would be detrimental to the sport as a spectacle and as an intense physical contest. This may produce absurd results. In football, the Football Association (FA) frequently rescinds red cards shown to players after the event. While this might soften the blow (by making the player available for games for which he would otherwise have been suspended), it does nothing to remedy the situation for the losing team where the sending-off is a major cause of a defeat.

22.02   Traditionally, good sportsmanship compels participants to accept the effect of these imperfections in the decision-making process. So long as there is no serious suggestion of bad faith,[3] these frustrating incidents are often shrugged off on the basis that "these things level themselves out over the course of a season". However, the increasing availability of technology and the growing commercialism in sport have led to repeated calls from high-profile sporting figures for "increased consistency" and the instances of review of such decisions by tribunals has increased.

Referees, umpires and stewards

22.03   These officials, who deal with "first instance" decisions, can do no more than make honest decisions in accordance with their view of events. They will generally have to make two decisions—a factual decision and what might be termed a "legal" decision as to how the rules are to be interpreted and applied. Generally, there is no system of "precedent"—that is to say that when a referee's decision is appealed the decision on appeal does not lay down guidelines for the resolution of similar incidents in future. This recognises the fact that no two incidents are alike, but it is submitted that it also makes it very difficult for the holy grail of "consistency" to be achieved. A comparison between the following two similar incidents that occurred in

---

[3] Such as the situation in the 2002 Winter Olympics when two gold medals were awarded in the ice-dancing after allegations of impropriety were levelled at the judges.

football's FA Cup over the weekend of February 16, 2002 shows the difficulty that match officials face.

In the match between Middlesborough and Blackburn at the Riverside Stadium on Saturday 16 February, the score was 0–0 with time running out, when the well-known referee Graham Barber sent off Blackburn's defender Lucas Neill for a "professional foul".[4] An incident occurred in which Neill and the Middlesborough player both fell to the ground to the right hand side of the Blackburn penalty area. The referee decided that Neill had committed a foul. Having decided this, he had to consider whether, in his judgment, the foul had deprived Middlesborough of a clear goal-scoring opportunity. He decided that it had, and sent Neill off. The referee's decision was met by almost universal criticism, both in the media and among the players and managers from both sides involved in the game.[5] Middlesborough went on to win the game 1–0. The reason that the criticism was so strong was that there appeared to be at least two fundamental problems with the decision. Not only did it appear that both players had been jostling for the ball, but the question whether a clear goal-scoring opportunity had been denied was open to debate.[6] Therefore both the factual and the "legal" basis of Barber's decision were open to question.

By contrast, the following day Newcastle took on Manchester City in another 5th round tie at St James' Park. During the first half Newcastle's pacey forward Craig Bellamy burst clear of the City defence. As Bellamy closed in on Nicky Weaver's goal, City's former Everton defender Richard Dunne, having been out-paced, stuck out an arm and held Bellamy back. The referee awarded a free kick and sent Dunne off. Again the reason was that Dunne had committed a professional foul. This time, however, the press, players and managers were unanimous in their view that the dismissal was the correct decision. Not only was the foul clear cut, but Bellamy was away from the last defender and in a central position.

The point of this illustration is to demonstrate the fact that the referees have complex split-second decisions to make, often in front of thousands of baying spectators. Even where incidents are reasonably similar to the untrained eye, the smallest nuances can have huge consequences and lead to major discrepancies. Had Blackburn beaten Middlesborough, they would have faced Everton at home in a quarter final, a game in which they might have expected to receive gate receipts of around half a million pounds.

---

[4] A professional foul occurs when a defender illegally impedes the progress of an attacking player so as to deny the attacking player a clear goal-scoring opportunity. Such a foul is deemed to warrant an automatic sending off. Usually, this situation will arise when the attacking player is running towards goal, and only the offender and the goalkeeper stand between him and the goal.
[5] The Blackburn manager, Graeme Souness, famously referred to it as a "minging" decision. Souness' reaction at the final whistle was even less sanguine and led to a report to the FA in its own right.
[6] There was also a suggestion that the Middlesborough player was offside.

Disciplinary tribunals

22.04   If a participant or a team wishes to challenge the decision of a match official, the usual means of recourse is to appeal to a disciplinary review board, or similar body. Such bodies are usually set up by the governing body of the relevant sport. Disciplinary bodies exist not only to review the decisions of match officials, but also to investigate more serious offences and those which are either not detected to take place off the pitch. The jurisdiction of disciplinary tribunals is usually established by contractual relationships. In team sports, contracts between clubs and the relevant governing body will establish the right of the governing body to discipline the club or its employees in accordance with defined procedures. These will be the same contracts that establish the right of clubs to compete in competitions organised by the governing body. In turn, the team will have a contract with its players requiring them to submit to the jurisdiction of the governing body.[7] Individual competitors may also be required to register with the governing body, thus establishing a direct relationship under which the governing body may exert their authority.

The governing bodies of most sports are aware of the potential impact of disciplinary decision upon participants, professionally and commercially. It is in the interests of the governing bodies of all professional sports therefore to put in place proper rules and regulations relating to discipline and misconduct, along with proper procedures for dealing with complaints about disciplinary decisions. Were professional sportsmen subject to stringent punishment without recourse to adequate rules and procedures, they would be likely to seek to challenge such sanctions in courts of law. This would harm the reputation of the sport as a whole and of the governing body in particular.

22.05   Although the reputation of bodies such as the Football Association or the Lawn Tennis Association may not seem particularly valuable, given the virtual monopoly they exercise in terms of control over their respective sports, it is to be remembered that such bodies are relatively weak compared with television companies and players or clubs in the most commercially successful sports. There is no guarantee for a body such as the FA that the most powerful and wealthy clubs will wish to continue participating in FA competitions. Over the last few years the major football clubs in Europe have threatened to break away from their respective national leagues to set up a more lucrative European league. The experience of World Cricket in the late 1970's, when Kerry Packer introduced the World Series as a breakaway from ICC condoned international competition shows that governing bodies in all sports need to be aware of the needs of their most powerful participants. The influence that clubs such as Manchester United, Glasgow Celtic and Real Madrid may therefore have over their respective governing

---

[7] And also to permit the team to discipline the player.

bodies ought not to be underestimated. This is one strong argument in favour of disciplinary powers being "contracted out" by governing bodies to independent bodies.

The next Chapter deals in detail with the power of the courts to intervene in disciplinary disputes in sporting matters, but as a general proposition, a participant who faces disciplinary action must be entitled to expect that minimum standards of fairness should apply. Although it is perhaps undesirable to equate disciplinary proceedings in sporting matters with legal proceedings, standards of fairness and the very concept of fairness itself tend to be imported from the legal sphere, and in particular administrative law. The sort of provisions to be expected in disciplinary proceedings therefore includes the right of the accused participant to make representations (whether orally or in writing) to the governing body and to call evidence where matters of fact are in dispute. Participants should also be entitled to know the rules to be applied and to have notice of the details of any disciplinary matter of which they stand charged. Beyond these basic requirements it is difficult to give details of procedural safeguards that exist across the board in all major competitive sports. In most instances, participants might expect to be accorded procedural rights such as the right to legal representation and/or assistance, an impartial tribunal with no conflict of interest,[8] and a reasoned decision. The courts have recently shown that they are not entirely unwilling to intervene in disputes between participants and sporting bodies to enforce proper procedures.[9] The following Chapter deals with these issues in detail.

Illustration—the Football Association

By way of an example, the English Football Association makes provision for the rules to be applied in their competitions, and establishes procedures for challenging referees' decisions and for investigating and penalising disciplinary offences. Its rules on disciplinary procedures make reference to such matters as time limits for lodging complaints, a procedure for determination of cases on written submissions and for dealing with cases in the absence of the alleged offender. It also makes specific provisions for conduct of hearings. In essence, such hearings follow the format of criminal trials, with a reading of the charge, a summary of facts put forward by the "Association",[10] evidence called by the FA with cross-examination if **22.06**

---

[8] So that it is, and appears to be unbiased. The test for bias in administrative bodies in English law is to be found in the judgment of Lord Goff in *R. v. Gough*. In many instances this may be a difficult allegation for disciplinary bodies to refute because of the potential influence of major teams or players (see above) and because often the governing body responsible for the constitution of the disciplinary tribunal may also be the employer of a match official against whose decision an appeal is brought.

[9] *Jones & Ebbw Vale RFC v. Welsh Rugby Football Union*, *The Times*, March 6, 1997, CA; *The Times*, January 1, 1998.

[10] Interestingly, the FA acts as the "prosecuting" authority.

required, evidence on behalf of the alleged offender and closing submissions (with the alleged offender having the last word). Interestingly, the rules make specific provision as to the standard of proof to be applied. Rule 5.2 provides,

> "The standard of proof shall depend on the seriousness of the misconduct alleged, requiring the Disciplinary Commission to decide on the balance of probabilities for misconduct considered to be of low seriousness, and to be satisfied beyond reasonable doubt for misconduct of high seriousness."[11]

The rules do not impose a general requirement upon the Disciplinary Commission to give reasons for their decision, although they are compelled to provide findings of facts, reasons for the decision and reasons for the imposition of any penalty on request from the alleged offender. A right of appeal lies to an Appeal Board. Clearly, if an appeal is launched, it will be necessary to have the written findings and reasons of the Commission.

22.07   The Disciplinary Commission is also the body that hears appeals from the decisions of referees and detailed (and distinct) rules exist in respect of the procedure to be adopted on such hearings.

The essential procedural elements of most sporting disciplinary hearings are very clearly articulated by the FA.

Tactical use of sporting disciplinary hearings

22.08   The proliferation of semi-formal oral hearings provides a potential advantage for alleged offenders. It is open to clubs and players to exercise their appeal rights in a way that is more akin to gamesmanship than sportsmanship. In most sports, a suspension or fine will not be executed pending appeal. If a team has an important match coming up for which a player is to be suspended as a result of either the decision of a referee or a disciplinary commission, it is in their interests to launch an appeal. This may result in the player becoming available for the game in question. At the time of writing, this very situation has arisen in respect of the England Rugby Union captain, Martin Johnson. He was caught on video clearly punching an opponent in a Premiership match for his club, Leicester. The referee saw the incident and showed a yellow card to both players. The RFU decided subsequently to refer the matter to a disciplinary panel. The panel did not sit for almost two weeks. Eventually, it decided that Johnson should be banned for three weeks. This would have meant that he would have missed the Six Nations game between England and France. However, at the time of writing his club Leicester have announced their intention to appeal on the basis that the referee took action during the match by showing the yellow card. Pursuant to an agreement between the RFU and the Premiership clubs at the outset of

---

[11] Unfortunately, there is no definition of which offences should be considered to be of "high" or "low" seriousness.

the season, the RFU were not supposed to refer incidents to Disciplinary Commissions where a referee had taken action during the game. They did not dispute that a three-week ban would be justified. Rugby League has deftly side-stepped these sorts of problems by providing for disciplinary hearings arising out of on-field misconduct to be conducted within 72 hours of the incident.

Alternatives to disciplinary committees

Internationally, the CAS (Court of Arbitration in Sport) has jurisdiction over some sports. The only way in which such bodies may assume jurisdiction is for governing bodies to submit to their authority. One advantage of such bodies is that there should be no suggestion of bias or undue influence. A dedicated national Sports Court would provide a firmer legalistic framework with more certainty for the parties involved and less chance of errors occurring (and therefore less opportunity for interference by courts of law). However, it might be expected to function less quickly and efficiently than specialist (and less formal) dedicated tribunals. It is submitted that the real value of a dedicated Sports Court would be to act as a forum for review or appeal of disciplinary bodies within individual sports. This would provide a more accessible avenue of recourse for those genuinely wronged than the High Court or Court of Appeal. **22.09**

Chapter 23

Challenging disciplinary decisions

"DEFENDANT: I don't recognise this court!
JUDGE: Why not?
DEFENDANT: You've had it decorated!"

Eric Morecambe and Ernie Wise, The Morecambe and Wise Joke Book, 1979.

Introduction

As the previous Chapter made clear, the potential importance of the deci-   **23.01**
sions of disciplinary tribunals is not to be underestimated. For a team or
player, such decisions are capable of costing millions of pounds and making
the difference between relegation and safety, glory or defeat and professional greatness or disgrace. Given the inherent imperfections in some
sporting decisions noted in the previous Chapter, it is perhaps surprising
that the courts have only rarely been called upon to intervene in such
disputes.

One sport in which the British courts have frequently been called upon to
intervene is boxing. It is not unusual for lawsuits to be brought to determine
whether a boxer is required under the rules of any one of the governing
bodies to defend his title against a particular opponent. Generally speaking,
such boxing cases tend to be based upon the ordinary law of contract.

Sporting bodies have traditionally been held not to be amenable to
judicial review as they are seen to be essentially private bodies, not exercising public law functions. That position is far from satisfactory, given the
stakes. However, over recent years, alternative avenues of redress have
become apparent through which the courts have felt themselves able to
adjudicate on sporting disciplinary matters. The first is demonstrated in the
case of *Jones & Ebbw Vale RFC v. Welsh Rugby Football Union*[1] and
Modahl v. British Athletic Federation Ltd,[2] and is based firmly in the law of
contract. The second potential basis for challenge is that the courts might
have an inherent supervisory jurisdiction to require disciplinary bodies to
act fairly (this is similar to the concept of judicial review, but lacking in the

---

[1] *The Times*, March 6, 1997, CA. For the facts of the case, see below.
[2] [2001] E.W.C.A. Civ. 1447.

powerful remedies available under that procedure; at the most a claimant could obtain a declaration or injunction, and there would be no action for damages) A third possibility is that the Incorporation of Article 6 of the European Convention on Human Rights and Fundamental Freedoms by the Human Rights Act 1998[3] provides athletes with a freestanding mechanism of challenging the decisions of disciplinary bodies, whatever the relationship between the parties.

23.02   In the case of *Jones*, at first instance, Ebsworth J. made the observation that in the past disciplinary decisions had been made from "wet and windy touchlines". She acknowledged that this was no longer acceptable given that sanctions imposed upon players had a real economic impact. The willingness of the court to intervene in the case of *Jones* was based upon the contractual relationship between the player and the Welsh RFU that arose out of the player's registration with the RFU. This contractual analysis provides a route by which a challenge may be made to the conduct of a disciplinary body. A similar approach was adopted by Lightman J. in *Korda v. International Tennis Federation*[4] where the claimant had made an application to participate in the Wimbledon Lawn Tennis Championships, in which he agreed top be bound by the rules of the ITF. A less straightforward contractual situation was considered by the Court of Appeal in *Modahl v. BAF.*

The contractual approach

Jones v. Welsh Rugby Football Union

23.03   It may be that a contract of registration between a player and a governing body contains implied terms of fairness as to the exercise of any disciplinary powers. It is important to bear in mind that the proceedings in *Jones*, both before Ebsworth J. and subsequently in the Court of Appeal, were respective applications for an interlocutory injunction. They were not full trials of the issues. As seen in the preceding Chapter, there will very often be well-defined rules of procedure set out by the governing body. It may be open to the relevant governing body to argue that an agreement by a club or player to submit to such rules limits the scope of any implied terms, or constitutes express contractual terms to deal with the resolution of disputes. Alternatively, the existence of such rules might be prima facie evidence of compliance by the governing body with any implied term.

The facts of *Jones* were that the Ebbw Vale player Mark Jones was caught fighting on the pitch. His conduct was the subject of disciplinary proceedings at which he appeared. He spoke with a stammer and was not allowed legal representation at the hearing. He was given a heavy fine and suspen-

---

[3] Which came into force on October 2, 2000.
[4] [1999] A.E.R. (D) 84.

sion. He complained that the rules were applied with undue rigidity and that they were unfair in themselves. Before Ebsworth J. he argued that the ability to challenge findings of fact were essential for a fair hearing. Further, it was argued on his behalf that in the modern professional era a more formalised approach than that adopted by the Welsh RFU, including representation by a lawyer, were required. The RFU's approach, which gave it total discretion to adopt whatever procedures it saw fit, was inappropriate.

Ebsworth J. held that there was nothing in the rules that required the disciplinary committee to watch a video or film of the incident in question, but that it was arguable that a system which denied a party the right to challenge the factual basis of an allegation made against him either by putting questions or calling evidence was lacking in basic fairness. It was also arguable that the committee had been wrong to refuse to depart from its normal practice and view the video. In the context of professional sport it was arguable that alleged offenders needed the right to defend themselves properly. An injunction against the suspension was therefore granted. The RFU set a date for a further hearing following the initial injunction. Jones and his club refused to attend and applied for a further injunction which was granted by Potts J.

The Court of Appeal upheld the decision of Ebsworth J. but overturned **23.04** the order of Potts J. Their Lordships reiterated the point that they were dealing only with applications for injunctive relief, and that Ebsworth J. had applied the correct test. The arguments put forward by the Welsh RFU were respectable and might well succeed at trial, but should not prevent injunctive relief being granted. The question that Ebsworth J. had had to answer was whether Jones and his club had put forward an arguable case on the basis of natural justice. Further, the Court of Appeal held that it had been correct for Ebsworth J. to find that there was a contractual relationship between the player and the RFU by reason of his signing the registration form which contained an undertaking to observe the by-laws, resolutions and regulations of the game.

It is worth noting that both the Court of Appeal and Ebsworth J. took the view that the parties ought to take steps to resolve the issues among themselves. While it is correct to say that this may be illustrative of a lingering reluctance for the courts to intervene in sporting disciplinary matters, it may also be explained by a recognition of the practical situation—*i.e.* that there is little to be gained for either party in a situation such as that before the courts in *Jones* in allowing the dispute to rumble on until a full trial of the issues takes place. It is clearly in the interests of a sporting body confronted with a criticism of its procedures (whether well-founded or not) to take steps to alter the situation of its own accord rather than having to resort to defending its position through litigation. Ultimately, the same governing body will have to decide the final punishment in any given case; it is not for the courts to decide how an alleged offender should be tried and punished.

Finally, it is worth remembering that the decision in *Jones* creates no binding precedent and sets down no broad legal principle. It is certainly not authority for the proposition that disciplinary tribunals are required to allow alleged offenders to be represented by counsel or solicitors.

Modahl v. British Athletic Federation Ltd[5]

23.05　The respective situations in *Jones* and *Korda v. ITF Ltd* were based upon the relatively straightforward situation where a sportsperson signs registration or application forms with a governing body. These situations fit easily into a contractual analysis. The Court of Appeal in the latest (and possibly the last) chapter in the saga of Diane Modahl, the distinguished former British 800 metre runner who failed a drugs test in 1994, was faced with a more complex web of relationships and obligations. Modahl was banned by a disciplinary committee of the BAF in 1994, but argued that there was strong evidence to suggest that the urine sample that had been analysed was likely to have been contaminated.

In 1995 an independent appeal panel (for which the BAF rules made provision) set aside the decision of the disciplinary committee on the basis of new scientific evidence. In 1999, Modahl's action in tort against the International Amateur Athletics Federation (IAAF) failed after the House of Lords held that it had no reasonable prospects of success and struck it out. She also claimed damages in contract against the British Athletics Federation (BAF). The Court of Appeal granted an interlocutory injunction against the BAF in imposing any ban in 1998.

At the subsequent trial, Modahl argued that she had a contractual relationship with the BAF by reason of (1) her membership of Sale Harriers Athletics Club, which was affiliated to the BAF ("the club basis"), (2) by reason of her participation in BAF events and events organised under the auspices of IAAF (to which BAF was affiliated) ("the participation basis"), and (3) also by reason of her submission to BAF rules and regulations ("the submission basis"). Finally she submitted that, if none of the three individual bases was sufficient to give rise to a contract, nonetheless the facts of her case required a contract to be implied. She further submitted that there had been a breach of contract by the BAF in choosing the members of the disciplinary committee, three of whom she alleged were tainted by bias. She claimed that the bias had led to her conviction by the disciplinary committee in 1994, and that this had caused her loss not withstanding her subsequent reinstatement in 1995.

23.06　In analysing the *Modahl* case it is vital to remember that her claim was for damages for breach of contract. Declaratory relief was of no use to her. It was therefore essential for her to establish a contract between herself and

---

[5] [2001] E.W.C.A. Civ. 1447.

the BAF, to prove that a breach had occurred and to show that the breach had caused her loss.

At first instance, Douglas Brown J. decided that there was no contract and also found that the allegations of bias had not been proved. He therefore dismissed the claim. The Court of Appeal found that the Judge had been correct to find that there had been no bias and that any loss had therefore not been caused by any breach of contract (much emphasis was placed on the fact that the only ground for allowing the appeal in 1995 was the availability of evidence that had not been available before the original disciplinary committee). Significantly, however, two members of the Court (Latham and Mance L.JJ.; Jonathan Parker L.J. dissenting) decided that there was a contract between Modahl and the BAF. Much consideration was given to the basis for the contract, and to the definition and scope of any implied terms. Equally significantly, Latham and Jonathan Parker L.JJ. appeared to accept (*obiter*, but following an exhaustive review of the authorities; Mance L.J. *dubitante*) that an athlete would be able to seek a declaration or injunction irrespective of the contractual relationship between the parties. This is a powerful doctrine and is discussed in detail below.

In finding that a contract existed between the parties, Latham and Mance L.JJ. accepted the claimant's arguments. Perhaps the most difficult basis for establishing a contractual relationship was the "club basis"—not only was the evidence in this regard far from complete, but the situation was compli-cated by the fact that the BAF (itself in administration at the time of the hearing) was in fact a successor to the body that had exercised control of British Athletics at the time Modahl joined her club. On the "participation basis", Latham L.J. was prepared to accept that the participation of Modahl (at the time of her disqualification a high-profile and well-regarded athlete) was given by her in consideration for the BAF's undertaking to apply the rules equally and fairly to all participants. Mance L.J. regarded the "submis-sion basis" as being the clearest rationale for the implication of a contract. The judgment of Mance L.J. makes it clear that he did not find that a contract had to be implied in the circumstances in order to give a potential remedy to the claimant. The judgment recognises (correctly, it is submitted) that there may be various different ways in which an athlete can obtain relief against an unfair finding by a disciplinary body. At paragraph 109 of the judgment he states,

"The fact that the courts have fashioned declaratory and injunctive relief, to assist claimants in private law cases where judicial review is not available and there is no contract, cannot of itself prevent the inference of a contract in other cases."

23.07 This allows claimants to have recourse to different legal mechanisms in different situations, and means that a claimant need not necessarily prove a contract with governing body in order to obtain an injunction against a suspension, but may nonetheless rely on the existence of such a contract at a trial of the hearing in order to claim damages.

As to the terms to be implied, Latham and Mance L.JJ. took the view that the correct approach was to see whether the proceedings as a whole had been unfair. This allowed the BAF successfully to argue that the fact that an independent appeal panel had considered the case and reached a conclusion which was accepted as fair by the claimant meant that there had been no breach. Modahl had contended that the alleged unfairness at the 1994 disciplinary hearing had caused her loss and that this situation was not remedied by the 1995 appeal. It is significant to note that their Lordships specifically found that any bias at the original hearing would not have been the cause of the loss of which the claimant complained. More importantly, however, Mance L.J. held[6] that,

" . . . the parties were implicitly agreeing to be bound by the ultimate outcome of the disciplinary proceedings taken as a whole and therefore including the independent Appeal Tribunal's determination. . . . A conclusion that the process should be looked at overall matches the desirable aim of affording to bodies exercising jurisdiction over sporting activities as great a latitude as is consistent with fundamental requirements of fairness . . . "

23.08   In other words, it is not open to a disgruntled athlete too point to one procedural flaw in a disciplinary process and therefore to claim that the process as a whole is contaminated where a proper appeal system exists so as to remedy that flaw, and the appeal system in fact works fairly. The rationale behind this is to allow sports administrators, so far as is possible, to put in place their own effective procedures rather than having sporting matters unnecessarily dealt with in courts of law. The judgment of Mance L.J. demonstrates that where a term is implied into a contract the term will be as limited and minimal in scope and content as is possible to give business efficacy to the contract. At paragraph 119, Mance L.J. cited the proposition from *Chitty on Contracts*[7] that,

"Ultimately the issue is what, if any, term should be implied either as representing the obvious though unexpressed intention of the parties or as necessary for the efficacy of the contract made on the terms of the respondent's rules. . . . Approaching the matter in this way, I can well understand it being said that the parties would obviously have intended, and that it was necessary for the efficacy of the contract, that the respondents should when selecting persons to sit on a Disciplinary Committee (or indeed an Independent Appellant Panel), (a) act in good faith and select only persons who they believed to be fit and appropriate, and (b) (probably) act with reasonable care in that respect. It is a different matter to

---

[6] At para. 115.
[7] 28th ed., Sweet and Maxwell, Vol. 1, paras 13–04 – 13–09.

suggest that it must have been intended or was necessary for the efficacy of the contract that the persons should in fact be free from some characteristic making them unfit, but of which the respondents neither knew nor had any reason to know. It is an even more extreme proposition that the respondents undertook that the persons selected would not, even during the disciplinary process let alone at some subsequent date, commit themselves to unwise statements demonstrating apparent, though not actual, bias."

It is submitted that the analysis of Mance L.J. demonstrates that where a court is persuaded to adopt a contractual analysis that gives rise to a duty on a governing body to act fairly, that duty will tend to be reasonably easy to discharge. The existence of written procedural rules and fixed penalties (or ranges of penalty) and provision as to the rights of parties will be evidence of compliance with the duty. Where the disciplinary tribunal has the benefit of such a framework within which to operate, then provided that it does not depart from those procedures, it will be difficult for a potential claimant to show that any implied term is being breached. Whatever the commercial considerations, it seems highly unlikely that the courts will require "Rolls Royce" justice. So long as there is no bias, a chance for each side to make representations and so long as decisions are made in accordance with the rules, and not to have been biased, it is unlikely that a governing body will be held to have failed in its obligations to the parties. Any standards required are likely to be minimum standards of fairness.

It is arguable that, since the introduction of the Human Rights Act 1998, **23.09** any implied term would be that the standard of fairness to be expected from a governing body would be that required by Article 6 of the European Convention on Human Rights and Fundamental Freedoms.[8] However, it is submitted that the courts would remain reluctant to read any stringent standards of fairness into a contract by way of an implied term where positive terms as to the disciplinary rules and procedures to be adopted were set out. That is not to say that those standards might not be required as a matter of general law by Article 6 itself.

It is also significant to note that their Lordships felt it was necessary for a claimant in Modahl's position to prove *actual* rather than *apparent* bias in order to succeed in an action for damages for breach of contract. This was a necessary element, as without actual bias the claimant could not prove causation.

Whether a contractual relationship exists, and the terms of any contract, will be a question of fact in any given situation. However, the approach of the courts in *Jones*, *Korda* and *Modahl* points the way to a potentially fruitful avenue of recourse for claimants who are aggrieved at the conduct of sporting disciplinary tribunals and wish to claim damages for loss sustained.

---

[8] Beloff, Kerr and Demetiou, *Sports Law*, Hart Publishing, pp. 203–6.

A public law approach?

23.10   Although sporting bodies may not be subject to the jurisdiction of the Supreme Court to order *mandamus* or *certiorari* it seems that they may be subject to a supervisory jurisdiction which compels them to act fairly. It is not clear at what point sporting activity becomes sufficiently important so as to render decisions taken in respect of it justiciable, but the Court of Appeal in *Modahl v. BAF* considered that there was ample authority to support the view that a court could intervene to prevent a sporting body from acting arbitrarily or to declare that its actions were illegal. Surely the existence of any such jurisdiction must be founded upon the concept of sport as a valuable factor in modern society and as a significant commercial activity, as it cannot flow from the powers or constitution of the disciplinary body,[9] and the courts would not intervene to resolve a dispute between amateur cricket teams playing a friendly match on the village green, not within the framework of any governing body.

In *Modahl* their Lordships relied heavily upon the decision of the Court of Appeal in *Nagle v. Feilden*[10] in which Lord Denning M.R.[11] held that a female horse trainer who had been denied a licence by the Jockey Club on the basis of her sex had a right to claim a declaration that the Jockey Club was not acting lawfully. In the context of a claimant's livelihood, Lord Denning M.R. held that a claimant was entitled to an injunction or declaration even in the absence of any contract. Although Mance L.J. expressed doubt as to whether this view had subsequently met with approval, it was clearly the view of Latham L.J. that it expressed the law, and Jonathan Parker L.J. also seemed to accept the validity of this doctrine.[12]

The Human Rights Act 1998

23.11   Article 6 of the European Convention on Human Rights and Fundamental Freedoms states,

> "RIGHT TO A FAIR TRIAL
> 6.1 In the determination of his civil rights and obligations or of any criminal charge against him, everyone is entitled to a fair and public hearing within a reasonable time by an independent and impartial tribunal established by law. . . ."

Section 6 of the Human Rights Act 1998 provides,

---

[9] For the reasons set out in the cases at n. 1 above.

[10] [1966] 2 Q.B. 633.

[11] Apparently ignoring his own judgment in the case of *Lee v. The Showmen's Guild of Great Britain* [1952] 2 Q.B 329.

[12] And see also *Stevenage Borough Football Club v. The Football League* [1997] 9 Admin. L.R. 109, *The Times*, August 9, 1996; *Colgan v. The Kennel Club*, unreported, October 26, 2001, Cooke J.

"6(1) It is unlawful for a public authority to act in a way which is incompatible with a Convention right."

By section 6(3) the phrase "public authority" includes "a court or tribunal".

While it is not suggested that sporting disciplinary bodies are likely to be held to be public authorities for the purposes of the legislation, it is clear that the courts must act in accordance with Article 6 when deciding cases. Provided that the matter in dispute between the athlete or team and the disciplinary body concerns "determination of his civil rights and obligations", the court will need to have regard to Article 6 in deciding whether to grant the relief sought. This may well involve the question whether the procedure put in place by the governing body, taken as a whole, complied with the requirements of Article 6. If a claimant can show that the disciplinary proceedings did not comply with Article 6 then the court may (pursuant to section 8 of the 1998 Act) award damages, but only where the court is satisfied that the award of damages is necessary to afford just satisfaction to the person in whose favour it is made, taking into account any other remedy or relief granted to the claimant in relation to the act in question and the consequences of any decision in respect of that act (section 8(3)).

There is ample authority on the issue of independence that shows that the mere fact that the first body to hear a case may not be properly independent (for example, the Disciplinary Committee) will not lead to a breach of Article 6 provided that a court or superior body exists to supervise the exercise by the lower body of its powers.

It is submitted that it is unlikely that the effect of the incorporation Article 6 will be to require vastly more stringent procedures of sporting bodies. However, it does provide a "free-standing" right for claimants to bring an action in the absence of a contractual relationship.

Conclusion

It can be seen from the cases of *Jones* and *Modahl* that the case law in relation to the jurisdiction of courts to hear challenges to the decisions of disciplinary bodies is developing rapidly. Following *Modahl*, the courts are likely to be disposed to find contractual relationships in situations where there is no clear and obvious financial consideration or offer and acceptance, or even any clear agreement between a participant and a disciplinary body, although each case will turn on its own facts. Even if a claimant is able to establish that a contractual relationship existed, it is still incumbent upon her to show the nature and extent of any implied term, breach of that term and a causal nexus between breach and the loss in respect of which damages are claimed. This is unlikely to be an easy task, and the standards required by any implied term may be limited by express terms as to the rules and **23.12** procedures to be adopted, and in any event will be the minimum standards required for the contract to have efficacy.

Where evidence a real risk of unfairness exists that would cause real prejudice to a claimant, he may be able to obtain injunctive relief against any suspension, even in the absence of a contractual relationship between herself and the disciplinary body in question. This, however, will not of itself give rise to an action for damages (evidence of a breach of contract or a tort will generally be required for damages to flow) and it may be that this "supervisory" jurisdiction will not be able to be invoked where the effect upon the claimant is relatively minor or temporary in nature.

The incorporation of Article 6 of the European Convention on Human Rights will affect the way courts deal with cases where the complaint arises out of an incident that took place after October 2, 2000, and this may provide claimants with a mechanism for claiming damages where no contract can be said to exist. However, it is unlikely to have a huge impact upon the standards required of disciplinary tribunals, as they already had a common law duty to act fairly.

23.13   A further point to be borne in mind is the ruinous financial effect on both Diane Modahl and the BAF of the litigation set out above. While it is understandable that sporting bodies should be wary of making their procedures so formal as to lead to delay and to increase cost (by, for example having legally drafted disciplinary rules and appointing lawyers to tribunals, or allowing representation by counsel at most hearings), surely this is preferable for them than to risk becoming embroiled in a marathon of litigation for which most sporting governing bodies are unfit.

Only time will tell how the law will develop in this area but as Simon Curtis of Barlow, Lyde and Gilbert Solicitors[13] says:

> "It seems highly likely that disciplinary tribunals are going to have to get used to the presence of lawyers ensuring that their clients get a fair hearing. The stakes are too high for it to be otherwise."

---

[13] scurtis@blg.co.uk.

Chapter 24

Drugs and sport

"Reality is just a crutch for people who can't cope with drugs."

Lily Tomlin.

Introduction

Drugs and sport are now synonymous with each other. Depressingly, no **24.01** major sporting event can pass without drugs featuring on the agenda. The list of banned substances is ever expanding. Any list of banned substances is likely to be out of date from the moment it is printed.

A professional athlete takes the risk of consuming a banned substance **24.02** even by using decongestants purchased from the local chemist. Most recently, the IOC stripped Alain Baxter, the British slalom skier, of his Olympic bronze medal (the first ever Olympic medal won by a Briton in an alpine event). He tested positive for methamphetamine. This is one of the many substances prohibited by the International Olympic Committee (IOC) on the basis that it is a stimulant (although recently it has been suggested that there are two forms of this drug; some commentators suggest of one of the two variants that there is little or no evidence to support the theory that it acts as a stimulant). Baxter explained that he had unwittingly inhaled the substance by using a Vicks nasal spray which he had bought across the counter in a chemist in Salt Lake City, USA. His case was that a similar variety of the nasal spray sold in Europe does not contain methamphetamine (whereas its American equivalent does). His doctor had declared that the European spray was free from prohibited substances. The IOC, despite these unfortunate circumstances, disqualified Baxter. The IOC operates a strict liability policy. If an athlete tests positive for a prohibited substance, he is guilty of a doping offence come what may. An athlete is responsible for any substance present in his bloodstream, consumed knowingly or unknowingly.

For every unlucky individual, such as Baxter, there are countless others who flout the rules with only one aim in mind—to obtain a performance advantage. The most notorious example case was Ben Johnson, the Canadian sprinter, who won the gold medal in the 1988 Seoul Olympics for the 100 metres in a world record time of 9.79 seconds. Both were taken away

251

from Johnson following a positive test for anabolic steroids. The story shocked the world, although few athletes. Carl Lewis, who finished second and was subsequently given the gold medal following Johnson's disqualification, had long been aware of the magnitude of the problem. The Canadian government set up an inquiry into drug usage in sport headed by Chief Justice Charles Dubin. The report is a lament for the ideals of sport and sees drug use in sport as a symptom of a "moral crisis". It condemned the "conspiracy of silence", a deliberate policy to hide the extent of drug use in sport. It is suggested that the governing bodies of sport had long known of the widespread use of drugs. Instead of highlighting the problem they attempted to blur the issue by pointing out the low number of positive tests at competitions. Competition testing was considered to be an ineffective means of detecting drugs that are primarily used as training aids, such as anabolic steroids. Therefore, suggesting that the number of in-competition positive tests reflected the extent of drug use in sport was deliberately misleading.

24.03   That analysis is supported by the fact that many athletes representing former Communist states, especially those from East Germany and the USSR, prospered during the 1970's and 1980's having been assisted by a systematic doping regime. The incidence of positive testing was surprisingly limited.

The risks of drug use are not limited to disqualification. At the same Seoul Olympics, the superstar of the Games was Florence Griffith-Joyner—known as Flo-Jo. She won gold medals in the 100 and 200 metre sprints and in the 400 metres relay. Griffith-Joyner set new world records, clocking 10.49 seconds in the 100 metre quarter final and 21.34 seconds in the 200 metre final. Those records still stand today. What is interesting is that few athletes since have come close to the times set by Griffith-Joyner. Her sudden death in September 1998 at the age of 38 of heart seizure raised suspicions of drug abuse. Speaking on BBC TV, the British sprinter Kriss Akabusi said Griffith-Joyner's career had been plagued by suspicion, especially when she retired only four months after the introduction of random drug testing.

Drug testing is now more frequent and sophisticated than it has ever been. At the same time, the drug abusers are more sophisticated.

Misuse of Drugs Act 1971 and the Medicines Act 1968

24.04   The Misuse of Drugs Act 1971 is the main legislative provision prohibiting the possession, use and supply of drugs in the U.K. Section 4(l) of the Act provides that it shall not be lawful for a person to produce a controlled drug or to supply or offer to supply a controlled drug to another. Section 4(2) provides that (subject to section 28), it is an offence for a person to produce a controlled drug in contravention of subsection (1) above or to be concerned in the production of such a drug in contravention of that subsection by another.

Section 28 provides that it shall be a defence for the accused to prove that he neither knew of nor suspected nor had reason to suspect that the substance or product in question was a controlled drug. This differs from the approach taken by the IOC, who apply a strict liability standard. Not all sports governing bodies apply such a standard. For example in *USA Shooting and Quigley v. Union Internationale de Tir*[1] the Court of Arbitration for Sport (CAS) overturned the decision of the UIT banning Quigley. He had tested positive for, amongst others, the banned substance ephedrine. It had been prescribed for bronchitis. The UIT accepted Quigley's explanation that he had not intended to consume a banned substance. The CAS, in finding for Quigley, was keen to point out to sports governing bodies the importance of drawing up clear and explicit rules on doping.

The Misuse of Drugs Act 1971 divides the substances into three classes, A, B or C. Class A drugs are considered the most dangerous, class C the least. Class A drugs include cocaine and crack; ecstasy; heroin, morphine and opium; LSD; psilocin, and cannabis oil. The maximum penalty for possession is seven years' imprisonment or an unlimited fine or both, and for supply, life imprisonment or an unlimited fine or both. Class B drugs include amphetamines, barbiturates, cannabis and cannabis resin. Maximum penalties are five years' imprisonment or an unlimited fine or both for possession, and 14 years' imprisonment or an unlimited fine or both for supply. Class C drugs include various tranquillisers and mild, amphetamine type stimulants. Maximum penalties are two years' imprisonment or an unlimited fine or both for possession, and five years' imprisonment or an unlimited fine or both for supply. Most of the substances which are prohibited fall within class C. The Police do not as a rule tend to prosecute individuals for possession of such drugs.

The Medicine Act 1968 also regulates the use of drugs in the U.K. It provides that a person may commit a criminal offence by selling or supplying a medicinal product. It places substances within one of five medical schedules, which determine whether a drug has any perceived therapeutic use, and whether or not it should be prescribed.

Challenging a positive test

As one might expect, athletes testing positive for a banned substance have **24.05** sought to challenge both the results of the test and the punishment meted out—on both legal and scientific technicalities.[2]

Sandra Gasser applied to the High Court for declaratory relief (following a ban imposed by the International Amateur Athletic Federation (IAAF))

---

[1] CAS 94/129.
[2] For a thorough analysis of this area, see *Sports Law and Litigation* by Moore and *Sports Law* by Beloff, Kerr and Demetriou, *ante*.

that the suspension was unreasonably in restraint of trade. Scott J. refused to grant relief but accepted that the principles of restraint of trade applied.

Katrin Krabbe had a ban imposed by the IAAF following a positive test for the stimulant, Clenbuterol. It was not on the list of the banned substances. The decision to ban Krabbe was taken on the basis that it was a stimulant. One of the bans imposed upon her was overturned.

The Dubin report effectively accepted that an athlete should be given the opportunity to challenge/test the validity of the results of the test. Positive drug tests by British athletes have hit the headlines on several occasions in recent years. The Scottish sprinter Doug Walker called into question the whole testing procedure. Walker insisted he had never taken any banned performance-enhancing substance. However, the most well-known case involved Sale athlete Diane Modahl. She made the same claim after a laboratory in Lisbon recorded a positive test by her in 1994.

24.06   She was subsequently banned for four years, but had the suspension lifted after a lengthy legal fight to clear her name ended with the Lisbon testing facilities being declared inadequate. She succeeded in establishing that there was a possibility that the urine sample had degraded by reason of the failure to store it in a refrigerator. Modahl unsuccessfully sued the British Athletics Federation (BAF) for more than £500,000. The House of Lords[3] rejected her argument that the BAF was in breach of contract with an athlete by suspending the athlete following the positive test. Lord Hoffmann indicated that suspension and commencement of proceedings involved no finding by the drug advisory committee that any offence had been committed or that the laboratory report was accurate. It would be inconsistent with the procedures of the IAAF and the BAF to imply a term that a national federation should not be entitled to initiate disciplinary procedures in accordance with the procedural guidelines if the laboratory had done something to vitiate its accredited status. That matter might not be within the BAF's knowledge. It was unreasonable to construe the contract so as to impose a potentially large liability in damages on it when it had simply been carrying out its duties under the rules of the IAAF. Modahl's claim was thus bound to fail and should have been struck out.

Modahl also claimed that the disciplinary committee's decision was tainted by bias. The Court of Appeal[4] rejected this argument. Modahl alleged that each member of the committee was, in one way or another, biased. For example, one member of the Committee was alleged to have said that all athletes were guilty of doping until proved innocent. The Judge considered the evidence and concluded that the the particular panel member was careless in his phraseology but did not carry into the committee a prejudice that athletes were guilty until proven innocent. Each of the other

---

[3] *The Times*, July 23, 1999.
[4] [2001] E.W.C.A. Civ. 1447.

panel members' impartiality was challenged—the allegations failed. In the Court of Appeal Parker L.J. stated[5]

"The judge's actual finding that the hearing before the Disciplinary Committee was not tainted by any actual bias seems to me to mark the beginning and the end of Mrs Modahl's case. Even if the selection of one or more of the members of the Disciplinary Committee gave rise to apparent bias—in the sense of a real risk of actual bias—the finding of no actual bias means, in my judgment, that a claim by Mrs Modahl against the BAF for damages for breach of contract based on apparent bias must fail since in the event no loss resulted."

In *Korda v. ITF Ltd (t/a International Tennis Federation)*[6] the claimant sought a declaration that the defendant was not entitled under section (V)3 of the ITF Tennis Anti-Doping Programme 1998 to appeal to the Court of Arbitration for Sport from a decision made by the ITF anti-doping appeals committee. Lightman J. said that in May 1998 the claimant signed an application form to enter the Wimbledon Lawn Tennis Championship by which he agreed, *inter alia*, that the meeting would be played under the rules of tennis as approved by the defendant, the ITF, and that competitors should be prepared to undergo drug testing. In July 1998 the claimant provided a urine sample which tested positive for a prohibited substance. The ITF's independent anti-doping review board concluded that there had been a violation of the anti-doping programme. The claimant appealed to the anti-doping appeals committee. The committee accepted the claimant's evidence that he did not knowingly take a prohibited substance and that he had acted reasonably. The committee decided that although a violation had occurred, in view of exceptional circumstances no sanction should be imposed beyond the mandatory sanction that the claimant should forfeit all computer ranking points and return to the ITF all prize money earned at the tournament. The ITF filed an appeal with the Court of Arbitration for Sport. The claimant sought a declaration that the ITF was not entitled to appeal to that court. His Lordship said that the ITF wished on appeal to contend that the sentence of the appeals committee was too lenient and that the penalty of a period of one year's suspension from participation in all ITF sanctioned or recognised tournaments or events should also be imposed. The claim by the ITF to the existence of a right of appeal rested upon the terms of section (V)3 of the programme which stated: "Any dispute arising out of any decision made by the . . . appeals committee shall be submitted exclusively to the appeals arbitration division of the Court of Arbitration for Sport . . ." The ITF contended that there was a contract in the terms of the anti-doping programme between the ITF and the claimant and that upon its true construction section (V)3 conferred upon both parties to that contract an absolute and general right of appeal on its merits to the court of arbitration.

24.07

---

[5] *ibid.*, para. 71.
[6] *The Times*, February 4, 1999.

The claimant argued that he was not a party to any such contract with the ITF, and certainly not to a contract which incorporated section (V)3. In addition the claimant contended that section (V)3 conferred no such right of appeal, but only a limited right to resolve questions raised by the decision of the appeals committee. Lightman J. accepted that a contractual relationship had been established. There was no written agreement signed by the parties and there was no oral agreement either. Such an agreement was to be inferred from the facts. The claimant submitted that the words of section (V)3 extended only to the validity, enforceability or construction of the decision. Lightman J. agreed, having considered language of the section. It assumed that a final decision had been made and was concerned with resolving questions as to the impact of that decision on the parties. Nothing would have been easier than to provide for appeals to the court of arbitration if that had been intended.

24.08   The ITF appealed to the Court of Appeal. The Court of Appeal found that the dispute arose from the decision of the Anti-Doping Committee and that the provision, which provided that the Appeal Committee's decision should be final, did not qualify the general jurisdiction given to refer matters to the CAS. Thus the case duly went before the CAS.[7]

In *Wilander & anor v. Tobin & anor*[8] Wilander and Novacek, professional tennis players, applied to the Chancery Division of the High Court for leave to re-amend their statement of claim in their action against Mr Brian Tobin and Mr David Jude, respectively the president and treasurer of the ITF, so as to plead that the provisions of rule 53 were void as incompatible with Article 59 of the E.C. Treaty. Rule 53, designed to detect and deter the use of prohibited substances by players at tournaments organised by the ITF, provided for random samples of urine to be tested. If both of two samples proved positive, a review board, before whom the player had no right to be heard or to adduce evidence or to make representations, could determine that a violation of that rule had occurred. Only then did the player have a right of appeal to an appeals committee. The application was refused by the Court of Appeal.

24.09   The Court of Appeal had earlier ruled in the same case that[9] it was neither unfair nor unreasonable that rule 53 reversed the normal burden of proof by requiring a player who had prima facie tested positive for drugs. The court refused to restrain the ITF from continuing with or acting upon proceedings against the appellants by reference to rule 53 of the federation rules. Citing *Conteh v. Onslow Fane*[10] and *Gasser*,[11] Lightman J. at first instance said that he could see nothing approaching unfairness or unreasonableness in the wording or procedure of the International Tennis Federation Rules. Neill

---

[7] CAS 99/223.
[8] *The Times*, July 15, 1996, *Independent*, January 24, 1997.
[9] *The Times*, April 18, 1996.
[10] *The Times*, June 26, 1975.
[11] *ibid.*

L.J., refusing the appeal, said that the appellants had not shown an arguable case that the ITF were in fundamental breach of contract, or that rule 53 was unfair or unreasonable and therefore void as being in unlawful restraint of trade, or that the anti-doping procedures followed by the ITF and its review board were so defective as to entitle the court to grant an interlocutory injunction restraining further proceedings by its appeal committee. It was important that the rules of international sporting bodies like the ITF should be absolutely clear and most carefully drafted to avoid the possibility of confusion and doubt. Different sporting bodies should, as far as possible, adopt in their rules common practices for drug testing.

Conclusion

This Chapter provides only a very brief introduction to this subject as it only **24.10** impinges on the periphery of the main subject. However, the issue is unlikely to go away as the money around sports gets greater and drugs become ever more sophisticated.

The claimant disagreed, and said the appellate had not shown an intention such that the ITF were to take upon a burdon of connect or that the 57 was unenforceable, and there is no reason to be unjustified enrichment or trade, on that the unfair ding procedures followed by the ITF and a ... new .... and seek ... directors ... to find the correct procedure for their ... resolution – strain in their proceedings, by its appeal committee. It was important that the rules of industrial sporting bodies, like the ITF should as all UEFA clear terms of careful drafted to avoid the problems of confusion and doubt that can arise in practice, bodies seek to anticipate in all of their rules enhance or prevent disputes, dispute, etc plan.

Conclusion

In this chapter we cover a wide area, which are of one occurs in the subject part at only £24,100. Comparison the primary military of the multinational. However, the matters unlikely to occur within the money issue in sports, law, property, and things b comp, are more topics.

Chapter 25

Insurance

"I . . . the Act of God designation on all insurance policies; which means roughly, that you cannot be insured for the accidents that are most likely to happen to you. If your ox kicks a hole in your neighbour's Maserati, indemnity is instantaneous."

Alan Coren, The Lady from Stalingrad Mansions, 1977.

Introduction

This Chapter looks at the need for organisations to insure themselves **25.01** against the risk of potential liabilities. This has been highlighted in recent years by the cases of *Elliott v. Saunders and Liverpool FC*,[1] *Smoldon v. Whitworth*[2] and *Watson v. British Boxing Board of Control.*[3] It also looks at whether there is a duty to insure, the potential for government intervention in this area and finally goes briefly to explore some of the different types of insurance which are available.

A useful chapter in this context is Chapter 9 of *School Sports and the Law* by Edward Grayson.[3a]

Cases highlighting the need for insurance

Elliott v. Saunders and Liverpool FC

In *Elliott v. Saunders and Liverpool FC*[4] Paul Elliott, playing for Chelsea **25.02** Football Club, failed to establish that Dean Saunders, then of Liverpool, had acted with such lack of care as to be in breach of his duty to exercise

---

[1] Unreported, June 10, 1994; Halsbury's Laws of England 1994, Annual Abridgement, para. 2056.

[2] [1997] P.I.Q.R. P133.

[3] [2001] Q.B. 1134; [2001] 2 W.L.R. 1256; I.L.R. January 11, 2001; *The Times*, February 2, 2001, CA; *The Times*, October 12, 1999 (Kennedy J.).

[3a] Craven. CCH Group Limited, 2001.

[4] Unreported, June 10, 1994; Halsbury's Laws of England 1994, Annual Abridgement, para. 2056. See Chap. 3, above, for more details.

reasonable care in all the circumstances, when the defendant's tackle had severed the claimant's cruciate ligaments.

However, despite the failure of the action it raised the profile of the potential liability of players on the football pitch. In particular, during the judgment of Drake J., he posed the question of potential comprehensive insurance within the professional game.

Following the case, Gordon Taylor, the Chief Executive of the Professional Footballers' Association ("PFA"), said that the case posed a dilemma. The PFA could ignore neither a player's right to sue nor the defendant being left isolated if his club's insurers refused to take responsibility. He said that an arbitration procedure and a no-fault insurance scheme had both been considered, but had been dismissed as unworkable.

25.03 Paul Elliott's claim was not driven by insurers seeking to cast the burden of paying his compensation onto the defendants' insurers. It was privately funded, and Elliott ended up having to pick up the substantial costs bill personally when he lost. He then had to rely on the benevolence of Chelsea's supporters to help him meet that cost by a testimonial match.

As Moore states in *Sports Law and Litigation*[5]:

"One can surely be excused for thinking that this was a thoroughly unsatisfactory outcome for a fine player like Elliott, who was rightly described by Drake J. as a 'gentleman'."

The compensation provided through the disability scheme administered by the PFA is extremely small, and with so much money passing hands in the modern professional game it is an astonishing state of affairs that more is not being done to protect its principal assets, its players.

The dilemma facing Paul Elliott, like many others, is that he only had third-party insurance[6] cover indemnifying him in respect of claims brought against him. Without comprehensive insurance[7] he was exposed to the predicament which he unfortunately found himself in.

Paul Elliott clearly needed his own personal insurance scheme, as do all other professional sportsmen and women, and advice to that effect is an essential responsibility of those involved in protecting the welfare of the players. Players and clubs alike would be well advised to ensure that adequate insurance cover is taken out to cover not only third party liabilities, but also the risk of injury to the player himself. If not, the only potential avenue open to an uninsured player who sustains serious injury during the course of a game, is to embark upon hazardous litigation.

---

[5] 2nd ed., CLT Professional Publishing Ltd, 2000.
[6] For an explanation of which, see below.
[7] For an explanation of which, see below.

Smoldon v. Whitworth

In *Smoldon v. Whitworth and Nolan*,[8] the Court of Appeal held that a   **25.04**
referee had been negligent and that this had caused the claimant's injuries
after a scrum collapsed. In that case Lord Bingham L.C.J. commented:

> "We are caused to wonder whether it would not be beneficial if all players were,
> as a matter of general practice, to be insured not against negligence but against the
> risk of catastrophic injury, but that is no doubt a matter to which those respon-
> sible for the administration of rugby football have given anxious attention."

Watson v. British Boxing Board of Control

Perhaps the biggest case highlighting the need for insurance against poten-   **25.05**
tial liabilities was that of *Watson v. British Boxing Board of Control*.[9] In
that case, the governing body of British boxing, the British Board of Boxing
was held to have been negligent in failing to provide adequate emergency
medical facilities at the world middleweight title fight between Chris
Eubank and Michael Watson.

As the Court of Appeal noted, the BBBC was a non-profit making whose
net assets at the end of December 1991 were about £352,000. Unfortunately for Mr Watson, despite its lack of assets, the board did not insure
against liability in negligence. This not only exposed the BBBC to unpro-
tected liability but more importantly left Mr Watson with serious doubts as
to whether he would ever be able to enforce his judgment.

This therefore highlights the need for compulsory insurance in areas such
as this to protect against similar situations happening in the future.

A duty to insure?

An interesting question arose in the case of *Van Oppen v. The Clerk to the*   **25.06**
Trustees of the Bedford Charity (Harpur Trust)[10] where a schoolboy was
seriously injured by a tackle in a house rugby match when he was 16 but
was not insured. The schoolboy claimed damages for alleged negligence
against the trustees of his former school. He alleged that the school had
failed to:

1. take reasonable care for his safety on the field of play by failing to
   coach or instruct him in proper tackling techniques and, in particular,
   the head-on tackle;

2. ensure that he was insured against accidental injury at the time of the
   accident;

---

[8] [1997] P.I.Q.R. P133. See Chap. 13, above, for more details.
[9] [2001] Q.B. 1134; [2001] 2 W.L.R. 1256; *Independent*, January 11, 2001; *The Times*,
February 2, 2001, CA. See Chap. 10, above, for more details.
[10] [1989] 1 All E.R. 273; affirmed [1989] 3 All E.R. 389, CA.

3. advise his father of:

(a) the inherent risk of serious injury in the game of rugby;
(b) the consequential need for personal accident insurance; and
(c) the fact that the school had not arranged such insurance.

The claim was dismissed on all the grounds complained of. As far as the first allegation was concerned, the trial Judge found on the evidence that what had happened could properly be described as "a tragic accident" due to a mistimed tackle, not by any coaching or training error, or omission.

25.07   However, the decision is more noteworthy for the finding that there was no duty on the part of the school to effect insurance cover. The relationship of school and pupil did not give rise to such a general duty.

The third limb of the claim failed on the ground that as there was no obligation on the part of parents to insure their offspring, a school cannot be under any higher duty. That finding was made by the Medical Officers' Schools Association ("MOSA") Report of 1979 which urgently recommended that schools should take out accident insurance for pupil rugby players. The Rugby Football Union's response to this was to activate it. Compulsory insurance was recommended but activated too late for the claimant in *Van Oppen*.

Legislation

Employers' Liability (Compulsory Insurance) Act 1969

25.08   There has, as yet, been very little legislative involvement in this area. The main piece of legislation is the Employers' Liability (Compulsory Insurance) Act 1969.

This Act makes employer's liability insurance[11] compulsory for most employees. Interestingly, local education authorities are exempt from the Act. However, a Department for Education and Employment Circular 2/94: *Local Management of Schools* makes it clear that LEAs will either act as insurers or arrange for insurance to cover the potential liabilities of employers, so in practice LEA maintained schools should have employer's liability cover.

The Act does cover private schools and this leads to the irony that if an employee of such a school, such as a P.E. teacher, had been injured playing in the same game as the claimant in the *Van Oppen* case, any failure on the part of the school to insure him against injury would have been an offence under section 5 of Act.

It should be noted, however, that the Act does not give rise to civil liability.

---

[11] For which, see below.

In the context of schools, it should also be noted that local education authorities are required by the School Standards and Framework Act 1998 to indemnify members of governing bodies of schools against any legal costs and expenses they may reasonably incur in the exercise of their functions as members of these committees.

Employers' Liability (Compulsory Insurance) Regulations 1998[12]

Even where the Act does not apply, a school should not have less than the statutory minimum cover required under the Act. This minimum level of cover is set out in the Employers' liability (Compulsory Insurance) Regulations 1998. The minimum cover in March 2001 was £5 million in the aggregate for claims arising from any one occurrence. **25.09**

The Regulations require this cover to be in force without any element of self-funding, that is without any excess or deductible being paid by the employer. The Regulations prohibit insurers from including certain policy terms and conditions which would otherwise allow them to avoid cover.

Proposals for the future

The above cases highlight the need for clubs, players, governing bodies and any others involved in sport to be fully insured against potential liability associated with their particular sport. This should apply to both professional and amateur sports. **25.10**

In addition, there is a strong case to bring in comprehensive insurance into professional sport to protect the participants against financial ruin following an injury blighting their career.

Moore in *Sports Law and Litigation*[13] suggests that:

> "an appropriate levy on transfer fees would surely provide an adequate large sinking fund to compensate players like Paul Elliott and Brian McCord, whose careers are blighted by injury, without the need to have recourse to law."

As he points out, a similar proposal was made by Lord Justice Taylor in his final report into the Hillsborough tragedy in order to provide the necessary capital for ground improvements.

In July 2000, the Sports Minister, Kate Hoey signalled her support for the introduction of a compulsory insurance scheme to benefit more than 500,000 amateur footballers.

The Football Association has also announced that it was considering funding a scheme to provide both personal injury and public liability cover for all its 43,000 affiliated clubs. The moves followed a campaign by a

---

[12] S.I. 1997 No. 2573.
[13] 2nd ed., CLT Professional Publishing Ltd, 2000.

Norfolk man who had to have part of his leg amputated as a result of a mistimed tackle in a village match.

Types of insurance available

25.11 There are numerous types of insurance available on the open market. The following provides a brief introduction to some of these. They are only general comments and the small print of each policy should be read to see exactly what they do in fact cover.

Employer's liability insurance

25.12 This enables employers to meet their legal liabilities up to the policy limit for claims arising from injuries, for example, to the employees.

Public liability insurance

This protects against the cost of claims by members of the public in relation to a business' activities.

Professional indemnity insurance

This provides cover in relation to a firm's staff's failure to show the necessary care and skill in the exercise of their professional duties.

Personal accident insurance

This provides cover for accidental injuries. It frequently has a tariff based on specific types of injury such as loss of an eye or limb. Some policies include related cover such as hospitalisation benefit. They pay out on the occurrence of a particular injury or loss and unlike employer's liability or public liability, it is the injury or loss of use rather than legal liability to a third party which triggers a payment under the policy.

Business interruption insurance

25.13 This covers loss of business income in the event of accidents such as fire.

Key person cover

This provides financial protection in the event of incapacity of key staff or in the sporting context, potentially, players. Such policies usually pay a lump sum to the insured upon the illness or injury of nominated persons which would help cover the costs of providing a temporary or permanent replacement and other expenses.

Permanent health insurance

This covers an agreed percentage of the salary of a member of staff or a player who is unable to work due to illness. This sum is paid to the employee, helping the business or club to avoid the need to pay both the sick person and their replacement. If the person is unable to return to work, the policy will usually pay an agreed percentage of their salary for a pre-agreed period, depending on their capacity to carry out other work.

Building and contents insurance

This covers what it suggests: a particular building and its contents in the event, for example of fire or theft.

Cover for governing bodies' liability

This would cover the potential liability of the governing bodies of sports such as that incurred by the British Boxing Board of Control in the case of *Watson v. British Boxing Board of Control.*[14]

25.14

Travel insurance

This will be relevant for those going on, for example, adventure holidays. People should be careful to check the small print and in particular that the activity they are undertaking is actually covered and is not excluded.

Legal expenses insurance

This provides cover against one a club's own legal fees and any legal costs against the club in the event of certain types of legal dispute. Cover is usually only provided where legal expenses insurers consider the club has reasonable prospects of winning or successfully defending the dispute.

Third party liability insurance

This is a general term which covers liability to third parties in circumstances set out in the policy.

---

[14] [2001] Q.B. 1134; [2001] 2 W.L.R. 1256; [2001] 1 L.R. 1; *The Times*, October 12, 1999. For which see Chap. 10 above.

Comprehensive insurance

This is another general term which normally not only covers liability from third parties in circumstances set out in the policy but also provides compensation to the policy holder in the event of certain circumstances.

Importance of full disclosure

25.15 Those taking out insurance are obliged to disclose all relevant information when asking an insurer to give them cover for the first time, and there is the same obligation on renewal. If the information is inaccurate or incomplete it could result in the insured having no cover at all. The person who looks after insurance for an organisation is responsible for making all the necessary enquiries so that full and accurate answers may be given to questions on the proposal form and any other questions insurers may ask.

Conclusion

25.16 The whole thrust of this book is that the risks of liability attaching to all sports is on the increase. In these circumstances, the best advice to all those involved in sport is to ensure that they are fully insured against such risks. In addition, professional sportsmen should consider obtaining comprehensive insurance to protect against an injury bringing their career to an end. An example of the awareness of the importance of taking out insurance is provided by the guidance given by the English Cricket Board on their web-site[15] where they say:

> "It is important for all those involved with young players to understand their responsibilities. It is also very strongly recommended that all those involved with young cricketers ensure that they have appropriate insurance cover, either individually or through their membership of the various cricketing Associations (*e.g.* the Association of Cricket Coaches, the Association of Cricket Umpires and Scorers etc.) or through their club or school."

Questions may always arise as to the definitions within the policies and insurers may well provide only restrictive policies. Difficulties may also arise for organisations in obtaining the cover. For example, the sport of skateboarding formed its own Skateboard Association under the aegis of the Sports Council but was forced to go to Holland for adequate insurance facilities.[16] It is interesting to note that for the more extreme sports, the organising bodies have taken the lead in this area by offering insurance as one of their member benefits. For example, the British Surfing Association (www.britsurf.co.uk) provides up to £2 million worth of public liability

---

[15] See www.ECB.co.uk.
[16] E. Grayson, *Sport and the Law*, 3rd ed., Butterworths, 2000, p. 441.

insurance worldwide, the British Kitesurfing Association (www.kite surfing.org) provides up to £5 million of third party liability insurance whilst flying any kite on water or land and the British Cycling Federation (www.bcf.uk.com) provides up to £5 million worth of third party liability insurance for cycling accidents in the U.K. and Europe. Considering that a kitesurfer apparently recently landed on top of a double decker bus on the Brighton Sea Front, this is perhaps a good thing.

Ultimately, this is an area which would benefit from government intervention in a similar way to that already implemented for employers and in another area, for car drivers.

Grayson, in *Sport and the Law*[17] makes the following points with regard to legal liability insurance: **25.17**

1. All clubs should have a "Public Liability" insurance in force, and it ought to include liability when the ground is loaned or hired for any purpose other than normal use, such as a boxing tournament. Club activities outside the ground and overseas tours should also be covered.

2. To insure a club's liability to its employees, a separate policy is usually required. The premium is calculated at a rate per cent on the total wages and salaries, and this cover is additional to any benefits that can be obtained under the National Insurance Scheme (see the Employers' Liability (Compulsory Insurance) Act 1969).

3. As so many clubs take part in overseas tours, clubs should ensure that, before they travel abroad, some sort of cover for medical expenses has been arranged. The cost of having a comparatively minor operation in some foreign countries is enormous, and there is no equivalent of our National Health Service in many areas.

4. Two complementary situations which can appeal to clubs and members collectively or individually are:

   a. group insurance schemes; and
   b. personal insurance which many participants obtain in particularly violent or physical pursuits supplementary to any cover.

5. Finally, a club committee and officers may find it prudent either by insurance or provision in their club rules to provide for general or specific indemnities. Once example, was the disclosure during Michael Watson's judgment against the British Boxing Board of Control on September 25, 1999 that notwithstanding its professional expertise among its well-known named Stewards, insurance cover did not exist.

---

[17] *ibid.*, pp. 441–2.

Part IV

Practice and Procedure

Practice and Procedure

Chapter 26

Bringing a sports injury case

"MORGANHALL: . . . if they ever give you a brief, old fellow, attack the medical evidence. Remember, the jury's full of rheumatism and arthritis and shocking gastric troubles. They love to see a medical man put through it."

John Mortimer, The Dock Brief, 1958.

Introduction

In practical terms, there is nothing to distinguish personal injury litigation **26.01** arising out of a sports injury from, say, an accident at work. This Chapter is not intended to be a complete guide to bringing an action to final hearing. However, it does hope to identify those matters to which litigants and their legal representatives should have regard when utilising the civil justice system. The civil procedure in England Wales underwent drastic reforms in 1999.[1] The Rules of Supreme Court (RSC) and County Court Rules (CCR), the rules by which civil justice operated prior to April 1999, were regarded as defective. Litigation was expensive, lengthy and overly adversarial. Lord Woolf, Master of the Rolls, in his final report on Access to Civil Justice set out his intentions for the civil procedure system. The Civil Procedure Rules (CPR) were the result. Underpinning the CPR is the overriding objective which is set out at CPR, r.1.1. The rules are a new procedural code intended to enable the court to deal with cases justly. Dealing with a case justly includes, so far as is practicable[2]:

(a) ensuring the parties are on an equal footing;

(b) saving expense;

(c) dealing with the case in a ways which are proportionate—

    (i) to the amount of money involved;
    (ii) to the importance of the case;
    (iii) to the complexity of the issues;
    (iv) the financial position of each party;

---

[1] Access to Civil Justice, final report by Lord Woolf M.R.
[2] CPR, r.1.1(2).

(d) ensuring that it is dealt with expeditiously and fairly;

(e) allotting to it an appropriate share of the court's resources while taking into account the need to allot resources to other cases

The court now has control of case management. In effect, this means that the timetable for the conduct of the litigation is set by the court. The times when cases were allowed to limp along year after year without ever reaching final hearing have long since passed. The emphasis is upon legal representatives and litigants to achieve as much as possible prior to the issue of proceedings. That includes settlement in appropriate cases.

Pre-action protocol

26.02   The pre-action protocol for personal injury came into force on April 26, 1999. The protocol is intended to allow parties to co-operate and resolve disputes prior to the issue of proceedings. The onus is on the proposed claimant to identify his complaint at an early stage to the proposed defendant and, if appropriate, their insurer. The protocol is intended primarily for actions which are likely to be allocated to the fast track,[3] more of which later. The claimant is required to send to the proposed defendant a letter of claim (para. 2.7), when sufficient information is available to substantiate a realistic claim and before issues of claim are addressed in detail. The letter is required to contain a clear summary of the facts on which the claim is based together with an indication of the nature of the injuries sustained and any other financial loss. The letter should be sufficiently detailed to allow the proposed defendant to commence investigations. A letter of claim is not intended to have the same effect as a statement of case. However, the letter should set out, broadly, the claimant's case.

   The protocol recommends that a defendant be given three months to investigate and respond to the claim before proceedings are issued. This may not always be possible. Where a party consults a solicitor close to the expiry of the limitation period it may simply be necessary to issue proceedings immediately. As a result of these investigations, and in an appropriate case, the defendant may have documentation to disclose. If the defendant denies liability he should enclose with his letter of reply, such documents in his possession which are material to the issues between the parties and which would be likely to be ordered to be disclosed by the court (para. 3.10) The aim of the disclosure of documentation is not to encourage fishing expeditions but to promote an early exchange of relevant information to clarify, and in an appropriate case, resolve issues in dispute. It is important to

---

[3] CPR, r.26.1(2) there are three litigation tracks—small claims, fast and multi tracks, CPR, r.26.6(4) the fast track is for claims which have value of between £5,000 and £15,000. The case will be allocated to the most appropriate track. The track, to a great extent, determines the way that the court will manage the case.

remember that there may in fact be no documentation. For example, in a case involving a reckless tackle during a football game, it is unlikely if there would be any documentation if the proposed defendant were a Sunday league footballer. However, if the proposed defendant was a footballer in the FA Premier League the defendant may have been the subject of disciplinary proceedings within his own football club. He may have possession of documents arising out such an inquiry.

If the claim is one in which expert evidence is likely to be required, the   26.03
claimant should identify in his letter of claim the names of proposed experts. Ordinarily, this would include a medical expert who will be required to give an opinion and prognosis on the injury sustained by the claimant. However, it is possible that expert evidence will be required on the subject of liability. For example, in the *Saunders v. Elliot* case a former professional footballer and now well-known football pundit Jimmy Hill gave evidence to the court. The defendant has 14 days to identify any objections to the named experts. The claimant must then instruct a mutually acceptable expert. However, if the defendant objects to all the named experts the parties may nominate their own experts. There may be costs consequences if either party is deemed by the court to have behaved unreasonably in failing to agree on a single expert to be instructed.

Evidence

Witnesses of fact

The claimant will be in a position to put his case effectively if the evidence   26.04
is garnered swiftly and proceedings issued at an early stage. In order to write the letter before action the claimant's legal representative will need to obtain a proof of evidence from the claimant. The solicitor with conduct of the matter would be well advised to obtain a proof of evidence from other potential witnesses. So, too, when notice of the claim is received, for the defendant.

Returning to the example of the reckless tackle, they may wish to obtain proofs of evidence from team-mates, the referee, lines-men (or referee's assistants) and spectators. It is likely that the referee and his assistants will be able to provide important evidence. Information which they will be able to provide includes whether or not a free-kick or penalty was awarded, did the player perpetrating the tackle receive a caution or were they dismissed.

Video technology

If the game was televised, video footage of the tackle should be obtained. As   26.05
television companies strive to out do each other in the quality of their sports

coverage, the number of television angles that can be provided of any one incident in a game is staggering. If the television company screening the match had those facilities at the game, each angle of the tackle should be obtained. Such evidence may, in fact, be of little value. Nevertheless, if there are 12 angles of a particular tackle available, then 12 angles should be available to the court.

A good example of this was provided in the case of *Pitcher v. Huddersfield Town Football Club Ltd*[4] which the claimant's lawyer, Mel Goldberg, a partner with London firm Grower Freeman & Goldberg, was reported as saying[5] signalled a new era in video evidence.

The claimant was a professional footballer playing for Crystal Palace. He alleged that that a player for the defendants had negligently tackled him and specifically that the tackle occurred after he had kicked the ball.[6] There were no witnesses to the sequence of events of the tackle except for Palace coach Ray Lewington.

The claimant therefore relied on video evidence. However, the video footage was not of good quality. KTV Limited, a video post-production house, used computer image enhancement to clarify and magnify the visuals, superimposing a time counter over the video. The finished video was then recorded on to a DVD to preserve the quality and to enable accurate timing and good slow motions.

26.06 The court saw the evidence using a five-speed replay system, and three magnifications. The DVD was also used to produce exact-frame stills. However, despite this and the expert evidence given on his behalf,[7] the claimant lost the case. Mr Pitcher's lawyer, Mel Goldberg, a partner with London firm Grower Freeman & Goldberg, was reported as saying[8]:

> "The reason we were unable to prove the case was because the angle of the video was unhelpful, but this technology means that football games can now be properly post-mortemed where necessary."

Physical evidence

26.07 Of course sport is not just about football just as evidence is not just about statements. There may be valuable physical evidence which needs to be collected. For example, take the not uncommon situation of a golfer or member of the public who is struck by an errant golf ball (the author has suffered that particular experience!). If the golf ball was struck from a driving range where the perimeter netting had been allowed to deteriorate

---

[4] Q.B.D., July 17, 2001, Hallett J.
[5] J. Fleming, "Video Scrutiny of Football Fouls" Law Gazette, September 7, 2001.
[6] See Chap. 3, above, for more details.
[7] For which, see below.
[8] J. Fleming, "Video Scrutiny of Football Fouls" Law Gazette, September 7, 2001.

into a state of disrepair such that there were holes in the net it would be essential to obtain photograph's of the holes in the net. Alternatively, it may be that the netting was not high enough. If golf balls are consistently hit out over the fence, evidence of this should be obtained. Other common accidents include trips and slips. Photographs of the cause of the trip or slip should be obtained before corrective measures are taken by the proposed defendant.

Medical evidence

As indicated above, if possible medical evidence should be obtained by way **26.08** of joint-instruction. The benefit of this is to save time and money. Proceedings for personal injury should not be issued without medical evidence to support the case. There are many medical practitioners who provide medico-legal reports. The cost and quality of such reports varies. The legal representative may have a number of medical experts whom he trusts and who provide consistently good reports. If you do not know of any practitioners then it would be worthwhile consulting a register of approved expert witnesses. It is usual to instruct a consultant in the relevant discipline to obtain a report. However, if the injury is minor a report from a registrar or a GP is likely to be adequate. As a general rule, if the claim is worth in excess of £15,000, the claimant should instruct a consultant. This is because the defendant may be given permission to obtain his own medical evidence. If the claimant has provided in support of his case medical evidence from his GP and the defendant then obtains evidence from a consultant, a court will almost certainly prefer the evidence of the consultant.

In selecting the expert, it is useful to know the amount of medico-legal work carried out by the practitioner in addition to the amounts of work which he does for claimants, defendants and on the basis of joint instructions. A court may be more persuaded by an expert who carries out an equal amount of work for claimants and defendants than an expert who does work exclusively for one or the other. Beware, they do exist and certain medical experts are known throughout the courts of the land for their lack of impartiality and their pro-claimant or pro-defendant stance. This has been remedied, to a certain extent, by the requirement for all experts to acknowledge that their overriding duty is to the court and not to the party or parties who pay them.

The medical report should set out how the accident occurred, the injury and symptoms suffered by the claimant since the accident, any relevant history gleaned from examination of the claimant's general practitioner and hospital records, the results of any examination carried out on the claimant and, finally, an opinion and prognosis. A court must find "on the balance of probabilities" whether the symptoms complained of by the claimant were as a result of the alleged negligence.

Non-medical expert evidence

26.09 Non-medical expert evidence may be necessary to support the claimant's case. Non-medical expert evidence may be required in many sports cases and can range from experts on defective sports equipment to experts as to how the game should be played.

A good example was provided last year in the high profile football case of *Pitcher v. Huddersfield Town Football Club Ltd.*[9] In a detailed judgment, Hallett J. made a careful of the examination of the expert evidence given by both sides. For the claimant, evidence was given by Sky Sports pundit Frank McLintock and [then] Crystal Palace manager David Bassett[10] and for the defendant evidence was given by Jimmy Hill and Frank Clark.

So, too, in the Court of Appeal case of *Caldwell v. Fitzgerald & ors*,[11] evidence was given by the distinguished experts John Francome and Carl Llewellyn.[12]

Parties should bear in mind the court's desire to keep expert evidence to a minimum. No party may call an expert or put in evidence an expert's report without the permission of the court.[13] No expert evidence will be allowed unless it will help the court. Evidence will only be allowed if the subject matter upon which it is proposed that evidence will be obtained is an "acknowledged body of expertise".[14]

26.10 In *Barings plc (in liquidation) v. Coopers & Lybrand (No. 2)*[15] Evans-Lombe J. stated in the context of whether or not investment banking was an acknowledged body of expertise that:

> "that expert evidence was admissible where the court accepted that there existed a recognised expertise governed by recognised standards and rules of conduct capable of influencing the court's decision on any of the issues which it had to decide, if the witness to be called satisfied the court that he had the necessary expertise to give potentially helpful evidence. Evidence meeting that test could still be excluded if the court concluded that calling such evidence would not be helpful in resolving any issue in the case justly, for example where the issue to be decided was one of law or was one which the court could reach a fully informed decision of without the hearing of such evidence".

The courts willingness to restrict non-medical expert evidence has been evidence most notably in personal injury litigation. Whereas care and employment experts were once commonplace, Judges now require consider-

---

[9] Q.B.D., July 17, 2001, Hallett J.
[10] Law Gazette, September 7, 2001.
[11] [2001] E.W.C.A. Civ. 1054, CA (Civil Division), Lord Woolf C.J., Tuckey L.J. May 27, 2001.
[12] See Chap. 3, above, for more details.
[13] CPR, r.35.4.
[14] See *Barings plc (in liquidation) v. Coopers & Lybrand (No. 2) The Times*, March 7, 2001 *per* Evans-Lombe J.
[15] *The Times*, March 7, 2001.

able persuasion before they will give permission for such evidence to be adduced. It is likely that litigants will be able to persuade the court of the need for non-medical expert evidence in sport's injury cases more easily if for no other reason than that such actions are novel.

Another example of a case where the argument succeeded that the case was not suitable for expert evidence is provided by *Liddell v. Middleton*.[16] In that case expert evidence was given in a claim for personal injuries suffered in a road traffic accident, specifically accident reconstruction evidence. The Court of Appeal held that the court had wrongly permitted the experts to draw conclusions from the facts which it was the Judge's task to draw, for example, the conclusion that the driver was grossly negligent. Their assertions were inadmissible and irrelevant. The Court of Appeal observed that the tendency for numerous experts to be instructed in road accident claims, which only served to increase the length and costs of the trial, was to be regretted. In such claims, it was the exception not the rule that experts should be required.

Parties should also be alive to the argument that any opinions given by non-expert witnesses as to fact should not be allowed in as evidence. Even if the witness as to fact is an expert, it may be argued that his evidence should be limited to facts and not opinions if the particular party relying upon his evidence does not have permission to rely upon any expert evidence from him.

Issuing proceedings

A claimant has three years from the date of the accident causing the injury to issue proceedings.[17] Time, for the purposes of limitation, does not begin to run for minors (those under the age of 18) until they reach the age of 18. Thereafter the claimant has three years to issue proceedings. Time does not run for patients (those who are incapable as a result of mental disorder). Where a claim is based upon trespass to the person, the limitation period is six years.[18] Where proceedings have not been issued within the relevant limitation period the court has a discretion to disapply the limitation period.[19]

26.11

The claimant commences proceedings by requesting that the court issue a claim form.[20] The claim form must be served on the claimant within four months after the date of issue.[21] Particulars must be served with the claim form or within 14 days after service of the claim form on the defendant[22]

---

[16] [1996] P.I.Q.R. P36; *The Times*, July 17, 1995.
[17] Limitation Act 1980, s.11.
[18] See *Stubbings v. Webb* [1993] A.C. 498.
[19] Limitation Act 1980, s.33.
[20] CPR, r.7.2.
[21] CPR, r.7.5.
[22] CPR, r.7.4.

save that the particulars of claim must still be served no later than the time allowed to serve the claim form.

The particulars of claim will set out the case which the claimant intends to bring. It may or may not be identical to the case which was set out in the original letter before action. The particulars of claim will usually set out the parties, their relationship, the duty or duties owed by one party to the other (whether they be contractual or otherwise), the facts upon which the claimant intends to rely and particulars of how it is alleged the defendant has breached duty owed to the claimant. In addition, where a claim is made for general damages for pain, suffering and loss of amenity, the claimant must include in the particulars of claim his date of birth and brief details of the injuries sustained.[23] Where medical evidence is relied upon this should be served with the particulars of claim.

26.12   The claimant may also claim special damages. Special damages are losses sustained by the claimant as a result of the alleged breach of duty/contract. For example, a claimant may have lost earnings or had to incur medical expenses which, but for the accident, he would not have incurred. These should be set out in a schedule of loss. This can include past and future losses. A schedule of loss should be served with the particulars of claim.

Defending proceedings

26.13   The defendant's opportunity to state its case is in the defence. The approach that a defendant must take in its defence is similar to that of the claimant with the particulars of claim. The defendant must state which of the allegations in the particulars of claim he denies. The defendant must also state which of the allegations are not admitted but which the claimant is required to prove and, finally, which are admitted. If an allegation is denied, the defendant must state his reasons for doing so and, if he intends to put forward a different version of events from that given by the claimant he must state his own version.

A defendant who fails to deal with an allegation which is raised in the particulars of claim will be taken to have admitted the allegation[24] unless:

   (i) the defendant has set out in his defence the nature of his case in relation to the issue to which the allegation is relevant[25]; or

   (ii) where the claim includes a money claim, a defendant shall be taken to require that any allegation relating to the amount of money claimed be proved unless he expressly admits the allegation.[26]

---

[23] 16PD para. 4.
[24] CPR, r.16.5(5).
[25] CPR, r.16.5(3).
[26] CPR, r.16.5(4).

If the defendant disputes any part of the medical report which the claimant has served in support of his claim, the defendant must say so and give reasons. Commonly, the defendant will in fact state that he neither agrees nor disputes but has no knowledge of the matters contained in the medical report. If the defendant has his own medical evidence upon which he intends to rely then he must serve the same with his defence.

Allocation and case management

The first procedural step that the court requires the parties to undertake is to file allocation questionnaires. The questionnaire invites the parties to identify the witnesses of fact upon whom each party intends to rely, in addition to each expert, to suggest which is the appropriate track, to attach proposed directions for the case and to indicate how long the final hearing of the matter will take. There are three tracks: small claims track, fast-track and multi-track.   **26.14**

Small claims — Civil Procedure Rules Part 27

The small claims track is the normal track for any claim for personal injuries where the financial value of the claim is not more than £5,000 and where financial value of any claim for personal injuries is not more than £1,000 (this only refers to the general damages element for pain and suffering and not other losses). Accordingly, it is unlikely that any sports injury cases will be allocated to this track. Only very minor injuries attract awards that fall below the £1,000 ceiling. Other matters relevant to track allocation include whether the claim is complex because of its facts or the law or evidence.[27] Since sports cases are still regarded as unusual, most judges will allocate to the fast or multi-track. The fundamental difference between the small claims track and the other two is that in small claims a party is not usually entitled to recover his costs of the action if successful. It was intended to be a swift means through which a litigant in person could resolve a low value dispute without the need to incur disproportionate legal costs. Only if a party has behaved so unreasonably in either bringing or defending a claim would a party be able to apply for his legal costs. This is a punitive measure and will only be utilised in extreme circumstances.   **26.15**

Fast track — Civil Procedure Rules Part 28

The fast track is the normal track for any claim for which the small claims track is not the normal track and which has a financial value of not more than £15,000. Moreover, the case will only be allocated to the fast track if the court considers that the trial is not likely to last for more than one day   **26.16**

---

[27] CPR, r.26.8.

and oral expert evidence will be limited to one expert per party in relation to any one discipline and in no more than two disciplines. So, where a claim for personal injuries is likely to exceed £1,000 in respect of general damages only, the case will be allocated to the fast track. The court will give directions as to the future conduct of the proceedings. In the fast track, the court will set a relatively short timetable for compliance with directions. The court may hold a case management conference if there is a significant difference of opinion between the parties on the appropriate directions.

A successful party whose case was allocated to the fast track would be entitled to recover his costs. However, fast track costs are subject to caps. For example, the maximum which is currently recoverable by the successful party for legal representation by a barrister at trial, for a claim worth between £3,000 and £10,000, is £500. The costs will be summarily assessed at the end of the hearing. Each party is required to attend the final hearing with a schedule of costs which has to be served 24 hours in advance of that hearing. This must identify the work carried out by that party's legal representative, their hourly charging rate and their experience. All disbursements must be identified. Unnecessary or exorbitant costs will not be recovered from the losing party. Of course, every case must be considered on its own facts. However, it may be of assistance to know that in the writer's experience schedules of costs and disbursements exceeding £7,000 or £8,000 are likely to attract considerable judicial scrutiny when it comes to assessment.

Multi-track—Civil Procedure Rules Part 29

26.17   The multi-track is the normal track for any claim for which the small claims or the fast track are not the normal track. Claims with a value in excess of £15,000 or where the issues are of sufficient complexity or where trial will, in all probability, take longer than one day will be allocated to the multi-track. The court will, more often than not, hold a case management conference. The parties will be given an opportunity to air their views on the appropriate timetable and the need for further expert evidence. The court will be less hostile to applications by a party to obtain its own expert evidence (as opposed to the jointly instructed expert if there is one). Where the amount in dispute is high it is difficult to see how allowing a party to obtain its own expert evidence is disproportionate. The parties will generally be given greater time to comply with directions in cases which are allocated to the multi-track.

Case management conference

26.18   The case management conference (CMC) is intended identify the real issues between the parties. Parties attending a CMC should be in a position to identify what evidence has been obtained, what is yet to be obtained, and why further evidence is necessary if either party is dissatisfied with that which is currently available. The legal representative attending on behalf of a party is expected to be fully conversant with the file and the issues. It is a useful opportunity to make specific requests for directions which would otherwise require a separate application. This can save cost. For example, pursuant to the pre-action protocol, there is a requirement to disclose relevant documents. If one or other party refused to provide a particular class of documents which the other considered disclosable then the aggrieved party can use the CMC to make a specific request. Where a party intends to make such a request they would be well advised to put the other party and the court on notice of that intention prior to the hearing.

Disclosure

The Access to Justice Reports recognised that the discovery process contrib- **26.19**
utes to the just resolution of disputes and should be retained. The case management powers of the court give the court the responsibility and the means to ensure that disclosure is limited to that which is really necessary in individual cases. The duty of disclosure is defined as "stating that a document exists or has existed".[28] A party is required to disclose[29]:

(a) documents upon which they rely;

(b) documents which *adversely* affect his own case, or which adversely affect another party's case or which *support* another party's case;

(c) documents of which disclosure is required by a relevant practice direction.

A reasonable research is required to identify documents in categories (b) and (c).[30] There is a right to inspect a disclosed document save where it is no longer in the control of the disclosing party, or that party has a right to withhold inspection or it would be disproportionate to the issues in the case to permit inspection. A document is in a parties control if it is in his physical possession or he has a right to possession or to take copies. A party may withhold inspection if, for example, the document was subject to legal professional privilege. So, the disclosing party would not be required to allow the inspecting party to seek counsel's advice on the merits of the case.

---

[28] CPR, r.31.2.
[29] CPR, r.31.6.
[30] CPR, r.31.7.

As mentioned above, if a party challenges the adequacy of the disclosure provided, that party may issue an application for specific disclosure. Any application must be made in accordance with CPR Part 23. Thus, the application should state what order is sought and must be supported by evidence. In certain circumstances an order for disclosure may be sought against a non-party.[31] However, in addition to satisfying the court that the document or documents sought meet the standard criteria, as set out above, to be a disclosable document, the party seeking disclosure from the non-party must also demonstrate that disclosure is necessary to dispose fairly of the claim or to save costs.

Example

Fraser Henderson is a squash racket developer. He decides to use a new form of twine developed by a company Green/Waring Poly Substances Ltd, a farming product developed to replace chicken wire. Fraser was unaware that the particular qualities of the twine were such that it would break and distribute shards of twine if hit by anything at speed. James and Hannah were playing squash when James' brand new "Henderson TK Racket" string broke causing a shard to go into his eye and injuring him. It was the first time the racket had been used. James sued Fraser who claims to know nothing about the problem with the twine. Green/Waring had carried out some scientific testing of the product before selling the product to Fraser and knew of these qualities. They had offered the report to Fraser before he bought the twine.

Is Fraser Liable?

Can James make a non-party disclosure application against Green/Waring?

Exchange of witness statements/expert evidence

26.20 At the CMC dates for the exchange of witness statements and expert evidence will be identified. The witness statements of fact relied upon by a party should have been taken prior to the issue of proceedings. Legal representatives should re-visit original proofs of evidence since it is likely that there will be fresh matters to deal with within the body of the witness statement. A witness statement is intended to be a party's evidence-in-chief when the case reaches final hearing. If a party wishes to raise new matters at trial the court will only allow a party to do so if there is good reason. It is therefore essential that everything is included in the witness statement.

It is worth mentioning that witness statements should be signed with a statement of truth. Indeed, virtually every document which is produced for the purpose of advancing legal proceedings should be signed with a statement of truth.[32] The statement of truth is an acknowledgment by the party signing that the contents of the document, witness statement or otherwise,

---

[31] CPR, r.31.17.

[32] A statement of truth is required on any statement of case (particulars of claim and defences), expert reports, any application issued pursuant to Part 23, witness statements, affidavits, etc.

are true to the best of their knowledge. It may be signed by the party's legal representative. A person who makes a false statement in a document or who makes a statement without an honest belief in its truth and signs it a statement of truth is in contempt of court. Legal representatives are required to explain to their lay client the importance of the statement of truth.

Certain expert evidence is likely to have been available at the commencement of proceedings. That evidence may or may not have been obtained on the basis of a joint instruction (depending upon how compliant the parties were with each other prior to issue). One party may be dissatisfied with the expert evidence which is available and can apply to obtain further expert evidence. If such an application is intended, it is unlikely to attract much sympathy unless questions have been asked[33] of that expert.[34] Questions are required to be put to an expert within 28 days of the service of an expert's report and should be for the purpose of clarification of the report (unless the court orders otherwise or the parties agree). If the answers are unsatisfactory and the court permits then a party may obtain further expert evidence. A date will be set for exchange of that evidence.

Where there is a mutual exchange of expert evidence, the parties must re-consider whether questions are necessary. Although an expert witness owes a primary duty to the court, there is a good chance that the "opposing" expert has provided an opinion/prognosis which is adverse to your case. It is important to allow "your" expert to examine that report and to make observations. In any case where the parties have their "own" experts the court will direct that the experts meet to discuss the issues raised in the reports. The court will require the parties to identify issues upon which they agree and disagree.   **26.21**

Final preparations

It was noted above that a party intending to claim past and future loss was required to set out those losses in a schedule of loss and serve it with the statement of case. The court will often make an order for service of an updated schedule shortly before trial. The defendant will then be required to serve a counter-schedule which sets out the arguments it intends to raise in response to the claims being pursued. Where there are complex legal issues to be determined, the court may order the parties to file skeleton legal arguments. The claimant will be required to provide indexed and paginated bundles of documents to the court and the defendant. You are now ready for trial!   **26.22**

---

[33] In *Daniels v. Walker* [2000] 1 W.L.R. 1382 it was held that where a party's reasons were not fanciful, permission to obtain further expert evidence may be obtained especially where the sum involved was substantial. The court indicated that where a party is dissatisfied with the expert evidence the disagreement may well be cleared up by written questions to the expert. See also *Cosgrove and another v. Pattison and another, The Times*, February 7, 2001.
[34] CPR, r.35.6.

Avoiding trial

26.23 The trial may be avoided by a number of means. I will deal with only two of the most common methods—summary judgment and settlement of the claim.

Summary judgment

26.24 Summary judgment may be given against a claimant or a defendant on the whole of a claim or on a particular issue if the court considers that the claimant has no real prospect of succeeding on the claim or issue or the defendant has no real prospect of successfully defending the claim or issue[35] and that there is no other compelling reason for a trial. An application for summary judgment should be made at the earliest possible opportunity. The respondent to a summary judgment application must be given at least 14 clear days' notice of the hearing and the issues the court will decide. Once again, the application is required to comply with CPR Part 23. The respondent may wish to rely upon evidence to resist the application and this must be served at least seven days before the summary judgment hearing. Any further evidence upon which the applicant intends to rely must be served within three days of the hearing.

The respondent can defeat the application by showing the court some prospect of success. It must be real. The inclusion of the word "real" means that the party must have a case which is better than merely arguable.[36] Where there is a factual dispute between the parties, a summary judgment application will, in all probability, fail. Returning to the example of the reckless tackle, where the issue is whether or not the tackle was reckless, the application will fail.

Settlement of claims and Civil Procedure Rules Part 36

26.25 Perhaps the most important part of the CPR is Part 36. It entitles the claimant to make offers to settle which, if not accepted, may result in punitive sanctions against the party refusing to settle. The claimant may offer to settle the claim for a fixed sum of money, say, £100,000. If the claimant subsequently recovers £150,000, the claimant may be entitled to punitive interest on the damages and costs incurred after the final date from which the Part 36 offer could be accepted (21 days after the offer). Alternatively, a defendant may make a Part 36 payment into court of, say,

---

[35] CPR, r.24.2 and CPR Part 24 generally.
[36] See *International Finance Corp v. Utexafrican SRPL* [2001] L.T.L. May 16 citing *Alpine Bulk Transport Co. Inc. v. Saudi Eagle Shipping Co. Inc.* [1986] 2 Lloyd's Rep. 221.

£50,000. If the claimant rejected that offer and recovered only £10,000, the claimant would be entitled to his costs only up until the final date from which the payment in could have been accepted (21 days after the payment in). Thereafter, the defendant would be entitled to his costs.

Chapter 27

Quantum of damages

"No brilliance is needed in the law. Nothing but common sense, and relatively clean fingernails."

John Mortimer, A Voyage Round my Father, 1972.

This Chapter provides a brief introduction to some of the general principles **27.01** involved in assessing the quantum of a personal injury claim and then goes on to look at some of the previously decided cases involving a sporting element.

General principles

It is not possible within the scope of this book to do anything more than **27.02** provide a brief outline as to the principles governing the assessment of damages in a personal injury claim. For a more detailed exposition of the subject, readers are referred to *McGregor on Damages*; *Clerk & Lindsell on Torts*; *Kemp & Kemp, The Quantum of Damages* and *Butterworths Personal Injury Litigation Service*.

General principle of compensation

The general principle of compensation for cases involving negligence is that **27.03** the court should award:

"that sum of money which will put the party who has been injured, or who has suffered, in the same position as he would have been if he had not sustained the wrong for which he is now getting his compensation or reparation."[1]

Aggravated damages

Aggravated damages are very occasionally awarded in addition to the **27.04** compensatory element. They are not awarded to punish the defendant but

---

[1] *Livingstone v. Rawyards Coal Co.* (1880) 5 A.C. 25, *per* Lord Blackburn at 39.

instead to reflect the greater degree of damage caused to the claimant in the circumstances in which the injury was inflicted.

They can be awarded for the damage caused to one's pride or for the humiliation during the commission of the tort. The circumstances in which the tort was committed and which may lead to an award of aggravated damages are varied.

The most common in the sports setting would be that the tort was committed in public, perhaps in front of a large audience or whilst being broadcast on television or the frustration at being unable to continue to play one's chosen sport. These factors could lead a court to consider that the damage suffered was more serious than the simple infliction of injury.[2]

In *Rogers v. Bugden and Canterbury Bankston Club*,[3] the New South Wales Supreme Court Common Law Division of Lee C.J., an award of A\$68,154.60 with costs against not only an offending player who broke an opponent's jaw in a professional rugby league match, but also the employer club,[4] was subsequently affirmed on appeal with an increase for aggravated damages.

Exemplary damages

27.05 Exemplary damages are purely punitive in nature and are best described as a civil fine. They should only be awarded in two cases. First, following unconstitutional behaviour by officials of the state or local government. This is an unlikely claim in the majority of sports situations. The second is where the defendant has committed the tort in a manner in which he knows that he will make a profit in excess of the damages awarded to the claimant from its commission. The exemplary damages award will take the financial profit element from the defendant and award it to the claimant. However, it is not restricted to moneymaking and exemplary damages can be awarded to teach the defendant that breaking the law does not pay. Such damages are means tested and will be added on to the compensatory award only if the defendant can afford to pay them.

In *Sports Law*,[5] Gardiner *et al.* refer to the Australian case of *Rogers v. Bugden and Canterbury-Bankstown*[6] and conclude from the reasoning of the court that exemplary damages would appear to be relevant only in instances of deliberate assault, not negligence.

The interesting thing they point out in respect of compensatory, aggravated and exemplary damages in the case is the role of the defendant club.

---

[2] Gardiner *et al.*, *Sports Law* (2nd ed., Cavendish Publishing Ltd, 2001), Chap. 16 and also the Australian case of *Rogers v. Bugden and Canterbury-Bankstown* [1993] A.T.R. 81–246.

[3] [1993] A.T.R. 181–248, CA (NSW).

[4] Unreported, December 14, 1990 and see [1991] All E.R. 246.

[5] 2nd ed., Cavendish Publishing Ltd, 2001, Chap. 16.

[6] [1993] A.T.R. 81–246.

From the case, they say it can be vicariously liable in terms of compensatory and aggravated damages. But where it can be proved that the club over "psyched up" or deliberately instructed players to injure an opponent, then they will be liable for a very large amount of exemplary damages. The court thought that this would have been so serious that the award would have been considerably in excess of double the remainder of the compensation.

Causation and remoteness

The loss for which compensation is claimed must be caused by, and not be too remote a consequence of, the defendant's tort. For the purposes of a typical personal injury claim, the defendant must reasonably have foreseen that his conduct would inflict a physical injury on the claimant but he need not have foreseen the impact that injury would have on the claimant in relation to his health of income.[7]   **27.06**

Mitigation

The claimant is under a duty to mitigate the losses resulting from the defendant's tort.[8] Strictly speaking this is not a legal duty since it cannot be enforced as such: failure to fulfil it simply entails a reduction in the damages awarded.[9] Further, damages are not generally recoverable for such losses as the claimant has avoided by taking action subsequent to the tort.   **27.07**

Distinction between special and general damages

Awards in personal injury cases are split into main categories: "general damages" and "special damages". General damage is that which the law presumes to flow from the wrong complained of and which need not be specially pleaded (though it should be averred that such damage has been suffered). Special damage means "the particular damage beyond the general damage which results from the special circumstances of the case, and of the claimant's claim to be compensated, for which he ought to give warning in his pleadings in order that there may be no surprise at trial".[10]   **27.08**

Special damages

Special damages in general amount to specific pecuniary loss and include such items as loss of earnings, medical and other expenses, damage to goods, the cost of care and the like. Sometimes these losses are continuing   **27.09**

---

[7] *Smith v. Leech Brain & Co. Ltd* [1962] 2 Q.B. 405.

[8] *British Westinghouse Co. Ltd v. Underground Rys. Ltd* [1912] A.C. 673.

[9] See *Clerk & Lindsell on Torts* (20th ed., Sweet & Maxwell, 2000), para. 29–08 and *Derbyshire v. Warran* [1963] 1 W.L.R. 1067 at 1075 *per* Pearson L.J.

[10] *Ratcliffe v. Evans* [1892] 2 Q.B. 524 at 528 *per* Bowen L.J.

at the date of trial in which case the court has to assess how long these losses are likely to continue. In addition, the court has to make a discount for the fact that the damages are being received now and not some time in the future. Currently the discount rate set by order of the Lord Chancellor under the Damages Act 1996 is 2.5 per cent.

General damages

Pain, suffering and loss of amenity

27.10 General damages, in general, amount to non-pecuniary losses and are different from pecuniary ones in that the objective of putting the claimant in the position he would have been had it not been for the accident cannot be applied literally to them: damages cannot restore a lost limb or happiness. They include items such as any claim for a disability on the labour market (pursuant to *Smith v. Manchester Corp.*[11]), for loss of congenial employment and for the loss of use of a chattel damaged in the accident. The most important head of general damages is generally that for pain and suffering and for loss of amenities.

Usually the judges make a single award to cover pain and suffering and loss of amenities. It seems clear, however, that the major element in this is the compensation to represent the injury itself (often called the loss of faculty) and the consequences that injury has on the claimant's way of life and therefore for his loss of happiness.

Damages are awarded so as to cover both the consequences of the injury and the injury itself and, as Lord Reid has pointed out,[12] the normal man is usually more concerned about the dislocation of his life than about his actual physical injury. Nevertheless, Judges tend to attribute an assumed loss of enjoyment of life to flow from different categories of injury when taking the starting point for assessing quantum in this regard. The conventional sums awarded for different types of injury are derived from the general experience of judges as manifested in previous comparable cases. In this respect, regard may be had to the cases cited in, for example, *Kemp & Kemp, The Quantum of Damages*; *Butterworths Personal Injury Litigation Service*; *Halsbury's Laws of England: Monthly Review* and *Current Law*. Judges may also take account of the Judicial Studies Board's *Guidelines for the Assessment of General Damages in Personal Injury Cases*.[13] The figures emerging are not fixed for all time: it has been stressed that in having regard to them Judges should take account of changes in the value of the currency.[14] Moreover, in *Heil v. Rankin*,[15] acting on the recommendation of the Law Commission, the Court of Appeal slightly increased damages for larger

---

[11] (1974) 17 K.I.R. 1; (1974) 118 Sol. J. 597, CA.
[12] *H. West & Son Ltd v. Shephard* [1964] A.C. 326 at 341.
[13] 5th ed., 2000, covering cases reported up to May 2000.
[14] *Heil v. Rankin* [2000] 3 All E.R. 138, CA.
[15] [2000] 3 All E.R. 138, CA.

cases of non-pecuniary loss because awards had fallen behind what was regarded as "fair, just and reasonable".

The starting figure derived from these sources may then be adjusted to take account of the special features of the claimant's case. The court therefore examines the circumstances of his life prior to the accident to see whether he was engaged in any special activities which he is now prevented from pursuing. As Lord Pearce said in *H. West & Son Ltd v. Shephard*[16]:

> "If, for instance, the plaintiff's main interest in life was some sport or hobby from which he will be debarred, that too increases the assessment."

Thus the deprivation of sexual pleasures,[17] the loss of a holiday,[18] the loss **27.11** of the comfort and companionship of marriage[19] and even the fact that the claimant had to give up employment which he clearly enjoyed[20] have justified a higher award. A substantial sum for non-pecuniary loss has also been awarded for a severe personality change, which led to the claimant being imprisoned for sexual offences on women.[21]

If such objective factors are relevant to increase the sum awarded, it might seem logical to reduce the prima facie figure where the claimant is rendered unconscious or is unable to appreciate his loss. However, in *Wise v. Kaye*[22] the Court of Appeal held by a majority that though this fact justified making no award for pain and suffering, it had no bearing on the damages for loss of amenities. Two years later this decision was confirmed by the majority of the House of Lords in the similar case of *H. West & Son Ltd v. Shephard*,[23] which itself was followed by the House of Lords in *Lim Poh Choo v. Camden and Islington Area Health Authority*.[24] So although the High Court of Australia has declined to follow *West v. Shephard* on this point,[25] and while there has occasionally been a reluctance to do so by English Judges,[26] it is settled that so far as English law is concerned it is the objective loss of amenities in respect of which damages are awarded. As Lord Morris said in *West v. Shephard*:

> "The fact of unconsciousness is . . . relevant in respect of and will eliminate those heads or elements of damage which can exist only by being felt or though or

---

[16] [1964] A.C. 326 at 365.
[17] *Cook v. J.L. Kier & Co.* [1970] 1 W.L.R. 566.
[18] *Ichard v. Frangoulis* [1977] 1 W.L.R. 566.
[19] *Hughes v. McKeown* [1985] 1 W.L.R. 963; *cf. Lampert v. Eastern National Omnibus Co.* [1954] 1 W.L.R. 1047.
[20] *Hearnshaw v. English Steel Corporation* (1971) K.I.R. 306, CA.
[21] *Meah v. Mcreamer* [1985] 1 All E.R. 367; *cf. Meah v. Mcreamer (No. 2)* [1986] 1 All E.R. 943.
[22] [1962] 1 Q.B. 638 (Diplock L.J. dissenting).
[23] [1964] A.C. 326 (Lords Reid and Devlin dissenting).
[24] [1980] A.C. 174.
[25] *Skelton v. Collins* (1966) 39 A.L.J. 480.
[26] *Andrews v. Freeborough* [1967] 1 Q.B. 1 *per* Willmer L.J. at 12, *per* Davies L.J. at 18 *per* Winn L.J. at 20.

experienced. The fact of unconsciousness does not, however, eliminate the actuality of the deprivations of the ordinary experiences and amenities of life which may be the inevitable result of some physical injury."

Loss of a chance

27.12 Claimants injured in the sporting context should particularly bear in mind the possibility of claiming damages for the loss of a chance.[27] In assessing the value of the lost chance, the usual civil standard of the balance of probabilities does not apply. In *Davies v. Taylor*,[28] Lord Reid said as follows:

> "When the question is whether a certain thing is or is not true—whether a certain event did or did not happen—then the court must decide one way or the other. There is no question of chance or probability. Either it did or it did not happen. But the standard of civil proof is a balance of probabilities. If the evidence shows a balance in favour of it having happened then it is proved that it did in fact happen . . . You can prove that a past event happened, but you cannot prove that a future event will happen and I do not think that the law is so foolish as to suppose that you can. All that you can do is to evaluate the chance. Sometimes it is virtually 100 per cent.: sometimes virtually nil. But often it is somewhere in between. And if it is somewhere in between I do not see much difference between a probability of 51 per cent. and a probability of 49 per cent."

Damages for loss of a chance are therefore to be assessed in proportion to that chance, subject to the *de minimis* principle that no account is to be taken of possibilities which are very small, speculative or fanciful. The assessment process must take uncertain events into account. As a matter of fact, an athlete's chances of winning a competition would turn on many contingencies such as his form at the time of the competition, the form of his competitors and the avoidance of injury. It is immaterial that such contingencies render the assessment of damages uncertain. In the case of *Chaplin v. Hicks*[29] the claimant lost the chance of winning a prize. Vaughan Williams L.J. said:

> "It was said that the plaintiff's chance of winning a prize turned on such a number of contingencies that it was impossible for any one, even after arriving at the conclusion that the plaintiff had lost her opportunity by the breach, to say that there was any assessable value of that loss. It is said that in a case which involves so many contingencies it is impossible to say what was the plaintiff's pecuniary loss. I am unable to agree with that contention. I agree that the presence of all the

---

[27] See *Chaplin v. Hicks* [1911] 2 K.B. 786, CA.; *Kitchen v. RAF Association* [1958] 2 All E.R. 241, CA. See also *McGregor on Damages* (16th ed.), para. 385 and Beloff, Kerr and Demetriou, *Sports Law* (1st ed., Hart Publishing 1999), para. 5.68–5.70. See also the cases referred to below and in particular *Mulvain v. Joseph* [1968] 112 Sol. J. 927.

[28] [1974] A.C. 207 at 213.

[29] [1911] 2 K.B. 786, CA.

contingencies upon which the gaining of the prize might depend makes the calculation not only difficult but incapable of being carried out with certainty or precision. The proposition is that, whenever the contingencies on which the result depends are numerous and difficult to deal with, it is impossible to recover any damages for the loss of the chance or opportunity of winning the prize. In the present case I understand that there were fifty selected competitors, of whom the plaintiff was one, and twelve prizes, so that the average chance of each competitor was about one in four. Then it is said that the questions which might arise in the minds of the judges are so numerous that it is impossible to say that the case is one in which it is possible to apply the doctrine of averages at all. I do not agree with the contention that, if certainty is impossible of attainment, the damages for a breach of contract are unassessable."

The leading case in this area with regard to sports is now that of *Langford v. Hebran and Nynex Cablecomms*.[30] It was an appeal by the defendants from the judgment of Klevan J., by which he awarded the claimant ("L") damages of £423,133 for personal injuries sustained in a road traffic accident, which included £57,379 plus interest for past and £326,368 for future loss of earnings. L, who was aged 27 at the time of the accident, had been working as a trainee bricklayer for five months prior to the accident. He was also a world champion amateur kick-boxer, had won his first professional fight, and was predicted to become a world champion professional kick-boxer as well as becoming a kick-boxing instructor upon retirement.

The Judge, following the approach approved in *Doyle v. Wallace*,[31] calculated the loss of earnings claim on the basis of:

i. a basic claim, which assumed that L would have had a professional fighting and teaching career of some nine years, during which he would have continued to work part-time as a bricklayer, following which he would have reverted to bricklaying until he was 60 years old; and

ii. a percentage of each of four alternative career scenarios based upon L's probable career as a kick-boxer and instructor.

In relation to stage ii. the Judge calculated the respective chances of each career scenario (in escalating success) on a "stand alone" basis as: (a) 20 per cent; (b) 40 per cent; (c) 30 per cent; and (d) 10 per cent. The defendants advanced a number of criticisms of the Judge's calculation.

The Court of Appeal held that only two criticisms of substance were made out. First, the Judge had assumed far too high a figure for L's potential earnings as an instructor. Secondly, the Judge's assessment of the career chances was illogical. It could not have been logically correct that L's chance of achieving career scenario (b) was greater than the chance of achieving

---

[30] [2001] P.I.Q.R. 13.
[31] [1998] P.I.Q.R. 146.

scenario (a), when L could only have hoped to attain scenario (b) by first attaining scenario (a).

They went on to state that this flaw fatally undermined the Judge's approach to the evaluation exercise. At the invitation of the parties the court considered that the appropriate percentage chances on an "additional claim" basis were: (a) 80 per cent; (b) 66 per cent; (c) 40 per cent; and (d) 20 per cent.

The net result of the approach that the court considered should have been adopted below would have been to reduce the total amount awarded by the Judge for lost earnings, past and future, by £11,677. That reduction was so comparatively small that it would not have been right to interfere with the Judge's award.

Another possible approach in this area would be for a court to make an award for a claimant's disability on the sporting labour market (pursuant to *Smith v. Manchester Corp.*[32]). For the guiding principles which govern such an award, the reader is referred to *Kemp & Kemp, The Quantum of Damages, paragraphs 6–151 to 6–161 and 6–700 to 6–724.*

Loss of opportunity to enjoy sport

27.13   It should also be noted that damages can be awarded for loss of opportunity to enjoy sport, for which see, for example, *Tsipoloudis v. Donald.*[33]

Case law on loss of ability to play sport

27.14   This section sets out some of the cases which may be useful in attempting to assess the quantum for the loss of an ability to play a particular sport. This may be permanent or temporary. It may also involve, for example, a loss of a chance to enter particular tournaments.

As explained, generally Judges will take a starting point based simply upon the physical injury of a claimant and will then go on to take account of any extra effects the injury may have had on his life. Generally, this will then be included in the overall award for pain, suffering and loss of amenity. However, where the circumstances are appropriate, Judges sometimes make a separate award in this respect.

Assessing the loss of ability or of a chance is an enormously difficult and to a large degree subjective task. Aside from the guidance already set out above, there are few guidelines or cases in this area and thus it is helpful not only to look at cases in the sporting arena but to look at analogous situations. Therefore, this analysis starts with cases on loss of congenial employment as they provide a good base for the analogous sporting cases. This is followed by the cases on dancers, musicians and then sportsmen and women generally. It will be seen throughout these cases that the level of

---

[32] (1974) 17 K.I.R. 1; (1974) 118 Sol. J. 597, CA.
[33] Unreported, December 11, 1998, CA. Referred to in Beloff, Kerr and Demetriou, *Sports Law* (1st ed., Hart Publishing, 1999), para. 5.70.

award is what many might consider derisory in comparison to the suffering involved.

Loss of congenial employment

Perhaps the best analogy for cases involving the loss of ability to perform a particular sport is those involving a claim for loss of congenial employment, where someone has had to give up a job they enjoyed either for a less enjoyable one or for no job at all as a result of their injuries. This often involves members of the fire service, police and nursing professions. It will be seen from the examples set out below that awards range from just over £6,000 for total loss of a career down to just over £1,000 for loss of one year of a particular career. **27.15**

Hale v. London Underground Ltd[34]: £5,000 (11/92) (≈£6,200 today)

Fireman, aged 39 at the date of the accident and 44 at the date of the trial, attended the fire at King's Cross underground station in November 1987. Medically retired in November 1990 from operational duty. He was transferred to a headquarters job but felt downgraded, entirely unhappy and took spells off work. He was retired from the fire brigade on grounds of disability in April 1991 but was immediately offered and took up employment on fire prevention duties. However, he went sick in September 1992 and had remained absent from work. The claimant was unlikely to continue his non-operational job with the fire service for more than six months. Thereafter he was likely to take a further two years before settling into new employment, and then there would be a further eight-and-a-half years up to normal brigade retirement age. He was expected to have an impaired capacity to gain employment, and his continuing vulnerability to stress limited the field in which he could seek employment. Court: (QBD) Queens Bench Division. Judge: Otton, J. **27.16**

Watson (Linda), Re[35]: £5,000 loss of congenial employment (1/97)

Female, aged about 27 at the date of the incident and 38 at date of assessment, sustained injuries to her coccyx and lower spine in an incident during her work as a police officer in September, 1986. Absent from work for six and a half months. Thereafter worked light duties for eight weeks. Had to return to light duties about 15 months after the incident and was unable to continue her work after June 1988 and was medically retired in May 1989. W had enjoyed her job, considered herself a "career woman" and had intended to work in the police force until she was 55 years old. Court: CICB (Durham). **27.17**

---

[34] [1994] C.L.Y. 1569; [1993] P.I.Q.R. Q30.
[35] [1997] C.L.Y. 1921; [1997] 97(2) Q.R. 6.

Sola v. Royal Marsden Hospital[36]*: £5,000 loss of congenial employment (6/97)*

27.18 Female nurse, S, aged 51 at the date of the trial in June 1997, was exposed to gluteraldehyde (in the form of "Cidex") over a period in the course of her duties as a full time theatre sister, which she commenced in September 1989, causing her to develop symptoms of breathlessness and lethargy. In November 1991 and January 1992 she suffered acute attacks, and occupational asthma was later diagnosed. She was retired on the grounds of ill health in August 1993. Court: CC (Clerkenwell). Judge: Recorder Russell.

Storey v. Rae[37]*: £5,000 loss of congenial employment (2/98)*

27.19 S, female, police officer, aged 33 at date of road traffic accident and 37 at trial, suffered fractures to her clavicle, right tibia and right lateral malleolus. She was fit for most forms of light or sedentary work. However, as a result of her injuries S was discharged on medical grounds from the police force. The judge found that S was a career officer and would have served another 13 years but for her injury giving her a total of 30 years' service. The award for loss of congenial employment reflected the fact S had for two to three years had difficulties at work but at the time of the accident was enjoying high profile work and was found to have prospects of promotion which were not negligible. Court: QBD. Judge: Judge Peter Crawford Q.C.

Worth v. Worcester and District HA[38]*: £1,500 loss of congenial employment (4/96)*

27.20 Male, aged 32 at the date of the accident and 39 at the date of the trial, sustained an injury to the lumbar spine when participating in moving a patient from an ambulance stretcher to a hospital trolley. W had to stop work as an ambulance man shortly after the accident, which the judge found was five years earlier than he would have done if there had been no accident. Loss of congenial employment awarded on basis that claimant was an enthusiastic ambulance man who had to give up his chosen career and obtain work at a lower status as an auxiliary nurse. Court: CC (Birmingham). Judge: Judge Taylor.

Richards v. Prodger[39]*: £1,500 loss of congenial employment (2/99)*

27.21 R, female aged 31 at the date of the road traffic accident and 35 at trial, sustained whiplash injuries to her neck and lower back. At the time of the

---

[36] [1997] C.L.Y. 1948.
[37] [1998] C.L.Y. 1692.
[38] [1996] C.L.Y. 2237.
[39] [1999] C.L.Y. 1469.

accident she had been employed as an assistant at a children's playgroup, an occupation which she enjoyed enormously and intended to pursue indefinitely, but she was unable to return to that work because of the lifting and bending involved. The Judge found that she would only be fit for light shop work. Court: CC (Gloucester). Judge: Assistant Recorder Wade.

Surrey v. Manchester Health Commission[40]: £1,000 loss of congenial employment for 12-month period (9/97) (≈£1,090 today)

S, aged 54 at the date of the incident and 58 at trial, was a female auxiliary nurse working on a hospital ward. She had not worked since the accident and took early retirement. S's life had revolved around her work and she was shattered by the early retirement caused by the accident. The judge found that an acceleration period of 12 months was attributable to the accident. Court: CC (Manchester). Judge: District Judge Griffiths.

Dancer cases

The next set of analogous cases involve people who lose their chance of being or continuing as professional dancers. This is highly vocational and takes exceptional talent, effort and training in order to succeed. This is reflected by the level of award which in the examples below range from just over £11,500 to approximately £8,500. **27.22**

Kirk v. Laine Theatre Arts[41]: £10,000 loss of ability to follow chosen career as a dancer (3/95) (≈£11,700 today)

Female, aged 17 at the date of the accident and 23 at the date of the trial, was a student at a theatre arts college with the ambition of becoming a professional dancer. She suffered from severe ligamentous and capsular strain in the lower back and around the right thigh whilst performing a box-splits exercise in a jazz dancing class. She tried to carry on dancing for two weeks after the accident but had to stop. She would never fully recover and would never be able to dance professionally. She would never be able to take part in sporting activities to any great extent without aggravating her symptoms. She had found employment as an airline hostess. The trial Judge held that the loss of her ability to follow her chosen career as a professional dancer was very different from cases where damages had been awarded for inability to follow a congenial employment as a fireman or policeman. This was a case where a young girl from the age of eight had set her heart on becoming a professional dancer. She had spent her last years at school giving up her free time to pursue this aim. He was satisfied that there was a distinct **27.23**

---

[40] [1998] C.L.Y. 1619.
[41] [1995] C.L.Y. 1712.

possibility of her being in the top flight of dancers bearing in mind the evidence that only a minute number of girls reach those heights. Court: CC (Nottingham). Judge: H.H.J. Heald.

O'Brien v. Martin[42]: *£7,500 loss of congenial employment (4/96)* *(≈£8,500 today)*

27.24   O, aged 25 at the time of the accident and 31 at the trial, sustained whiplash injuries to the cervical and thoracic spine in a road traffic accident. She had been a scholar of the Royal Academy of Dancing and had then studied dancing full time for a further two years. As a professional dancer her earnings were modest, but the Judge found that those earnings were likely to have increased in the future but for the accident. Immediately after the incident she decided to train as a masseuse to supplement her income. When she realised that she could not continue as a professional dancer, she began retraining as an actress. The award for loss of congenial employment was at the top end of the bracket although the Judge took into account the limited career span of a dancer and the fact that acting was not going from one extreme to another. Court: Court not stated. Judge: James Goudie Q.C.

Musician cases

27.25   Similar to the dancing cases are those relating to musicians. The following are examples of both a professional and amateur musician. Whilst the professional musician received approximately £8,000 which is similar to the dancer awards, the amateur received only about £2,150−£3,250 for both the loss of the ability to play his instruments and also for loss of congenial employment.

Byers v. Brent LBC[43]: *£7,500 loss of congenial employment and pleasure derived from playing double bass (4/98) (≈£8,000 today)*

27.26   B, female, aged 25 at the date of the accident and 31 at trial, tripped over a paving stone, falling heavily on her right (dominant) hand. She was diagnosed as suffering reflex sympathetic dystrophy. The injury was permanent but with a small chance of some reduction in pain and increase in mobility. B was an exceptionally gifted double bass player and had studied the double bass at the Royal Academy of Music and in Italy under the foremost double bass musicians in the world. She had embarked on a career as a double bass soloist with early success. The evidence was that even if she

---

[42] [1996] C.L.Y. 2215.
[43] [1998] C.L.Y. 1645; (1998) 98(3) Q.R. 7.

had not succeeded as a soloist she would have obtained a post in a leading orchestra. As a result of her injuries, however, she could no longer play the double bass. She was unable to contemplate returning to professional music in any capacity. After the accident whilst still being treated, B commenced an M.Phil. degree. B withdrew from the course and commenced work which she found fulfilling as a church youth worker at a modest wage. It was contended that B had failed to mitigate her loss and that she should only be awarded damages for loss of earnings to compensate her for the difference between what she would have earned as a double bass musician and the salary she could have been expected to earn had she continued her studies or used her degree in music to obtain a more highly paid job. The Judge found that in the context of losing one vocation B had acted reasonably in selecting a career which offered her challenge and self fulfillment. The Judge took into account the precarious nature of a career in music in assessing lost earnings and the difficulty of achieving success as a double bass soloist. Court: (QBD) Queens Bench Division. Judge: Deputy High Court Judge Harvey.

Atkinson v. Whittle[44]: *total general damages: £8,000, of which ≈£2,000—£3,000 would be for loss of congenial employment and of P's music (3/98) (≈£2,150—£3,250 today)*

P, male aged 46 at the date of the road traffic accident and 54 at trial, suffered a soft tissue whiplash injury to his cervical and lumbar spine. The accident caused a minor degree of aggravation of the symptoms for 12 months. Subsequent to the accident P suffered almost constant pain in the neck although he adjusted his daily activities to cope. The Judge found that the accident had accelerated the symptoms in his neck by four years. At the time of the accident P had been employed as a deputy headmaster in a special school, but was medically retired from his post shortly after the accident. P was an accomplished musician, principally on the clarinet and saxophone, but he had been forced to give up playing those instruments due to the symptoms in his neck. The judge took account of loss of congenial employment and of P's music in the award for general damages. General Court: (QBD) Queens Bench Division. Judge: Judge Grenfell.   27.27

Sports cases

There are a number of cases which involve injuries to sportsmen and women. Unfortunately, most do not actually specify how much is awarded for the injury and how much for the loss of the ability to perform the sport and the resulting disappointment. For ease of reference, the cases are split   27.28

---

[44] [1999] C.L.Y. 1479.

up below into those where the injury resulted in a permanent disability to participate and those where it was only temporary.

Permanent disabilities

27.29 Awards for permanent sporting disabilities (in themselves) seem to go up to just over £26,000 from the examples given below.

Singleton v. Knowsley Metropolitan Borough[45]: *£12,000 (≈£26,300 today) for loss of chance of boxing career and employment in consequence of such career (2/82)*

27.30 Male, aged 20 at date of accident in May 1978 and 24 at date of hearing. "Top class" amateur boxer, who had won several schoolboy titles and that of Territorial Army Featherweight Champion of Great Britain, amongst others, and who had "a very considerable future." Had intended to turn professional later in 1978. At date of accident employed as refuse collection bin man. Largely ambidextrous, but wrote with right hand. As result of being caught by compressing ramp of refuse lorry, right hand and wrist were severely injured, necessitating surgical amputation through middle of fore-arm; dislocation of left acromio-clavicular joint; lacerations of chest wall. Dislocation had largely resolved, leaving him with only occasional symp-toms of discomfort, and would resolve completely. Suffered continuing phantom limb sensations, occasional pain at stump and chilblains in winter. Disability assessed by D.H.S.S. at 60 per cent Had been provided with two kinds of prosthesis, neither of which he liked. Had lost chance of successful boxing career and income from boxing and openings likely to have resulted from having been a boxing personality. Now employed as cleaner at Sports Centre with continuing loss of earnings. Court: Liverpool. Judge: Butler-Sloss, J.

Gibbens v. WJ Curley & Sons[46]: *£3,500 (≈£41,800 today) general damages (1/65) (of which perhaps £20,000 or so for loss of amenity possibly although unclear from report)*

27.31 Male, aged 22. Oblique fracture of right thumb, fractures of right ankle, right tarsal scaphoid, dislocation of lower end of right tibia, and complete severance of right ankle tendons. Spent seven months in hospital and underwent 12 operations. Use of foot restored but unable to play football, "an occupation dear to him." Had played for county and for England as schoolboy. Before accident had signed amateur forms with professional club; possibility he might have bright future as professional footballer. Now unable to take part in sporting activities and worked as toolmaker. Judge: Glyn-Jones, J.

---

[45] [1982] C.L.Y. 840.
[46] [1965] C.L.Y. 1141.

Girvan v. Inverness Farmers Dairy (No. 1)[47]: probably approximately £15,000 to £20,000 estimated as a reasonable award for mental anguish of being unable to clay pigeon shoot (although jury awarded more)

A Scottish case in which G sustained a fracture of the right elbow and **27.32**
lacerations to the head and knee. As a result, G was no longer able to
continue his interest as a dedicated clay pigeon shooter, in which he had
enjoyed considerable competition success. G claimed that he had been
deprived of the thrill of competition, a high profile, a reputation, and the
companionship which came from competing in the sport. In the first action,
G was awarded £120,000 solatium by a jury but this was set aside on appeal
and sent back for assessment. In that case, it was argued for G that in
England the amount of the award just for the physical injuries would be
between £35,000 to £45,000. Lord Justice Clerk (Ross) stated: "Even if the
starting point was £45,000, the special feature in relation to the pursuer's
shooting could never justify the award being increased to anything in the
order of £120,000." At the second trial, he was awarded £95,000 by a jury
and again the defenders appealed on the ground that this was excessive. The
House of Lords decided not to set aside the award on the basis that they
would not interfere with the jury's award since although a Judge would not
have awarded so much, juries can significantly differ in their judgments.
Reference in particular was made to the working rule in Scotland in such
cases that awards were generally only considered to be excessive if they were
more than 100 per cent of what a Judge would have awarded. Lord
Kirkwood stated that a reasonable jury could have awarded as much as
£45,000 for the injury and £15,000 to £20,000 "in respect of the mental
anguish he had suffered by reason of the fact that he could no longer take
part in clay pigeon shooting." Probably what can be taken from this case is
that a judicial award would be around £15,000 to £20,000.

Watson v. Gray[48]: £25,000 general damages (7/99) of which perhaps approximately £10,000 to £15,000 reflected the enhanced loss of amenity to a professional footballer of such an injury, together with the loss of congenial employment as a result of his likely premature retirement from the game

W, male, a professional footballer, aged 25 at the date of injury and 28 at the **27.33**
date of assessment, sustained a comminuted transverse fracture of the right
tibia and fibula as a result of a negligent tackle by an opponent during a
First Division league match. The fracture was surgically repaired under
general anaesthetic with a plate and screws. A butterfly wedge of bone was

---

[47] [1995] S.L.T. 735; (No. 2) [1996] S.L.T. 631; [1998] S.L.T. 21, HL.
[48] [1999] C.L.Y. 1510; (1999) 99(4) Q.R. 5.

discarded. The plate and screws were removed six months post injury and W was in plaster for a further two months after which, he began to increase his level of exercise. W's rehabilitation programme was interrupted by a third operation to repair a hernia which had developed on the lateral aspect of the fibula, and by pain in his right groin which required surgery. The court found that the groin pain was unconnected to the original injury. He made a good functional recovery from his physical injuries with no increased risk of premature arthritis. There was a small discrepancy in leg lengths of approximately 6 mm. Despite initial fears that he would never play football again, W was available for first team selection 18 months post injury. However, he was left with muscle scarring to his right leg which exacerbated the tendency of his right foot to pronate. Experts agreed that he had lost the pace and sharpness essential for a top striker. He also lacked confidence when tackling and being tackled and was unable to perform to his previous level. At the age of the assessment hearing, 27 months post injury, he had not played a full first team match. The judge found that W's career had been blighted and that he had been deprived of the opportunity of playing football at the highest level. He was likely to end his career in the lower divisions at a greatly reduced income and had a low residual earning capacity outside the game. W's injury fell within the description of injury in section (K)(b)(iv) of the JSB Guidelines. The agreed general damages award reflected the enhanced loss of amenity to a professional footballer of such an injury, together with the loss of congenial employment as a result of his likely premature retirement from the game. Court: (QBD) Queen's Bench Division. Judge Michael Taylor.

Dibble v. Carmarthen Town Council[49]: settlement of £20,000 general damages and loss of earnings

27.34 Andy Dibble, 36, a goalkeeper, suffered "horrific" burns from pitch markings when he dived to make a save. The former Welsh International was scarred for life by pitch markings drawn with hydrated lime. At the time of the incident, in December 1998, he was playing for Barry Town in the League of Wales, against Carmarthen Town at their council-maintained ground. At the time of the report, he played for Stockport County. He did not realise how badly he was hurt until he took his shirt off after the game and discovered a four-inch wide strip of flesh had been burnt off from his shoulder to his hip. He was taken to hospital in Wales where he underwent skin grafts before being transferred to Withington Hospital in Greater Manchester. His solicitor said the incident had totally changed the direction of Mr Dibble's career. The former Manchester City goalkeeper had been planning to move to America to pursue his ambitions. Mr Porter said: "It would have been a very lucrative move for him. Instead he had to stay in this

---

[49] Unreported, 2001.

country and scrabble around for a club when he recovered in 1999. The story about his injuries had been widely covered and that affected his bargaining power." Mr Porter added that the injuries on his chest had been "horrific". He said: "He had to undergo skin graft surgery, which is very painful, and has been left with scarring which is very embarrassing to him in the showers after games." (© 2001 Ananova Ltd).

Cooper v. William Press & Son[50]: £3,000 pain, suffering and loss of amenities (11/73) (≈£22,000 today, of which perhaps approximately £10,000 to £15,000 for loss of ability to continue wrestling)

Male, aged 34. Steel erector. Fracture of right radius at level of elbow joint restricting movement to 20 degrees loss of straightening and seven degrees loss of bending. Twenty per cent reduction in grip. Unable to resume full pre-accident work. Also unable to engage in pre-accident recreation as amateur wrestler. Had won several area championships and had hoped later to be selected for 1972 British Olympic team. Judge said loss of prospects of appearing in future championships were serious matters affecting award. Judge: Stocker J. Judgment date: November 2, 1973.   **27.35**

Temporary disabilities
Depending upon their severity, from the examples below awards for temporary disabilities appear to range from £10,000–£15,000 for six years away from top class rowing to £1,000–£2,000 for loss of a season's horse-riding competitions.   **27.36**

Ostling v. Hastings[51]: £20,000 general damages (11/97) (≈£22,000 today) of which it is estimated approximately £10,000 to £15,000 awarded for loss of six years' rowing, possibly less

The claimant, male, 23 years of age at the date of accident and 28 at date of trial, suffered injuries to both knees, his left wrist and an abrasion to his left buttock when he was knocked from his motorcycle. The most serious injury was that to the right knee where there was an extensive wound around the right patella extending into the knee joint with an 80 per cent disruption of quadriceps tendon. There was some compression in the small area of articular cartilage on the back of the patella. The quadriceps tendon was repaired with sutures through drill holes in the patella. The claimant was in hospital for two weeks, in plaster for seven-and-a-half weeks and thereafter attended intensive physiotherapy for a period of five to six   **27.37**

---

[50] [1973] C.L.Y. 805.
[51] [1998] C.L.Y. 1677; Kemp PRI–005.

months. The claimant was left with a 10 inch inverted U shaped scar to his right knee and a 1.5 inch scar to his left knee. He experienced occasional insecurity in his right knee and his sleep was disturbed in cold weather. He had a restriction in bending which was permanent, resulted in an inability to squat for more than one minute and caused difficulty in his work as a motor mechanic. The right knee remained stiff and clicks. There was a slight risk of osteoarthritis with a possibility of a patellectomy in future. The claimant had been an élite rower, a member of the Leander Club and had represented Great Britain at under 18 and 23 levels. He had potential to make the 1996 Great Britain Olympic squad. He was unable to return to rowing at the previous level. He had attempted to return but found his ability limited. The Judge found that he had lost six years of élite rowing. The Judge regarded this as an exceptional case involving a young man at the top flight of his sport whose progress had been frustrated. Furthermore, he came from a family in which his father had achieved sporting success at the highest level of rugby football. There was a small risk relating to future employment which was taken into account in the award of general damages for pain, suffering and loss of amenity.

Mulvaine v. Joseph[52]: *£1,000 (≈£11,000 today) general damages for loss of opportunity of competing in five tournaments, the ensuing loss of experience and prestige, and loss of chance of winning prize money (11/68)*

27.38　The claimant, an American club professional golfer, suffered minor injuries to his left hand on a visit to the U.K. for the purposes of competing in seven tournaments. As a result, he failed to qualify in two tournaments and decided not to compete in the others and returned to America without completing his programme. The object of the trip was to gain experience of tournament play in Europe, to improve his game, to acquire publicity and prestige and to win some of the money prizes. Thompson J. said that the issue of damages raised novel and interesting questions of law. He awarded damages under the following heads: (1) loss of opportunity of competing in tournaments; (2) ensuing loss of experience and prestige which might have resulted in his becoming a tournament professional in America; (3) loss of a chance of winning prize money. The report in the Solicitor's Journal of Thompson J.'s judgment concludes: "The figure was bound to be spec-ulative, but he would award under that head [broken down as numbered above] £1,000 damages . . . including damages for disappointment felt through the frustration of his plans." In addition, £140 was awarded for the usual head of pain and suffering (although the Current Law report suggests that this was for pain and suffering and special damages).

---

[52] [1968] C.L.Y. 1118; *The Times*, November 7, 1968; Sol. J. November 22, 1968.

Gudge v. Milroy[53]: £7,250 (1/00) (of which perhaps approximately £1,000 to £2000 for missing a season of horse riding competitions)

G, female, aged 24 at the date of the accident and 29 at trial, suffered severe **27.39** whiplash injury to her neck with immediate pain radiating from her neck to her shoulders with some restriction of movement. G was a keen horse rider who competed in national events. The accident prevented her from competing in the 1996 season. It was found that G had experienced significant pain and discomfort over the first two to three months and thereafter less significant pain up to four months after the accident. G was left with intermittent residual symptoms in the nature of a nuisance which would appear after exertion, particularly after competing on her horse. It was accepted that those symptoms were likely to be permanent. Court: CC (Hitchin). Judge: Judge Serota Q.C.

Another case referred to simply by its facts is mentioned in Grayson's *Sport and the Law[54]*:

" . . . while these pages were being processed, a Criminal Injuries Court Board awarded a 31-year-old disabled athlete fit to carry on his sport but proscribed in the job market £70,000 general damages for pain, suffering, loss of amenity and loss of future earnings, applying the *Smith v. Manchester City Council* (1974) 118 Sol. J. 397, 17 KIR ICH) formula for assessing general damages."

Finally, Edward Grayson in *Sport and the Law[55]* provides three examples of civil assault cases:

Hamish v. Smailes (unreported, Epsom county court, 1983)[56]

Involved a head butt causing a broken nose and black eyes to a 38-year-old **27.40** local player in a local league match. The defendant was held liable for civil assault (trespass to the person). £400 general damages awarded plus £5.80 proved special damages and costs.

Vermont v. Green (Unreported, Basingstoke, 1989)[57]

Kick during course of play to opponent causing two nights in hospital **27.41** adjudicated to have been deliberate in spur of moment. Defendant held liable for civil assault (trespass to the person). Awarded £400 general damages but claim for aggravated damages refused.

---

[53] [2000] 4 Q.R. 6.
[54] 3rd ed., Butterworths, 2000.
[55] *ibid.*, p. 279.
[56] Provided to Edward Grayson by H.H.J. John A. Baker DL from Court archives.
[57] E. Grayson, *Sport and the Law* (3rd ed. Butterworths, 2000), p. 279; provided to Edward Grayson by Oliver Sie, Barrister.

May v. Strong (Teeside county court, 1990; Halsbury's Laws MRE 92/62
[1991] All E.R. 313; [1991] B.P.I.L.S. 2274)

27.42   Serious foul play and violent conduct to a 19-year-old semi-professional
footballer. Defendant sent off by referee and recklessness held by the judge
to amount to an assault. £10,000 damages to a 19-year-old semi-
professional footballer (£6,000 pain, suffering and loss of earnings (one
assumes this is "amenity"): for compound fracture of tibia and fibula;
£4,000 special damages for net loss earnings for nine months).

Moore in *Sports Law and Litigation*[58] also refers to the last of these cases,
May v. Strong.[59] He adds that the injury was a result of a very late tackle
from behind. He also states that the award for general damages would have
been worth approximately £8,000 in 2000, although the religious application of inflation multipliers can have a distorting effect on awards made in
old cases, and an attempt therefore should be made to locate the most recent
comparators.

Conclusion

27.43   There is a paucity of both guidance and decided cases in this area. Clearly,
each case will depend upon its facts. However, it is hoped that the above will
at least help in some way to start to bring some order and, perhaps in the
future, some consistency to this area of law.

---

[58] 2nd ed. 2000, CLT Professional Publishing Ltd.
[59] [1991] B.P.I.L.S. 2274.

Chapter 28

Costs and funding

"To see some of our best-educated boys spending the afternoon knocking each other down, while thousands cheer them on, hardly gives a picture of a peace-loving nation."

Lyndon Baines Johnson, quoted in the "New York Times", 1967.

Introduction

As with all personal injuries cases, the issue of costs may in itself raise a number of issues. Since the introduction of the Civil Procedure Rules this issue has perhaps left the specialist realm of costs draftsman and stumbled into the general practitioner's area due to the fact that costs are now much more frequently assessed summarily after at the end of a particular hearing. **28.01**

However, despite the often very broadbrush approach which is taken it should be remembered that costs is a particularly technical area and this Chapter provides merely a brief review of some of the main issues and readers are referred to the specialist texts on the issue for more details. In particular, the authors have found *Assessment of Costs under the CPR* by Nicholas and Michael Bacon[1] and *No Win No Fee—No Worries* by Kerry Underwood[2] to be particularly helpful in this area. See also *Kevan on Credit Hire* by Tim Kevan.[3]

Indemnity principle

General

If there is no conditional fee in place, parties should be aware of the indemnity principle which provides that, in general, a party can only claim costs for which he is liable to pay his own legal representative. **28.02**

---

[1] EMIS Professional Publishing Ltd (www.emispp.com), 2001.
[2] EMIS Professional Publishing Ltd (www.emispp.com), 2nd ed., 2002.
[3] EMIS Professional Publishing Ltd (www.emispp.com), 2001, Chap. 15.

In effect, a party's right to claim costs from the other side is a (partial) indemnity against the costs he has incurred with his own solicitor. As Bramwell, B. said in *Harold v. Smith*[4]:

"Costs as between party and party are given by the law as an indemnity to the person entitled to them; they are not imposed as a punishment on the party who pays them, nor given as a bonus to the party who receives them. Therefore if the extent of the damnification can be found out, the extent to which costs ought to be allowed is also ascertained."

This reasoning was upheld in *Gundry v. Sainsbury*.[5]

Extent of the need for proof

28.03 In *Bailey v. IBC Vehicles Ltd*,[6] Henry L.J. observed that the signing of the between-the-parties bill by the solicitor as an officer of the court was effectively a certificate that the receiving party's solicitors were not seeking to recover in relation to any item more than they had agreed to charge their client; the signature was normally sufficient to enable the court to be satisfied that the indemnity principle has not been breached. This position was endorsed in the Supreme Court Costs Office's "Guide to the Summary Assessment of costs".[7]

It is exemplified in *Hazlett v. Sefton Metropolitan Borough*[8] in which it was held that it would not normally be necessary for the client to have to adduce evidence that he would be personally liable for his solicitor's costs, there being a presumption that he is liable.

However, this case went on to say that where there is a genuine issue by the paying party as to whether the receiving party had properly incurred liability for costs, the position would be different; if it was alleged that the receiving party was not liable to pay his solicitor's costs (perhaps having entered into an unlawful/unenforceable conditional fee agreement or for any other reason) he would be at risk in relying on the presumption and not supporting it with evidence that he had incurred liability for costs; in the absence of evidence he would be unlikely to recover his costs. For the same reason, if the indemnity issue is being challenged, the receiving party's costs should not be summarily assessed.

In this regard, it should also be remembered that in *General Mediterranean Holdings SA v. Patel and Patel*,[9] Toulson J. held that in an application for a direction that privileged documents be disclosed to the court, CPR, r.48.7(3) was held *ultra vires*. This type of argument allied with

---

[4] (1860) 5H&N 381.
[5] [1910] 1 K.B. 645, CA.
[6] [1998] 3 All E.R. 570.
[7] November 1999, at para. 24.
[8] [2000] 4 All E.R. 887; [2000] Env. L.R. 416; [1999] N.L.J.R. 1869.
[9] [2000] 1 W.L.R. 272.

the right to privacy under the European Convention of Human Rights (ECHR) will be open to those claiming costs in the future whilst those defending such claims may potentially be able to rely upon Article 6 of the ECHR and the right to a fair trial.

Ex parte Larkin

In *R v. Clerk to Liverpool Magistrates' Court, ex p. McCormick Regina v.* **28.04** *Same, ex p. Larkin*[10] it may be argued that the indemnity prnciple to some extent was watered down by the Divisional Court. In particular, it held that costs were incurred by a defendant within the meaning of section 16(6) of the Prosecution of Offences Act 1985 merely if he was contractually obliged to pay them and there was no requirement for the defendant to prove that he had in fact paid, or was likely to pay, the costs.

The claimant in the first case, *McCormick*, had signed a standard contract with his solicitors when first instructing them which stated:

"You are of course responsible for our costs for advising you and representing you in court."

His solicitors acknowledged that often it would not be cost effective for the firm to seek to recover costs from a client if he could not pay them. The justices' clerk had taken the view that the claimant had known when entering into the contract that he could not make, and would not be expected to make, any payment not covered by public funds, and accordingly had incurred no liability to pay the pre-legal aid costs, within the meaning of section 16(6) of the 1985 Act, and regulation 7(3) of the Costs in Criminal Cases (General) Regulations.[11]

The claimant submitted that the sole question was whether there was a **28.05** contractual liability to pay. If there was, and there was no agreement that whatever happened the defendant would not have to pay, then the costs had been incurred, even though there was little prospect of any payment being recovered in fact.

He relied on *R. v. Miller (Raymond)*,[12] which concerned a predecessor of the current legislation. In that case the applicants were funded by their unions and so did not personally have to pay their costs. Mr Justice Lloyd said[13]:

"Costs are incurred by a party if he is responsible or liable for those costs, even though they are in fact paid by a third party . . . "

[10] [2001] 2 All E.R. 705; *Independent*, December 18, 2000; *The Times*, January 12, 2001.
[11] S.I. 1986 No. 1335.
[12] [1983] 1 W.L.R. 1056.
[13] At 1061D.

Elias J. (with whom Rose L.J. agreed) agreed with the claimant's analysis. He had no doubt that if the claimant were to win the lottery the firm would look to him for payment. The fact that they did not expect to be able to recover the costs, unless there was subsequently a defendant's costs order made in their favour, did not prevent the liability being incurred by the claimant. Liability to pay was incurred if there was a contractual obligation to make the payment and not merely if it was likely that the sum would have to be paid.

Thai Trading agreements

28.06　A particular area of controversy in recent years in this area has revolved around what became known as "Thai Trading agreements" deriving their name from the case of *Thai Trading Co. v. Taylor.*[14] In effect, they consisted of contingency agreements in which legal representatives agreed to waive their fees in the event of losing the case.

In *Thai Trading* itself, the Court of Appeal ruled that contingency agreements were no longer contrary to public policy and the fact that the agreement in question infringed Rule 8(1) of the Solicitors Practice Rules 1990 did not make the agreement unenforceable.

Under Rule 8(1) of the Solicitors Practice Rules 1990 such agreements were prohibited unless they conformed with section 58 of the Courts and Legal Services Act 1990. Rule 8(1) stated:

"A solicitor who is retained or employed to prosecute or defend any action, suit or other contentious proceeding shall not enter into any arrangement to receive a contingency fee in respect of that proceeding."

However, in *Hughes v. Kingston Upon Hull City Council*[15] the Divisional Court refused to follow this line of reasoning and they decided that the case had been decided *per incuriam* as the case of *Swain v. Law Society (HL)*[16] had not been cited to the Court of Appeal in *Thai Trading*. The House of Lords in *Swain* had ruled that the Solicitors Practice Rules have the force of subordinate or delegated legislation. (The relevant power arising from section 37 of the Solicitors Act 1974). Lord Diplock stated[17]:

"The Solicitors Act 1974 imposes on the Law Society a number of statutory duties in relation to solicitors whether they are members or not. It also confers on the council of the Law Society, acting alone or with the concurrence of the Lord Chief Justice and The Master of the Rolls or of the latter only, power to make rules and regulations having the effect of subordinate legislation under the Act."

---

[14] Above.
[15] (1999) 2 W.L.R. 1229; [1999] 2 All E.R. 49; [1999] Env. L.R. 579; *Independent*, November 16, 1998; *The Times*, December 9, 1998.
[16] [1982] 2 All E.R. 827.
[17] At 830b.

Lord Brightman concurred and stated[18]:

> "The rules have the force of a statute . . . just as much as if the rules . . . were set out in a schedule to the Act."

It was successfully argued in *Hughes* that Rule 8 had statutory force and because there was a contingency agreement, which fell foul of the rule, it was unlawful and therefore unenforceable.   **28.07**

Following the decision in *Thai Trading*, the Council of the Law Society decided to change the Practice Rule, however this was not done before the decision in *Hughes*. The new Practice Rule 8(1), which was amended with immediate effect on January 7, 1999, reads:

> "A Solicitor who is retained or employed to prosecute or defend any action, suit or other contentious proceeding shall not enter into any arrangement to receive a contingency fee in respect of that proceeding, save that permitted under statute or by the common law."

However, a court will probably look at the Rule in force at the time the agreement was made. The newer rule is not retrospective and does not deal with agreements entered into before January 7, 1999. Leave for the claimant in *Hughes* to appeal to the House of Lords was refused, albeit on a technicality.

Hughes was followed in *Wells & anor v. Barnsley Metropolitan Council* and *Leeds City Council v. Carr*[19] both of which were heard together by the Divisional Court.

In the Court of Appeal decision of *Geraghty & Co. v. Awwad and Another (CA)*,[20] *Thai Trading* was again not followed and *Swain* was held to be decisive. In *Geraghty*, a conditional fee arrangement was held to be unenforceable; not only because it breached the old Rule 8(1) of the Solicitors Practice Rules but because it was also contrary to public policy. It now seems that the current judicial line is that the assertion in *Thai Trading*, that the contravention of a professional rule does not make the practice contrary to law, was made *per incuriam*.

Obviously, this will be subject to the Access to Justice Act 2000 and new Rules on conditional fees.

Solicitor's retainer

Issues may arise if there is no mention of costs within the retainer. This is contrary to the Solicitors' Costs and Information and Client Care Code 1999, which reflects the state of solicitors' obligations. Before this, the relevant provisions on costs information were provided by Rule 15 of the   **28.08**

---

[18] At 840f.
[19] [2000] C.O.D. 10; [2000] Env. L.R. 522; *The Times*, November 12, 1999.
[20] [2000] 3 W.L.R. 1041; [2000] 1 All E.R. 608; *Independent*, December 1, 1999.

Solicitors Practice Rules, which is headed "Costs Information and Client Care". There has always been a provision under Rule 15 of the 1990 Rules for the Law Society to draw up a code on costs; however the 1999 Code seems to be the first example of such a code.

Under Rule 15(a), solicitors shall "give information about costs and other matters". In the notes to this Rule, part (i) states that:

"A serious breach of the code, or persistent breaches of a material nature, will be a breach of the Rule, and may also be evidence of inadequate professional services under s37A of the Solicitors Act 1974."

Part (ii) states:

"Material breaches of the code which are not serious or persistent will not be a breach of the Rule, but may be evidence of inadequate professional services under section 37A."

If inadequate amounts of information were given in a case, potentially it may be possible to argue that this amounted to a serious breach, although from the wording of part (ii) of the note it looks as though the court would regard this as merely a material breach.

The remedy available to the client under this route includes the possibility of his solicitors being disallowed all of their costs. It seems that any person is entitled to make a complaint, not just the client of the defaulting solicitor. However, any determination by the Office for the Supervision of Solicitors would have to take effect before the assessment of the costs.

Further and in any event, there is still the possibility that some or all of the costs may be allowed.

28.09   Under the old Rule 15 there does not seem to be an express obligation for such information to be given in writing. Solicitors may seek to rely upon an implied term of reasonable remuneration being added into the contract of retainer under section 15 of the Supply of Goods and Services Act 1982.

According to *Cordery on Solicitors*, para. 402 obligations deriving from the contract of retainer can include:

"those which are implied by law in circumstances where the parties have not reached express agreement".

Cordery, at para. 405 goes on to state:

"The question of costs must also be discussed with the client both at the outset of the transaction and at any time thereafter if it appears that the solicitor's previous estimate of costs is likely to be rendered inaccurate by subsequent events. Information as to costs should be given in writing." (However, it seems that this is a qualification added by the implementation of the 1999 Code.)

The Law Society certainly encouraged firms before the 1999 Rule to put such information in writing (see the standard Letter of Confirmation of

Retainer) but there does not seem to have been any express obligation to do so; which is now the case. Under the old regime, it seems that solicitors were possibly able to escape without directly referring to costs in the retainer. There was also the possibility of a reasonable price for the services being implied.

Much will depend upon the particular facts of each case and also as to what regime was in place at the time.

Liability of third parties for costs

Jurisdiction to award costs against third parties derives from section 51(1) of the Supreme Court Act 1981. The procedure in this regard is covered by CPR, r.48.2:   **28.10**

> "(1) here the court is considering whether to exercise its power under section 51 of the Supreme Court Act 1981 (costs are in the discretion of the court) to make a costs order in favour of or against a person who is not a party to proceedings—
>
> > (a) that person must be added as a party to the proceedings for the purposes of costs only; and
> > (b) he must be given a reasonable opportunity to attend a hearing at which the court will consider the matter further.
>
> (2) This rule does not apply—
>
> > (a) where the court is considering whether to—
> >
> > > (i) make an order against the Legal Services Commission;
> > > (ii) make a wasted costs order (as defined in 48.7); and
> >
> > (b) in proceedings to which rule 48.1 applies (pre-commencement disclosure and orders for disclosure against a person who is not a party)."

Defendants may want to find out who is funding the action. In *Condliffe v. Hislop*,[21] the Court of Appeal held that a claim may be struck out as an abuse of process if pursued champertously or financed by a third party who is not going to meet the costs if the case fails. Exceptionally, a court may order the financing party to be identified, or for the action to be stayed pending such identification or the giving of security: *Abraham v. Thompson*,[22] reversed on the facts in *Abraham v. Thompson*.[23]

It should be noted that with regard to the issue of security for costs, Article 6 of the ECHR may come into play. Potentially, it may be argued that such orders bar access to the courts. This may be open to argument. However in *Tolstoy Miloslavasky v. United Kingdom*[24] the court held that

---

[21] [1996] 1 All E.R. 431; [1996] 1 W.L.R. 753.
[22] (1997) 141 Sol. J. L.B. 114, *The Times*, May 15, 1997.
[23] [1997] 4 All E.R. 362, CA.
[24] [1995] 20 E.H.R.R. 442.

at least in respect of appellate proceedings a requirement that the appellant give security for costs was no violation of Article 6(1). However this might potentially be different if access to the court of first instance was precluded.

28.11   The case of *Murphy v. Young's Brewery*[25] involved the question of third party liability for costs. The case concerned a legal insurance policy. Phillips L.J. stated[26] in particular that where the test for maintenance propounded by Lord Mustill in *Giles v. Thompson*[27] is satisfied:

"I would expect the court to be receptive to an application under section 51 that the meddler pay any costs attributable to his intermeddling".

This was confirmed in *Nordstern Allgemeine Versicherungs AG v. Internav Ltd.*[28]

In *McFarlane v. E.E. Caledonia Ltd (No. 2)*,[29] Longmore J. ordered a non-party to pay the successful defendant's costs. The non-party was a commercial company which had funded a claimant's unsuccessful claim for damages for personal injury on a contingency fee basis under which the non-party accepted no responsibility for the defendant's costs.

Two more recent cases in which insurers have been held liable for the successful party's costs are: *T.G.A. Chapman Ltd & anor v. Christopher & anor*[30] and *Pendennis Shipyard Ltd & ors v. Margrathea (Pendennis) Ltd (in liquidation).*[31] See also *Globe Equities Ltd v. Legal Services Ltd & ors.*[32]

Wasted costs

28.12   Solicitors and barristers may sometimes be at risk of a costs order against themselves. Provision is made for "wasted costs orders" by the Supreme Court Act 1981 section 51(6) and (7) which provide:

"(6) In any proceedings entioned in subsection (1), the court may disallow, or (as the case may be) order the legal or other representative concerned to meet, the whole of any wasted costs or such part of them as may be determined in accordance with rules of court.

---

[25] [1997] 1 W.L.R. 1591.
[26] At 1601.
[27] [1994] 1 A.C. 142.
[28] [1999] 2 Lloyd's Rep. 139; *The Times*, June 8, 1999, CA.
[29] [1998] 1 W.L.R. 12; [1998] 2 All E.R. 873; [1998] Lloyd's Rep. I.R. 1; [1997] C.L.C. 1306.
[30] [1998] 1 Lloyd's Rep. 315; (1997) 94(35) L.S.G. 35; (1997) 141 S.J.L.B. 185; *The Times*, July 21, 1997, CA.
[31] *The Times*, August 27, 1997 (Raymond Jack Q.C. J., QBD).
[32] *The Times* April 14, 1999; *Independent*, March 15, 1999; [1999] B.L.R. 232.

(7) In subsection (6), wasted costs means any costs incurred by a party—

   (c) as a result of any improper, unreasonable or negligent act or omission on the part of any legal or other representative or any employee of such a representative; or

   (d) which, in the light of any such act or omission occurring after they were incurred, the court considers it is unreasonable to expect that party to pay."

In *Ridehalgh v. Horsefield*[33] the Court of Appeal gave general guidance for the exercise by courts of their jurisdiction in this area. The Costs Practice Direction Section 53[34] confirms the three stage process applied in *Re a Barrister (Wasted Costs Order) (No. 1 of 1991)*[35] and approved in *Ridhalgh*, namely:

1. Had the legal representative of whom complaint was made acted improperly, unreasonably or negligently?

2. If so, did such conduct cause the applicant to incur unnecessary costs?

3. If so, was it in all the circumstances just to order the legal representative to compensate the applicant for the whole or part of the relevant costs?

Costs on separate issues

It should be noted that Part 44.3 of the Civil Procedure Rules allows the court to take account of whether a party has succeeded on part of his case, even if he has not been wholly successful. Whilst the general rule remains that costs follow the event, this, along with the opportunity to make Part 36 payments and offers on separate issues means that the courts may potentially allocate costs according to the success of each issue fought.   **28.13**

Small claims track: unreasonable conduct

Part 27.2 of the Civil Procedure Rules excludes the application of Part 36 offers to settle and payments in from the small claims track. It should also be noted that in *Afzal v. Ford Motor Co.*,[36] the Court of Appeal stated that offers were not usually appropriate in small claims court. However, unreasonable conduct is a question of fact. Further, Calderbank offers, *i.e.* offers   **28.14**

---

[33] [1994] Ch. 205.
[34] CPR PD 48.
[35] [1993] Q.B. 293.
[36] [1994] 4 All E.R. 720.

headed "without prejudice save as to costs" may be appropriate on occasions".

There are a number of cases in which offers to settle have been made and when a claimant has failed to reach that offer, costs have been awarded against that claimant on the basis of unreasonable conduct: *Coady v. Hankins*[37]; *Ashby v. Wiggins*[38]; *Stonard v. Dunster*[39]; *Somasundarum v. Wickes*[40]; *Scotchford v. Joannou.*[41] They would appear to be based upon the principle set out in *Bloomfield v. Roberts*[42] that the test for unreasonable conduct is an objective one. *Fronda v. Jackson*[43] states that when assessing costs, the award of costs for unreasonable conduct is a punitive measure.

Such an approach may be argued by either claimants or defendants depending upon who has made the settlement offer. It may potentially be opposed using *Afzal* and the argument that Part 36 is expressly excluded for a reason, namely that offers to settle and payments in are not appropriate.

It still remains to be seen how the courts practice will develop in this regard under the CPR.

Costs only proceedings

28.15 In *Bensusan v. Freedman*,[44] Senior Costs Judge Hurst gave general guidance on costs-only proceedings. In that case a detailed assessment in costs only proceedings was brought under CPR Part 8 in a personal injury claim. The claimant sought damages for shock and anxiety which she alleged she had suffered as the result of dental negligence after a piece of dental equipment fell onto her tongue during root canal treatment and she involuntarily swallowed it. Five weeks after her solicitors sent the defendant a letter of claim, the claimant accepted an offer to settle for £2,000 plus costs to be assessed if not agreed.

Although the defendant was based in Essex and the claimant lived in Kent, the claimant had consulted a specialist dental negligence practice in Nantwich where both partners were qualified dentists. The claimant had entered into a conditional fee agreement with a success fee of 50 per cent. She did not have an after-the-event insurance policy. The parties failed to agree the costs payable and the claimant issued a Part 8 application in Crewe county court to commence costs only proceedings under CPR, r.44.12A.

---

[37] [1998] C.L.Y. 489.
[38] [1997] 11 C.L. 189.
[39] [1997] C.L. 155.
[40] [1996] C.L.Y. 699.
[41] [1997] 3 C.L. 78.
[42] [1989] C.L.Y. 2948.
[43] [1995] C.L.Y. 4015.
[44] Supreme Court Costs Office (Senior Costs Judge Hurst), September 20, 2001.

The claimant's bill for assessment totalled £3,419.69, which included a base fee of £1,170, with the work carried out by a grade 1 fee earner, and a success fee of £864. The following general points of principle arose:

(i) the location of the claimant's solicitors, their appropriate hourly rate, and the linked issue of venue for issue of the proceedings;

(ii) the appropriate grade of fee earner; and

(iii) the success fee.

The court was also asked to give general guidance on costs only proceedings.

Senior Costs Judge Hurst held, applying *Truscott v. Truscott : Wraith v. Sheffield Forgemasters Ltd*,[45] which was considered in *Sullivan v. Cooperative Insurance Society Ltd*,[46] although it was open to the claimant to instruct whichever solicitors she chose and there might be dental negligence cases in which it would be reasonable to instruct a distant specialist practice, it was not reasonable for the claimant to instruct specialist solicitors in this case. However, the disparity between hourly rates in Nantwich and in Tunbridge Wells, Kent, worked to the defendant's advantage. Therefore, it was appropriate to allow the rate for the area where the work was done.

The commencement of proceedings in Crewe county court was purely for the benefit of the claimant's solicitors. It appeared that if substantive proceedings had been issued, the court would have made an appropriate order for transfer either on its own initiative or on an application by one of the parties.

This case was a clear and straightforward negligence claim of the type   **28.16**
routinely dealt with by grade 2 fee earners, especially by legal executives. Therefore an hourly rate of £110 was allowed rather than the £180 per hour claimed.

It was clear from *Callery v. Gray*[47] that the requirement to act reasonably would mean that solicitors would have to consider using a two-stage success fee in future. *Callery* was specifically limited to straightforward claims in road traffic accidents and could only provide a starting point for deciding the appropriate success fee in this case. In the light of the complexity of this claim and the solicitor's knowledge at the date when the conditional fee arrangement was entered into, the appropriate success fee was 20 per cent.

The new costs only procedure appeared to be being misused by both claimants and defendants in breach of the overriding objective. If a claimant

---

[45] [1998] 1 W.L.R. 132.
[46] *The Times*, May 19, 1999.
[47] [2001] 1 W.L.R. 2112; [2001] 3 All E.R. 833; *The Times*, July 18, 2001; *Independent*, July 24, 2001. See now the House of Lords' judgment [2002] 1 W.L.R. 2000; [2002] 3 All E.R. 417; *The Times*, July 2, 2002, see below.

was forced to commence proceedings under CPR Part 7 rather than costs only proceedings under CPR Part 8, defendants would find themselves having to pay not only the reasonable and proportionate costs of the claim itself, but also the costs of the Part 7 proceedings and any related assessment proceedings. If the defendant had acted unreasonably in compelling the commencement of Part 7 proceedings, the court would consider making an order for costs on the indemnity basis.

The procedure under CPR, r. 44.12A was as follows:

(i) the parties reached an agreement on all the issues, including which party was to pay the costs;

(ii) the agreement was made or confirmed in writing;

(iii) no proceedings had been started and the parties had failed to agree costs;

(iv) the costs only proceedings should be issued (by either party) in the court that would have been appropriate if substantive proceedings had been brought;

(v) the claim form had to identity the claim or dispute, state the date and terms of the agreement, set out a draft of the order sought, state the amount of the costs claimed, and state whether costs were claimed on the standard or indemnity basis;

(vi) the evidence in support of the claim had to include the documents proving the defendant's agreement to pay the costs;

(vii) the matter would not be placed before the Costs Judge or District Judge until an acknowledgement of service had been filed;

(viii) the claimant could ask the court by letter to make the order sought once the time for filing the acknowledgement of service expired;

(ix) the court could make an order for detailed assessment or dismiss the claim;

(x) a claim would not be treated as opposed and be dismissed if the defendant disputed the amount of the claim or stated that it was issued in the wrong office; and

(xi) the court could make an order by consent that differed from the order sought in the claim form.

In no circumstances should a District Judge or a Costs Judge hear the application and then immediately embark on a summary assessment of the costs in dispute. A summary assessment was made by a judge who had decided the substantive issue. In costs only proceedings the only issue decided by the Judge was whether there should be a detailed assessment of the costs. Judgment was given accordingly

After the event insurance premiums

Section 29 of the Access to Justice Act 2000

With the introduction of section 29 of the Access to Justice Act 2000, for the first time premiums for after the event insurance policies became recoverable from the other side. Specifically, the section provides: 28.17

> "Where in any proceedings a costs order is made in favour of any party who has taken out an insurance policy against the risk of incurring a liability in those proceedings, the costs payable to him may, subject in the case of court proceedings to rules of court include costs in respect of the premium of the policy".

There are numerous issues which may potentially arise surrounding this section and no doubt further litigation will arise in the future. For the moment, the two leading cases are *Callery v. Gray and Russell v. Pal Pak Corrugated Limited*[48] ("*Callery v. Gray (No. 1)*") and *Callery v. Gray (No. 2)*.[49] It should be noted that since the writing of this book, the House of Lords have given judgment in *Callery v. Gray*.[49a] Thus is dealt with briefly below.

Callery v. Gray (No. 1)

In *Callery v. Gray (No. 1)*, the Court of Appeal held that where a reasonable uplift was agreed at the outset of a straightforward personal injury claim and after-the-event insurance was taken out at a reasonable premium, the costs of each were recoverable from the defendant if the claim succeeded or was settled on terms that the defendant pay the claimant's costs. However, the maximum uplift recoverable in a straightforward claim arising out of a road traffic accident was 20 per cent.   28.18

Two appeals had been brought in costs-only proceedings concerned with the arrangements for financing the cost of personal injury litigation. Both appeals arose out of personal injury claims that settled pre-action. Only the first related to after the event insurance premiums.

---

[48] [2001] 1 W.L.R. 2112; [2001] 3 All E.R. 833; *Independent*, July 24, 2001; [2001] E.W.C.A. Civ. 1117.
[49] [2001] W.L.R. 1 2112; [2001] 4 All E.R. 1; [2001] E.W.C.A. Civ. 1246.
[49a] [2002] 1 W.L.R. 2000; [2002] 3 All E.R. 417; *The Times*, July 2, 2002.

In that appeal, the defendant appealed from the decision of H.H. Judge Edwards who held that it was entirely reasonable for the claimant to have taken out insurance as early as possible and agreed with the District Judge's decision to allow recovery of the after-the-event ("ATE") insurance premium in full.

With regard to ATEs, the appeals raised three main issues:

1. whether an ATE premium could be recovered in costs-only proceedings;

2. the stage at which it was appropriate to enter into an ATE policy; and

3. the reasonableness of the claimants' ATE premiums.

The Court of Appeal held that the "proceedings" referred to in section 29 of the Access to Justice Act 1999 were proceedings advancing a claim for substantive relief. CPR, r.44.12A was introduced to enable pre-action costs to be recovered where an action had been settled before substantive proceedings commenced. The meaning of "costs" in CPR, r.44.12A was the costs that would have been recoverable in the proceedings if the proceedings had been commenced. By reason of section 29 of the Act, such costs could include the costs of an ATE insurance premium taken out in contemplation of the commencement of substantive proceedings. Accordingly, an ATE premium could be recovered in costs-only proceedings.

In both appeals the claimants' solicitors reasonably concluded that the claims had every prospect of an early settlement of both liability and quantum. The vital issue was whether the court should allow recovery of an ATE in those circumstances or whether it should require litigants to defer taking out an ATE until the defendant's response to the claim was known.

28.19   It was held that insurance premiums benefited defendants as they ensured payment of the defendant's costs when a claimant was unsuccessful. Premiums taken out at an early stage were substantially cheaper than when it was known if the defendant was going to contest liability. Further, it would assist access to justice for solicitors to offer legal services on terms that the claimant will not pay costs whatever the circumstances. Consequently where at the outset ATE insurance at a reasonable premium was taken out the cost of it was recoverable from the defendant in the event that the claim succeeded or was settled on terms that the defendant pay the claimant's costs.

Finally, they held that it was not possible on the evidence to form a conclusion as to the reasonableness of premiums charged for ATE insurance and stated that a separate judgment would be provided on that point. This was *Callery v. Gray (No. 2)*.

Callery v. Gray (No. 2)

In *Callery v. Gray (No. 2)*,[50] the Court of Appeal gave guidelines as to the **28.20**
recoverability of an after-the-event insurance premium under section 29 of
the Access to Justice Act 1999.

The circumstances of the appeal have been summarised above. This
judgment dealt with that remaining issue after the commission of a report
on the make up of ATE premiums by Master O'Hare. Master O'Hare's
report dated July 23, 2001 raised issues of general importance in relation to
ATE insurance. The principal issue raised by this appeal was whether the
cost of insuring against failure to recover one's own costs could be recovered
under section 29 of the Access to Justice Act 1999.

The Court of Appeal held that although annexed to this judgment,
Master O'Hare's report did not have the status of a judgment. This judgment only addressed those issues identified in the report that arose on the
facts of this case.

The jurisdiction to include an ATE insurance premium in an award of
costs was conferred by section 29 of the Act. The phrase "a liability in these
proceedings" was imprecise and did not define the nature of the liability,
although it was not in issue or doubt that the liability was restricted to
liability for costs. It was necessary when considering whether or to what
extent a premium was recoverable to ask whether it was consideration paid
for insurance against the risk of incurring a costs liability in the
proceedings.

The court also had to consider whether the premium was reasonable.
Insofar as the court found that the premium was not reasonable it could be
reduced. In this context it was important to distinguish contractual entitlement to benefits from the use made by the insurer of the premium. The court
was only concerned with whether the premium was a reasonable price to
pay for the benefits it purchased and a litigant who purchased his insurance
from an insurer who conducted his business in an extravagant manner
might be disentitled from recovering the full cost of the premium.

It was desirable in the interests of justice that an effective market devel- **28.21**
oped in ATE insurance. Solicitors were encouraged to take advantage of
such sources of information as www.thejudge.co.uk and the magazine "Litigation Funding" published by the Law Society. It was open to the insurer to
place evidence before the court about the reasonableness of his premium.
However, satellite litigation on the point was unsatisfactory and a judge
could only be expected to give broad consideration to such evidence.

The court considered in detail the elements responsible for the size of the
insurance premium as set out by Master O'Hare. This appeal was concerned
with a premium fixed on an individual basis. No objection was taken to the
parts of the premium that covered risk/profit cost, or administrative costs.

---

[50] [2001] W.L.R. 1 2112; [2001] 4 All E.R. 1; [2001] E.W.C.A. Civ. 1246.

No objection in principle was taken to that part of a premium that covered commission payments. The court commented that in the longer term market forces would prevent premiums being unreasonably inflated by extravagant commission payments.

The court also considered in detail the benefits provided in exchange for the premium paid. The primary liability covered by the claimant's policy was for the opponent's costs in the event of court order, withdrawal, discontinuance or settlement with the insurers' prior approval, all of which fell within the meaning of section 29 of the Act.

To the extent that the premium provided collateral benefits, it could fall outside the scope of section 29 of the Act.

28.22 The claimant's insurance entitled him to an indemnity in respect of his own disbursements in the event that his claim failed. The government had indicated that the cost of own costs insurance would be recoverable. Whilst there was a suggestion that it was the intention of the Lord Chancellor that own costs insurance was an alternative to a conditional fee agreement, there was nothing to suggest that there was an intention that claimants were to be entitled to pass on to the defendants the cost of insuring against failure to be awarded costs on the ground that they had been unreasonably incurred. Section 29 of the Act could and should be interpreted to treat the words "insurance against the risk of incurring a costs liability as meaning "insurance against the risk of incurring a costs liability that could not be passed on to the opposing party". The circumstances and terms on which own costs insurance would be reasonable so that the whole premium could be recovered as costs would have to be determined by the courts in individual cases, assisted if appropriate by the Rules Committee. The whole of the claimant's premium, including the small element of cover for own costs insurance, fell within the description of insurance against the risk of liability within section 29 of the Act and was recoverable.

Accordingly, there was no reason in principle to refuse to award any part of the claimant's premium under section 29 of the Act. It was not correct to presume as a starting point that a premium was reasonable unless the contrary was shown. The court had to consider the evidence of the relationship between the premium, the risk and the cost of alternative cover. In this case the premium was tailored to the risk and the cover was suitable for the claimant's needs. Therefore, the premium was reasonable. However, that did not mean that a premium of £350 would always be reasonable in cases such as this. There was no reason in principle why £7.50 insurance premium tax should not also be recoverable.

On these bases, the appeal was dismissed. However, the House of Lords granted an application by Charles Gray seeking leave to appeal in this case on January 25, 2002. The Appeal Committee had made a provisional unanimous decision to grant leave following a consideration of the applicant's petition and had invited objections from the respondent on December 4, 2001.

Sarwar v. Alam

In *Sarwar v. Alam,*[51] a separate issue arose regarding the recoverability of **28.23** the ATE insurance premium by a claimant car passenger where he had failed to enquire whether the driver's before-the-event insurance was available to him.

The Court of Appeal held that it was recoverable because it was not reasonable to require the claim to be conducted by his opponent's insurers. The court also prescribed guidelines for similar future cases.

The appeal was in costs-only proceedings concerned with the arrangements for financing the cost of personal injury litigation. The claimant ("C") was the passenger in a car being driven by the defendant ("D") which was in a collision with another vehicle. C commenced proceedings with the benefit of an ATE policy. C's claim was settled for £2,250 together with reasonable costs. In the subsequent costs-only proceedings D's insurers disclosed for the first time that D's before-the-event ("BTE") motor insurance policy contained a provision for legal expenses insurance ("LEI"), which would have covered a claim by C against D as a passenger in a vehicle being driven by D. Both the District Judge and the Judge below held that this BTE insurance was available to C such that it was unreasonable for him to have incurred the cost of an ATE premium, the recovery of which was consequently disallowed. In particular, the judge below held that C and/or his solicitors should have made enquiries of D and/or his insurers about the existence of the BTE policy.

The Court of Appeal held that it was not incumbent on C to use D's BTE policy. The policy provided for legal representation to be arranged by D's insurers, who were, of course, the insurers for C's opposing party, and further provided for those insurers to retain full conduct and control of the claim. That was not, in the circumstances, a reasonable alternative to representation by a lawyer of C's own choosing.

They went on that the position might well be different, however, if BTE insurers generally were to finance some transparently independent organisation to handle claims such as C's, and made it plain in the BTE policy that they were so doing.

In the ordinary course, however, if a claimant making a relatively small (*i.e.* under £5,000) claim in a road traffic case had access to pre-existing BTE cover which appeared to be satisfactory for a claim of that size, then it should be used.

A solicitor should normally invite a client, by means of a standard form letter, to bring to the first interview any relevant motor and household insurance policy, as well as any stand-alone LEI policy belonging to the client and/or spouse or partner. However, regard had always to be had to the

---

[51] [2002] 1 W.L.R. 125; [2001] 4 All E.R. 541; [2001] E.W.C.A. Civ. 1401.

amount at stake, and a solicitor was not obliged to embark upon a treasure hunt.

In addition, given the frequency with which motor insurance policies now provided LEI cover for a claim by any passenger of the insured, the solicitor should ordinarily to ask his client to obtain a copy of the driver's insurance policy, if reasonably practicable. The question of practicability was necessarily fact-sensitive.

In these circumstances, the appeal was therefore allowed.

Conditional fees

Sections 27 and 28 of the Access to Justice Act 1999

28.24   The Access to Justice Act 1999 also allows solicitors to act on a "no win no fee basis". If successful they will be able to recover their normal costs from the loser with their own client making up any shortfall. The client is still responsible for the other side's costs if the case is unsuccessful.

Specifically, section 27(2)(a) of the Act defines a conditional fee agreement as:

> "an agreement with a person providing advocacy or litigation services which provides for his fees and expenses, or any part of them, to be payable only in specified circumstances".

Further section 28 covers litigation funding agreements which are agreements where a funder agrees to fund the provision of advocacy or litigation services to another person and the litigant agrees to pay a sum to the funder in specified circumstances.

28.25   The regime is subject to numerous regulations and it would not be appropriate to attempt to cover them all here. However, it is worth looking briefly at the leading cases in this area, that of *Callery v. Gray* and *Russell v. Pal Pak Corrugated Ltd.*[52] It should again be noted that since the writing of this book, the House of Lords has given judgment in *Callery v. Gray.*[53] This is dealt with briefly below.

As mentioned above, the case involved two appeals in costs-only proceedings concerned with the arrangements for financing the cost of personal injury litigation. Both appeals arose out of personal injury claims that settled pre-action.

In the first appeal, the defendant appealed from the decision of H.H. Judge Edwards on January 29, 2001 upholding a District Judge's decision to allow a success fee of 40 per cent in a straightforward claim following a road traffic accident. He found that an appropriate figure for the uplift

---

[52] [2001] 3 All E.R., *The Times*, July 18, 2001; *Independent*, July 24, 2001.
[53] [2002] 1 W.L.R. 2000; [2002] 3 All E.R. 417.

would have been 33 per cent so that in the circumstances the District Judge was not wrong to assess the figure at 40 per cent.

In the second appeal, which was also a straightforward claim following a road traffic accident, the defendant appealed from a decision of H.H. Judge Marshall Evans on January 25, 2001 to award the claimant a success fee of 20 per cent, reduced from 30 per cent.

The appeals raised two main issues with regard to conditional fees:

1. the stage at which it was appropriate to enter into a conditional fee agreement ("CFA");

2. the reasonableness of the claimant's percentage uplift.

The Court of Appeal held that in both appeals the claimant's solicitors reasonably concluded that the claims had every prospect of an early settlement of both liability and quantum. The vital issue was whether the court should allow recovery of an uplift in those circumstances or whether it should require all solicitors to defer agreeing an uplift until the defendant's response to the claim was known, so that the risk of failure could be assessed on an individual basis.

If the latter approach was adopted, liability for success fees would be **28.26** borne in much larger amounts by those unsuccessful defendants who persisted in contesting liability. This would not result in an equitable sharing of costs between unsuccessful defendants. Additionally, in claims arising out of road traffic accidents where defendants were insured, the same insurers would often be sharing the costs involved. Further (with regard to ATE insurance premiums as well), it would assist access to justice for solicitors to offer legal services on terms that the claimant will not pay costs whatever the circumstances.

Consequently where at the outset a reasonable uplift was agreed, the cost of it was recoverable from the defendant in the event that the claim succeeded or was settled on terms that the defendant pay the claimant's costs.

Where a CFA was agreed at the outset in this category of claim, 20 per cent was the maximum uplift that could reasonably be agreed. That figure assumed no special feature in the claim and this court's conclusion was based on very limited data at an early stage in the new costs regime. It would be desirable to review that conclusion once sufficient data was available to enable a fully informed assessment of the position.

Turning to the first appeal, the 40 per cent uplift was too high and was reduced to 20 per cent. The second appeal could not succeed unless it was established as a matter of principle that a CFA should not have been entered into when it was, and there was no such principle. The first appeal was therefore allowed to the extent indicated and the second appeal was dismissed.

Post script: Callery v. Gray (House of Lords)

It should be noted that since this book was written the House of Lords have given their judgment in *Callery v. Gray.*[54] It is not intended to provide a detailed examination of that judgment here. However, it is noted that they held, dismissing the appeal (Lord Scott of Foscote dissenting) that the responsibility for monitoring and controlling the developing practice of funding personal injury litigation by way of CFAs under the Access to Justice Act 1999 lay with the Court of Appeal and not the House of Lords which would only intervene in an exceptional case. This was not such a case and in any event the Court of Appeal was not purporting to lay down rules applicable for all time but was only giving provisional guidance to be reviewed in the light of increased knowledge and experience. The issues were essentially ones of practice and the House of Lords was not satisfied that the Court of Appeal's decisions were wrong.

In his dissenting speech, Lord Scott of Foscote stated that the Court of Appeal was wrong to hold that it was reasonable to take out an ATE policy at a time when litigation was highly unlikely. If the expenditure was not reasonably required for the purposes of the claim it would be contrary to long-established costs recovery principles to require the paying party to pay it. In this case the likelihood of litigation being necessary in order to pursue C's claim was always very remote. The appeal should be allowed to the extent of disallowing the ATE insurance premium. The Court of Appeal also did not have the evidence on which it could properly conclude that the amount of the premium was reasonable.

Conclusion

28.27 It is perhaps ironic that reforms intended to increase access to justice have perhaps in some ways hindered it by causing a myriad of satellite litigation. It will be no surprise if this continues in the future, particularly in the areas of ATE insurance premiums and conditional fees.

---

[54] [2002] 1 W.L.R. 2000; [2002] 3 All E.R. 417.

Part V

Conclusion

Chapter 29

Conclusion

"Blue moon, I saw you standing alone, without a song in your heart, without a love of your own."

Another song of the long-suffering Manchester City faithful.

The law in this area promises to develop further in the next few years and **29.01** litigation is likely to increase.

With this in mind, the best advice for anyone taking part in or organising a sporting event would be to make sure that they are insured against the risks inherent in the particular activity undertaken.

In the meantime, it is to be hoped that the government may introduce legislation providing for compulsory insurance for those organising any such events.

Index